Social Psychology

Social Psychology
Society and Self

Jeffrey Nash
Macalester College

West Publishing Company

St. Paul   New York   San Francisco   Los Angeles

COPYRIGHT © 1985 By WEST PUBLISHING CO.
50 West Kellogg Boulevard
P.O. Box 64526
St. Paul, Minnesota 55164–0526

Printed in the United States of America

Library of Congress Cataloging in Publication Data

Nash, Jeffrey E.
  Social psychology.

  Bibliography: p.
  Includes index.
  1. Social psychology. I. Title.
HM251.N353 1985   302   84–17337
ISBN 0–314–85281–6
1st Reprint—1985

COPYEDITING: Katherine W. Teel
COVER ART: *Golconde* by René Magritte.
             Private Collection. Reproduction
             rights granted by the
             Menil Foundation.

Photo Credits

1, 3 Mike Mazzaschi/Stock, Boston. **8** Hazel Hankin/Stock, Boston. **9** Owen Franken/ Stock, Boston. **11** Owen Franken/Stock, Boston. **13** Jill Cannefax/EKM-Nepenthe.

22, 24 The Bettmann Archive. **30** The Bettmann Archive. **38** Jeffrey Grosscup. **39** AP/ Wide World Photos. **44** Jill Cannefax/EKM-Nepenthe.

50, 52 Pam Schryler/Stock, Boston. **56** Burk Uzzle/Woodfin Camp and Associates. **58** Michael Hayman/Stock, Boston. **64** Robert V. Eckert, Jr./EKM-Nepenthe. **67** Charles Gate- wood/Stock, Boston. **70** Peter Vandermark/Stock, Boston.

78, 80 Mimi Forsyth/Monkmeyer Press Photo Service. **83** Elizabeth Crews/Stock, Boston. **85** Jean-Claude Lejeune/Stock, Boston. **87** Tom Ballard/EKM-Nepenthe. **89** Bill Anderson/ Monkmeyer Press Photo Service. **94** Gabor Demjen/Stock, Boston. **97** Robert V. Eckert, Jr./ EKM-Nepenthe.

104, 106 Jim Anderson/Woodfin Camp and Associates. **108** Judy S. Gelles/Stock, Boston. **119** John Marmaras/Woodfin Camp and Associates. **121** Ellis Herwig/Stock, Boston. **123** Richard Balzer/Stock, Boston. **125** Freda Leinwand/Monkmeyer Press Photo Service.

Photo credits continue after index

Contents

Chapter Twelve   Life in Public Places   306

Chapter Thirteen   Worlds of Emotion   332

Preface

Two overarching purposes guided me in writing this book. One was to present a version of social psychology informed by those schools of thought which stress the importance of understanding the real-life experiences of people, and to use the perspectives and insights gained to address and view topics of theoretical and research interest within social psychology. This first purpose is a part of a descriptive attitude that grounds much of social psychology. In this attitude the researcher approaches the people he or she studies in order to learn from them. Hence, the social psychologist has to be sensitive to the language that people use and the interpretations that they make in their everyday activities. In this book I devote many pages to conveying a sense of the experiences of ordinary people who are sometimes engaged in some extraordinary activities.

The second purpose of the book is twofold: On the one hand, I acknowledge the topics typically studied by those in the field—those human activities which show the bond between society and self—and, on the other, I exercise a descriptive and analytic perspective in understanding the ways in which people accomplish both a sense of who they are and who the others who make up their social worlds are.

Towards these ends, the book moves the reader through a section in which perspectives for understanding the subjective character of social phenomena are presented. Next, the reader will find materials which introduce concepts of and approaches to the study and comprehension of social life. The student will find introductory sections on some of the most influential thinkers in social psychology. By studying these early thinkers and pulling ideas of lasting significance out of their theories the reader should become more familar with the language and concepts of social psychology. I believe such familiarity should lead the reader toward seeing everyday life in a social psychological relief.

In the middle chapters of the book, the reader will discover treatments of some of the major concerns of social psychology. Socialization, groups, language, inequality, deviance, gender identity, aggression, collective behavior, and emotions are the topics which are submitted to social psychological scrutiny.   Throughout the chapters dealing with these topics there are descriptions of the phenomena under investigation.   These descriptive accounts are not merely examples of concepts, but are in a very real sense the data of the book.   The actual life experiences depicted in this book are designed to appeal to undergraduate students and to serve as reference points for the process of making sense out of what is read.   Such acts of interpretation are, of course, at the heart of constructing and maintaining the very subject matter of the text.

A concluding chapter reviews the many-sided nature of social psychology as it is developed here.   Although readers will see how schools of thought divide the efforts and energies of analysts and researchers, they will also understand the common themes which weave this work into a comprehensive social psychology.

Acknowledgments

In a most profound sense, this book is a tribute to my deeply missed friend, James P. Spradley.   When I first joined the faculty at Macalester College, he suggested that we collaborate on a text so that the materials and ideas of the sociologists who studied everyday life would be accessible to undergraduate students.   We worked for several years on a book in which we wanted to integrate his interest in urban anthropology with mine in the sociology of everyday life.   The book was never to be.   But the ideas that he instilled in me, the style he inspired me with, his insistence on examples, and his keen appreciation of the diverse and intrinsically interesting nature of the fine-grained details of social life guided me through the writing of this book.   It is my fondest wish that he would have approved of the work I have done.

Of course, the actual writing of the book would not have been possible without the understanding of Clark Baxter, an editor who hared the purposes of this text from the very beginning and whose supportive attitude really helped.   Reviewers, I understand, are supposed to concern themselves with the "nuts and bolts" issues of a book, and the principal readers for this text did their job well.   They gave criticism and instruction which ranged from my misreading of literature to where to dot the i's and cross the t's.   These criticisms from the reviewers, careful and sympathetic, made the text possible.   The reviewers were Brad Stone at Oglethorpe University, J.M. Calonico at the University of New Orleans at Lake Front, Marnie Sayles at the University of Akron, John M. Johnson at Arizona State University, and Charles W. Tucker at the University of South Carolina at Columbia.   To all the reviewers—I'd gladly do it again.

This book has been tested on my often unsuspecting students at Macalester.   They tried the exercises, heard the lectures, and some even read the manuscript.   Most of them liked it, and a few offered telling criticisms and helpful suggestions. They are responsible, in part, for the idea of this text. A special thanks to Susan Lowry who may have a future as an editor.

Finally, my family was a part of this project in ways that go far beyond tolerating me. Their lives are a part of my sociological imagination. There are three of them. I know one understands and I hope the other two will come to with time. To Anedith, Marc, and Jason.

Social Psychology

Chapter One

The Discipline: Its Purposes and Methods

OUTLINE

The Discipline:
Its Purposes and Methods

Several years ago a tragic event occurred in a large eastern city. A police car sped into a Latin-American neighborhood and pulled to an abrupt stop alongside the curb; uniformed officers jumped out of the car. People on the street and in nearby homes observing this action began to converge on the scene. What they saw sent a shudder of horror and anger through the growing crowd of spectators. The policemen had a helpless woman pinned to the ground; she appeared unconscious, and one officer was beating her on the chest with his fist. The other made furtive glances toward the increasingly larger number of onlookers while he held the woman to the ground.

In a matter of seconds, the neighborhood became electrified. Word spread from those at the front to newcomers, and the crowd began to grow more agitated; people pointed, talked, and cursed. Enraged at what they saw, they suddenly rushed at the policemen, knocking them away from the woman. A melee followed. Several minutes later, after cooler heads prevailed, the brawl ended. Lying on the ground was the dead body of the woman.

In the angry confusion that followed, people began to discover another interpretation for the actions of the police officers: they learned that the woman has suffered a serious cardiac arrest, the officers found her alive but unconscious when they arrived and immediately attempted to administer external cardiac massage to get her heart started again. In the midst of their efforts, the crowd of neighbors and friends had intervened, interpreting the police officer's actions in completely different terms. The woman died in a matter of minutes.

2

How many times have you heard the expression, "Do you know what I mean?" Apparently, at least in our society, we are not always sure about other people's intentions and motives. Much of what occupies our everyday lives consists of trying to figure out what is happening to us and to the people who make up our social worlds. Even though the process of making sense out of each other's actions may be problematic, as members of society we learn to guess what other people intend, and most importantly, we know how to act on the basis of those guesses.

This book is about efforts of social psychologists to understand how people learn to live together. The focus of the book is on everyday life. However, I will also discuss how people behave in the artificial environment of the laboratory and in unusual circumstances like accidents and emergencies. The discipline of social psychology draws on many areas of research and on several theoretical traditions. I will introduce the reader to most of these, but at the outset, I want to make it clear that this approach is a part of what is sometimes called the qualitative movement in social science. This means that in the study of social psychology, we are concerned with the feelings, thoughts and language of ordinary people, and hope to preserve in the prose the flavor of the experiences that make up their social existence.

In these pages I will introduce the reader to a sociological perspective of social psychology. My aim is ambitious: I work from an assumption that virtually every aspect of social life can be understood from the perspective of social psychology.

SOCIAL PSYCHOLOGY AS PERSPECTIVE

Social psychology seeks to understand human experience. From the moment of conception, human beings live out their lives under the influence of other people. And, although death is an individual experience, it is also a profoundly social experience. Society pervades our lives; it even affects parts of our lives that we do not ordinarily think of as concerning other people. For example, how we sleep, the decor of our bedroom, and even the content of our dreams may be influenced by a magazine we have just read, a relationship we just ended, or the last video game we played. It is impossible to escape the bonds of our fellows. The Japanese soldier who hid in the Philippine jungles for twenty-five years waiting for the end of World War II still lived under the constraint of the distant society to which he belonged. His refusal to surrender made perfect sense to him in terms of his understanding of the social values of the Japanese society. Ours is a social existence, one created and shared with other people. Hence, to understand a person is to understand people. The social and the psychological are inseparable in this task of understanding.

Social psychologists seek to understand the web of social influences that surround every human being. They address a series of questions whose answers help them to understand. What is it about the species that people everywhere, in normal conditions, seem to need their own kind? What is society? Of what is it composed? What are social pressures and how do individuals deal with them? What are the differences, if any, between the social lives of males and females? How do children learn the ways of their social worlds? Why are people so inclined to communicate? What are the purposes and forms of aggression? These and hundreds of other questions guide social psychologists in their study of social and psychological phenomena.

One of the fundamental questions in social psychology has to do with method: "How shall we study humans in groups?" This question has been debated throughout the history of the discipline, and differences of opinion continue to the present day. Among the diverse answers to this question, two are especially important for our purposes.

On one hand, many social psychologists insist that social psychological research should follow as closely as possible the canons of rigorous scientific research. Wanting to emulate the techniques of physics, chemistry, and biology, they seek to make objective, detached observations about social life. Their ideal is to gather data under carefully controlled laboratory conditions. For the purposes of research, human beings and their social situations are treated as equivalent to the kinds of objects and creatures studied by the natural sciences. The goal of this kind of social psychology is to identify the causes of behavior and, ultimately, to make accurate predictions of the behaviors of individuals in groups.

On the other hand, advocates of social psychology as a part of the sociological perspective maintain that although the techniques of the natural sciences provide significant information about some aspects of people living with people, alone these techniques fall short of providing an adequate understanding of the social dimensions of human existence. In its search for rigor, social psychology as a specialty of the science of psychology may miss some essential social phenomena, namely the subjective intentions and motives of individuals. Humans have intentions, wishes, reasons, motives, and meanings that enter into social interaction. Social phenomena are not objective entities but are the results of relationships made from subjective meanings. The essence of any human group is the set of realities created by group members themselves, including people whose primary preoccupation seems to be figuring out what everybody else thinks is real. In this text, the purpose of social psychology is to understand the complicated ways in which social life is accomplished. Like many aspects of life, the principles that underlie a phenomenon may seem simple. Indeed, as we shall learn, often a simple rule will underline the organization of a conversation, such as the understanding that one person speaks at a time. It is the practice of that rule, however, that gives us an appreciation of the sophisticated skills of our species.

Social psychology as a part of psychology has, by and large, followed the model of the natural sciences, and this tactic has paid off in certain respects. For instance, from studies we know a great deal about formation and maintenance of attitudes. Likewise, we have amassed impressive information on how people react to group pressure and how they transmit messages through various group structures. Succeeding chapters will sift through those findings to present the strongest and most compelling knowledge available about the behavior of people in social settings.

Still, in this book, a different kind of appreciation of the social world is presented. Just as a scientific psychologist assumes that humans can be studied as "subjects" in an experiment, the sociologist who uses social psychology as a perspective also makes assumptions. Chief among these is the assertion that humans have a unique quality distinquishing them from other animals and from the world of things. People do not merely respond, they act and react in terms of how they interpret their environments. People have purposes to carry out, plans to organize their actions, and methods that they employ to join in the building, and even the destroying, of social worlds. In a very real sense, all persons act as scientists do when they plan and carry out an experiment. Everyday life is purposeful, full of intentions and meanings; it does not just happen.

The approach taken in this book, which we are calling social psychology, has a venerable history. Its goal is to understand social life in a way that fully accepts a "human coefficient." It begins with the conviction that the study of social life concerns subjective meanings, the socially constructed realities people live by. This belief requires that we preserve the points of view of the people we study both in terms of their beliefs, feelings, and actions, and in the idioms we select to communicate about these matters. We will learn how to use experimental observations, survey data, and information gathered in a variety of sometimes ingenious ways. Throughout, our target is to comprehend the relativity of social life while searching for the principles that make such relativity possible.

Basic Elements of Social Phenomena

Social phenomena involve subjective meanings   We might say that the event which was related at the beginning of this chapter was a social event merely because people were involved—human beings interacting with one another. Communication occurred between the policemen and among some individuals in the crowd which had quickly assembled. From a strictly objective point of view, we could contend that what was social in this situation involved the physical presence of people together and their observable behaviors. We might even assume the perspective of an outsider and try to depict behaviors and their patterns without asking the people involved what happened. There are times in the work of the social psychologist when such a stance can help greatly in understanding how a particular strip, or string of events, can take place. Using this tactic, we could learn the age, sex, ethnic background, and skin color of the participants all of which are important facts. We can also learn about the physical setting that served as a backdrop for this human drama. But if we know nothing about the subjective world of people—their thoughts and intentions and, most crucially, the meanings they read into situations—the events will remain a mystery. In sociological social psychology, we begin with this hidden world of subjective meanings and seek to describe it.

The observable events and actions that took place in our example have both an objective and a subjective reality. This is another way of saying they can be viewed from the outside or the inside. Objectively, the policemen knelt beside a woman lying unconscious on the ground. One man repeatedly raised his hand, bringing it down in a hammer-like fashion, striking the chest of an apparently helpless woman. We could objectively describe this behavior in more detail but the question would still remain: "What did the police officers do to this woman?" The answer takes us to another level of understanding. It leads us from the objective reality recorded by an outside observer to the subjective reality as seen by the various persons participating in the situation. And as we have seen, there was more than a single subjective reality operating among the people at the scene. This leads us to our next point about social phenomena.

The subjective meanings that constitute social phenomena are arbitrary   By **arbitrary** we do not mean that you can call what the policemen did anything you like and still understand their motives. Further, when we say meanings are arbitrary, we do so in full awareness that human beings are restricted, in the same way that all life forms are, by laws of biology and psychology. For example, all people must eat, but the matter and customs of eating are arbitrarily defined by the culture to which one belongs. We can be specific about what we mean by arbitrary: the meaning of a social action is said to be arbitrary whenever that action has a significance that, in some sense, was put there by people. By implication, arbitrary meanings vary from person to person and group to group.

On this point social psychology aligns its perspective with those of many other disciplines. Anthropologists regard culture as arbitrary. Linguists write of languages, with their rules and content, as arbitrary. The great sociologist Emile Durkheim wrote that there is nothing intrinsic in any act that makes it have one meaning over another. For example, nothing in the nature of a person striking another human being demands that we understand it as a hostile or even aggressive act. A football player strikes a teammate on the buttocks with a resounding blow as they start to run on the field together. What does this act mean? A young man strikes his friend on the shoulder with his fist. A father asks his young son to hit him in the stomach as hard as he can, as the father flexes his abdominal muscles. Two youths attack an old man, hitting with their fists on his chest. A policeman strikes a woman repeatedly on the chest as she lies on the ground. Do all these similar actions mean the same thing? All are social acts, but their meanings vary. More importantly, each of these actions can have numerous meanings depending on the circumstances in which they occur. In the language of social psychology, we say that meanings are **situated**.

In human societies anything imaginable can take on subjective meanings and become part of the social process. A slight movement of one eyelid or a tiny movement of the head may arbitrarily be assigned meaning. A person stands among a group of friends motionlessly and in silence; the absence of behavior in this instance may be quite meaningful. A young man runs along a city street, and the meaning of his behavior changes with the time of day, whether late afternoon, early evening, or three in the morning. And what his behavior means varies from the observer to the actor, and from one observer to another.

The **arbitrary meanings** which make up social life take on even greater importance when we look at societies other than our own. It is easy to see that the sounds of languages have different meanings, but we might overlook such subtleties of behavior as how close people stand when they talk. In Latin-American societies the physical distance between people in normal conversations is much less than for our own society. Although this subjective meaning assigned to "talking distance," as the anthropologist Edward Hall calls it, is largely outside of awareness; still we know if someone stands too close when talking. Hall observed two businessmen, a Latin- and a North-American, talking. The former would move a bit closer to feel comfortable with the conversation. The subjective meanings assigned by the American businessman to this new proximity raised feelings that the other person was pushy, and he began to feel ill at ease. He stepped back. In a few seconds as the conversation continued at full clip, the Latin businessman stepped forward; the American retreated. And so the pair marched down a long corridor, unaware of their own rules, but acting on them nonetheless. Each had learned an arbitrary meaning for how close to stand when talking. Sociological social psychology takes as its first task the understanding of the subjective meanings that make up the very fabric of social life.

Social phenomena are more than subjective: they are intersubjective In the examples we have given we have portrayed situations where individuals do not share completely the same meanings for a particular event. Misunderstandings occur frequently in complex societies and lead to the disruption of social interaction. But in all societies, the subjective meanings that constitute social phenomena are, to some extent, shared, or **intersubjective**.

Two police officers are speeding toward the Latin-American neighborhood. As the driver of the car increases speed, the other interprets his action as reasonable given the urgency of a citizen's report. They share similar definitions of "appropriate speed." One says, "It's a cardiac arrest," and the other nods his head. Somehow they share in the subjective meanings of a complex condition they have not actually seen. "Let's go," says the other officer as the car comes to a screeching halt and he opens the door. Both know what is meant by this short utterance. Both view the woman lying on the ground in much the same way and begin their joint efforts to administer first-aid. In some strange way that we will

Make a list of five possible subjective experiences which could be the reason this group is gathered. In groupings like this one the existence of the gathering does not depend on all the people having the same common experiences. They must, however, think they are working toward a common end. Social reality is constructed out of intersubjective phenomena.

try to uncover and analyze in this book, these two men achieve a form of mutual consciousness. They have come to share the subjective meanings of the situation, or at least they think they share these meanings and act on them as if they in fact shared them.

If we merely assume the stance of an outsider, it is easy to miss the significance of this intersubjective element in social life. The policemen appear to share the same physical space, the squad car; they have similar clothes; they look about the same age and size; both are white. But these are external characteristics the observer thinks they share. From the participant's vantage these commonalities may be totally irrelevant to this specific happening. They select, as it were, from a host of characteristics the ones that they can use in order to accomplish a practical act. The sense of sharing that they achieve for the moment is a relative thing. Many subjective meanings can function as a sufficient reason to act. Some of these are so thoroughly shared by members of a society that they are rarely talked about. These are the hidden assumptions which we all have learned about the nature of life and the grand purposes of existence. Other meanings are quite specific to a certain setting, like the idea of "this is a

In collective or mass order, minimal intersubjective experience supports social reality. When we do not have much information about the actual experiences of others, we rely on their appearance to figure out what they are doing and we expect them to judge us accordingly.

woman who has just had a heart attack." Some meanings are easily accomplished and rarely result in problems for those who seek to use them. Greetings are good examples of these. Other meanings may be so elusive yet still regarded as of such importance that interactions based on them are almost always highly problematic. Love is perhaps the best example of this.

Social phenomena consist of socially constructed realities For some social psychologists, human beings are like complex computers, carefully programmed with social attributes and knowledge, reacting to situations in ways they were programmed to act. Although few would defend this analogy to the last detail, there are whole schools of thought which, depending on where they start, argue that people are not especially distinctive among forms of life, or that it is not a wild pipe dream to envision computers with human capabilities. We think this analogy seriously distorts both the nature of computers and the character of human social life.

When people interact they do so on the basis of their intersubjective understandings of a particular situation. To be sure, we will learn that they do follow rules somewhat like computers do, but the understandings on which the social world is built are never static. Each situation requires a creative solution, a working-out process, or, in the idiom of social psychology, a **negotiation** or *definition of the situation.* The Latin-Americans who stood as spectators did not automatically react to the policemen, nor did they merely follow a rule about how to act around white policemen. Instead, they made judgments about what was happening. They weighted possible interpretations of the event taking place before them. Communications flitted back and forth among the people watching, by gesture, word of mouth, posture, facial expressions, and bodily movement. A social reality was constructed, shared by some but not all, and action flowed out of this subjective assessment of the situation. That action, of course, was gravely real in its consequences.

The essence of human social life is a construction of meanings which people find sufficient for living their lives. The approach to social psychology we have called sociological social psychology takes as its primary task the careful description and analysis of these meanings and the realities that derive from them.

As we mentioned earlier, an important question of social psychology is how we know about social phenomena; in other words, how do we go about understanding the lives of people? Although there are volumes devoted to this question, we can outline one major distinction which researchers follow when gathering information about social phenomena.

KNOWING ABOUT SOCIAL PHENOMENA: DEDUCTIVE AND INDUCTIVE OBSERVATIONS

Simply from living in a conscious state, all of us have learned a great deal about social phenomena. In our ordinary state of mind, however, we rarely question seriously how we learned what we know and do. It is enough for the practical purposes of everyday life to know how to do something.

The social psychologist follows a different path, one that requires a continuous inquiry about how we know what to do. The act of doing social psychology, then, is extraordinary. A goal of this inquiry is to be able to make the grounds of social interaction explicit so that others may understand precisely how social life is carried on.

The social psychologist must simultaneously live and act in the ordinary world and also view that world as a whole in order to reframe and present to others a version of how the world works. This is a difficult job which demands not only a thorough awareness of living in society but also a thorough mastery of devices for distancing oneself from experiences. It is obvious that no single social psychologist can have all, or even a significant portion of the array of experiences for all members of society.

Although the subjective experiences which serve as the components of social reality may vary from individual to individual, to the observer social reality often appears to be a uniform and regular phenomenon.

In the complex, modern world, the prospect of appreciating all the various ways in which people make sense out of their social lives overwhelms the individual. However, concentrating on an understanding of only our own accomplishments, our little corner of the world, is equally undesirable. So we can easily see that the social psychologists must have help to escape the dilemma of too much experience versus not enough experience. The escape comes in the form of methods that allow us vicarious and indirect experience. A major part of social psychology is, then, concerned with discovering the nature and range of human experience.

We are trying to understand two types of people: those who have had experiences and those who wish to understand those experiences. There are two general methods used to reach this goal. The first is a cumulative and indirect approach and the second is creative and direct. The first type of inquiry we will call understanding through **deductive observation** and the second, understanding through **inductive observation**. The reader should note that I will be using the terms deduction and induction in a way that is subtly different from the traditional one. I use deduction to refer to the act of understanding specific experiences from the application of more general ideas, or concepts, while induction is an understanding which emerges in its general expression from specific and context-bound experiences. Both processes of understanding are part of the encompassing effort of the social psychologist to understand social phenomena. Hence, the separation of the two observational methods is itself somewhat arbitrary, but necessary for the purposes of distinguishing ways to know about social realities.

Deductive observations are remarks, comments, and interpretations of the experiences of others that are guided by a systematically organized way of thinking. Whenever we judge some action to have a meaning by relying on a body of knowledge that we know already exists—usually in books, lectures, or conversations among those who have read the books and heard the lectures—we are making deductive observations. At the level of common sense (common sense can be both an ordinary concept and a scientific one) we can say that the Latin-American crowd misunderstood the actions of the policemen. When we say this we go beyond the description of the events in terms of their subjective meanings. At least, we are evaluating these meanings by comparing them and finding them dissimilar. Although we may not be very articulate in relating to another person just how we made the comparison and drew the conclusion, nevertheless, we did it.

In social psychology it is required that we be explicit about how we make our evaluations. We follow this requirement in order to meet at least some shared expectations about the scientific status of our inquiry. By being explicit we allow others the opportunity to make alternative evaluations, and we make public our techniques for acquiring knowledge of experience. What makes this process essentially deductive is that it is a process of discovering meaning through the application of ideas, typically the ideas of others who have attempted to understand social experiences and to relate that understanding to an audience.

Discovering meaning through the application of ideas may be depicted according to stepwise phases. First comes the concept itself; second, the experiences (observations); third, the intellectual act of matching concept with experience; and fourth, the formulation of a **theme** or **hypothesis** that evaluates the experience in terms of the concept. (See figure 1.1)

The act of observation is fundamental to all scientific inquiry. In order to observe subjective experiences and how these experiences become the stuff of social reality, some special types of observations are required, but the attitude of the curious observer is still essential.

Phase one which we have called concepts requires that the social psychologist be conversant with the ideas of the discipline. We have already mentioned that social psychology has a history which is available to us in the form of written texts. Of course, this book is a part of that history. To do a deductively organized study, the student first must understand concepts of social psychology. You acquire this understanding by communicating with others who have it.

Concepts are arranged in the textual materials of social psychology according to plans and schemes. Some of these ideas have been worked on by many scholars and researchers who have organized them into tightly woven systems of sentences called **theories**. In sociological social psychology, there are theories of attitude formation and change, self concept development, and even of turn taking in conversations. Theories may be **grand** in the sense that they pertain to experiences which are general,

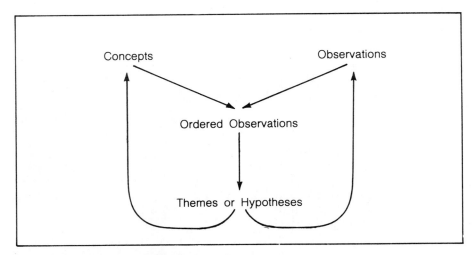

Figure 1.1   Deductively Organized Observations

shared by all or large portions of a population of people, or they may be **delimited** to a specific population, like a people who practice acts regarded by others as perverse or deviant.

Not all concepts are so well organized. Those that are new, just articulated in the latest journal, or recently conceived but which seem to have the potential to become more fully developed, we call **theory sketches**. Social psychology has many of these as we will soon learn. Last, there are ideas that have profound impact on our understanding of some aspects of social experience, but which consist of a single idea, sort of a big insight. These are referred to as **isolated concepts** (Wilson and Dumont 1967; Ogles 1980).

A concept may be gotten from any one of these three sources: theory, theory sketch, or isolated concept. Of course, the power and the degree to which a particular study contributes to our understanding depends on the relationship between the study and the concept. A study may seem to disprove a whole theory, or suggest a possible new theory, or simply be provocative.

Observations are sets of awarenesses which we associate with our experience. They can be treated as information in social psychology by packaging them as data. We can do this by recalling what we know in the form of strings of happenings, telling stories about our past or about the actions of others. Or, as social psychologists, we may simply watch other people; however, we must be on the scene, be there first hand.

There are many strategies for watching people. These range from becoming a full participant in the social phenomenon (being an actual member of the group, for instance) to merely standing by, watching and wondering about the goings-on before you. No matter which strategy proves to be most useful to a particular study, the sense of being there must be conveyed in the report. Being in the presence of the social reality forces the observer to figure out what is happening, to use vicarious or newly acquired experiences to capture the essence of what is seen.

Among the many ways that experiences may be readied for analysis are talking with people (the **interview**), writing up the totality of a person's experiences (the **life history**), or asking people to write or tell you about their experiences. Some of these methods of social psychological research will be introduced in more detail throughout the text. Now, I want to review the organization of deductive observations and provide an example.

Observations that are guided by concepts are deductive because they move from abstract generalizations to specific instances of experiences. Deduction in traditional logic has a stricter definition; it refers to following steps of reasoning to draw conclusions about events from law-like sentences of which the syllogism is the classic example. However, our use of the term captures the procedure of analysis which allows us to use ready knowledge to interpret sets of actual social happenings.

A study that I did in 1980 exemplifies this process. Suppose as social psychologists, we are interested in the general concept of well-being. First we would read several books that offer definitions of well-being. We discover that well-being is measured by asking people how satisfied they are with their place of residence, jobs, family relationships, and what their outlook is for the future (Institute for Social Research Newsletter 1983). We also know that a valid principle for understanding how people assess their experiences is that these assessments vary a great deal from situation to situation. If you ask a person about his view of the future, you are apt to get quite different answers depending on what that person just heard from Payne Weber.

Well-being, as we understand it has to do with feeling good, being satisfied, and generally optimistic. We also are aware that much of the classic theory of sociology properly stresses how difficult it is to feel well in modern society. Durkheim wrote of anomie, Marx of alienation, Weber of disenchantment. Contemporary sociologists like Goffman and Irwin suggest that modern life is shallow, consisting of the acts of manipulating appearances for the purposes of getting what you want from other people (Goffman 1959) (Irwin 1977). Hardly the stuff of well being, we conclude.

So from all these concepts, some of which are tightly woven into theories and others just loosely articulated ideas, we come up with a conceptual problem of our own. We wonder how in the world people manage to feel well in modern society? We look for people who seem to consistently be well. We hope that a careful analysis of what these people mean by feeling well will provide us with some clues to solving our conceptual problem. We aim to sharpen the concept of well-being (Nash 1980).

Literally millions of men and women perform a strange ritual everyday. They put on specially designed, scanty clothes, shoes that bear exotic names, and they run for long distances for no apparent reason through the streets of every major city in the country. You can see these folks everywhere. Chances are you have even engaged in this rite yourself. When we talk to these people about their experiences, they tell us that they cannot live without the ritual. They say that the ritual changed their lives, improved their physical and mental condition. In short, it seems to promote well-being. How do they arrive at such meanings for an experience that requires the exertion of energy, and may, on occasion be painful?

First we find several of these ritualists, and get to know them as best we can. We talk to them, ask them to tell us about their experiences, and we may even try the ritual ourselves. In time, we start to appreciate how runners make sense of their experiences. We find that they evaluate their performance by timing themselves, they record the distances they travel, and they meet on weekends to test themselves against one another by running prescribed distances. We notice that only one person wins these weekend races, and yet people who do not win seem perfectly satisfied, indeed even elated, about not winning. We probe deeper and discover that racers compare themselves with others according to all sorts of provisos: how old they are, how much they train, the weather on race day, the course layout itself, and a host of idiosyncratic concerns. After sifting through the information we have gathered about how these people make sense out of their ritual, we discover that they all see running as an event, a special occasion organized just for their needs as runners. We find that some of these people have made a career out of organizing racing and running events. We gain a thorough understanding of this organization and then we formulate our own conceptual sentences.

We conclude that the state of well-being seems to be an outcome of participation in events that have a certain organization. These events are generally recognizable to all who believe running is good. Yet, they are flexible enough to allow each participant his or her own version of their performances. We hypothesize that it is participation in events so organized that allows a person, in spite of the great odds against him or her, to feel well. Well-being, then, is not so much an attribute of an individual's psychology as it is a result of interaction in situations of a distinctive organization.

There are many variations on the study just reported, but all deductively arranged observations are guided by concepts that we find. We apply these concepts, change them in the process, and gain a full understanding of social phenomena.

Inductively organized observations (see figure 1.2) can be thought of as a process of discovering meanings through experienced interpretations. Some of these studies seem exotic in comparison with deductive approaches. Most of us are familiar with the general outline of the study of well-being. However, the inductive approach requires that we do a little mental gymnastics.

The inquirer starts with an idealization, namely pure experience. Obviously, no such thing exists as pure, uninterpreted experience; however, it

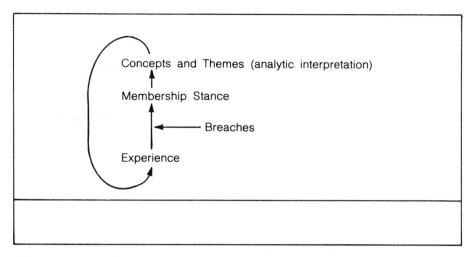

Figure 1.2   Inductively Organized Observations

can be imagined. The researcher proceeds from a mental state in which he or she assumes that nothing whatsoever is known about the phenomenon in question. Starting with this assumption of naivety allows the social psychologist, at least figuratively, to become the phenomenon. Social psychologists say that whenever this state is achieved, the researcher has accomplished a **membership stance,** meaning that he or she can think, act, and feel like the people being studied.

After having arrived at this level of knowing, the researcher then can draw on another set of rules to decide what is happening; here his or her expertise as a social psychologist comes into play. The analytic task is identical to that in deductive observation. Concepts, theories, and ideas from the literature of social psychology are applied in order to gain a fresh perspective on the experience. However, the researcher must not miss the significant differences between deduction and induction. In the deductive approach, the analyst's consciousness builds on existing knowledge of the social world. In the inductive approach, he or she builds on experience itself. Often the acquisition of membership knowledge is a dramatic occurrence.

Since the researcher is purposely naive, when the point of view of the members is actually seen, consequences might be shocking. For example, one researcher reports precisely how a hit man learned to control his emotions during the act of murder. After several months of visiting the hit man and listening to his stories, the researcher was able to at least empathize with the man. In this case, we are allowed to understand and appreciate how a man coolly and deliberately kills another; it seems that part of the secret is in not looking into the victim's eyes, an interesting comment on the power of nonverbal communication.

More generally, the research on the hit man (Levi 1981) shows how hit men learn to disassociate the ordinary meanings of human interaction. Levi interviewed one hit man, Pete, who described this ability to disassociate as "heart," which he defined as "coldness." The hit man just "blanks out" when he kills. He learns a negative routine which helps him transform his victims into targets. Hit men reframe their experiences so that features of their victims are now attended in a negative way:

> [The victim was] a nice looking woman . . . She started weeping, and [she cried] "I ain't did this, I ain't did that . . . and [Pete, how the informant referred to himself] said that he shot her. Like it was nothing . . . he didn't feel nothing. It was just money (Levi 1981, 59).

The assumption of membership stances can be hastened through the use of certain techniques, devices and equipment. For example, the researcher may attempt to draw maps of the occasions of experiences as if he or she were leading a stranger into his or her house. This is a task much like playing a fantasy game where someone must find a way out of a dungeon by giving instructions to a stranger in a limited language (Fine 1983). Or, the researcher may actually wear special glasses that invert the usual perception of the world thereby forcing the wearer to become conscious of his or her ways of knowing the ordinary world.

The occasion of having one's experiences disordered is called a **breach**. Breaches may happen naturally, as when you begin talking to someone whom you mistake for a close friend, only to discover that the person is a stranger; or when you believe you are alone and act accordingly only to look up and see that you are being observed. Breaches may also be contrived; they may by the result of carefully designed behaviors. A well-known illustration of this is the assignment Garfinkel gave his students to behave as if they were visitors in their own homes over a Christmas vacation. Garfinkel also devised an experiment which shows the extent to which people go to discover subjective meaning in their experiences. He used a breaching procedure. He requested that students participate in what he called "an exercise." They were informed that they were a part of an experiment to explore alternative means to psychotherapy as a way of giving people advice about their personal problems. The students were to discuss any problem they wished into a taperecorder as they sat before a one-way mirror in front of a desk. They were to phrase their questions in such a fashion that the questions could be answered with a simple "yes" or "no" by the counselor on the other side of the one-way mirror.

Actually, on the other side of the mirror was an experimenter who responded with random yes's and no's to the questions submitted. The students, undaunted by these meaningless responses, searched out patterns of meaning. They presumed the existence of a qualified counselor and made sense out of apparently contradictory advice: this advice was the breach. When asked his opinion of the advice he received after the experiment was concluded, one student replied:

The answers I received, I must say that the majority of them were answered the same way that I would answer them to myself knowing the differences in types of people. One or two of them did come as a surprise to me and I felt the reason perhaps he answered these questions the way he did is . . . that he is not aware of the personalities involved and how they are reacting or would react to a certain situation (Garfinkel 1962, 696).

A final method to arrive at understanding is imaginative reconstruction, or the use of fictive devices. Frequently, it is impossible to observe, talk with, or elicit information from those we wish to understand. For many reasons, face-to-face contact may not be feasible. In such an instance, the social psychologist does not forgo research and analysis. Instead, he or she exercises his or her imagination to reconstruct what the phenomena of interest may be like, or used to be like. The researcher relies on all the materials he or she can get: historical accounts, diaries, case and life studies, court opinions, newspaper stories and reports, and other data. Then, the researcher imagines the context, or surroundings, and interprets the phenomena in appropriate or plausible ways. The researcher tries to imagine the phenomena as if he or she were there.

Sometimes this imaginative exercise employs another device called the **ideal type**, a concept I will discuss more fully later. For now, the ideal type is defined as a fictitious construction, invented by the social psychologist, for the purposes of finding out what a given social phenomenon is like. For example, in order to imagine what the parents of a deaf child might experience, we, as social psychologists, can suggest a type of parent we will call the "sign changer." These parents, our information indicates, believe that some form of manual communication, using the hands as the sole instrument of communication, is necessary for their child to learn normal communicative competency. However, they do not wish their child to master the sign language of the deaf because they believe that that language is less desirable than English. So they have a positive attitude toward manual communication and a negative one toward deafness. This predisposes them to look for a means of communication other than that used by deaf people. They select their own language, English, and change the signs to fit English, inventing articles (sign language has none), and reordering sign sequences to conform to English word order.

Our type of parent may not exist as a real person at all. We admittedly exaggerate to create a fictitious character. But our imagining of a plausible type of person allows us to discover trends, interrelationships, and overall patterns in social phenomena.

SUMMARY

Social psychology seeks to understand social life by recognizing the importance of subjective meanings. It must attend to the distinctive qualities of these experiences—their arbitrary, intersubjective, and constructed nature. The goal of understanding can be realized by following procedures and rules that social psychologists have devised for conducting studies. These procedures and rules can be summarized according to how observations are organized, either deductively or inductively. Deduction begins with established understanding in the form of theories and various kinds of concepts. These are applied to sets of experiences which the researcher acquires directly or indirectly. The theories or concepts turn out to be valid, or they are modified or discarded.

The inductive approach moves the researcher from naive or unanalyzed experience to social psychological understanding by ways of processing or reorganizing ordinary happenings. In the task of social psychology, special attention is given to capturing the sense of the experience in the description and in higher-order understandings of observations.

EXERCISES IN SOCIAL PSYCHOLOGICAL UNDERSTANDING

1. Next time you are at a public restaurant, take notes on the activites of the people around you. Notice how they are eating, what they are doing with their hands, and their general posture and over-all appearance. Do not eavesdrop and do not be concerned with finding out what they are actually talking about. After you have about three pages of detailed observation, think of three different versions of what they may be doing. Match the details of your versions with the details from your observations.

This exercise will increase your conscious awareness of how we impute meanings to the actions of others in everyday life. Since you will probably be able to support all three versions with your observations, it will also help you appreciate the nature of social phenomena. It is a good idea to show how each version you have of what is going on addresses the features of social phenomena (subjectivity, arbitrary definitions, intersubjectivity, and constructed realities).

2. When you are out about town, pay attention to people who exercise in public. A city park is an excellent site for doing this work. See if you can classify them into different groups—joggers, bicyclists, walkers, etc. Try to come up with at least four groups. Describe the range of appearances within each of the groups. Now, think of a label which depicts the activities of each group, with at least two words or phrases for the variation within the type. You should be able to draw a simple table with labels and sub-labels from your observations. This exercise should help you understand how to induce concepts from observations.

KEY CONCEPTS

Social phenomena
Subjective meanings

Arbitrary
Situated
Arbitrary meanings
Intersubjective meanings
Negotiation
Deductive observations
Inductive observations
Theme or hypothesis
Concepts
Theories
Grand theories
Delimited theories
Theory sketches
Isolated concepts
Interview
Life history
Membership stance
Breach
Ideal type

SUGGESTED READINGS

A good way to become familiar with social psychology is to read some examples of it. Introductory materials can cover a wide range of topics which will be treated later in the text under special headings. For now, the interested student should read a few pieces to get the feel of social psychology. We suggest Levi's article for its appeal and dramatic impact; Georges and Jones' for the way they deal with the subjectivity of research and the range of information one can get from them; and finally, for the more serious methodologically minded reader, Ogles' paper both introduces the reader to the types of observational research done and to a novel idea about how to come up with valid concepts.

Georges, Robert A., and Michael O. Jones. *People Studying People: The Human Element in Fieldwork.* University of California Press, 1980.

Levi, Ken, "Becoming a Hit Man: Neutralization in a Very Deviant Career." *Urban Life: A Journal of Ethnographic Research* 10, No. 1 (April 1981):47–63.

Ogles, Richard H. "Concept Formation in Sociology: The Ordering of Observational Data by Observational Concepts" in *Theoretical Methods in Sociology,* ed. by Lee Freese. University of Pittsburgh Press, 1980.

Chapter Two

The Origins of Social Psychology

OUTLINE

The Origins of
Social Psychology

Two students walk across campus on their way to class on a warm spring day. "What class are you goin' to?" says Ben. "Sociology," replies John. "Oh, I took a soc class one time. All the prof did was talk about what some guys said a long time ago about society and self. Seemed to me just like a bunch of different opinions." "Yeah, I know what you mean; but I guess there might be some good ideas in some of that stuff," John responds. "Maybe," Ben concedes, "but I'm glad it's your class and not mine."

They walk on in silence, then John says, "You know, I disagree. Those ideas aren't just opinions. I think it's not so much that they are valid or invalid, true or false, but they represent ways of seeing the world, perspectives on what things mean to people. Some of those ideas are pretty interesting." "Yeah, well, I still prefer math. It has real answers!" Ben counters. "See you for lunch."

THE influential social psychologist, Gordon Allport, pointed out that a history of social psychology need not be a "tour through a museum of oddities and antiquities" (Allport 1968, 1). However, the study of its history can be justified to the extent that it shows the relevance of present-day theory and research. This relevance can be appreciated by casting previous thinking and research in a contemporary context. The accumulation of knowledge is crucial to science. The ideal is for the researcher to stand on the shoulders of giants, or in other words, to build his or her thinking on the foundations of earlier theories and facts. While there can be little doubt that much, if not all, of scientific knowledge accumulates, it

24

is not as clear whether experiences and common-sense knowledge accumulate. Certainly, we learn from the past, but we also seem to repeat mistakes in our personal lives. Ideas must be applied and experienced to become a part of the social worlds in which we live.

Sometimes the adage "there's nothing new under the sun" seems particularly appropriate with regard to the history of social psychology, for many of the ideas forming the basis of modern sociological social psychology come from thinkers who lived at least eighty years ago. My justification for spending an entire chapter on history is grounded in my perspective itself. Each generation, or class of readers, must learn and interpret ideas in ways that make the ideas relevant to them. This process amounts to building identities on which certain concepts can be hung. When we read about Durkheim, Weber, Mead, Thomas, and others, we are reconstructing their ideas for the purposes of our understanding. These people become abstractions, or as Goffman said "identity pegs" (cf. Goffman 1959).

Since our concern is with the sociological side of social psychology, our history will be biased. We will study persons whose writing and ideas still appear in contemporary literature. To the degree that social psychology is "an attempt to understand and explain how the thought, feeling, and behavior of individuals are influenced by the actual, imagined, or implied presence of others" (Allport 1968, 3), we want to stress the "presence of others" portion of this definition.

Traditionally the "presence of others" has been understood from several different perspectives, each of which persists in modern social psychology. First, there is the notion of social reality itself; second, questions of the nature of the individual; and, third, efforts to explain the links between the individual and social reality.

Although there are many exceptions to this rule, European scholars have seemed to be preoccupied with the nature and power of social forces, while American scholars have worked hard to preserve a place for the dignity of the individual in the face of strong and overpowering social influences. We will work our way through these two tendencies and, then, in the next chapter appreciate the reconciliation of them in the thinking of an Austrian immigrant whose insights have integrated and stimulated modern social psychology.

EMILE DURKHEIM (1850–1917): THE SEARCH FOR SOCIAL EXISTENCE

Emile Durkheim, the great French sociologist, is not usually treated as a founding father of social psychology because his name is so often counted among the fathers of sociology proper. We want to give his work ample appreciation since we believe that social psychology depends first on a strong concept of social reality, and then on an equally persuasive concept of the individual.

Durkheim argued that the word "social" does not simply refer to more than one person. Social life exists, in a sense, independently of individuals; it is simultaneously within and outside of the individual. Although social reality depends on individuals for its creation and continuation, it also influences the individual.

Our ideas of what is socially right and wrong depend upon two interrelated processes:

1. the existence of an external social reality
2. the development of our individual consciousness from that social reality.

We can illustrate these two points with a simple example.

At a northern college, a teacher assigned students the task of constructing snow igloos as part of a class on techniques of winter survival. He gave the students the following instructions: "You will work in groups of three. The igloos will be completed within four weeks; you can use an illustrated handout of a completed igloo as a guide. Each group will use only one tool, a shovel, which you can pick up and return to the supply house near the gymnasium." The instructor offered no explicit rules of conduct or organization. During the month of working on the task as individuals, social realities emerged for each group of students. We will focus on one such group.

After the first day of class, three students met as assigned and decided to get organized. They talked briefly about the task and agreed to meet at 2:30 that afternoon on the field where they would build the igloo. It did not seem necessary to make individual assignments for the tasks involved. At 2:30, eager to begin their work, Don, Jane, and Dawn met on the snow-covered field. "Where's the shovel?" Don asked. "Who has the illustration of the completed igloo?" said Dawn. The shovel was still at the supply house and the illustration, it turned out, had been left in Jane's dormitory room. "This will never do," remarked Dawn. "Let's assign tasks. Don, you get the shovel; Jane, you bring the plans, and I will select a site." "Wait a minute," Don interrupted. "Why should I get the shovel? You're a female chauvinist! I don't like to carry heavy things." "OK, OK," Dawn replied, "I'll get the shovel, you choose the site." "That's better," Jane added. "I don't mind bringing the plans, I have them anyway. See you guys here, same time, tomorrow afternoon."

The next day all three students appeared at 2:30, equipment in hand, ready to start. After a few minutes of shoveling Dawn complained, "I'm tired. You two are just standing around; it's your turn." She laid the shovel down and started looking over the illustration on Jane's paper. Don started to shovel a little faster, piling snow higher and higher. Ten minutes later, he stopped and yelled, "I'm beat. Hey, Jane, work up a little sweat here, will'ya?"

They worked for an hour this way, taking turns shoveling and interpreting the illustration. This routine continued for about four hours a day for four days, until they had an enormous pile of snow. The igloo had begun to take shape, the pile was tall enough to hollow out an entrance and the main cavity. Now the work assignments shifted. This time Jane recommended one of them start to hollow out an inside cavity, one work on the walls to protect the entrance, and one complete the task of piling snow. They decided to rotate tasks every ten minutes. But when the time for rotation arrived, the following conversation took place:

DON: I'm really into this cavity. I don't want to stop. Let me do this, and you two take turns on the entrance and the shoveling.

DAWN: Wait a minute. We decided to rotate, and you can't change that.

JANE: That's right, we all agreed.

DON: But I'm into this; look, it has my style to it. I'm hollowing out two cavities with a wall between. Just look.

JANE: Yeah, listen, you look. I don't want trouble; just get yourself out of there right now!

DAWN: This is a group thing. It's not your igloo.

JANE: If we keep this up, we'll never finish. Frank's group is already farther along than we are—their pile is twice as high as ours. We've got to work together.

DON: I don't care about that. Go build your own igloo.

DAWN: But we all worked to get this far. You can't quit now. We will still have this one as ours for the class even if Jane and I start over.

DON: All right, all right! I'll rotate, but don't mess up my partition in there, Jane.

JANE: Sure, sure . . . Let's finish this thing and get out of here.

Our common-sense view might lead us to conclude that this project involved only three individuals, each engaging in certain activities. If we take Durkheim's position, we can see social processes operating in this situation. The three students created and participated in a group. Although their agreements contributed to the formation of the group, the interaction they constructed involved much more, including each person's understanding of what working in a group required, and forces outside of their group that influenced how they resolved problems.

They might have decided to go together to Jane's room to get the illustration, then all go get the shovel and work on the same task, two of them using their hands and the other using the shovel. But because of their previous experience, each student had to subjugate a personal preference for a particular task to the social arrangement they called "taking turns." Even Don had to give up his identification with the igloo and conform to the requirements of the group goal.

Durkheim referred to group processes as a social reality. He insisted that the group with its larger manifestations, institutions, and society could be thought of as existing, as he put it, in and of itself. The behavior of individuals, to a sometimes surprising degree, could be accounted for in terms of these group-level phenomena.

For Durkheim two facts were fundamental to all groups: **constraint** and **integration**. Constraint refers to the capacity of the group to compel persons to act and think in particular ways. For instance, Don began to think about his work on the igloo in an inappropriate fashion; he thought as an individual, not as a group member. Jane and Dawn articulated the facts of their existence as a group. As individuals, they might have agreed that people should "get into things," but that viewpoint was inappropriate, given the rotating division of labor which had emerged as a characterisitic of their group. Don's personalistic attitude impeded the accomplishment of group goals and the life of the group itself. Although none of those involved liked the situation, they participated as members of a group, not as isolated individuals. Their performances and decisions—such things as rebuking Don or taking turns—were derived from a deeper phenomenon, called social constraint.

Integration is defined as the degree of personal involvement that a group requires of its members. Our igloo makers were in a loosely integrated group. It was held together by a weak attachment to a task assigned for the purposes of a college class. The arrangement of the task performance subordinated individual attitudes to group imperatives. Rotation, or turn-taking, depends first on an awareness of the necessity to subjugate one's wishes and desires to those of the group. It also depends on the demands of organization; for example, stopping and starting work according to a schedule is such a demand. This type of group arrangement does not require much integration.

Other groups require intense personal involvement. If these three students suddenly found themselves lost in some northern wilderness, the conditions for survival would create a group reality with a high degree of integration. We have several journalistic and personal accounts of how strong group pressures can become under survival conditions. For example, cannibalism was performed and condoned by plane crash survivors stranded in the mountains of South America. Our own students would in all probability arrive at agreements and a division of labor requiring they cooperate much more closely if they were to actually experience survival conditions.

Durkheim argued that once groups, with their customs, traditions, and codes of behavior come into being, they shape and educate individuals who subsequently become members of the group. Without ignoring the importance of the individual, Durkheim placed emphasis on the group. Without strong group life, a collection of people would lose its capability to engender moral commitment in its members.

Durkheim held that if we want to understand a social phenomenon like the group constructing an igloo, we must look for its relationship to many other things. From this perspective, a seemingly trival activity such as students making igloos takes on new meanings. This igloo-making was part of a college course. The course was listed in the college calendar for the month of January when such off-beat learning became admissible and even welcomed. The faculty and administration, who at other times of the year might view such an activity as foolish now saw this as a learning experience, one that demonstrated how the college curriculum was flexible, interesting, and practical. Ultimately, the idea of igloo making expressed a basic value of the college: innovative, practical learning can be a desirable component of liberal arts education. This kind of activity can attract prospective students who are looking for evidence of innovation and flexibility in a college. Along with faculty meetings, courses in organic chemistry, and registration lines, igloo-making is thus one other expression of the social reality of this particular college.

The greatest contribution Durkheim gives us is his emphasis on the importance of social realities. In the relationship between individual and society, it is society that defines the parameters of individual performances. Erving Goffman, a leading exponent of the study of the details of everyday life, writes:

I personally hold society to be first in every way and any individual's current involvement to be second (Goffman 1974, 13).

Still, following Goffman, the sociological social psychologist is concerned with what individuals do within social parameters, with how the latitude that a person finds there is put to use. Given the social facts of a situation, what are the relationships among individuals, and how might the actions of individuals alter the social boundaries of their existence?

MAX WEBER (1864–1920)

The German scholar, Max Weber, did more than any other thinker to show how the concerted actions of individuals can have profound influence on the parameters of society itself. In this sense, he is a major figure in the history of social psychology.

The task of inquiry, as he saw it, is to discover how the meanings of social life emerge and develop into patterns, and how these configurations relate to one another. Weber was acutely aware that people live within subjectively defined and created social worlds. Although he appreciated the search for scientific laws and causal explanation in the cultural sciences, he also stressed the importance of subjective experience. In fact, he warned that the search for scientific laws could either result in trivial generalization or, more often, obscure the researcher's understanding of unique cultural and social innovations. The social psychologist must focus on uniquely occurring events, those intersections of meanings that occur rarely and give rise to new configurations. From this base of understanding, explanations which incorporate subjective experiences and their meanings can be made.

"Action is social insofar as, by virtue of the subjective meanings attached to it by the acting individual (or individuals), it takes account of the behavior of others and is thereby oriented in its course" Max Weber, The Theory of Social and Economic Organization. *New York: Oxford University Press, 1947, page 88.*

The social scientist pursues the goals of understanding and interpretation. These goals may be achieved by observing, thinking, and feeling, and even acting as the people being studied do. However, as observers we can reach only partial understanding of others. We are always bound by our own lifestyles and place in society. We could actually convert to the lifestyles of those we study, but that would limit our range of interests, and we would probably lose the desire to communicate what we know to an audience. We can, however, experience a kind of controlled conversion. By thrusting our imagination into another way of life, we can know vicariously what it is like to live under a particular set of social circumstances. Weber referred to this imaginative exercise as the **mental experiment**, and although he suggested that the exercise be used with extreme caution, he regarded it as a powerful method for achieving understanding of social phenomena.

By compiling the results of many such experiments and comparing them, the social psychologist can begin to portray the organization of values and meanings for larger constellations: groups, societies, and even cultures. For Weber, the culmination of such studies was the identification of the unique happening. With this method the social psychologist can say what characterizes a group, what is distinctive in one group and missing in another, and, with good fortune, what constitutes the emergence of new social forms that influence the course of societal development.

Weber gave us some guidelines to follow in the performance of the mental experiment. Imaginative endeavors are highly individualized, varying with the creative impulses of each person. However, we need not worry about endlessly searching for understanding on an individual basis. There are some criteria that allow us to communicate our operations of understanding to others and likewise allow them to evaluate the accuracy and usefulness of our work.

The primary tool of imagination in Weber's research is the **ideal type**. The ideal type is a composite concrete case (a personality, social situation, or institution) invented by the researcher from his knowledge of the relevant aspects of the investigated subject. The ideal type is constructed for the purposes of comparisons with other types or for the discovery of some unnoticed dimensions of a phenomenon.

For example, in order to find out about sexism in American society, we may invent the character type of a male chauvinist. All of the aspects of chauvinism, such as the unquestioning association of housework with women and the uncritical payment of unequal wages to males and females for the same labor are concentrated and exaggerated in the type. No single real individual would possess all these aspects. However, a single case or ideal type can serve as a specimen for characterizing the aspects of the phenomenon. In a brilliant article, Richard Ogles (1980) shows how Archie Bunker of television comedy fame can be used as a **specimen case** to identify the aspects of bigotry as they are typically understood in American society.

Ogles (1980, 159–164) selects two charactersitics of bigots: their derogatory language and their imperviousness to criticism. He then shows how Archie Bunker can be considered a specimen case. The distribution of these two characteristics in the remarks and actions of Archie allows us to develop a concept of bigotry that is empirically grounded and flexible enough to permit recharacterization. It is also suggestive of hypotheses as well as sufficiently clear to serve as a concept in the language of social psychology.

Whereas Ogles' specimen case does describe reality, the ideal type does not. It is a careful distortion of reality designed to uncover essential meanings. It can be modified by constant movement to and from actual descriptions of the reality and the type itself.

Although an ideal type does not contain actual descriptions of action, the thoughts, actions, and patterns it does describe must be possibilities. We refer to this as the plausibility of the type. The male chauvinist may not actually pass over a competent female for a less-qualified male in an executive promotion, but that kind of action is a possibility.

Part of the work of a social psychologist is the construction of types. These are not classifications of the facts of social life or moral judgments about how things should be; they are selective arrangements of facts chosen to make a point, to achieve a state of understanding. Such types are always provisional and can be discarded if they do not operate to produce understanding. They are framed by the researcher (Martindale 1980). They are imaginative projections of consciousness into other times, other situations, and other people's minds.

The Calvinist Experience

Let's explore the way in which Weber himself used the ideal type. He was convinced that the modern industrial order was the most significant social development in human history. He believed that the advent of this new social order in the nineteenth century could not be fully comprehended by referring to cheap labor, deep river ports, navigable rivers, and other specifics. The industrial revolution and capitalism resulted, he reasoned, from a unique contact between two independent configurations of meaning in the lives of people. The merger of religion and economic aspects of societal phenomena shaped a new reality.

Weber saw capitalism as a rational system of calculated exchange which ensured individual profit. A certain kind of person, the successful business man, symbolized this system. He—or she, as we update Weber—is hardworking, well organized, tedious in habit and mannerisms, and above all goal oriented. The existence of such persons impressed Weber as unique in world history. To Weber, the entrepreneur seemed overcommitted to his work. In a figurative sense, he becomes his business. He defines his qualities, aspirations, hopes, and dreams, in terms of the continued and spectacular success of his business. This person drives himself, works day and night, and is totally consumed by the economic enterprise. His private and public life as a businessman merge into one reality. Indeed, Weber's description brings to mind the work currently being done on the Type A and Type B personalities. The Type A, prone to heart attacks, is a contemporary version of Weber's businessman. Weber reasoned that such a total merger of self and outside activities could not be motivated solely by concern with making a living. Such zealous activities go beyond economic necessity and seem to characterize men anxious about the destiny of their souls. So Weber tried to imagine where these fervent men came from and why they were part of such a frantic economic system.

His search led him to the second part of his analysis. He found another special mentality among zealots whose religious belief systems rested on practical concerns. Weber was not interested in the truth or falsity of religious dogmas. He focused on what happens in the everyday lives of people who hold a particular belief. He knew that the beliefs occur within complete social context and religious principles have meanings in everyday life that go beyond their theological significance.

The belief he examined was the doctrine of predestination espoused by the Calvinists. Predestination is a belief that God is all-knowing, grants eternal life, plans in detail the lives of mortals, and saves souls. However, since He knows all, He knows whose souls are already saved, or will be saved. He has preordained the salvation of some souls. There is, then, as election of souls, something like a celestial ledger, which enumerates the saved and excludes the lost. According to the doctrine, all of this is basically outside the control of the individual believer. It is God's business and beyond human comprehension.

Weber was interested in the practical reasoning this doctrine engendered. He asked his readers to imagine what it would be like to live among people who fervently believed in this doctrine. He imagined that a person would experience anxiety and a perpetual battle of faith to believe that he really was one of the chosen. No one could really prove this to himself or others. Every believer faced the problem of reconciling daily activities with nagging doubts about his fate.

How would you react? What would you do? How would you live your life? Imagine yourself always under the canopy of the doctrine, always in the presence of others whom you presume share your religious convictions. Weber's imagination identified three possible reactions which are portrayed in the following soliloquies.

Life with reckless abandon   Since I have nothing to do with my soul's destiny—that's God's affair—why do I worry about it all the time? This anxiety is burdensome; I can't take it anymore. What does it matter? My preacher says that I'm saved by the grace of God. Seems to me I've got that or I don't. Doesn't matter what I do, so why not just do what I want? What's to stop me from just having fun? Women, drink, dance and revelling! Why not? These things don't really have anything to do with my soul.

But wait, what will others think? The Reverend, my friends, my family. If God predestined my life and I do all these sinful things, how will others think of me as one of the elect? They will never believe it. How could God will such a life of indolence, waste, and self-indulgence for one of his children?

Religious questioning   I just can't go on this way. I guess I never will know if I'm really chosen—if I'm really one of the flock. My parents tell me, "Stop doubting, it's God's affair. He will take care." But, I can't get the picture of that list out of my mind. That list without my name on it. What can I do? Nothing seems to matter. I don't see any reason for doing anything. Why not just wait? My faith is strong, at least as strong as other people's. I guess I really believe. Wait! I know it. I am chosen. My heart rejoices. There's no more fear. Now I will wait for my destiny.

It has been four months since I worked down at the shop. My father was patient at first. I told him it was God's will. He listened, but now he says that God never sanctioned such laziness, that God gave me talents;

He could never have intended this kind of life for His chosen few. So my father says things like "Maybe my son is not one of us."

Activism: By their deeds you shall know them   Sure everybody has doubts. God told us that, but we must overcome them. It's all in God's plan. If our faith is strong, if we are really in the flock, then God's will be done. God is good. Always, He is there to show the way, the way He planned. He tests us with bad times, but He has a purpose: we must accept. Yet, I know He is good. He will help me, my life will be rewarded, and this will be evidence of my soul's security. I have a seed faith. It grows, and God reveals more and more of His divine plan to me.

My good fortune, my hard work, my toil is what He intended. Its fruit is His, I share it and put it back into the earth. Such a good life, full of all my talents, full of activity. This is what God wants for His children. How could a sinner and a cursed heathen be so blessed?

Each of these three ideal type reactions are objectively possible. They could, and to some degree, do happen. But our purpose in formulating the types is to discover which one fits best with the self-driven, committed businessman of modern capitalism. We are after a kind of relationship that we can understand, which informs us about the similarities between two previously unrelated sets of meaning configurations.

The Spirit of Capitalism

The third reaction is the one which made the most sense to Weber. The easiest way to convince your fellow believer of your soul's fate is to prosper on earth, to use your God-given talents, and to realize His ambitions and wishes for you—ambitions and wishes which can only be recognized in terms of earthly success. The harder one works, the more accomplished, the more certain one could be of his chosen status. Living under these conditions produces frantic activity and total immersion in work. By their hard work, frugality, and judiciousness you shall know them.

The mentality necessary for a modern economic system took shape and was nurtured in religious thought. Historical circumstances led to an intersection of economic and religious meanings for human action. The two systems for deciding the sense of human existence had an elective affinity for one another. They merged to form a third, unique meaning system composed in part of both previously independent systems.

Weber looked for another ideal type to illustrate the merger, and he found the life and writings of Benjamin Franklin. This man, Weber believed, clearly represented the consequences of the historical intersections of systems. Here was a secular, business-like man whose ethical proclamations and zeal for work were like those of the earlier Calvinists. Franklin gave "hints to those that would be rich" and advice to young aspiring businessmen. He wrote of money "in almost idolatrous terms"

(Zeitlin 1968, 125). He emphasized a commitment to industry, frugality, and punctuality. He ascribed his recognition of the utility of virtue to a divine revelation which was intended to lead him in the path of rightousness. Why should men make money and what should men make of money? Franklin's answer was biblical: "Seest thou a man diligent in his business? He shall stand before Kings" (Weber 1958, 53).

Weber showed that even in the rational economic system of modern society there is a *heart* that comes from the psychological burden which ordinary Protestants carry. Unsure of their fate, they seek outward signs of their inward grace. These signs they find in worldly success. While the sacred meanings may have slowly eroded with the advance of modern society, the zeal and frantic spirit of making a buck remained.

GEORG SIMMEL (1858–1918)

We move a step closer to a fully developed concept of social and psychological reality with the teachings of another German scholar, Simmel. He wanted to identify a set of conditons which make up the state of affairs we refer to as society. He borrowed a term from philosophy to name such a set of conditions: **a priori**.

We have learned that individuals act, know, and feel in many different ways. When they meet in a concerted social activity however, their individuality merges. The social entity they create does not merely derive from its component parts; it is more like a container with a definite shape that molds whatever goes into it. Keeping with this metaphor, many kinds of fluids can be poured into the container, but some cannot. They may leak through the sides or be too thick to enter the vessel. Simmel referred to the containers as **forms** and what went into them as **content**.

Social activities have definite forms that can be identified and described separately from the actions that they contain. Statements made about these forms are depictions of a priori conditions of social activity, or **sociation** as Simmel called it. Talking about form without reference to content is a little like describing a thermos bottle while ignoring the liquid inside. A complete social psychology requires a description of both form and content, and most importantly of the interaction between them. The first step, though, is the identification of the forms or a priori conditions.

Social forms can be identified in every area of a society. In order to illustrate Simmel's concept of form, let us look at one type: conversational form. Often the smoothness and ease of social exchange depends not so much on what is said as it does on the form, or the way in which the exchange is organized. In the same way that we use a grammatical form for organizing words into a sentence, we learn to use conversational forms for organizing our encounters with other people. We talk, not merely to transmit information, but to accomplish social ends, including talking for the sake of talking. Conversation can be an end in itself.

Take the case of two friends who live in distant cities and meet for a brief time in an airport. They exchange information about the weather in their respective cities, the nature of their travels, and their families. Two things have taken place: the exchange of information and the participation in a conversational form. On other occasions these two friends may meet and decide they simply want to talk. A person without such a friendship to serve as a form may turn on the television to a favorite talk show which is actually based on this same social form.

The guests on a standard talk show are selected for something distinctive in their identity, an accomplishment, or a reputation. They range from witty and informative to dull and ordinary. They are selected so that they cover a wide range of social backgrounds and different occupations. The nature of the form of a talk show becomes especially apparent on radio talk shows where anyone can phone in and be on the show. The various backgrounds of people appearing on the show, as well as who these people are and what they say can be thought of as content. However, in this case, the variety of content hardly influences the form at all. Guests know the rules of breaking for a commerical, of turn-taking, and of what can and cannot be said over a public medium. In radio talk shows, the moderator assumes control over the conversations to make sure they conform to the form. He may chide a caller to hurry with his question or comment, or he may talk over the caller to preserve an appropriate format for the show.

In a very careful study of radio talk shows, Ellis, et al. (1981) show how rules for tying together statements, demonstrating who is talking about whom, and when requests for additional information are appropriate all operate to create an organization for radio talk shows which allows the listener to recognize and even participate in the talk as conversation. It is remarkable that we can so easily distinguish among the various forms of talk in our everyday worlds.

Perhaps most significantly, all parties to this form of communication realize the obligation to keep up the talk, to talk through errors or disruptions of speech. The announcers or hosts develop favorite stories and techniques for moving the show along that function as formulas for creating an illusion of fresh talk (Goffman 1981). So familiar are we with this form that we have no difficulty at all in recognizing a talk show and the friendly chitchat which comprises both the character and the appeal of the form.

Social psychology has as one of its goals the discovery and portrayal of social forms. Simmel showed us that the contents of activities alone would never provide us with sufficient information about social life. Forms must be isolated and grammars of social interaction must be written in order to reveal the a priori nature of social life. With these grammars we can achieve an appreciation of the finely grained nature of everyday life.

CHARLES H. COOLEY (1864–1929)

The American social psychologist, Charles H. Cooley, was familiar with the European conception of society as a super-individual, and especially with the ideas of men like LeBon who thought of society and the crowd as having minds and vitalities of their own. Cooley could not relegate the human imagination to external forces or to natural instincts. For him, societal and psychological matters were inseparable.

He wrote that society actually consisted of the imaginings that people have of one another. When two friends meet and embrace or shake hands, each brings to the encounter a wealth of images and ideas of the other person as well as the ideas he has of himself. The solid facts of society exist in the minds of people. Because we think of society as an objective thing, it seems strange to say that society exists in our minds.

Society exists in my mind as the contact and reciprocal influences of certain ideas named "I," "Thomas," "Henry," "Susan," "Bridget," and so on (Cooley 1922, 84).

Cooley meant that in order to describe what society is like, we must discover what people think, how they think, what categories they use in thinking, and most importantly, how these categories are interrelated and interdependent.

The Looking-glass Self

Just as we make contact with our image in a mirror by knowing that it is a reflection of ourselves, so we make contact with others by seeing our own images reflected in the actions of those around us. Here the term **contact** does not refer to direct physical touching but to a symbolic meeting of minds through the medium of imagination. If you talk to your mother on the telephone and she tells you how lonely she is and how much she longs for you to visit her, you understand this request through your own qualities reflected in her request. The qualities may be ideas of your obligations toward your parents or even more generally, your views of kindness and being a good person. Your own feelings about being alone and, the opposite, enjoying the comforts of companionship, are mirrored in her request.

You may decide not to visit, but you and your mother have contacted each other in a symbolic act. Although we rely on our own particular ways of knowing, the social sense of knowing, which Cooley called society as a psychic phenomenon, depends on the imaginative reflection of ourselves in others. When you imagine turning down your mother's request, you hear her disappointment or the disgust in her reply. What is heard is your own understanding of how you would act if positions were reversed. You hear over the telephone line your ideas about yourself as a good son

Although this person is engaged in solitary work, he still gives off messages about his social identities. What messages do you get about who this person is and what he is doing?

or daughter, or as a responsible adult. Thus one way to think about society is as a result of individual minds in reflective contact.

Self and Society

The human capacity to extend consciousness, to guess at what is inside the head of another person, creates society. On the basis of guesses, we add or subtract some qualities from our felt worth. We can now summarize briefly Cooley's ideas:

1. We imagine our appearance to other people.
2. We imagine their judgment of that appearance.
3. We feel some self-worth or the loss of it—pride or self-mortification.

We acquire our sense of belonging in society by slowly accepting over long periods of time the personal histories assigned to us. It is not that we acquiesce in this process, but our consciousnesses merge with those of the others around us. Cooley believed this process took place in what he called the **primary groups** of society.

Like a family or group of teenage girls in a boarding school, primary groups involve intimate, face-to-face contact, not casual acquaintances of impersonal relationships like the ones you might find riding the bus to work each morning. Also, primary groups demand of the person undivided attention. People in primary groups share a wide range of subjective meanings; they have spent a great deal of time inside each other's minds. These groups are not like the groupings of people who gather on the street corner to wait for the bus. The urban world as we will learn is basically a world of strangers (Lofland 1968). The primary group is a world of the familiar and the intimate.

A third important distinction of the primary group is that it encompasses the entire person, providing the direct mirror images of newly forming individuals (the young), as well as stable, historical images of the older members. Our sense of self-identity emerges from and continues to be maintained by our membership in primary groups.

We imagine how we appear to others and react to how we imagine that others evaluate our appearance. Cooley said that we see ourselves reflected in the reactions of others. This group of punkers clearly wishes others to see them in a special way. What do you suppose these punkers think that others think of them?

Lastly, the primary group produces and develops a character from the total society of which it is a part. Likewise, the quality of a society can be assessed by a careful examination of the primary groups in it. This insight underlies much research in social psychology. In the primary group individuals learn the meanings and shared realities of society as these have been created and maintained over the generations.

For Cooley, society and the individual are two sides of the same phenomenon. Society is collective consciousness, organization of minds in concert, thoughts arranged in categories and related to one another. On this point Cooley concurred with another early social psychologist who is perhaps the dominant thinker on the road leading to social psychology.

GEORGE H. MEAD (1863–1931)

Mead, who was in the philosophy department at the University of Chicago, taught a course entitled "Social Psychology". This course and its impact on those who took it were among the most significant influences in social psychology. In his class, Mead tried to show that although people are endowed with contemplative powers, a person is typically not alone in his or her quiet world. Mead anticipated the writing of Ortega y Gasset (1973, 217) who pointed to "Man's power of virtually and provisionally withdrawing himself from the world and taking his stand inside himself." This power ironically makes possible the creation of a distinctively human phenomenon—society.

For Mead the primary problem of social psychology was to unravel the relations between the individual and society. Which came first, the individual with his contemplative power and his individual ways of doing things or the society with its organized and customary ways for individuals to think, feel, and act? This is no chicken-and-egg question in Mead's estimation. The pure case of a man within himself, without some reference to shared categories of thought, even if these are simply words, cannot exist. Without society, there can be no individual.

Mead's position was clear: no society, no individual. Any individual escape must itself depend on an aspect of social life. A contemporary social psychologist, Harvey Farberman (1980), makes a similar point with regard to the role of fantasy in modern society. He points out that just when we reach out to achieve our innermost fantasies, we become vunerable to the forces of society. Our ideas of our worth and of who we are and what we do are reflections of these same subjects in the aggregate we call society. In the final analysis, we are society; it is in us. It may even teach us to value withdrawal from it. Herbert Blumer summarized Mead's thinking as follows:

For Mead, the self is far more than an "internalization of components of social structure and culture." It is more centrally a social process, a process of self-interaction in which the human actor indicates to himself matters that confront him in the situations in which he acts, and organizes his action through his interpretation of such matters. The actor engages in this social interaction with himself, according to Mead, by taking the roles of others, addressing himself through these roles, and responding to these approaches. This conception of self-interaction in which the actor is pointing out things to himself lies at the basis of Mead's scheme of social psychology (Blumer 1975, 68).

The Emergence of Self

Mead described the emergence of the human mind and self in the process of social interaction and communication. A child is born with a potential for interaction. Almost immediately he begins to use it, reaching out to his surroundings. He discovers the involuntary things he does like crying or cooing bring facial expressions and responses from others. He learns to discriminate among people, the sounds they make, and finally his own sounds and movements. The child is becoming a member of a family, and in the process, society begins to enter the consciousness of the child.

With the acquisition of language during the first four years of life, the child learns to **take the attitude of the other.** This involves mentally projecting his understanding of a set of actions, words, and feelings into the imagined situation of the other person. Mead called the limits of this mental projection—the boundaries of the community and the attitudes of the community members—the **generalized other.**

Older children and adults are more discriminating about whose attitudes they take as their own. Take the serious jogger, for example. Such a person no longer cares when a person she passes remarks that her running style is sloppy and tense. But when a fellow jogger, after a daily workout, discusses the merits of relaxed hands, arms and shoulders, when she points out that these matters increase the benefits of running, thereby further decreasing the chances of heart failure, the jogger attends, notices, ponders, and takes in the attitude of the other (Nash 1976, 1980).

The Nature of the Self

Mead was concerned with another basic question: Is a person made up totally of attitudes and actions of others? His response to this question is often either ignored or passed over in the discussion of his work. What he had to say, however, is of importance to social psychology.

He puzzled his students with the suggestion that the individual is not totally composed of social influences. He contended there are two parts to every social self: that which is the result of having absorbed others' attitudes and actions as one's own, and that which is unique to the individual. The first part he called the **me** and the second the **I.**

He defined the I as the creative, spontaneous aspects of the self. One way to think about this division in the self is to imagine the direction of influence on thought, feeling, and action. He defined the me as those instances when the influence originates outside the self, from the pressures put on us by others, and then those pressures are taken in as part of the self. When we share with the boss the belief that he has the right to tell us what to do for instance, the direction is from external to internal. Social psychologists refer to this process of absorbing outside pressures and influences as socialization.

Most research in this area has been concerned with the acquisition of the me. For example, many studies and experiments have been conducted to show how alarmingly easy at least in some situations it is to get people to take on attitudes other than their own. Zimbardo (1973) and his associates set up a simulated prison and assigned students the roles of playing prisoners and guards. They were shocked by the ease and rapidity with which the students took to these roles and subsequently at the harassment and even brutality that the role-playing "guards" gave to the "prisoners."

Other researchers have demonstrated that the qualities we attribute to ourselves are those we think others attribute to us. If we believe we are attractive then we believe others think we are attractive, whether or not they actually do. Myiamoto and Dornbusch (1956) conducted a study in which they asked sorority sisters to evaluate themselves and other members of their sorority on qualities like physical attractiveness, friendliness, and intelligence. They were also asked to say how they thought others evaluated them. The strongest relationships were between what the sisters believed their fellow sisters thought rather than what they actually thought.

Mead's distinction between the me and the I tells us that these studies are focused on the me and therefore provide an incomplete picture of the social self.

If we were to compare, behavior by behavior, a me-derived action with a similar one derived from the I, we would discover the two seem externally indistinguishable. But they may have been motivated by quite different forces. The I part of the self is the motivational part, the energy source.

A person can be in control of his bodily functions, feign an attitude or feeling, or play act, and all of these matters can be discussed as autonomous phenomena. Let us consider the example of courtship in which two persons play, rehearse lines, and act. A woman and a man can speak and act in similar ways, but the meanings of their actions can differ in terms of intentions and motivations. The situation may involve three separate but interrelated phenomena:

1. the intentions and motives of the first party,
2. those of the second,
3. those that each accepts as sufficient grounds for the accomplishment of "good times."

One may say to the other, "I love you," and the other may reply, "I love you too." Both act similarly, and the verbal utterances are followed by embraces, smiles, laughs, and a good time in general. Yet each knows they have different reasons for their actions and emotions, and each knows that the actions expected from one another are different. One partner believes love can be exercised with many different partners without adversely affecting the various relationships. The other person is a "one-woman man," yet for intimate and personal reasons, he accepts this shared partnership as "good times."

The woman may never articulate her feelings of love for this one man, nor how these differ from those she has for other men. The man may never make explicit his version of fidelity. Nevertheless, when they are together each accepts what happens, the things they say and do, the ways they look at each other, and the way they hold hands, as manifestations of a good time.

In an insightful study Judith Katz (1976) shows how the conditions of mutual perceptions of love are quite a problem in our society. We may be able to understand that two people may love each other in different senses, but when one partner wants evidence of the love from the other, problems develop. We assume that one who loves us knows what we want, understands our tastes, likes, and dislikes, and wishes to do unselfish acts on our behalf. Whenever we have to ask, or remind our partner of our tastes, or whenever the nice things he does for us turn out to be something he wanted to do for himself, we find the belief in that person's love fading in its credibility, and we begin to question it. If he has to ask, maybe he really doesn't love me; if he gives me something I don't like, or if he invites me to accompany him bowling when he should know I hate bowling, maybe love is lost.

Mead maintained that we cannot truly understand social interactions without probing the consciousness of the parties involved. External influences, like the strong cultural importance of love as the sole criterion of intimacy in our society, find their way into the details of personal relations, transforming that lonely place into a social gathering with the symbolic presence of others. But in spite of socialization processes, the individual retains his or her unpredictable uniqueness, and Mead felt this to be an essential aspect of human social life, its creative and spontaneous nature.

W.I. THOMAS (1863–1947)

Thomas' major contribution analyzes the part that consciousness plays in giving meaning to social life. He was especially concerned with identifying social situations in which people carried on their daily lives, and with the definition of these situations.

The Social Situation

Thomas thought that a **social situation** was composed of objective conditions like the physical aspects of a room or the buildings of a city, along with the objects of human attention. Thus, any social situation may be thought of as a physical shell within which are found people with attitudes and values—the objects of attention. For Thomas there are no unchanging attributes of the social world. Instead, the social world is created by people who act in it. As Thomas said, the social world is defined as real; it is comprised of definitions about what is real. We may think of it as the arena of action, the place within which the processes of society unfold.

Thomas' social situations are of two varieties: those created and defined by tradition, and those we create for ourselves and others. Whether we deal with the givens or the novel situations, every activity may be thought of as a "solution to recurrent problems." The people involved in the situation of social action bring with them their past experiences, and they apply them to give meanings to the present situation. Any individual has to define the situation in a way consistent with the definitions of others.

Definitions of Situations

There is always competition between the spontaneous, personal **definitions of the situation** and those provided by society. Although we are always

The process of defining the meanings of social situations can have a powerful influence on the actions of people. Although we take for granted that these girls are cheerleaders, can you imagine them looking like this in other social situations? Make a list of at least three situations other than cheerleading under which a group of high school girls like these might assume such a posture.

deciding for ourselves what a setting means, we do so within pre-existing meanings we have learned. The social experience attempts to assign meaning to our surroundings.

Thomas demonstrated that such mental exercises actually create situations. Whenever people define situations, these definitions influence behavior. This is true, for instance, in the example in the first chapter in which the policemen attempted to revive a woman, the victim of a heart attack. The dramatic consequences of this instance can be related to two conflicting definitions of the same situation. The policemen defined the situation as a medical emergency, whereas the spectators defined it as police brutality. People's respective interpretations, then, provide bases for action. When a situation is believed to be real, it is real in its consequences.

Thomas' work shows us the constant interrelationship between the social world as it has been defined in the past and as it is collectively defined at the moment. His research was, in part, a description of the characteristic ways in which these definitions of situations took place for different people.

SUMMARY

The works of the Europeans we have discussed converged on core concepts. They stressed a full appreciation of the autonomous nature of the social aspect of human life. This does not mean that these men overlooked the part the individual plays in social life. Each in his own way dealt with the constructed qualities of social reality. Nevertheless. compared to the Americans, they clearly wanted to expand their understanding of society as a compelling and influencing agent in the lives of people. Taken together, the thinking of these giants of sociology points toward a description of social reality.

The three Americans we discussed emphasized the indivisibility of society and individual. Society and individual are best comprehended as two aspects of the same phenomenon. Each thinker expressed this idea according to his focus. All three wanted to depict the continuing interplay between social and psychological reality.

From the ideas of these early social psychologists we identify several basic propositions:

Society is essentially a creation of human minds   Cooley called society "psychic phenomenon." Thomas gave many illustrations of socially defined situations, and Mead describes the genesis and maintenance of society in the me. They all relied on some preconceptions. They all demonstrated the mind in the presence of other minds as inventor of the social world.

Society has an autonomous existence   Once created, the society, as well as its content, acquires a history. It is passed on from generation to generation and even moment to moment. Both Durkheim and Simmel stressed that the product of persons coming together does not equal the mere sum of what each brings to the encounter. Also, the product of social interaction exists as an entity capable of making itself felt in subjectively experienced, real ways.

We must recognize, however, that a great intellectual problem is embodied in the way we are talking about social reality. We refer to the interactive outcomes of people mentally and emotionally taking each other into account as social reality; and we say that those outcomes do not merely derive from the backgrounds of the respective people. Still, the danger here is a kind of thinking philosophers call **reification**, or thinking about social reality as a type of inanimate phenomenon. The student should be aware of the long-standing debate about precisely what social reality is. For our purposes, as Thomas teaches, a thing is real in its consequences if it is thought of as real. People do think of society as real in a variety of significant ways. It is in this sense that society has "autonomous existence".

Knowledge of society requires understanding To achieve a genuine, workable body of knowledge about society, social psychologists must attempt to find out what society is like for those who experience it. This may of necessity be a vicarious understanding, but it should evoke feelings and thoughts which are much like those of the members of society. Social psychologists involve themselves in the lives of the people they study. Weber's treatment of the origins of modern capitalism illustrates this. Since understanding may emerge from imagining the interplay of intersecting circumstances, it is often the once-occurring situation that sheds light on major societal and psychological phenomena. Thus, social psychologists seek out the details of life.

Society consists of forms that provide a structure for ongoing activities These forms give meaning to individual lives. Many different things can happen within a given form. Forms allow and disallow thoughts, feelings, and actions according to their appropriateness to the form.

Society may be understood from the perspective of the individual and from the perspective of organization The first step in understanding is to describe individual and collective processes of intentions and actions. The second step builds on the first to analyze the forms or organizations.

EXERCISES USING CONCEPTS OF SOCIAL PSYCHOLOGY

1. Write a brief description of yourself—your looks, intelligence, how well you get along with others, etc. Now ask another member of your social psychology class to write a similar description of you, and you write one of him or her. Both of you write what you think the other thinks of you. This exercise works best if you know the person outside of class.

According to Cooley's concept of the looking-glass self, you should find your description of yourself agrees more with what you think the other person thinks about you than with what they actually think. Did your results show this? If not, can you think of why not?

2. In our soceity, home ownership is very important. However, the average price of a home far exceeds the yearly earnings of the typical American family. Still, people buy and sell homes using a complicated way of thinking about money which we call the mortgage. See if you can depict the idea of mortgage as a kind of definition of the situation?

3. Many of you have had driver education classes in high school. In those classes, you learned about defensive driving. Compare the basic task of defensive driving with Mead's ideas about how essential the task of "taking on the attitude of the other" is to social relationships. Does this way of conceiving of social order tell us anything about traffic regulations and the nature of accidents?

KEY CONCEPTS

Constraint and integration
Mental experiment
Ideal type
Specimen case
A priori
Form and content
Sociation
Contact
Primary group
Taking the attitude of the other
Generalized other
I and me
Social situation
Definitions of the situation
Reification

SUGGESTED READINGS

There are many excellent secondary sources on the origins and varieties of social psychological concepts. The student should also be aware that the thinkers discussed in this chapter were all prolific writers and their books and papers are readily available in the university library. We suggest three sources for the interested reader. Sheldon Stryker in a recent article reviews the origins and developments of the kind of social psychology we are pursuing in "Symbolic Interactionism: Themes and Variations." This is technical and a somewhat difficult paper written for the professional.

A more accessible secondary source is Meltzer, Petras and Reynolds. Their small book covers both the history and current state of symbolic interactionist social psychology.   Finally, in a delightful book written for the beginning student, Donald A. Hansen introduces the thinking of George H. Mead in the context of social involvement.   His book deals also with Weber's theory but in a more general way than I have.

Hansen, Donald, *An Invitation To Critical Sociology.* New York: The Free Press, 1976.

Meltzer, B.N., J.W. Petras, and L.T. Reynolds, *Symbolic Interactionism: Genesis, Varieties And Criticism.* London: Routledge, Kegan Paul, 1975.

Stryker, Sheldon, "Symbolic Interactionism: Themes and Variations" in *Social Psychology: Sociological Perspectives,* ed. by Rosenberg and Turner. New York: Basic Books, 1981.

Chapter Three

Consciousness and Social Interaction

OUTLINE

HUMAN CONSCIOUSNESS
Receiving Information
Encoding Information
Actively Manipulating Symbols

THE SOCIAL ORGANIZATION OF CONSCIOUSNESS
Typified Knowledge
The Life World
The Life Plan

CONDITIONS FOR SOCIAL INTERACTION: THINKING ABOUT THE OTHER PERSON'S MIND
Reciprocity Thinking
Filling-in Assumptions
Assumptions of Typical Experiences
Temporality or Sense of Time

BASIC ELEMENTS OF SOCIAL INTERACTION
Memories and Background Knowledge
Linguistic and Communicative Skills
Motivations and Emotions

SUMMARY

EXERCISES IN UNDERSTANDING INTERACTION

KEY CONCEPTS

SUGGESTED READINGS

Consciousness and
Social Interaction

They squinted their eyes as they emerged from the dark movie theater. Neither said much at first. The movie had been both a powerful experience and a strange one. Bill spoke first, "I really can't believe a person like 'Chance the Gardener' could exist. It must just be Kosinsky's way of criticizing TV." "Maybe, but, I think he is more than that. To me he is almost like one of those experiments Garfinkel did where students interpreted random 'yes' and 'no' answers to these questions according to what they thought should be said. You know, the thing about interpreting," Susan replied. "Yeah, you're right." Bill agreed. "You read the book, right?"

They walked to the school dorm. Susan still had the movie on her mind. Back in her room, she picked up her copy of Kosinsky's Being There *and leafed through it. Her eyes stopped at a particular passage on page nine:*

When one was addressed and viewed by others, one was safe. Whatever one did would then be interpreted by others in the same way that one interpreted what they did. They could never know more about one than one knew about them.

Jerzy Kosinsky, Being There

Tʜᴇ way we think and write about consciousness and social interaction is heavily influenced by Alfred Schutz (1899–1959). This important man's ideas were not discussed in the last chapter because his approach to understanding is so central to our study that it deserves an entire chapter. Alfred Schutz was trained in law and social science. He knew many of the great European thinkers of the 1920s and 1930s, including Husserl, the father of modern phenomenology. When the Nazis came to power, Schutz, like many others, escaped to America where he established a successful business and kept up his academic interests at the New School for Social Research in New York.

Because of his knowledge of Weber, Mead, Cooley, and influential European thinkers, Schutz could articulate a synthesis of theories according to his design for establishing a vital phenomenological sociology. His way of conceptualizing social interaction makes possible a strong version of social psychology. We follow his lead by considering the nature of interaction.

Interaction among human beings is a universal experience. People touch one another, hold hands, embrace, and make contact in other physical ways. We have visual experience of others as we see their actions, and as we watch them even when they are unaware of our presence. We talk with people in close, intimate conversation, or speak into electronic devices which carry our words around the world or even into outer space. These diverse and wide-ranging human happenings all embody the universal feature, social interaction.

We define **social interaction** as the process of interaction and mutual influence that involves contact between two or more minds. Any definition of social interaction includes assumptions about human nature. In order to make our assumptions clear, let us look first at interaction among some physical objects in a bowling alley. These red, white, and blue wooden objects, although only a few inches apart, are not in contact. They do not have desires for each other, nor do they think about making contact. They do not know of each other's presence. On initial inspection, as naive observers, we would attribute only inanimate qualities to bowling pins.

Suddenly, a black ball rolls down the floor toward the group of wooden pins, striking some of them with considerable force, and a chain of reactions follows in rapid succession. The pins begin to influence each other in a jumbled confusion of movements. Some pins fly up in the air, knocking others into motion. Their positions change in relation to each other and in a fraction of a second, the once orderly group lies in a new formation, some pins resting on others, some lying horizontally in isolation. One solitary pin remains standing. In all this violent commotion, its position was not influenced by the movement of the other pins.

How should we study this kind of interaction? Given our assumptions about the inanimate, nonconscious nature of such wooden objects, we would want to maintain a detached, outsider's vantage point. We could study the motion of the pins by recording and measuring angles, lines of force, and points of contact. In such a study we do not need to assume anything about the desirability of interaction or anything whatsoever about the pins as agents in the interaction. To be sure, the motion of a particular pin can only be appreciated in terms of its complex relationship to other pins, the speed of the ball, and other matters.   But no social interaction took place.

At the other end of the bowling alley are a group of people engaged in social interaction.   They touch each other, make noises, change their positons, push, shove, laugh, and show in their actions, or lack of actions, their awareness of each other.

Bowlers and bowling pins are different qualities of phenomena.   If one of the bowlers clasps the hand of another, pulls her to a standing position, and gently pushes her towards the line of bowling balls, saying "It's your turn," this sequence of events carries with it a hidden world of thoughts, intentions, and meanings.   Not only have two bodies briefly touched, not only has sound traveled between two persons, but contact has occurred between two minds.   And all others, including those who have observed this happening, have participated in it.

To understand the special nature of social interaction as conscious, mental encounters, we must first examine human consciousness itself.

HUMAN CONSCIOUSNESS

Consciousness, of course, has its physical and chemical basis in the central nervous system.   Recently, the subject of much research has been how the brain operates, which portions of it are the sites of which functions, and precisely how information and learning are accomplished in the brain. Although this research is of utmost importance, especially for its implications in treating abberations of the brain, it is not necessary for social psychology to explore the basis of consciousness.   However the brain works, it succeeds in providing connections of imagination and attention sufficient for the construction of the social world, the subject of social psychology.   As a medium for the work of interaction, the **human consciousness** must allow for receiving, encoding, and actively manipulating information.

Receiving Information

All life must coordinate its activities with its environment.   At least in the animal world, such coordination, whether for reproduction, protection, or acquiring food requires that the animal have some awareness of itself as well as its external world.   Humans share with the rest of the animal kingdom this capacity to receive information.   Human consciousness, then, allows for the **receiving of information** from outside the organism.

Encoding Information

One of the most important features of human consciousness is our ability to **encode** information.   This means an object, event, quality, or relationship can stand for some other object, event, quality, or relationship.   Mead called this symbolic communication.   Instead of depending on our immediate awareness of temperature, for example, we let such things as snow, the wind blowing through trees, a mercury column in a thermometer, or the words, "It's twenty below zero," stand for a certain state in the environment—coldness. This capability makes possible the element of social life Goffman referred to as theatricality. In a theatrical mode we know information enters a relationship to other information. This knowledge allows us to act as if we were someone or something else. The images on the screen evoke the meaning of coldness, even if the actual temperature in the theater is uncomfortably warm. Or, in everyday life, theatricality may refer to a speaker's attempts to pretend his last remarks were not intended to insult, or the listener's attempts to ignore the insultive intent and pay attention to other aspects of the speaker's remarks.

There are many ways to encode information. Human consciousness makes predominant use of symbols to accomplish this important task. A symbol is any object or event which has been assigned meaning. A smile, the simple human act of turning up the corners of the mouth, can be assigned such meanings as "I like you," or "I won and you lost." Symbols couple with their referents, the meanings or things they stand for. Language is a complex system of symbols allowing us to encode anything conceivable in human experience. But human consciousness makes use of other symbolic systems such as the clothes we wear, the arrangement of furniture in our houses, the way we move our bodies, and even the distances we stand from people. Symbols allow us to talk about the past and the future, to be aware of things outside of our immediate presence. Perhaps, the most important feature of human consciousness is this capacity to encode information symbolically.

Actively Manipulating Symbols

Those animals depending on direct input from their environments or limited in their encoding capabilities tend to respond only to the world around them. Stimuli are taken in which may or may not stand for other things, and the animal selects some behavior from its repertoire. Although human beings also react in this fashion, most of our behavior is **symbol-manipulative**. We work with our environment, attempting to use, change, modify, or, in some cases, ignore it. Some researchers have discovered, for example, that people who live in northern climates in larger urban settings, often dress and act in a way which communicates to their fellow residents their disdain for winter behavior. They do this by simply displaying symbols of warm weather. Hence, they will resist putting on boots even if it means ruining a new pair of shoes (cf. Nash 1981).

Symbols may be rearranged to create new worlds of fiction having no external reality at all. People may have failing memories and reason in ways that would get failing marks in a college logic class, but all these things do not mean people are "judgmental dopes" (Garfinkel 1967, 66–75). We invent stories, believe in stereotypes, lie to others, and change the reasons we give for our conduct. Human consciousness always includes an

Through the socialization process we learn to associate meanings with particular gestures. Can you make up a story for this scene which would give explicit meaning to the gestures these men are making?

active, creative element, and it is this feature which distinquishes us from all other animals. Chimpanzees can respond to arbitrary symbols. They can be taught to communicate with gestures or colored chips, but they are not able to employ these devises to create some new myth about the origin and history of chimpanzees.

THE SOCIAL ORGANIZATION OF CONSCIOUSNESS

What we take for granted—like our presumptions of memory in others, the styles of thinking we enact, our common sense attitudes—is all socially organized. The mind without interaction with other minds remains merely a potential, an empty form. Consciousness involves systematic relationships among minds.

Typified Knowledge

The process by which we come to think of the world as typical reveals the meaning of consciousness as socially organized. As Weber taught, sometimes the typical understandings people have can combine in practical action into new and more general ways of thinking about the world. Weber explained how a form of religious consciousness was necessary to modern thinking about capitalism. In everyday life, we all place our actions and those of others within categories of typical knowledge. Alfred Schutz wrote that this typical knowledge is what we refer to in the vernacular as common sense. The runner, for example, who speaks of "steady pace" is referring to an organized body of knowledge shared by other runners. He or she knows what it means to run with a steady pace, and how to tell if his or her own movements fit this category. When we explore the full context of this expression "steady pace," we discover several typified ways of thinking.

First, it is runners who use this expression. As a type they assume certain identities and attitudes. They think of themselves as people for whom running is an organizing theme in their routine, everyday worlds (Nash 1976). They have a runner's attitude. They judge running as a central or core value in their awareness of their world. Thus, all other occurrences are interpreted from that stance. The birth of his baby means, among other things to the runner, missing two days of training runs.

Second, this phrase points to an organized set of categories. A steady pace assumes its meaning within these categories that are part of the runner's consciousness. It contrasts with jogging and racing pace; the first refers to a warming up exercise and the second to a deliberate, studied running style. The steady pace can be used during a training run but not in speed work. It can also apply to different paces like a steady racing pace.

Consciousness, then, is composed of **typified knowledge**—classes of events, things, and most importantly, the ordering of their contexts. One runner's steady pace differs from another, and the outside observer can know the meaning of the term only by discovering how runners as types of people think about the various kinds of running activities they engage in. The following example illustrates how typifications may operate within a given context.

During mid-July in suburban Hopkins, Minnesota, several thousand runners congregate for the Raspberry Festival Five-mile Open. The race is held in conjunction with a community celebration. There will be a parade, shops will be decorated, and the town officials will speak. For the runners, this is a popular race, one in which the finish is defined as fun because there is always strong competition, and of course, there is the crowd. For the runners, Hopkins means a race, not a festival. The racer ignores or reinterprets the signs all around him of different ways to interpret the event. The people who line the street may be parade watchers. They are there anticipating the start of the parade; watching the runners is secondary. Some may even taunt the runners, while spectators with small children must placate them by reminding them that soon after the runners finish the parade will start. To drivers on their way to a summer outing, or heading to the office for some catch-up work on this Saturday summer

Conciousness of being together or having similar life experiences is enhanced by symbols. These children are acquiring a sense of who they are by sharing a common experience, their interpretation of which may well shape how they think about other people.

afternoon, the racers are indeed an annoyance. What is seen as the place for a parade by some is seen as nearing the finish, a place to pick up the pace, for others, and for still others as an unnecessarily crowded intersection.

Often, social markers indicate the shift from one typification to another. Consider the parade route at Hopkins. Ordinarily it is a street with typical understandings of its use for residents and visitors. It is a two-way street with no parking; it has four stop lights and a speed limit of twenty-five miles per hour. For a few hours on the Raspberry Festival Day, these typical understandings are suspended and another set comes into operation to transform the meaning and use-value of the street. The speed limit is relevant to usual street traffic, but not to a parade, and certainly not to a foot race; the bus stop sign posted on the street means nothing, except that the would-be rider must look for a new stop today—something he knows if he has ridden this bus regularly, or something he will discover if he tries to behave as usual on this day. Consciousness of which typification operates "street" or "parade route," defines one typification as relevant and the other as irrelevant. While the parade is in progress, the curb may be sat on. Goffman (1974) suggested that we think of shifts in the set of typifications employed to define the appropriate meanings for a situation as a process of **framing**. We have just depicted a **reframing** process.

In the case of the parade, the social marker is often dramatic, helping people understand that a reframing is taking place. People who know of the coming of the parade gather; others merely wonder what is happening. Children not yet experienced in reframing see the street without traffic as an opportunity to play. The confused bystanders and playing children learn what is happening when a motorcycle, flashing its red lights and mounted by a uniformed policeman clears the street, proclaiming that the transformaton has taken place.

The Life World

Consciousness is organized around life situations. Thomas pointed out that our social experiences are influenced by predefinitions of situations. By predefinitions he meant that the situation is thought of before interaction takes place. If we extend this idea, we realize that each of us lives in worlds of ready-made meanings associated with persons and events encountered in the pursuit of the pragmatic objective of living (Wagner 1970, 320). These worlds can be described according to the characteristic consciousness they engender. Those patterns of consciousness social psychologists call, after Schutz, **life worlds**. A life world may be thought of as a form of ready-made meanings. A person is aware of different meanings associated with different activities. Each person has a life world, or a typical way that he or she begins the understanding of social life.

An example of one life world will help show how this concept informs our analysis of everyday life: Fred rolls out of bed at five A.M. It's still dark, and anyway, his eyes can't focus enough after last night's six-pack to see what kind of day it is. He switches on the radio to catch Earl Finkel's "meteorological forecast." Earl says over the radio: "Well, people, we are lucky again—mid-November, no snow, and low 40's. How much longer can it last?" Fred moans and swears. "I could have used the rest," he mutters.

Fred is a construction worker. The company he works for landed a good contract to repair the sewers in an old neighborhood. Fred operates a crane and makes good money. Construction is seasonal here in Minnesota, just as it is affected by weather conditions virtually everywhere (cf. Reimer 1979). Workmen can't do certain kinds of jobs in inclement weather. So the men have been pushed to finish excavation before the hard freeze. The work is hard, and recently, with union approval, they have been pulling down overtime, time and a half, trying to finish. Fred is beat. He could use the day off. November is usually a slow work month. Some years it means lots of beer and icefishing. This year it's a different story. "Looks like another beautiful day." Fred is really depressed. Here what counts as beautiful can only be understood from the perspective of Fred's life world.

In modern society most of us operate comfortably and unreflectively in many life worlds. We use the concept of life world much as the older concept of role was used by G.H. Mead and other early social psychologists. We have learned to be different people according to our definitions of the situations in which we find ourselves. In the concept of role, the ideas we have about what is the expected behavior for a particular situation guide our actual behavior. In the life world concept we account for expectations and their influences on actual behavior by locating the expectations in an agent, namely a conscious person.

For example, let's imagine a middle-aged woman, and think about the various life worlds in which she could live. On occasion, she may think of herself as a wife and a mother. On other occasions she may think of herself much differently. During any ongoing occasion, whenever she simply makes sense out of her world, the mentality she assumes for that occasion is called by Schutz a "natural attitude." In an average day the natural attitude of the housewife may well end with the kids off to school or breakfast finished. When this same woman dresses for a day at the office and goes to the corner to wait for the bus, she becomes a bus rider. As a bus rider she knows how to time the arrival of the bus, read a schedule, where to sit to avoid conversation while on the bus, or conversely, how to encourage it. She is familiar with the objects of the bus world— tokens, passes, transfers, route maps, side seats, rear seats. When she arrives at work, she then becomes an executive, instructing her secretary, setting a meeting time, pondering the consequences of cutting out part-time people employed in her school district, and thinking up strategies for going after federal grant money.

In the language of social psychology, this woman is doing much more than acting on expectations. She is symbolically and literally becoming a different person with each varying stituation. She is able to make transitions from life to life because she has mastered the art of gearing into and out of qualitatively distinctive communicative settings. In order to accomplish this feat, she must be competent in applying rules, making judgments, and mutually recognizing the intentions of those with whom she interacts. Each life situation is organized, and in each there is a given consciousness which we can uncover only by observing and describing the perspectives and competencies of conscious persons in the respective settings. We make no judgments about the contexts or interrelationships among these forms before the descriptions are completed, but we do expect personhood to be multidimensional.

The Life Plan

Thomas showed us that if we take a very broad view of individual lives we can see the patterns in how people organize their social worlds. He called this pattern **life organization**. Such plans underlie the often conflicting realities of the everyday world. The life plan does not necessarily unite these life worlds, but it does serve, even if in vague ways, as an overall objective and guideline for an individual's life as a whole. This can start with specific or limited plans and motivations provided for in the life world. We call this supreme system a **life plan** and quickly note that it does not need to be deliberate. It may be imposed and it certainly can change throughout a person's life (Wagner 1970, 319).

A father advising his son speaks from a confidence he believes one acquires only with maturity. He advises from his vantage point. He and his son may share many life worlds. They both are football fans, fishermen and bus riders, but the overall sense each makes of their respective worlds, their underlying consciousnesses, differs. The father recommends trust and faith that "all things will work out." The son may not be able to articulate his stance, but he is sure it is different. The father's roots, his sources of security, and the signs of his happiness—like home, provisions for the son, and even the son himself—are for the son unbearable chains, symbols of dependency. The son's frustrated attempts to change his father's understanding highlight the operation of two different life plans. Life plans, with their varying interpretations of the same events are sometimes associated with age or cohort grouping. When this occurs, we speak of generations, and in this sense, of generation conflict (cf. Mannheim 1938).

Forms of consciousness, the organization of everyday life worlds, and the judgmental activity of social life take place on a tacit level. If you ask someone what their life world for the moment is, they cannot necessarily tell you. Just as I do not need to know the formal rules that linguists use to describe a grammar of a language in order to speak that language, so, in everyday life, people do not often formalize their knowledge systems.

CONDITIONS FOR SOCIAL INTERACTION: THINKING ABOUT THE OTHER PERSON'S MIND

One of the primary tasks of social psychology is to show how unspoken knowledge that people have of each other makes possible social interaction. We can, like Cooley and Schutz, think about this knowledge as assumptions we make about what is in the minds of other people. In some situations so much is assumed that what people do or say makes no sense to someone who is not party to that specific conversation. Consider the following example:

JIM: Your SL–76s looked great—did they help?

JOHN: A little, but I still have that quad problem.

JIM: Thought that was taken care of?

JOHN: Me too, but that's why I got the SL–76s; they did help, but can't say they're worth the bucks.

JIM: In the kick I thought I saw you pull up.

JOHN: Yeah—same old story.

In order to understand the meaning of this conversation, we would have to know about the context of the interaction between Jim and John. Because they share the social knowledge of a life world (the runner's world) they do not have to explain everything to each other when they talk about running. They both know, for example, that SL–76s are special shoes of a class known as running shoes. SL–76s are one of eight different types of training flats manufactured by one shoe company. A flat is a shoe that uses the whole of the foot. Flats contrast with spikes designed for short fast races, putting more of the stress of running on the toes. Flats are either racing or training. Racing flats are lighter and provide less support for the foot. Some training flats, like SL–76s, are popular for use in long distance races of two or more miles.

Jim knows John recently purchased the 76s because they have a reputation among runners for having a well supported heel. The reputation takes on significance when paired with John's allusion to a "quad problem." He means he has been having pain in the front part of his thighs while running and believes this has something to do with the worn heels on his less-supported Brook-Drakes, another type of running shoe. He switched from the Drakes to the 76s because of the heel support and its specially shaped, rounded heel which he thought would minimize wear, prolonging the life of the less painful heel-striding posture. Jim knows this as well and was curious about the outcome of the experiment. John and Jim thought the 76s would fix up the problem. Apparently, John feels he has experienced less pain, but is unsure of the advisability of the purchase of the more expensive 76s.

Jim and John also share a long history of competitive running. Their emotional involvement in this competition is controlled. After all, they belong to many other life worlds; they hold jobs, have families, and belong to organizations. John has never beaten Jim at a race. A "good race" for the two friends is one in which Jim pushes John to run faster. John's "quad problem" has prevented him from running all out (at top speed) in the finish of races. Jim usually beats John "in the kick." In last Saturday's Eight-miler, John's leg hurt on the final half mile, preventing him from catching Jim, even with his SL–76s. "Same old story."

Jim's remark, "In the kick, I thought I saw you pull up" was not a reflection of just good sportsmanship, interest, or controlled exhilaration of the winner. Within their running relationship, Jim acts like his winning is unimportant to him, and he periodically acknowledges John's accomplishments, personal record times, and John's role in pushing Jim to run faster. Winning is important, but not as important as having a "good race."

The friendly competition between Jim and John is part of the reality of their relationship as runners. To uncover the meaning of their conversation, we must be aware of the unspoken understanding between them. In this example, its expression is so subtle that if we were just looking for general rules of good sportsmanship, we would miss the richness of the interaction. When observing social relationships and describing them as life worlds, we must recognize the operation of many idiosyncratic ways of talking, double meanings, implications, and general rules.

John and Jim presume a common life world between them. They assume that each possesses similar knowledge of the objects of the runner's world, like shoes and personal records. Each thinks the other knows more or less the same things about running. In the conversation, Jim guesses about whether John understands him, and John allows any vague comments that Jim may make to pass on the grounds that they will become clear in future remarks. These assumptions allow their interaction to continue.

Recent writers have singled out an essential aspect of these assumptions which they refer to as **mutual intentionality recognition** (Cegala 1982, 83–85). They suggest that human beings signal to each other their intentions to engage in communication. When they mutually recognize these intentions, they give each other a certain latitude in the precision of what is said that is taken up in their respective knowledges of their common experiences. Without this mutual recognition, persons engaged in conversation tend to turn inward, touching their own faces or folding their arms as they talk on without regard for whether their remarks are being received or not. Alternatively, gesturing away from the body and towards one's communication partner is thought to reflect an outward intent to communicate.

Jim and John interact with ease as they feel secure in assumptions about each other's intentions and the level of understanding between them. They make good guesses about each other's motives and intentions. Without the ability to make, recognize, and act on such guesses, the social world could not exist at all.

We can analyze several of the tacit assumptions people make about the thinking and intentions of others. Schutz called these assumptions **reciprocity thinking, filling-in assumptions, typical experiences,** and **temporality.** The contemporary sociologist, Aaron Cicourel (1974, 52–54) first discussed these in systematic fashion for the purposes of a social psychology. These are basic to social interaction; we cannot go out and observe them, but we can infer their existence from what people say and do.

Reciprocity Thinking

Reciprocity thinking occurs when one person assumes that for the moment—for the sentence being spoken or the thing being requested—the mind of the talker and of the listener are interchangeable. For the purposes of interaction this assumption is taken as valid by both parties until further notice (Cicourel 1974). Reciprocity thinking about others is never valid in the sense that we can somehow test and know that we know the other person's mind. We guess at what is on the person's mind. We have guessed this way for a long time, since probably even before we could talk, and we boldly decided what others intended by using our confidence in our own ability to know others.

The ties that bind. These two men are engaged in a form of interaction which requires that they make many assumptions about each other. See if you can list at least four assumptions that might be necessary for this interaction to occur.

When we say "pass the salt," and someone hands us the salt shaker, we assume an interchangeability of standpoints with the person of whom we made this request. When we receive the salt shaker we hold that in fact, or for this limited purpose, we have interchanged mental stances. But did we really? Whether it is really possible or not is irrelevant to social life, for the reality is defined or constructed by those who live within it.

We do not hold such assumptions forever in a kind of blind faith. We can't test them by gathering direct evidence, but the way the other person responds provides a kind of support for this assumption about the other person's mind.

In our example, John responded in a way that Jim interpreted as appropriate for his question, so John continues to assume that his subjective conditional way of thinking is true. Had John replied about the SL–76s, "Yeah, but it uses too much oil," Jim would have been puzzled. Jim knows SL–76s use no oil and presumes that John also knows that. But John's response is inappropriate; it does not make sense. Therefore, it is possible that either Jim's presumptions about John are false, Jim made a mistake, John has misunderstood Jim, or John is joking—putting Jim on. In any event, the remainder of the conversation cannot proceed. Probably, in this case, Jim would take John to be joking or to have misunderstood and then request a clarification, for a different way to establish reciprocity thinking must be found or else the interaction ceases. Jim might reply, "Sure man, my pair are down a quart all the time," and move on to the rest of the conversation; or else, Jim could say, "Not your TR 3, man, your SL–76s." John might then say, "Oh, I thought you were talking about my car." Both of these examples function to restore the form of thinking we are calling reciprocity.

Hence, we have learned that all interaction depends on the mastery of a particular way of thinking about what others are thinking. We must learn to think we know what the other person is thinking.

Filling-in Assumptions

Two or more persons depend on the vagueness of each other's talk in order to engage in talk at all. This reflects the assumption that the other person can fill-in what we do not express. In other words, if people require of each other definitions of all the terms in everyday conversation, there could be no social interaction at all. The dialogue between Jim and John would expand to one hundred times its present size if Jim were to specify what quad problems are. Instead, Jim assumes that John knows. If there are misunderstandings in future conversations, Jim can always find out what John means; at least he assumes he can!

Of course, this all means that a great deal of talking and social action can take place on very little knowledge. Often only a name or label is required to serve as sufficient grounds for the continuation of a social world. New words never heard before or events never seen, can be interpreted and can acquire meaning.

The policeman knows the territory which he patrols. He fills-in in order to interpret objects in his environment. He cannot tell you in so many words how he knows. He just knows that open drapes in a certain home mean trouble. The light off in the second tier above the shop means something is wrong. Neither of these events occurred before; they are novel. Yet the policeman can reply, "I felt something was wrong." The policeman has acquired a history of idealizations about the appearances of his beat. He notices kids darting around the corner of a building because the movement of the kids is an instance of a "unique feature emerging from the backgound of routine features" (Mehan and Wood 1975, 78). The policeman may not fully understand the movement, but he takes it to be suspicious and investigates without completely knowing whether or not a law has been broken. Policemen decide law violation neither from a formal legalistic vantage point or from applying their background knowledge of their beat and its typical appearances. They judge such problems by allowing the routine practices to fill-in with the web of practical circumstances the incidences of applications of the law. A law, then, is not evenly enforced, just as Jim and John do not really need to know about SL–

76s in precisely the same way. The meaning of the law, or a particular law, and the reference to the shoes both depend on being within a context of other meanings, assumptions, and sketches of knowledge which are sufficiently vague and incomplete, a context that becomes clear only after future events take place (Garfinkel 1976a, 210–213).

Assumptions of Typical Experiences

As we discussed earlier, people organize their social worlds into categories, grouping together things that are different and unique and treating them as if they were the same. In interactions with other people, we make assumptions about whether or not experiences are typical. In the example of the policemen deciding something is wrong from some clue in the appearances of his normally perceived environment, he made the judgment on the basis of his contrast between typical and extraordinary features. He relies on his own stocks of knowledge to determine a sense of what is routine and what is not. "Things are quiet tonight," the policeman tells his partner. "Let's take one last swing around by the liquor store then request a Code 7 (coffee break)." As the patrol car pulls up in front of Tom's Liquor Store, the men look at the store's appearance and notice that the lights are on and the doors look locked. "Looks OK—let's go," they agree. The judgment, "looks OK," depends upon an attitude or common-sense assumption that social life can be normal or routine. In order to arrive at any judgment regarding meaning, an assumption that there are "normal or typical experiences" must be made.

Let us look at an example to clarify this assumption. Frank tells his son, six-year-old Bobby, that the family might purchase a jeep. But jeeps are expensive, and Frank is not sure the family budget will allow for such a large expense. One Sunday morning Frank says to Bobby, "Let's go look at jeeps. Probably, the showrooms will be closed, but we can look around." Frank and Bobby head for the local AMC–Jeep dealer. Upon arrival they find the showroom locked, and the particular model they want priced inside. Bobby reads the sign on the door, "Open 2:00–8:00 Sundays." It is now 11:00 A.M. He grabs the door and pulls it hard. Frank looks at Bobby and admonishes, "It's locked. Please don't pull on it." Bobby stops. They decide to go out on the lot once more to read sticker prices on the new cars. Frank walks back to the showroom window and hears the faint sound of bells inside. He does not give it a second thought.

They continue browsing the lot commenting on the costs of cars. "This one is $6,000," says Frank. Bobby says "Wow, this one is $48,000,000. Let's get this one, Daddy." Frank ignores Bobby and walks to the next car. They see two men drive up in front of the store and look through the windows, then glance around the grounds. They spot Frank and Bobby and say nothing. They talk briefly to each other, go inside the shop through a side door, using a key, and then they depart. Frank and Bobby peer longingly one more time through the showroom window at the green

The motives that we impute to each other in interaction often clash. What do you think this policeman might be saying to the man who is sitting on the sidewalk?

Commando inside. Frank does not hear the bells. They get back into the old family sedan and drive home.

This episode rests on assumptions of typical experiences: shopping, Frank's fatherly attitude toward Bobby's behavior, the cost of automobiles, and the like. We want to show how the principal feature of the story—the meaning of the alarm bell—relates to typical understandings. Bobby set off the burglar alarm when he pulled hard on the door. The two men, on-call security guards, did not suspect that a crime had been committed. They did not call the police. Instead, they simply inspected the property themselves and pronounced everything as normal and went back to their homes. Now, what typifications, or normal forms, underly this decision-action sequence?

From the guard's point of view, they know, first of all, that real criminals rarely set off a front door alarm. The shop is equipped with a dual alarm system, one wired to windows, side, and back doors (typical entrances for criminals) and the other to front doors which face a busy city street. Secondly, Sunday morning is not a typical time for a burglar, especially for one using a front door entrance. Third, criminals engage in purposeful action; they plan their heists. In short, they come prepared with the equipment they need and with planning required to carry out the burglary. Generally, such planning does not include bringing children on the job.

Upon arrival at the dealership, the guards found no open doors, nothing disrupted inside, and no one who looked like a burglar on the scene. They concluded, therefore, that the alarm went off accidentally and that they should recommend that it be checked for mechanical defects first thing Monday morning (when repair people typically work). They decided that this was another instance of rowdy children or curious pedestrians jerking over-zealously at the door, and the appearance of Frank and Bobby did not suggest that either of these two were criminals. The guards close the sequence for the moment by thinking of the incident as a case of an infrequently occurring, but nevertheless typical, false alarm.

From Frank's perspective, the faint noise of bells was not understood as an alarm until several days after the incident when it dawned on him what had happened. The presence of the two guards in streetclothes did not precipitate an unusual scene for Frank. The men had keys to the show-room, which they knew how to use. They knew each other, and they were doing something inside the store, a normal set of activities for those whose life worlds include this location. Frank felt no need to call Bobby to account for his disruptive action, setting off the alarm, nor did he feel he himself should explain to the men what happened: they were looking around and two guys came to check the place out—two typical occurrences.

In this example, we see how participants in interaction make assumptions about the existence of typical experiences and how these assumptions become the basis for their social action. They do not treat all the events and actions of others as entirely unique nor of equal importance. Some things are routine and ordinary— even false alarms. No false alarm is like any other in all its details; still, every false alarm has common features which we can describe. The meaning of the event derives from these features.

Temporality or Sense of Time

Social time is another feature of the conditions of consciousness that makes possible social interaction. In our natural attitude, we have a variety of ways of experiencing time, such as calendar time and clock time. However, for the purposes of sociological understandings of experience, as Schutz pointed out, a person's sense of the lived-through dimensions of time is what is important.

Contemporary writers of social psychology have turned their attention to describing how time is experienced. Weigert (1980) shows how the meanings of time derive from the social purposes to which time is put: hence, "time is money"; we have "time to kill"; we put "time" into a job; and we take "time out" from our daily rounds. The multiple and varied meanings which time can have in everyday life and the continuity of social interaction itself depends on a state of mind which Cicourel (1974) referred to as the **"retrospective-prospective"** sense of occurrence. This awkward but precise phrase contains several aspects.

There is the assumption of "I-can-do-it-again." This way of thinking about the future allows us to assume a continuity of time.

What has been proved to be adequate knowledge so far will also in the future stand the test (Schutz 1971, 286).

We assume, until proven otherwise by actual experience, that the future and the past are connected in a way we can understand. It is our ability to expect routine and even novel occurrences that gives us the confidence to go about the task of reciprocity building. Our anticipations and expectations do not refer to future occurrences in their uniqueness, but to the future as typical.

For example, even if we know our plans could go awry when we plan for a Friday night party, we invite friends over, buy beer and wine, and prepare food on the assumption that a good time is possible in this fashion as it has been before. Such a way of thinking links our understandings of our past with our projected future, allowing us to anticipate the future, and in this case, giving us sufficient grounds to go ahead with the planning of Friday's party. Still, as Schutz put it, "Any experience carries its own horizons of indeterminacy" (Schutz 1971, 286). We hope, therefore, that the party will be a success, but we cannot be certain until Saturday morning. Hence, all social interaction depends upon assumptions about the past having relevancy for the future. An attitude of "having done something in the past, I can go and do it again, more or less" grounds social life.

Simmel's search for the a priori conditions of social interaction has been continued in sociological social psychology. That search has led to descriptions of how consciousness operates as conditions out of which interaction emerges. These conditions are not directly observable since they are essentially assumptions. They constitute, however, the foundation for all social interaction. What actually transpires between persons in an interaction will depend on the individual's definition of situations and the precise nature of the typical thinking they practice.

Inferring a present, building a background. Although senses of time change from situation to situation and from life phase to life phase, all social acts depend on tying together a sense of what is happening at the moment with what happened in the past. Interactions build a person's background which, in turn, is used by a person to create present meanings. The child in this picture is acquiring a background while his mother renews her sense of who she is.

BASIC ELEMENTS OF SOCIAL INTERACTION

The outcomes of social interaction, what actually gets done in interactive work, can never be anticipated in every detail. Instead, the meaning of interaction must be thought of as a result of what people bring with them to the interaction and their individual contribution to it.

In a communicative encounter, each party comes prepared, in a sense; they have prefabricated meanings which they intend to use in a given interactive encounter. These stocks of prefabricated meanings contain memories, knowledge systems (some of which are widely shared by the members of society and others which encompass much smaller domains), special skills and approaches to communication, and motivations. Any encounter among socialized persons can involve many levels of meanings often layered on top of one another (cf. Goffman 1974) and they can occur sequentially or simultaneously. These levels, as the illustration with Frank and Bobby shows, need not be shared in the sense that all parties actually think, feel, or act in the same manner.

There are elementary skills and experiences which a person must possess and must presume that others possess in order to engage in interaction. These break down into **memories** and background knowledge, linguistic and other communicative skills, and motivations and emotional involvement. All three elements are contained in what we will call the individual's **biography** (Berger and Berger 1974; Schutz 1961). Biography is a personal and public social history of the individual. Interaction between two persons entails the contact of biographies.

Memories and Background Knowledge

Human beings both know and remember what they know. A detailed description of the knowledge of everyday life for even the most trivial of happenings is an elaborate undertaking. A simple greeting such as "Hello, how are you?" activates our knowledge of the appropriate organization of conversation in which certain responses are admissible. Several researchers have identified the characteristics of this organization. For example, Susan Ervin-Tripp (1972) has isolated rules for addressing one another in American society. These rules she depicts as alternating in their application depending on several factors such as how the person reads and interprets such matters, whether or not the setting is a status-marked one, whether one person is at least ten years older than the other, and what is the sex and kinship of the person being addressed.

In regard to the performance of the rituals of everyday life, such as a greeting, we have learned that the organization of the exchange is so powerful that, in a sense, "everybody has to lie" (Sacks 1975). For example, we may reply, "Fine, thank you," when in truth, we have just learned some distressing news. In her personal account of the trials of becoming a widow, Lynn Cane (1974) reports her own loss of the ability to enact the knowledge of the amiable greeting. When asked by a total stranger why she seemed nervous during a business trip on an airplane, when a noncommittal reply would have been appropriate, she replied, "No, I'm not scared of flying. My husband has cancer. He's dying." (p. 31), whereupon the conversation ended.

In crossing a busy intersection, we act on the basis of pertinent information, such as our knowledge of traffic, the meaning of different colored lights, and times of day (rush hour, for example). Some of us become specialists in interpreting traffic, hypothesizing that cars with oversized tires on the rear (raked) are more likely to speed through a red light and hence must be watched more carefully than a station wagon. We guard our exposure to the raked, modified auto, while strolling in front of the wagon without a second thought. Of course, our knowledge of the behavior of cars may be inaccurate, or we may forget something about cars we once knew, but we act toward the car as an extension of the qualities we attribute to the drivers. That is, we think we know what types of cars go with what types of people.

Our enactments of what we know depends on what we can remember. When a policeman becomes a specialist in reading the intent of a person from his demeanor, dress, and general appearance, he must remember fine details pertaining to these matters. In order to make a judgment about whether a person should be stopped for questioning, the policeman must remember what constitutes a normal appearance and compare the appearance of the suspect to this normal or typical case. Upon discovering an incongruity—such as a person dressed as a mailman "delivering letters" on a street the policeman knows receives its mail by way of a central distribution system—he feels justified in making a stop and inquiring about the suspect's motives and actions. Under such conditions, he feels he is minimizing the chance that he will bother an innocent person or, in the converse of this problem, fail to stop a guilty person. Likewise, a dentist must be able to recall every detail in the steps of doing a root canal, even though he or she allows forgetfulness of the patient's first name. Obviously, in our modern society, those actions that require the most detailed recollection are least likely to be left to informal recall, that is, instructions are written down and stored in a fashion that allows them to be displayed when the situation requires detailed knowledge. The expression "write that down" is synonymous with "that's important."

The content of interaction between two persons derives from the background knowledge systems they have learned and their recall of those systems. A person's knowledge of what is typical, normal, or ordinary within a recognizable setting forms the basis for the construction of the reality of a social interactional encounter.

Linguistic and Communicative Skills

In the social world memories and knowledge are expressed symbolically. The medium of language transports knowledge, capturing it in phrases and sentences and making it useful for whatever purposes people have in mind. Hence, the precise linguistic skills and knowledge possessed by the people involved in interaction becomes a major contributor to the character of the interaction. In a conversation with a friend, you may wish to express a delicate point which you know is contrary to your friend's own views. Strongly committed to your own opinion, you feel compelled to speak out. Still, you value the friendship. To escape what may become the negative consequences of your remarks, you prepare your friend with a few well chosen remarks: "You and I are good friends and we are both moral people, but your objection to a neighborhood abortion clinic is simply outrageous." This verbal device has been called a **credentialing disclaimer** (Hewitt and Stokes 1975) and is one among many tactics available to a speaker designed to smooth over the anticipated negative consequences of a remark. By acquiring skill in such verbal techniques, we can present our knowledge about a subject like abortion without implying an identification with some undesirable group, like radicals, rednecks, pro-lifers, or whatever designation might be judged offensive in this particular setting. The skill we possess in such talking allows us to avoid pejorative associations and, thereby, maintain the integrity of the assumptions that ground the interaction in the first instance. In the preceding example, you are telling your friend that his friendship is of higher value than your view of abortion, but that you do have strong feelings about abortion and these feelings are a part of your general relationship.

Even after having been caught in the performance of some unacceptable act, we can try to talk our way out of its consequences. Two social psychologists, Scott and Lyman (1968), provide a classification of types of accounts which they define as linguistic devices intended to justify or excuse a person from the consequences of his or her actions. Sleeping through an important chemistry examination may be excused if the offender can "talk" to the professor in the correct manner. For example, a student may say, "I just can't understand it. That clock of mine never failed before. I've used it all semester and on this of all mornings it breaks down! Must be a broken part, and it's a new clock too."

The way in which something is said, the mannerisms, gestures, and facial expressions accompanying an utterance can be just as important as the actual words themselves. We refer here to styles of communications, nonverbal elements such as body gestures and postures. An account, whether it is an excuse or a justification, must be framed in the appropriate style. A professor may not lecture his wife, nor a lawyer brief her husband. In both cases, the same information can be conveyed in different styles. The professional, consultative, or lecture style must be switched to a casual or intimate style, a style that highlights the character of the relationship of that occasion. Every person expresses at least part of what he or she knows in language. They may be inept or clever in anticipating the reactions of others to what they say. They may avoid the negative attitudes of others by disclaiming or accounting for their intentions and actions, or they may become trapped by others more skillful in the games of language. Those lacking **communicative skills** often find themselves in sympathy with the line from an old popular song which referred to lawyers who could "put you where they choose by the language that they use."

The final character of interaction must be judged, at least partially, by the communicative skills of the participants. The give-and-take of testing the conditions of social life, the searching for mutually sufficient grounds for interaction, the shifting of those grounds from impersonal to personal, all occur within the framework of symbolic communication. Talking, then, is the currency of social interaction. It is through conversation and its related phenomena that the character of interaction is discovered.

Motivations and Emotions

Each of us possesses the potential for different levels of involvement with others, and we are capable of having a variety of reasons for those involvements. Although we have learned that all interaction rests on tacit background features, there are varying degrees of tacitness required for interaction. Our relationships with others, then, may entail a rather thoroughgoing and encompassing way of thinking about the other person. An example of minimal involvement occurs whenever we purchase an item at a large discount store. We expect of the clerk to have only limited knowledge of us, knowledge pertaining to the act of exchanging money for goods; our personal histories become irrelevant to the task of acquiring a tube of toothpaste. On the other hand, when we complain to a close friend, we expect that he or she will interpret our disgruntled disposition in a fashion consistent with our friendship. For instance, if we think, "He should know I feel rotten if I don't get my morning coffee," then we could point to interference with our morning routine to aid our friend's interpretations of our state. However, such a tactic used on a testy clerk by an irate customer would probably yield quite different results.

Thus involvement of emotional depth ranges from superficial to intimate, the former requiring minimal presumptions regarding the other and the latter maximal. The actual qualities associated with involvements vary from situation to situation. Clerks in hardware stores may feign helpfulness in order to make a sale. One partner in love may exploit the vulnerability in the other that comes from assuming states of mind in order to procure some object or information that would be regarded by the other lover as outside the scope of the relationship. A classic example of this situation is the female spy using her wiles to extract secret attack plans from an enemy general.

Motivational systems provide the reasons for engaging in interaction. The reasons are taken for granted (institutionalized) in such a way that parties to the interaction are not tempted to wonder why they are doing what they are doing. Reasons for interaction also emerge from the character of the interaction itself and are transitory and highly situational.

Throughout the text, I will use motivation as a key concept. I will refer to reasons people have as to why they will do something as **in-order-to motives,** and the reasons they give for why they did something as **because motives**. I will preserve the stance of the act, describing whether the actor is attributing motives to himself or to another. Weigert (1978) has written in a very explicit style about the various concepts of motivations that Schutz developed. These are important because they capture the lived-through sense of the reasons we find and devise for the actions of ourselves and others. It is through a description of the motivational systems that operate in interactional encounters that we understand why people do what they do and say what they say about what they do.

Although we have discussed the elements of social interaction as if they were separately occurring components of a social situation, actually they are dependent, intermingling, and mutually influential. Any social interaction may be discussed in terms of background knowledge, communicative skills, and motivations, but a single instance of a social act contains all of these aspects and, no doubt, many more. Our description of an encounter or social event must be attentive to each of these elements and their interrelationship with the others. Of course, the task is doubly complicated by requirements of the word "social." We always deal with at least two persons even if one of these persons is imaginary.

SUMMARY

This chapter introduced the central concepts of social psychology for understanding the basic elements of social life. These concepts were depicted as ways of thinking about the nature and the actual practice of social interaction. After conceiving of interaction as part of a conscious process, the social organization of consciousness itself was described in terms of typified knowledge, the life world, and plan.

Moving to a treatment of how people accomplish interaction, necessary conditions of thought were identified. These are reciprocity thinking, filling-in assumptions, assumptions about typical experiences, and a sense of time. When we understand interaction as a process of thinking about other people, we can further appreciate and describe the range of elements implied when two or more people interact with and among themselves. We give to those with whom we interact backgrounds of knowledge and linguistic and communicative skills, as well as motivations and emotions. The versions of these elements that we impute to others become the material for building social meanings.

EXERCISES IN UNDERSTANDING INTERACTION

1. A: How are you today?

    B: Fine. Did'ya get those papers?

    A: Didn't have time. Too much goin' on at work.

    B: That's OK—probably too early anyway.

    What are these two people talking about? Of course, you can imagine a variety of topics which this conversation would fit. Select one and rewrite the conversation so that it is not ambiguous. Now, identify the precise forms of the conditions necessary for interaction. What is the version of reciprocity thinking operating in the conversation; what matters are purposefully left vague, what typical experiences are assumed; what sense of time is used by the people talking?

2. Look at the above conversation again. Repeat the exercise, but this time show how the conversation can take place even though the two people talking actually have two quite different things in mind. If you saw the movie *Being There*, you will recall many examples of this happening in conversations between Chance the Gardner and the people he interacted with, including the President of the United States.

KEY CONCEPTS

Social interaction

Human consciousness

Receiving of information

Encode

Symbol-manipulative

Typified knowledge

Framing

Reframing

Life worlds

Life organization

Life plan

Mutual intentionality recognition

Reciprocity thinking

Filling-in assumptions

Typical experiences

Temporality

Retrospective-prospective

Memories

Biography

Credentialing disclaimer

Communicative skills

In-order-to motives

Because motives

SUGGESTED READINGS

Much of the literature from which this chapter was drawn is highly theoretical, and not the easiest reading one can do. However, there is a very good secondary book by Monica B. Morris which covers many, if not most, of the basic ideas of this chapter. In addition, in the book mentioned the reader will find some exciting research illustrating approaches to understanding meanings in people's lives, especially the meanings of being old in modern society. Also, the undergraduate student should not be afraid to tackle Schutz himself. Wagner edited a volume several years ago which makes Schutz accessible to the average reader with a thin wallet. Finally, the popular writer Jerzy Kosinsky is a master at depicting the confusing and complicated ways people decide what each other means. His novels amount to exercises in understanding social interaction. *Being There* is as good as any ethnography for showing how social reality is constructed from the details of everyday interaction.

Kosinsky, Jerzy. *Being There.*   New York: Bantam Books, 1978.

Morris, Monica. *An Excursion Into Creative Sociology.* New York: Columbia University Press, 1977.

Schutz, Alfred. *On Phenomenology And Social Relations.* Edited by Helmut Wagner. Chicago: University of Chicago Press, 1970.

Chapter Four

Socialization: Learning How to Interact

OUTLINE

Socialization:
Learning How to Interact

A family sits at the dinner table. It is 5:30. There are four of them: the father, the mother, a four-year-old girl, and an eight-year-old boy. The father wonders out loud about the wisdom of a recent repair to the aging family car. A brief discussion ensues between the father and mother about the remaining years of service they can expect from the auto. The four-year-old topples her milk and the other three spring into action — paper towels and a mop soon take care of the minor spill. They resume eating. The eight-year-old speaks, "Dad, you know about that story? Well, you see, I thought maybe, you know Sam, from my school, I saw him up at the playground, and he is going to the game today, and you know those watches they're givin' away, well he says they are really neat, and . . . . " The father interrupts, "Jimmy, I can't take you to the ball game today." Jimmy is disappointed and remarks, "Gee, all you ever do is work." The parents look at each other and smile.

Soon, the meal is finished, and while cleaning up the dishes the father says, "Jimmy has a strange way of asking me to do things. I wish he'd just come out and say it." "Don't worry, dear. He'll learn, after all he's just eight." "I guess so, but I don't remember ever having so much trouble talking and being so self-centered when I was a kid. I wonder what the world will be like when these kids are grown?" They retire to the den to watch some television.

THERE are two distinct meanings for the concept of socialization in social psychology. The first stresses how an individual adapts and conforms to role expectations, opinions of others, and the norms and values of society (Gecas 1981, 165). The second emphasizes the development of the individual, how he or she passes through stages and confronts crises. In this view, people are different at different phases of their lives. How they deal with pressures from society depends in large measure on the various competencies they have acquired.

The individual is thought of according to the primary interests of the analyst. Hence, we may see the individual as relatively stable undergoing changes in a patterned fashion. These changes can be influenced by the demands of social environment, but the order that we call society is rooted in some inherent characteristics of individuals. Or, we may think of the individual as malleable, shifting form and content as a result of contact with others.

The first conception depicts socialization as a means by which society perpetuates itself, a means that by definition operates against the natural dispositions of the individual. In the second conception, socialization is "largely . . . a matter of the shaping of self concepts" (Stryker 1979, 177). The question of how order comes about at all is answered from the vantage points provided by the conceptions. Is order imposed on the individual? Is order an outcome of forces which operate on individuals, or is it a resultant effect of individuals interacting; in other words, is it something that emerges from the basics of social life?

Our title serves to remind us that we seek a wholistic view of the individual and society. Just as Mead and Cooley insisted on tying self and society together, so we will see socialization as a concept that describes how individuals adapt to the social pressures they experience through the social competencies they have mastered. Socialization, then, refers to the lifelong process which is often patterned into phases and stages in which a person acquires the skills necessary to interact with others. There are different kinds of social competencies which operate in their respectively appropriate contexts. These can be characterized by the qualities they manifest. The contexts of socialization vary from intimate and informal to impersonal and formal, from the family and peer context to that of school and occupation.

At birth the human infant can engage in simple kinds of social interaction. Although a part of an elaborate social network, the object of much conversation, and even the recipient of greetings and questions, infants cannot return the talk or respond in appropriate ways. In fact, adults often do the responding for the infant, answering their own questions, and providing their own cooing sounds. As children grow physically, they also grow socially. First comes the smile, usually in response to a parent's presence. Next come responsive sounds, movements, and finally words. Then these give way to fluent conversations and the complex process of social interaction. But learning to interact does not stop at childhood or adolescence. It continues for a lifetime.

LANGUAGE AND THE SELF

As a child acquires knowledge, language, and motives, he or she also acquires self. A very young child may say, "Julie want cookie." Implied in this early utterance is a motivation that goes beyond mere hunger for a specific type of food. Both "Julie" and "cookie" reflect the child's growing awareness of the world, a knowledge about herself as an object and about a particular kind of edible substance. In this simple use of language, she has taken an important early step toward acquiring a sense of self.

Fundamental to the development of self is the complex task of taking the role of the other. This involves learning to think in the manner we have identified as reciprocity thinking. The child must learn to think what others are thinking—to project herself into another person's position and try to see the world from that other person's perspective. At first, the child engages in reciprocity thinking in a distinctively childlike fashion, in a manner much less complex than that mastered by adults. Most of us have learned to imagine distant places and persons with the greatest of ease. Although we may take for granted this skill, we often become aware of reciprocity thinking when we interact with children. Consider the following example:

Ann's mother tried to explain why Ann should eat wheat bread rather than the white bread she begged for. "Honey, scientists now think that our bodies require roughage to stay well. White bread has all the roughage removed. So, when Mommie says you should eat whole bread, it is for your own good." "But Mommie," Ann replied, "white bread is softer."

This misunderstanding between mother and child suggests that the mother's speech and the child's are not comparable in a strict sense. The child tries to think what her mother is thinking but is unable to go very far with this. Mother, on the other hand, projects her confidence into the imagined activities of distant scientists who presumably work for the purposes of improving human health. The mother thinks in complex reciprocities. She assumes she knows "scientists;" she can guess the importance of their work, and she can interpret that portion of their knowledge of nutrition that pertains to feeding her family. The six-year-old daughter is also capable of reciprocity thinking, but at a much different qualitative level. To her, bread has meaning only in so far as it relates to some immediate action, such as the amount of energy she has to expend chewing food. We can say her thinking lacks a long-term future orientation. She does not give consideration to what the health of her colon will be when she is fifty years old. The conversation between mother and child has a note of futility about it. They talk past one another, each operating from different knowledge systems, with different levels of linguistic skills, and from distinct motivational vantage points. One speaker operates from a base acquired through years of refining the

Socialization is the process through which people acquire the skills necessary for social interaction. Although most of these skills are learned incidentally, some of them are learned directly from others. How the skills are imparted and the form they assume vary with the quality of the relationships between people.

application of knowledge, and the other from recently acquired skills barely tested out in the practical consequences of daily living.

The child learns about the world by extending her imagination beyond her immediate concerns. The adult has developed an extensive repertoire of different modes of imagining the presence and the nature of the other person. The problem of what kind of bread to eat must be resolved on grounds mutually understandable to mother and daughter: "Mommie demands you eat the wheat bread," or "Do what you want, it's your colon." In the first instance, threats are mutually understandable, and in the second, mother and daughter may maintain their respective views. The daughter gets her soft bread and the mother continues to believe that wheat bread would be better for her daughter's health, but the daughter is capable of making decisions about her body. This latter position may be interpreted by the child in several ways including, "Good, I get white bread," or, "Mommie doesn't love me anymore."

Children mature socially as well as physically, moving from a phase marked by a refusal to allow thoughts and awareness to fall under any perspective or interpretation other than their own to an increasing ability to "take on the attitude of others." A seven-year-old boy requests of his friend playing outside in the front yard, "Please be quiet. You must realize my father is a writer." Or a girl replies to her father's request that she clean up her room, "As you may realize, Daddy, I had my cast off only today." (Adapted from Cook-Gumperz 1975, 157–58.)

The acquisition of language develops the ability to identify. Children learning to use the language of their culture develop mental capabilities to become the other person, which means to the extent that those others carry the culture of the group, children learn about how to be social beings by participating in groups. In social psychology, we say that this process entails "learning to play a series of roles, to assume a series of conducts or linguistic gestures" (Merleau-Ponty 1964, 109).

The development of language parallels and is indistinguishable from the growing ability of the child to perceive other people. O'Neill (1973) demonstrates this point by discussing childhood jealousy. The birth of a new baby in a family often results in behavioral regression on the part of older siblings, seen in incidents such as bedwetting or reverting to baby talk. There may even be open hostility toward the baby. The older child sees the new baby as an affront to what he assumed was his "eternal presence." In other words, he thought of his family as a constant, making up the totality of himself. Before the new baby, he was not required to distinguish between himself as a member of the family and the family itself. To him these two phenomena were identical. Now the presence of the younger child calls into question this reasoning. He must learn to think, "My place has been taken," which necessitates a new form of linguistic expression. Linguistically, this process may be referred to as a verb conjugation, from present to future perfect. Socially, the process takes the form of "I have been the youngest, but I am the youngest no longer, and I will become the biggest."

This example does not imply a causal relationship between learning grammar and overcoming jealousy. The actual relationship depends upon many factors, like the developmental level of the older sibling and the parents' responses to the jealousy. I simply wish to make the point that the mastery of language also requires the mastery of socially appropriate action. For the child, language functions as a social principle. Language, literally, is society, not just a representation of it. The rules of language usage and the socially appropriate actions the child must exhibit are identical at this phase of socialization.

What we are saying here about the socialization process is substantiated by some important psycholinguistic research. The child's early speech can be interpreted as **iconographic:**

". . . that is, the setting, shared history of the participants as well as presently occurring events for the participants are treated as a single communicative context in which verbal utterances and their prosodic features form a single unit for interpretation by the child. All parts of the message and context contribute equally to the possible interpretation. *ALL COMPONENTS ARE CONSIDERED TO CONTRIBUTE SIMILARLY TO THE UNDERSTANDING FOR BOTH THE CHILD AND HIS RECIPROCAL PARTNERS.* (emphasis added) (Cook-Gumperz 1975, 151).

Another way to grasp this complicated point is to think of the differences between child and adult speech. The de Villiers (1979) sum up these differences according to three features. In adult language, there is a freedom from the here-and-now, an ability to take into account variation in shared knowledge, and an awareness of language form. In the earliest forms of child language, communication is bound by circumstances. Even seven- and eight-year-olds have difficulty communicating when they are separated by a screen obscuring their view of one another. Likewise, anyone who has phoned a family household and tried to relay a communication through the child who answered the phone knows how tedious this task can be. However, with the acquisition of language comes the ability to escape the confines of circumstance. In the end, the adult human uses language to create circumstances (de Villiers 1979, 86).

Children can and do learn for themselves, even if they are working on specially designed projects. What they learn, however, depends in part on the way they use language. The literal nature of their communication defines the limits of their views of the world.

Language contains all the necessary knowledge for assumptions about the character of others and for assessing intentions and motivations. Its mastery and its many varieties and uses provide us with the keys to understanding social life.

PRIMARY SOCIALIZATION

Although linguistic aspects of communication like the learning of tensing and mood are of importance, the development of the social self involves more. It includes all the subtle and explicit influences that come from the social context of communication. All of us learn to adapt, to do what is appropriate, to break rules in some situations, and to work out relationships with other people. In social psychology, it is convenient to distinguish between two kinds of socialization, each highlighting the importance of varying social context: **primary** and **secondary**. The former includes all the learning experiences which occur within the family and other primary groups. The latter refers to socialization taking place in less intense, less total context. This secondary socialization is also called **adult socialization**, and can be as profound and compelling in its effects on the individual as primary socialization.

Earlier we introduced Cooley's notion of the "looking-glass self." That concept helps us understand how we think of ourselves as we believe others think of us. Cooley felt the primary group, that is, the social context characterized by face-to-face contact, demanding all of the person's consciousness and encompassing the entire person, produced society. Thus, groups with these characteristics constitute the context for primary socialization.

Let us consider a typical interaction between father and son to see how self-concepts are formed in primary groups. Sam, the father, says, "I don't know why you always make such a mess! Why can't you just leave things alone?" Son Freddie answers, "I can't help it." Sam then relates the history of Fred's development for the child's benefit. "Sure, always been that way. When you were three you got into some old paint cans in the garage and poured out all the paint, all over the floor. Took me a week to clean up that mess. Guess you can't change a leopard's spots." Freddie answers with silence.

We do not intend to convey the impression that Freddie is messy because his father thinks he is. The formation of self is more complicated than that. However, in this passage we can see that Sam does offer an interpretation of his son's behavior. He characterizes it, casts it in biographical relief, and judges it with implications for the future. In their daily lives with their families children receive literally thousands of such character references. They are told they are bright, sensitive, dull, clumsy, quick, or slow. Often, these definitions can take on great importance in influencing actual behavior.

A series of experiments by Rosenthal (1966) demonstrates the part played in learning and education by **self-fulfilling social expectations**. He did studies with both animals and humans and found that the definitions experimenters had about the nature of the animals and children they were working with influenced the actual behavior of subjects in the experiments. For instance, when teachers were falsely told that certain children's I.Q. tests indicated they were about to "spurt ahead" in their school work, those children often surpassed their classmates on I.Q. tests taken a full year later (Rosenthal and Jacobsen 1968).

Fortunately for the child perhaps, parents' and other adults' reactions are often inconsistent and expressed in a form which is not immediately comprehensible to the child. This vagueness about what the parent or teacher really means leaves room for the child to select and formulate personal ideas about who he or she is that are sometimes at variance with his parents' judgments. Freddie may think Sam just "bitches all the time"

Practice makes perfect. Many of the images we have of who we are result from working out our own meanings for what we see happening in the world around us. The little girl in this picture has her own version of the meanings of the acts of those people in her immediate environment. What do you suppose she is thinking?

and that he, Fred, does not think of himself as messy at all. After all, Fred's friend Adam is the biggest mess in the world. As Fred likes to say "Adam's room is so dirty he sleeps in the living room."

Primary socialization, then, is crucial to the acquisition of selfhood. Within intimate social contexts, whether dominated by the family or fragmented among different people and groups, the materials necessary for becoming a social self are found. The materials are assimilated, organized, and used by individuals personally reflecting their unique experiences and endowments.

SECONDARY SOCIALIZATION: REFERENCE GROUPS

After people develop selves, they still confront groups which make demands and exert pressure on them. Certainly the impact of these groups on the self can be profound. But these groups require distinctive competencies of the individual. In a sense, we meet these groups when we step outside the door of our homes. They are comprised of our neighbors, strangers, friends, and enemies. As the child learns to identify the other, he learns to differentiate kinds of people. The kind of learning which takes place, learning which allows the categorization and classification of people, is the basis of secondary socialization. Secondary socialization builds on primary. Think of primary socialization as a necessary condition for secondary. Having acquired the rudiments of language use and selfhood, the person matures into a discriminating adult, picking and choosing the groups toward which he or she compares his or her behavior. Such groups are called **reference groups** (Merton 1957).

The reference group supplies the basic information and experiences of secondary socialization. A reference group can be defined as those persons in the social world whom an individual uses as standards for making sense of his or her own actions. A reference group, also, serves as a symbolic guide to producing behavior. It is a person's understanding of others as that understanding plays a role in the interpretations the person makes regarding the significance of his or her own actions. As the child moves out of the primary context of immediate family, friends, and relatives, the influences of these people are replaced by others less intimately known. Important others become reference groups—peers at school, the boys down the block, the girls in Campfire, the members of a football team, or the members of the lodge to which one desires admission. Even if a person does not actually interact, in face-to-face contact, with these others, they may be an important influence on the self. Let us look more closely at how reference groups operate in secondary socialization.

To be selective in the discussion of groups possessing referential significance for the individual, I will sketch how such groups enter into the socialization picture. The processes described here transform the capability for thinking reciprocally in general ways to thinking about the other according to very specific contexts.   For the child, everybody's opinion matters.   When a seven-year-old boy becomes preoccupied with whether or not his outfit for the day "looks funny," he is worried about people in general thinking he is strangely dressed.   The teenager who knows his blue-jeaned, layered shirt, leathered tennis shoe look is offensive to his elders, disregards that potential censorship in favor of the positive judgment he believes his peers give to his style of dress.   Both the seven-year-old and the teenager are capable of knowledge of the generalized other, but only the teenager distinguishes significant others from the array of possible groups.   The teenager has selected a reference group.

The process of becoming more and more discriminating about who is significant for the purposes of acting is developmental.   The adult may distinguish many different significant others for particular situations.   Thus, in the neighborhood store, in the presence of clerks and co-residents, the jump-suit leisure attire of the lawyer gives him the feeling of being properly dressed.   Upon returning home with the groceries for the night's dinner party, he changes into a leisure suit, denim-look, with boat shoes.

Breakin' in new meanings.   Sometimes people use the skills of interaction they have to invent new ways to express themselves.   At times, these new forms of expression capture the attention of a larger audience, but even popular forms like breakdancing carry messages from the original group contexts.

The next morning as he prepares for a day in court, he chooses a white shirt, a subdued tie, a dark suit, matching socks, and black shoes. All these outfits have been carefully selected with reference to different groups.

The adult's ability to imagine himself in different situations is the hallmark of secondary socialization. Secondary socialization involves the internalization of specific forms of reciprocity thinking, forms which possess definite limits and partial applications. Groups of people whose imagined standards are referred to by the socialized person may or may not actually adhere to those standards. The lawyer may be regarded as overdressed by his colleagues, or as an out-of-date, unhip casual dresser by his dinner guests. As Cooley, Mead, and Thomas taught, it is what the lawyer thinks others think of him and his reaction to this imagined opinion that determines his actions.

The importance of self-concept in mediating the actions of people has long been recognized in social psychology. The studies of the American soldier during World War II indicated, for example, that the morale of troops could not be assessed by objective factors such as whether or not promotions or pay rates came fast and easy. Instead, such objective factors were interpreted by soldiers according to the way they compared them-selves with others (Stouffer, et al. 1949). The meanings they attached to slow or fast promotions depended on which reference group they used to compare their understanding of their own position. In the air force where promotions were rapid, airmen who had advanced a grade in six months might express discontent since some of their fellow corps members ad-vanced two grades in the same time period. On the other hand, in the army, making a corporal's grade in three years was regarded as normal progress, and the fact that one was still a private after six months was no cause for discontent. Of course, the knowledge that one was in the army instead of the air force could be just cause for low morale among members of the army.

During the Vietnamese War many army officers were dismayed when what they thought was their humane treatment of recruits failed to produce an appreciative attitude among the recruits. Officers, many of whom were career soliders, remembered well the often dangerous, and clearly arduous training they had received as young recruits. During the Second World War, training consisted of long hikes, experience with live ammunition, and uncomfortable living quarters. Indeed, there were many deaths as the result of training accidents. In the modern army, training routines are monitored and evaluated. Whenever live ammunition is used, it is under the strictest supervision. Long, forced marches no longer are used to push recruits to the limits. Trainees ride in trucks on hot days, take shorter marches, and enjoy much greater freedom on bases than was the case in the army many "Lifers" recalled. All of these managed training routines appeared to be "soft living" to the career soldier. But, they were still interpreted as horrors of army life by the draftees who did not judge their present life style by previous army practice, but by the civilian life from which they had been snatched. To the career drill sergeant, the award of a meritorious service certificate meant a high honor. To the draftee such an award became evidence of how well he was able to "pull the wool over the sergeant's eyes," while making the best of a highly undesirable, hopefully temporary situation. The sergeant would be angered, or at least confused, at the draftee's ridicule of or outright disgust for the award. He would expect the piece of paper to be honored in a special place, perhaps framed and hung on the wall. The draftee instead hangs it upside down in the bathroom or simply throws it away.

We explain these differences in the interpretation of meaning and attribution of significance according to the different socialization experiences of the two men. Each came from a learning background which provided identification with different reference groups. A person evaluates his present circumstances by comparing himself with those whom he regards as relevant points of references. Hence, feelings of deprivation are relative. The young draftee regards the practices of World War II basic training as irrelevant to his current plight.

This concept of the relativity of feelings of deprivation helps us understand why blacks in the sixties who were "absolutely" better off than their ancestors were angry enough to riot. It also reminds us of the importance of the immediate standards from which judgments of having been wronged derive. Homans (1974) writes about the sense a person has of the distribution of rewards in a way that is consistent with our use of the concept of **relative deprivation**.

Distributive injustice occurs when a person does not get the amount of reward he expects to get in comparison with the reward some other person gets. He expects to get more reward than the other when his contributions . . . rank higher that the others, equal reward when his contributions and investments are equal to the other's, etc. Though many men in many societies implicitly accept this rule, they may still disagree as to whether the distribution of rewards is just in particular circumstances, because they do not admit the same dimensions of reward, contribution, and investment as relevant. In their assessments of distributive justice, persons are more apt to compare themselves with others that are close or similar to themselves in some respect than with others that are distant or dissimilar (Homans 1974, 268).

A major consequence of adult socialization for an individual is the shifting that occurs almost daily among various standards of different groups with which the individual comes into contact with. Some shifts are dramatic, entailing conversions; others are minor, matters of taste and preference. But regardless of how minor or trivial a shift in reference group may seem, it may become a part of the complex method a person uses to judge how he or she is doing. Hence, the way the person feels, whether we are talking about the child's sense of having been wronged, or the adult's, is bound up in a person's symbolic powers of comparison.

Our discussion of significant references and their acquisition in the adult's life emphasizes that a person need not actually achieve membership in a group for that group to become a significant reference. In fact, all that is necessary is anticipated membership.

For the individual who adopts the values of a group to which he aspires but does not belong [conformity to nonmembership group norms] may serve the twin functions of aiding his rise into that group and easing his adjustment after he has become a part of it (Merton 1957, 265).

But as Merton suggests, there are several consequences of this type of reference group behavior which may be dysfunctional as well. If people shape their behavior in accord with a group to which they want to belong and then fail to acquire that membership, they may become **marginal**. They will have changed their behavior so that they now act in ways inappropriate to their old group. Hence, it is only in relatively open social structures that provide for mobility that **anticipatory socialization** operates smoothly.

INTERPRETATIONS OF RULES:
ACTION AND THE REFERENCE GROUP

Another way to stress the importance of describing the precise form of reciprocity thinking that results from identification with specific groups is to examine how rules for action are interpreted. The same explicitly stated rule manifests itself in many different forms of action. Our understanding of the use to which a rule is put depends upon a full description of the context in which it is used, its interpretation, and, perhaps most importantly, the socialization level of persons involved.

Consider the **application of rules** of behavior at a public swimming pool. Often these rules are written down and displayed on bulletin boards near the pool. I have seen as many as thirteen rules for a single, small motel pool. Let's look at some of the more common ones: "Don't eat or drink near the pool." This rule seems clear enough and straightforward in application until we sit by the pool and observe the actions of people. We may see a mother fully dressed, sitting at a table six feet from poolside, sipping a Coke. The lifeguard, we note, makes no comment. On another occasion, an eight-year-old boy clad in swimming trunks walks to within fifteen feet of the pool, sandwich in hand, and the lifeguard yells, "Hey kid, don't eat near the pool!" Obviously, the rule is applied differently in the two instances. The matters of interpretation which distinguish applications of rules may be expressed as questions: What does "near the pool" mean? To whom, or to what kind of person do the rules apply? What constitutes eating or drinking?

With regard to the first question, we see that in the mother's case, position in relation to the pool, is defined as "not near", probably because, as the lifeguard tells us, she is not swimming. Thus, the application of the rule to situations depends on a judgment with respect to who is swimming and who is merely poolside. This is apparently decided by the attire of the person, although even this determination becomes complicated by the presence of people clad in swimsuits who do not swim. Thus, a nonswimming person, wearing nonswimming clothes may actually move closer to the pool than a swimsuited person and still not be "near" for the purposes of the rule.

"Eating and drinking" depends on what is eaten or drunk and under what circumstances. Regarding what constitutes eating and drinking, drinking pool water while swimming is not "drinking." Then, a person who walks to the side of the pool and with methodical intent begins to sip pool water through a straw would presumably come under a different rule than "Don't eat or drink near the pool." Or a formal poolside dinner, for which tables are set up, suspends the rule. An adult may consume food in small quantities, sunflower seeds from a plastic bag, for example, without prohibition, while the consumption of a candy bar by a child would evoke blasts from the guard's whistle.

Thus, from our observations, we must conclude that the meaning of a simple rule depends on the lifeguard's interpretation of nearness on the part of different kinds of people and under various circumstances which can be ranked in terms of the departure from what is presumed to be the normal activities of swimming. Adults know the rule and may, therefore, break it judiciously or with formal sanction. Children, on the other hand, willfully flaunt the rule and must be admonished.

Similar points can be made for other rules such as "Don't run." Children may be more sophisticated than we realize in how they apply rules. A six-year-old girl, gleefully and repeatedly diving from the pool's board, develops a gait that looks like a walking racer's waddle. She beats other children to the head of the line for the board and still avoids "running." On one occasion, the guard blasts a whistle at her, to which she replies, "But I wasn't running!" "Running," then is not a matter of technical definition of foot-pavement contact and forward motion. It is essentially a realization of a motive. The crucial question which the guard must decide is, did the girl intend to run, or is she really running even if she does not appear to be running? Such everyday applications of rules are only partially related to official reasons for the rules, such as safety. They reflect to some degree personal involvements of the people at the poolside and, chiefly, the interactional character of such encounters, in other words, contacts among socially defined selves.

More often than not, how we decide to apply rules for the preliminary matters of defining the meanings of a given situation depends on the available cultural definitions for situations. Stebbins (1969) hypothesized that individuals enter a setting with particular intentions, and that certain aspects of the setting will confirm these intentions. Taken together, those aspects of the surroundings and the individual's intentions will lead her or

These rules are the starting points for the interpretations that visitors to the beach make of appropriate behaviors. The way that officials, like lifeguards, and people on the beach mutually decide the proper application of these rules can vary greatly according to the motives and knowledge of the respective participants. Follow the rules, and above all, have fun.

him to select a cultural definition of the situation. This definition will then direct the individual's actions.

Stebbins demonstrated how regular and uniform the culturally given interpretations of situations can be by staging a classroom disruption. In this enactment two visitors to a lecture class interrupted the instructor and accused him of polluting the students' minds, calling him an outsider, an atheist, and a communist. The subject of the day's lecture had been evolution and the school a part of a "community where religious matters are taken seriously." After a heated five-minute debate, the two were expelled from the classroom, and the experimenter entered, explaining how the confrontation had been staged.

The students who witnessed this scene then filled out open-ended questionnaires which asked their impressions of the pair's intentions as well as their personal feelings about what happened. There was a remarkable consistency in the students' accounts which Stebbins interpreted as culturally given definitions of the situation. The general impressions were that the two men were religious figures of some sort whose beliefs were being challenged by the lectures, and as a result the men wanted the lectures corrected or stopped; their activities were considered outrageous and highly resented. Other students felt that these two men were only nonstudent intruders who somehow decided that the lectures were having a bad influence on the students, and as a result wanted the lectures either corrected or stopped. Their activities were regarded as mildly disgusting.

Although this research does not prove that culture provides ready-made interpretations of situations, it does show that in ambiguous situations people tend to rely on what they see as generally appliable interpretations. How we interpret the meanings of situations and the specific way in which rules are applied is conditioned by the generally available cultural meanings of situations and the concrete applications of rules to a given situation.

EXTREME CASES OF SECONDARY SOCIALIZATION

Sometimes in the course of one's life major changes in identity occur. These changes produce a different organization in the self, an altered identity. Others recognize a person as a social object according to his or her own announcements (Stone 1962, 93). Hence, a person may announce a new identity which varies from an older one, but may be equally complete. These extreme changes in identity, usually in adulthood, take place after a person has accumulated considerable socialization experience. They are, however, similar to primary socialization since they involve the entirety of the person, the total social self.

As we have noted, secondary socialization complicates and fragments the self. It gives us many life worlds, adding some, causing us to drop others. Our primary socialization experiences function to organize these many facets of the self into a whole, or a life organization. Now we focus on secondary experiences so extreme they function to alter life organization in a radical fashion.

Prisoners of war during the Korean or the Vietnamese wars, for example, discovered they lived in profoundly altered life situations. Everything about their lives was externally manipulated by their captors. Old routines like grooming habits or sleep patterns were controlled by strangers. Even encounters with soldiers from home were transformed into occasions for mistrust, since a buddy may turn out to be a collaborator.

Studies of the reactions of prisoners of war to extreme brainwashing techniques reveal that coercion frequently produced a **"ritualization of belief"** (Schein, Schneier, and Barker 1961). The prisoner or inmate transformed his beliefs from matters of primary self concern or relevant life plan expressions to secondary levels of verbal expression. He said what he was supposed to but without inward conviction. He learned to feign, to express himself and his beliefs, often ideological precepts, moral dogma, and the like, in ways that would satisfy his torturers. Those of us who see and hear an air force colonel denounce the American system as imperialistic on national television may not be able to tell that the testimony reflects ritualization. To us, it may ring with authenticity, but the colonel's former friends, those who knew him well, notice a strange difference in his manners, speech, and posture. Upon returning home after release, the colonel may have to account for his action to the armed forces authorities. In most of these cases, military courts have ruled that such expressions of belief were the result of duress and did not reflect a genuine conversion. These decisions seem to recognize the social psychological distinction between primary and secondary socialization.

Another finding from studies of prisoners concerns the phenomenon of **ritual identification** with the captors. During the atrocious treatment of Jews in Nazi concentration camps, prisoners frequently esteemed articles of Nazi clothing worn by the guards. They would bargain for these articles and wear them under their own clothing. Or, they would even fashion symbols of their captors like the swastika and display them outwardly on their clothing. As with ritualized belief, close examination of these practices indicated that they did not respresent genuine or deep-level reorganization of the prisoner's self. His or her primary experiences remained intact to resurface and manifest their true nature after the extreme pressure lifted.

In less dramatic but similar fashion, extreme pressures for conformity exerted by schoolteachers over students, or the close supervision of a foreman over his workers can produce a characteristic ritual adaptation. One sociologist has termed this form of adaptation **"chameleon conformity"** (Rosow 1967). He points out that extreme external pressures for the proper behavior without regard for internal or value states of behavior produces a self-presentation in which a person does what is expected of him or her for potential or actual rewards. They behave for instrumental reasons. Their actions are merely a means to an end and not necessarily an expression of their deeper self-identities. We all do what we must—work at the summer job or accept a menial job after school to earn extra money. However, we do not regard these activities as reflecting our real selves. A student may drive a cab at night, but he does not think of himself as a cabbie. He is instead a student. Or in another instance, a person goes to school to become a lawyer, but she does not really think of herself as a student. We act as chameleons, changing our colors to conform to the demands of a situation, but we retain our underlying identities.

This identity shows up in times of stress, according to Rosow. If another summer job becomes available, we do not forgo wages to stay with the first one on the grounds that former job is "really me." We simply move on to another job. Top level executives express loyalty to their firms until a better job comes along. Their loyalty shifts appropriately. This does not mean that the executives have no life plans, but just that affiliation with a particular firm is interpreted as progress toward a personal goal such as success.

Secondary socialization methods are obvious and direct, and designed to denigrate the individual. Uniforms, harassment, and drills strip persons of their identities so that they can acquire new ones.

The work of recent theorists like Goffman can be seen as part of an effort to assess the effects of socialization in societies that are organized so that major portions of everyday life are taken up in interaction with strangers. When we interact with those whose core self-attributes we do not know, and whose authentic selves are largely irrelevant to the instrumental purposes of going about our daily rounds, we tend to develop facility at presenting a version of our selves to others, a version we think of as appropriate to the situation. Goffman formulated several concepts designed to help understand the nature of interactions in an impersonal world. His theory has been referred to as dramaturgical, or, more colorfully, as the view of society as the "big con." His ideas will be discussed in more detail later; however, his cynical view of socialization as impression management is consistent with what we are singling out as the effects of secondary socialization, namely the **ritualization of the self**.

To understand chameleon adaptations, we must know whether the experiences in question involve deep level identities or secondary ones, whether we are talking about essential attributes of self or techniques the individual has developed to simply get along. Both deep and surface, private and public attributes of selfhood are acquired through reciprocity thinking and taking the attitude of others, but the former functions to organize the experiences of the latter. The experiences of prisoners of war and the instrumental actions of the employee represent learning which modifies the self, making it more complex, adaptable or manipulative. There are, however, some secondary socialization experiences which apparently modify core self identities.

The popularity and vitality associated with the Jesus movement surprised many in light of the secular character of most youth movements in the 1960s and the early 1970s. The very youth who had rebelled against the puritanical moral code of their parents now embraced the brotherhood of those who know the love of Jesus. Yet, often they kept their long hair and hip clothes, or changed them for wardrobes even more unconventional. Jesus people were not the Christians of The First Presbyterian Church. Still their conversion to Christianity rang with authenticity as they changed their ways of life, giving up drugs, forgoing the use of swear words, and, most importantly, devoting much time and energy to "the work of the Lord."

It appears that we have, in this case, an instance not just of an individual passing through stages that shift the focus of selfhood, but changes in the core of the self brought about through secondary socialization. At least we can conclude that significant alterations have occurred in the way these believers think of themselves. However, detailed descriptions of the types of belief changes characterizing the Jesus people show that primary socialization continues to play an important role. In fact, one observer hypothesizes that "the Jesus movement combines elements of the moral code into which these young people were originally socialized as well as elements of the youth culture into which they were later socialized" (Gordon 1974, 159). He illustrates that a self-change which he calls **"consolidation"** takes place, and apparently contradictory socialization experiences synthesize into a new self-identity.

The Jesus person speaks a language which is a synthesis between religious discourse and the argot of the hip. He or she is a hip Christian. Dress, casual style of work and worship reflect the impact of youth cultural values, while the religious belief system itself represents a conventional expression of basic institutional values of society. However, the changes necessary to become a Jesus person may involve movement from many backgrounds: from the youth-drug culture, from the conventional secular life, or from Christian fundamentalism. A move from conventional, not-saved backgrounds to Christian fundamentalism represents an ordinary conversion. Here the values of the institutions implicated, like family organization and marital fidelity, remain unchanged.

Typically, a person finally espouses religious values that have been indirectly introduced earlier in his or her life. When a fundamental Christian becomes a Jesus person, the belief changes often symbolize rebellion against conventional or institutional expression of belief. He or she assumes a new identity built upon old belief systems. It is the change from fundamental to youth-drug to Jesus person which activates the consolidation experience. Drifting from the ways of the Lord or straying from the fold is only temporary. The return is effected by the style of life picked up while in the wayward life of the hip. Jesus personhood reconciles these background features. Sometimes this reconciliation occurs indirectly: a person loses faith and becomes a conventional, secular person only to regain the lost faith of childhood by way of a hip expression of it.

I mention these phenomena of conversion and consolidation to show that, generally, consolidation involves only a modification of the self. Most adulthood learning, even if it appears to have radically altered the self, builds on the interactional effects of primary and secondary socialization.

SUMMARY

Socialization is a term used to refer to the lifelong process in which a person acquires the skills necessary to interact with others. Children accomplish the task of learning through the mastery of both social and linguistic problems. Socialization proceeds according to ever-increasing complexity in a person's capacity to think as though she or he were someone else. Of course a variety of factors can modify this trend toward complexity, such as psychological aberrations and senility.

Interactions, then, are influenced by the uses to which people put their version of reciprocity thinking. Those skills acquired within the context of the primary group generally result in core qualities of the self; whereas with some extreme exceptions, experiences mediated by specific ways of thinking about others complicate and diversify the self. We call the first type of socialization primary and the latter secondary.

EXERCISES FOR SOCIALIZATION

1. Two very important skills acquired throughout the socialization process are senses of time and space. These are fundamental to many of the processes of comparison (reference group membership, distributive justice, etc.) discussed above. By using techniques designed to help you recall your primary socialization experiences, you can gain a greater appreciation of how these senses were formed and sharpened in our own childhood.

Professor James P. Spradley devised several exercises which accomplish this appreciation.

a. The task is to select a period of your childhood, say when you were ten to thirteen years of age. Then, recall where you played and associations between play and area of play during this period of your life. Professor Spradley suggested that you draw a turf map. This map will represent your recollection of your territory of play. It should include your home, a sketch showing layout of your friends' homes, playgrounds, etc. Figure 4.1 is an example of a turf map to show you what one looks like. Of course, these will vary with the person's experiences, the kind of neighborhood, the family composition, and other factors.

b. Compare your completed maps with others in your class. Notice if there are differences between men's and women's maps, between those of people who grew up in cities and of people who were socialized early in rural or suburban environs. You can spend hours with these maps. You should discover that they tell you a great deal about how you acquired a sense of membership in groups and the general notion of who you are.

c. Professor Spradley used a device he called the life chart to illustrate how we mark and sense time. To draw one of these, first sit down with paper and pencil and make a list of the events in your life which you think represent significant changes; Spradely called these "marker events." Pare them down to categories which gloss the events, e.g., neighborhood life, junior high dating, making the cheerleading team, etc. Now arrange these according to the lived-through sequences of your life experiences. Figure 4.2 shows one example of a life chart.

d. Again, compare life charts with others in your class. You will discover how these charts convey the sense of self which you currently hold. How you mark your life can be seen as representing the core attributes of your sense of self. Notice how there are both similarities and differences in life charts. Generally, people with similar charts share interactive competencies.

2. Much of the socialization experience consists of learning how to use rules. Spradely invented an exercise to help students appreciate the great variation and complexity in the practice of "rules-in-use." A simple version of this exercise requires that you recall how eating took place when you were, say fourteen years old. Recall a typical weekend at your home. Write a paragraph about each meal of the day. Then, state the rules which governed eating at your house. For example, there may be assertions like "Don't chew with your month open," "Food will be served to mother first, then boys according to age," or "Sunday is the big meal, everybody must attend". By comparing these rules for eating among your classmates, you will discover the consistency and the variation of rules-in-use in everyday life. You will also find out there are often rules for not following rules. These make life interesting on occasion.

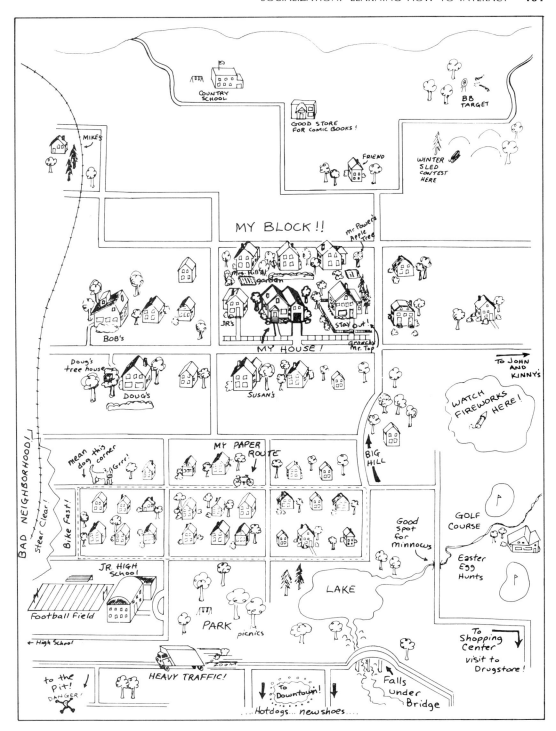

Figure 4.1   Turf Map

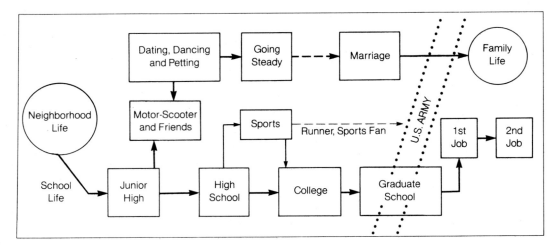

Figure 4.2   Life Chart

KEY CONCEPTS

Iconographic speech
Primary socialization
Secondary socialization
Adult socialization
Self-fulfilling social expectations
Reference groups
Relative deprivation
Distributive injustice
Marginal
Anticipatory socialization
Applications of rules
Ritualization of belief
Ritual identification
Chameleon conformity
Ritualization of the self
Consolidation

SUGGESTED READINGS

The concept of socialization is so encompassing in social psychological literature it is difficult to single out a book or article on socialization. However, we have introduced the concept to refer to the ways and manners of accomplishing social interaction. Books about socialization are books that depict precisely how and why people learn to think of themselves in certain ways and how and why they act as they do.

Three sources are highly recommended here. The first is a technical but readable account of how prisoners of war during the Vietnam conflict learned to communicate with each other by simply tapping on the walls of their cells. A prisoner of war himself for several years, Phillip Butler documents a fascinating resocialization experience. Edmund W. Vaz recounts the learning experiences of young hockey players as he explains what is actually learned from the playing of youth hockey in the highly hockey-conscious nation of Canada. Finally, in a personal account written from the parent's point of view, Spradely and Spradely relate how a young hearing-impaired girl and her family learn the social meanings of a serious physical handicap.

Butler, Phillip. "The Tap Code: Ascribed Meanings in Prisoner of War Communications." *Urban Life* 5, no. 4 (1977): 399–416.

Spradley, Thomas S., and James P. Spradely. *Deaf Like Me.* New York: Random House, 1978

Vaz, Edmund W. *The Professionalization Of Young Hockey Players.* Lincoln, Nebraska: University of Nebraska Press, 1982.

Chapter Five

Group Phenomena:
The Self and Others

Group Phenomena:
The Self and Others

At first we were just a bunch of guys. Sure each of us had experience playing college ball, but we were not together as a unit. We had the talent all right. There was never any question about that. It was the team thing. That first season nothing really jelled. We had our moments, but as the season wore on, all of us knew we were not playing as a team. Too much "star" stuff, not enough team work. We had to come together as a group before we had any chance at the championship. The coach knew that, so at the start of the second season, he changed our training camp. He insisted that we do everything together. He even isolated us from our families. We ate together, traveled together, shared rooms. The worst thing was that any time one of us broke a curfew or a training regulation, we all got demerits. Demerits added up to fines and that hurt. There was that time Verl skipped a morning "skull" session, and we all got fined $100.00. I can tell you I got pretty sick of those guys before the season started.

But you know, now as I look back on it, that training camp brought us together. We started anticipating each other's moves better, on and off the court. We became a team almost like I remembered when in high school we won the state championship. We were older and wiser — more experienced, but the team thing, that never changes. And, that's what gave us the edge that championship season. We played as a unit, a single effort, not just five "hot shots" who happened to be on the court at the same time.

I NTERACTION, socialization, and self are the three principal concepts necessary for understanding the nature of social life from a social psychological point of view. The results of the interrelationships among these three phenomena emerge as the group. Although groups originate in individual thought and feeling processes, they are the outcome of thinking about and imputing motives to others in more or less regular ways. Groups exhibit clearly identifiable patterns of self-other relationships.

THE NATURE OF THE GROUP

According to Simmel, social **form** is somewhat independent of **content**. As noted in an earlier chapter, one can discuss many different topics such as sport or religion within a recognizable form known as the "conversation." The form of the conversation is distinct from its content as well as from other ways of talking; for example, lecturing about sports differs from talking about baseball with friends at the barbershop. Or, children may engage in games—some simple, others complex, some cooperative, others competitive—but all of these games constitute a social form called "play."

When we talk of groups, we are discussing a social form. Whereas the content of different groups shows enormous variation, there is more order and stability in the form; hence, sociological social psychology pays attention to form over content in the task of analyzing social life. Of course, this does not mean content never influences form, nor that form never changes; some very subtle interactions can take place between content and form. By stressing form over content, social psychologists simplify the amount of descriptive observation necessary before analysis can begin, and they follow, in observation, powerful concepts depicting human sociability.

What distinguishes a group from the aggregate of individuals and the specific behaviors of individuals is the form displayed. In a situation where three men are talking together, what they converse about may be irrelevant to the form of their group, but the manner in which they converse is quite relevant: they seem to presume a great deal about one another, using first names only; they touch each other frequently, patting backs, and hitting each other on the shoulders; they laugh at remarks which do not seem funny to the outsider; they use words that sound familiar but apparently possess special meanings for them. Although we cannot comprehend all that transpires in this group, we do gather from the tone and character of the interaction we observe that these men are friends.

In another instance, we see three other men. They are dressed quite differently from the first three, and they speak in formal terms of address, using Mr., Dr., and other honorific verbal designations. One of the men is called by his initials, T.J. The only body contact we notice is handshaking. They seem distant, intent upon a specific purpose. One man remarks repeatedly, "What have we got so far, T.J.?" and, "Now let's sum up our progress on that." It is obvious that the character of these two groups

All groups include and exclude members. This boy is clearly being excluded from the collective piano playing of his friends.

differs significantly. The first is informal, familiar, and expressive, in the direction we have identified as primary; the latter is formal, instrumental, and in the direction we can call secondary. Friends and business associates, even if they are actually the same individuals, manifest distinctive forms in the group level of reality. It is the character of the social interaction that reveals the form or nature of the group.

TYPES OF GROUPS AND THEIR ORGANIZATION

A group possesses a characteristic organization depending upon the manifestation of the three features of interaction in the group's form. The three features are background knowledge which ranges from tacit to explicit, communicational skills which vary from casual to formal, and motivation and emotional involvement which vary from complete and intense to partial and superficial. The various combinations of these features define the type of group form. A **primary group**, for instance, manifests tacit knowledge backgrounds, casual communicative expressions, and intense, complete motivation and involvement. A **secondary group** displays explicit knowledge systems, formal articulations, and requires only partial and incomplete motivational and emotional involvement with the group. Further, mixed combinations of features are possible producing forms which, generally speaking, are predominantly primary or secondary, but which, in practice, are neither. We now turn our attention to the description of features of each of these types of group forms: primary, secondary, and mixed.

The Primary Group

We have already learned the primary group is characterized by intense, intimate communication and tacit understandings among its members. The theoretical importance for the study of primary groups has been developed by several social psychologists. Among the most convincing is a work by G. C. Homans, *The Human Group* (1950). In this book, he states that it is in the primary, small group that the observer can find the origins of norms, the very rules that make social order possible. By studying the human group, the elementary features of all social life can be uncovered. According to Homans, the accomplishment of social order for whole societies is, in part, a process of transferring the order and strength of the small group to society.

At the level of the small group society has always been able to cohere. We infer, therefore, that if civilization is to stand, it must maintain, in the relation between groups that make up society and the central direction of society, some of the features of the small group itself. If we do not solve this problem, the effort to achieve our most high-minded purposes may lead us not to Utopia but to Byzantium (Homans 1950, 468).

Such a "high-minded" charge requires some clear thinking about small groups, and Homans supplies just that. He draws upon some classic studies from social science literature: the bank wiring room studies, the Norton Street gang study, and the ethnography of the family in Tikopia. Each of these studies is famous for producing a theoretical insight.

The study of the bank wiring room was conducted by groups of researchers at the Western Electric Company's Hawthorne (California) plant during the 1920s. It concerned the relationship between group organization and worker productivity. As reported by Mayo (1933), the researchers originally expected that physical characteristics of the work situation along with matters of employee-employer relationships would be the determinates of productivity in a bank wiring room (the room where the bottom parts of telephones were wired together). However, much to Mayo's surprise, any factor which he varied, even such counterproductive ones as dimming the lights, tended to increase worker output. Mayo came to the conclusion that what was varied was not nearly as important as the mere fact that attention was being paid to the workers.

This finding, known as the **Hawthorne effect**, is generally interpreted as showing that workers in any setting can not be viewed as isolated individuals but as part of well-organized small groups. Further studies on the work groups at Western Electric demonstrated that management efforts to control productivity were often thwarted whenever those incentives or policies conflicted with the norms of the work group. Hence, members of the work groups who either overproduced or underproduced were brought back in line through the exercise of informal social controls. An effective means of control at Western was "binging," a practice male employees had of hitting each other on the shoulders. Whenever a person departed from the group's standards for what was a good day's work, he found that the friendly hits on his shoulder became more violent and he might even be ostracized.

William Whyte's *Street Corner Society* is an early study which shows that street gangs are not just random collections of boys with time on their hands. Instead, they are elaborately organized social systems adapted to their environments. The Norton Street gang had a complicated leadership structure, and rules that were so powerful that they even influenced the leisure time activities of gang members. For example, Whyte found that the results of bowling contests were correlated with the youth's ranking in the gang.

Homans cites these studies as well as Firth's description of the complicated kinship structure of the Tikopia as evidence for his theory that small groups can be understood as a system of interrelated elements. These elements are **activity, interaction, sentiments,** and **norms**. Activity he defines as what people do. The essential feature of interaction is contact with others, and sentiments are matters of the emotional states of people relevant to the activities of the group. Norms are inferences people make about what is expected of them and their use of these inferences for the purposes of establishing conformity to inferred group standards.

These elements make up a set of hypotheses. Homans argues that specific predictions are possible based on the nature of the small group as a social system. The more people engage in the same or a similar activity, the more they will contact each other. They will experience sentiments with increased contact, and these sentiments must be controlled if the group is to cohere. Hence, with increased activity comes increased interaction and feelings and finally the creation of norms. The norms are exceedingly important because they govern, in turn, the activities of the group. His theory allowed him to formulate the hypothesis that the more frequently a person interacts with another, the more probable it is that those people will like each other, their liking being an outcome of norms that emerge to control sentiments.

Although Homans' theory has been subject to criticism, and he himself has modified the basis of his theory in his recent writing, the underlying rationale of his ideas is consistent with our viewpoint. It is out of mutual contact and recognition that the rules governing social action emerge. Rules emerge within the context of groups, and these rules are applied and interpreted within these same contexts. Hence, the practices of everyday life in the primary group setting offer keys to understanding the nature of entire society. In the primary group selfhood develops and skills in interpersonal relationships are acquired. In the setting of the small group, the very essentials of social life are revealed.

What we learn in such groups subsequently influences other relationships and interactional encounters we might have. In fact, the total arrangements of all parts of society, of its institutions and even the forms that these parts assume (the structure of society), rest on the work, interpretations, and learning that develop within primary small groups. A society in which individuals have lost their capacity to form primary groups is in danger of failing to transmit itself from generation to generation. Without the vitality of the primary group, members of society may lose their ability to trust and know each other.

Although the primary form may express itself in many different contents, for the purposes of describing the form itself three will be mentioned: the **love-couple, friendship,** and **family** groups. Each kind of primary group has definitive characteristics; furthermore, the form a group takes is not rigidly set but worked out. Friends can become lovers, and brothers can become friends. Like all social life, the primary group depends on constant negotiation among people working out their interactional encounters.

A Love-Couple Sally and Ivan remember when they first met: they laugh about it. He was nervous because it was so much like a conventional date. He dressed up, groomed for more than an hour, and rehearsed his conversation. He thought about which topics he should discuss and what she might think about him. He had been surprised that she accepted his invitation to go to the movies. After all, Sally was the most gorgeous woman in their senior class. That first date was typical. Everything they talked about seemed artificial. He avoided saying anything he imagined might be offensive to her, and she waited for him to take the lead, to suggest where they should eat and which movie they should see. Still, it was a pleasant evening warranting a second date.

The second date was an improvement. Each began to relax and try to be more natural, and that is when, as Ivan put it, "things began to click." They discovered, for instance, that both liked health foods and yoga, and that they seemed to believe in similar life philosophies. They discussed for hours such topics as "tactics for survival in a hostile world" and "the meaning of life for them." Continued meetings become more and more informal. Soon they could introduce topics by using shortened phrases or words. If Ivan said, "I think there's a yoga approach to long distance running," Sally knew what he meant without further explanation. Sally could ask, "Could you buy me a loaf of bread," without fear he would bring home white bread. As they became "closer," they decided to live together. Long discussions ensued about whether or not to tell their parents:

SALLY: My mom's hip, very modern. She'll understand.

IVAN: Maybe so, but hostility depresses me. I really want to avoid hassles, if possible.

SALLY: She knows about love, and trusts me. She doesn't want me hurt. All I have to do is say it's what I really want. It'll be OK.

IVAN: I hope so. My parents are no sweat. They live so far away. We'll hold off telling them to see how things work out.

In the conversational form of the primary group, most of the meanings associated with expressions are tacit: "It'll be OK" and "to see how things work out." Sally and Ivan mutually presume that the meanings of these remarks will become clear to both of them in more or less the same way. They decide to live together and change their names to mark the new era in their lives. Both become "Skipper," a singular designation for the new reality they have created. They are now "together," a couple serious about one another. When friends inquire, they explain, "Yes, we've got a relationship."

As this newly built social reality endures, it will expand the degree of tacitness which grounds it. It will be renegotiated as crises threaten the assumptions from which the meanings and reality of the relationship derive. For example, Ivan gets a job in another town and Sally must decide whether she will continue her schooling or accompany Ivan. They argue:

SALLY: Skipper, you know I love you, but I have one year left to finish my thesis.

IVAN: I know, Skipper, but if you really love me, you'll quit and come with me. You know I need you.

SALLY: Oh, Ivan, you're just being self-centered and old-fashioned. I don't want that kind of relationship.

By discontinuing the use of "Skipper," Sally indicates to Ivan a change in her understanding of the meanings that undergird their relationship. As problems force each person to be more explicit, it becomes clear that their understandings of "love" are not identical and the assumed reciprocity on which the relationship was originally founded must now be renegotiated or ended.

Like all primary groups this one rests on trust and a certain degree of unqualified acceptance (Garfinkel 1963). The love-couple presumes an intensity of interpersonal involvement in which the meaning of the cliché "love is never having to say you're sorry" becomes clear. As we can readily guess, the building of such primary relationships from "scratch," that is, based exclusively on the feelings and interaction between two persons, results in a fragile relationship which is easily influenced by outside pressures. Conversely, whenever something happens to upset routines within such groups, the more likely one will respond emotionally to the disturbance (Handel 1982, 69). Similarly, one will be willing to do a great deal of work to restore the trust that grounds a relationship. In experiments in which he purposefully upset the routines of social life, Garfinkel discovered that whenever subjects were given random yes/no answers to personal questions by someone they presumed to be a counselor, they searched for an underlying pattern in the yes/no sequences, trying desperately to use what they believed about such settings to restore sense to a trusted relationship. Perhaps this is a part of what Homans was suggesting about the vulnerability of a civilization that does not protect and support primary group formation.

Friendship   Friendships are also classified as primary groups. The difference between love and friendship is often obscure. We may love our friends, of course. But generally the difference between having a friend and being in love is one of the degrees of tacitness, informality, and involvement. We presume less of a friend than of a wife or husband. As Goffman would have said, those with whom we are in love are allowed "back stage," are privy to matters of the self behind the "front." For example, if we experience a radical change in mood, this is more likely to be misunderstood by a friend than by a lover. Rage may be interpreted by a friend as the termination of the friendship, but by a lover as a mood change signaling a need for intervention or simply as evidence in support of the proposition "that's the way he is sometimes."

Friendships can develop in unlikely situations, such as on the assembly line, in the bar, or during a bus ride; however, we can describe the typical friendship according to a process. In other words, it does not depend on specific kinds of activities. Thus, it resembles the love relationship since it generates a complete environment for itself as the following example shows:

Bud and Gene grew up together on the Sand Springs line, a working-class suburb of a larger midwestern city. They played together as children, shared the experiences of trouble, joy, disappointment, and grief. When they were growing up neither really imagined an existence without the other. Gene went to war, and Bud stayed home, a 4F. They corresponded for awhile, but soon they simply stopped writing. Gene wrote home to his wife frequently, and Bud would occasionally find out from Gene's wife how things were going. When Gene returned, they revived their relationship, spending long evenings together telling stories about their childhood adventures and Gene's wartime exploits. Bud had married during Gene's absence, and the wives, of course, accompanied their husbands on visits to each other's houses. But the men carried on the conversations, and the women often left the room whenever Bud and Gene started talking about old times.

There was more to this friendship than just conversation and reminiscences. Bud worked at a local high school in the athletic department. He was able to get tickets to all the football games, and since he managed the concessions at home games of the local university, he could allow Gene and his family free admittance. In return, Gene, a handyman, installed central air-conditioning in Bud's house, kept his plumbing in repair, and helped out with jobs Bud could not handle himself.

There were also limits to the friendship. It was lifelong and it endured many crises and even bitter quarrels, but where each other's families were concerned a "hands off" agreement existed. Bud's children "went wrong." His son became a homosexual and moved to California; his daughter dropped out of high school and had several run-ins with the law. Finally, family tension over these problems led to divorce. Throughout these difficult times Gene was there to listen, sometimes for hours on the phone. Never did Gene give Bud explicit advice. Each understood that such matters were part of family life and mixing family and friendship could have a devastating effect on their friendship. Bud remarried after several years, moved from job to job, state to state, finally reappearing in their hometown where Gene had remained since the Second World War. The two men resumed contact, and their respective lives, which by now were considerably different, seemed to have little effect on their friendship. The content and operation of their friendship had been established long ago. The version of reciprocity that served as the foundation of their friendship was stable and enduring, protected by an elaborate defense from outside pressures.

Family The family is the primary group form par excellence. It is in the context of the family that the strongest, most consistent manifestations of tacitness, informality, and intense involvements are found. In essence, a person does not achieve a family. Families are given, members find them ready-made, appropriate for re-interpretation, re-organization and renegotiation. A husband and a wife do invent their relationship out of a social base comprised of mutual assumptions, as we have learned. But this family is their second, built to some extent on experiences of the first. A marriage reality is created and sustained through years of practice, and may have a distinctive and even idiosyncratic character (Berger and Kellner 1964). Children and others who confront it must discover its nature.

Years ago the sociologist Durkheim suggested that a fundamental fact of all social life is the degree in which interactions and meanings of everyday life are integrated into the structures of society. When we discuss forms of primary groups and identify these forms according to their features, it should be clear that we are also discussing how closely integrated organizational form is to larger patterns of organizations for society. The love-couple as a form is the least well integrated, the family the most well integrated, and the friendship an intermediate form. In other words the meanings for a love-couple relationship are more problematic since they are not part of taken-for-granted, commonsense knowledge—what everybody knows. Family forms, on the other hand, are precisely understood in terms of what everybody knows. One way of thinking about integration is to focus on the problematic character of the form. The less problematic the form, the more integrated it is, and conversely the amount of ambiguity associated with the form is a reliable indicator of low integrative linkage to other societal forms. Keeping within a Durkheimian idiom, we can say that dyads like the love-couple are egoistic. We should not be surprised to find a wide variety of meanings for primary relationships.

A recent study of blue-collar patrons of a bar (LeMasters 1975) gives some indication of the variety of content possible within the family form. To young middle-class couples who attempt to use the love relationship as the sole foundation for their families, the practices described by LeMasters may seem strange. For example, the men who become regulars at the bar, spoke of their wives and their marriages in terms like these: "My wife is a good gal, but I just don't know anybody I'd like to be married to for thirty years."; and, "Hell, man, you can't live without'em and you can't live with'em." The wives often talked of the "raw deal" that marriage is for them and commented that if they had known then what they know now, they would at least have "waited awhile to marry."

In short, wives and husbands may actually interpret their involvement in marriage quite differently. However, the segregated sex roles that mark these blue-collar families "can be quite stable and satisfying if both sexes accept the arrangement" (LeMasters 1975, 45). The reasons for staying together vary. For the wife from a conservative rural background "catching" and staying with a man who can provide "a good living" may be the motivation; or the husband may be satisfied with a "homemaker" and a "good mother for his children." Within the marital relationship these reasons remain tacit and function to the mutual satisfaction of the couple. Since the form is primary, we expect tacitness to prevail and should not be misled by pronouncements from the individuals involved. Like the author of this study we must search for the "bedrock" features of the relationship. For example, LeMasters reports this conversation with a married couple:

"You know, Professor," one of the older wives said to me, "Bob and me have never had an argument in our forty years of marriage." "That must be a record," I said. The husband looked at his wife and said: "That's a lot of bull-shit—what are you trying to do; feed the Professor a lot of crap?" The wife stopped talking, resuming her beer drinking, and the husband took over the conversation. "I'll tell you what, Doc." he said. "Marriage is a 50–50 proposition and people who don't know that better stay single." He drained his beer and ordered another one. "Now you take this wife of mine—she's a good sport. During the depression when a man could hardly earn a dime, she stuck right by me and saved every penny she could." He paused to light a cigarette.

"Another thing—she always took care of our kids. If I had a woman that let her kids run around dirty the way some women do, I'd kick her right out of the house." The wife didn't say anything. Then the husband continued. "Her only trouble is she talks too damn much—and some of the stuff she says don't make sense—like that thing she told you tonight about us never having an argument! Christ Almighty, I wouldn't have a damn woman in the house if I couldn't fight with her once in a while." The wife was looking in her purse for some snapshots of their grandchildren she wanted to show me. I looked at the pictures and admired the children—they were handsome. "A hell of a lot better looking than their grandparents," the husband said. He turned to his wife, "Come on, Mother, Harry [the bartender] says that all grandparents have to be home in bed by 10:30. Let's go!" The wife protested that she wanted another beer. "Nope, you've had enough for an old lady"—and out they went (LeMasters 1975, 45).

Our point with regard to primary groups can be succinctly stated: the primary group form establishes informality. It rests on an assumed content that cannot be explicated without changing the nature of the relationship. As with any relationship built on degrees of tacitness, as long as the parties do not question the assumptions, the relationship endures. Informality demands tolerance and unquestioned loyalty to the emotional basis of the relationship. It requires familiarity and longtime interactions which can be patterned and intuitively grasped by the participants. Primary forms occupy a major portion of a person's social existence. They provide continuity for social life.

Secondary Groups

In a complex society in which there are many different primary groups and persons from these groups must interact, the base for interaction can not always be tacitness and informality. If we do not know a person's background, if we cannot assume we know his or her self, we cannot relate to that person immediately in a way that allows intuitive understanding between us. Nevertheless, we find it necessary to interact with others. A particular person may have a commodity we desire, or he or she may be important for an intended activity. Thus, it is obvious that grounds other than those provided by the primary group must be established so that the affairs of everyday life in a world of strangers (Lofland 1973) can be carried out.

The German sociologist Ferdinand Toennies (1940) wrote systematically about the social psychological basis of interaction in social contexts varying by degrees of formality and tacitness. He was particularly concerned about the changes occurring in society from relationships built on familiarity and natural association to those resting on objective, rational grounds. In modern social psychology, we think of these differences in social encounters as **expressive** or **instrumental**. Primary groups are essentially expressive and secondary groups instrumental.

Writing at the beginning of the twentieth century, Toennies noticed the railroads which connected small German villages were bringing together for the first time people of markedly different backgrounds. The social problem of the stranger, the person whose motives and intentions could not be readily ascertained, become paramount. We can think about this as a problem of trust. Although the railroads were constructed for the purposes of commerce and industry, the effect was far more profound. How could lifelong residents of a village, tightly knitted into a community, relate to other people about whose character and identity they knew little. In short, Toennies focused on the problem of finding grounds for interaction which could substitute for natural, taken-for-granted grounds of common experience crucial to a sense of community. He discovered that such a basis existed in thought patterns that had already developed concurrently with increasing industrialization of Germany and Europe. He pointed out that if a set of specific goals could be defined by all the persons involved in the interaction, then a form of organization relevant to these goals emerged.

The storekeeper and the customer are one example. The storekeeper need not know a stranger to take his or her money in exchange for an item. All that is required is a precisely defined and delimited reciprocity thinking between them. All the storekeeper needs to know is that the other person possesses money and is willing to exchange it. And from the perspective of the stranger wishing to purchase clothing, all he or she needs to know is the location of the store, minimal standards of civility, the kind and availability of the item and the necessary exchange. A customer does not have to know about the storekeeper's family life, about the details of the children's activities in school nor their mischief at play. The storekeeper, on the other hand, does not need to know about the purchaser's recent good fortune in a card game.

Toennies' observations led him to suggest that, within given societies, two basic forms could be identified: one in which the primary group form prevails, and the other which is "rational" or "goal specific." The first, he believed, was "natural" and engendered feelings of belongingness and security, while the latter resulted in mutual suspicion and distrust. The first kind of society he called **Gemeinschaft** and the second **Gesellschaft**. The Gesellschaft, composed of secondary group forms, solved the problem of how people with radically different backgrounds could interact by offering a superficial and artificial foundation for social relationships. Toennies referred to this foundation as "rational will." The Gesellschaft society requires that we learn to treat all persons as strangers. In the language we have chosen to use, we say the basis must be explicated or formalized so that it can be learned readily without regard to differences in socialization experiences. The secondary group form establishes minimal requirements for interaction. It generates a formal system for interpersonal relationships, a system with a definite reason for being.

As with the treatment of primary groups, the aim is to describe the form; therefore, I selected the case which most clearly demonstrates the characteristics of a secondary social form, the bureaucracy. Its basis is explicit; its language is formal, and its requirements for involvement and the motivational systems it activates are minimally specific. In the Gesellschaft society, the bureaucracy functions as the standard for all social relationships. Social life within bureaucracy retains a secondary character. It comes after something else, building on experiences already present in those whom it recruits as members. In essence, one does not belong to a rational exchange, rather one works with it.

PROPERTIES OF RATIONAL SOCIAL FORMS

Precisely what are the properties of the **rational** organization? Another classic German sociologist whose writing has already been discussed, Max Weber, depicted the form of bureaucracy in explicit terms. He enumerated five basic features: the bureaucratic form is 1) **formal**, 2) **impersonal**, 3) **technical**, 4) based on **an ideal of merit**, and 5) **hierarchical**. By formal, Weber meant that organizational principles transcend any person or the activities of people connected with the organization. These principles are essentially formal, written down, and expressed as abstract guidelines for the determination of admissible practice and policy. A rational organization has a charter, a constitution, and a statement of purpose and intent. Of course, this is expected in the secondary form, for the form must accommodate and educate newcomers. The procedures for doing this are formal. The conscious characteristic of interactants operating within this form is ordinarily known as bureaucratic action.

A judge, for instance, can be removed from his bench for unprofessional conduct in affairs of law. While acting in the role of judge, a person must follow abstract rules. These rules define a set of actions as being instances relevant to the court room. These judgments depend on an abstract legal notion which must be enacted by certain kinds of people. A judge who consistently rules in a biased fashion violates the principles defining a court and may be admonished by a higher authority, thus, the intent of the phrase, "Equal justice under the law."

The feature of impersonality signifies equal relationships among people within the boundaries of the rational exchange. This property forbids primary experiences. It requires background knowledge be considered irrelevant, and allows such knowledge to become relevant only if it is consonant with the abstract principles presumed to govern the occasion. Thus, if two people are neighbors, close friends, or even relatives, these facts are not to be considered pertinent to any rational operation of a bureaucratic nature. A special deal on a new car for a friend is officially forbidden; or a separate set of books used to allow friends to avoid administrative steps at a welfare agency likewise is prohibited.

A third feature of rational exchange in everyday life is the influence of technical competency. Durkheim's early writing referred to this as "the division of labor." Within any given social organization, there are tasks to be accomplished. The manner in which the group separates performances relevant to the accomplishment of the tasks is the division of labor. In societies without a rational foundation, which are societies predominantly primary in group form, there may be little technical skill required to do work. For example, clearing a patch of jungle for planting corn and the actual planting of the corn may require the same tool, an ax; nevertheless, the group may sharply delineate the former work as masculine and the latter as feminine. In this instance, it is not the technical basis of the

Rarely does one see a bureaucratic image more clearly. Although this picture was staged for a promotional purpose, it shows many features of the bureaucratic organization. Can you identify all of these features in the picture?

activities which separates the two kinds of labor; custom, religious beliefs, or other elements of culture function to define who does what.

The bureaucracy, however, minimizes the role the traditions of a particular group play with regard to task accomplishment. In this ideal type, the rational grounds for task accomplishment is the technical requirement of the work. Thus, if a division exists within an organization, it is because of some technical reason. A motor pool platoon within an army division is organized with a person in charge, a staff of trained mechanics, and a parts inventory because the division needs motorized vehicles and this equipment must be maintained. Or a corporation selling information-processing machines must have a research branch to develop and improve computers and software to do that job. Thus, rationale for the ideal expression of the bureaucratic form rests on a technical requirement, whether this is hardware or knowledge of a technical nature.

Weber's fourth bureaucratic feature stated that merit predominates in a bureaucracy. The merit dimension of the rational organization means that the occupant of any technically created position has the job because of his or her skill in its performance. Personnel who fill the positions, ideally, should be those individuals with the highest accomplishments. Hence, the best mechanic gets the job in the motor pool or the brightest research technician heads the study of the latest miniaturized computer circuitry.

Finally, the bureaucratic levels within the naturally derived organizational form are ordered according to a principle of hierarchy. Each level is accountable to the one directly above it. More fundamentally, all the divisions or levels are not only technically grounded, but they are also stacked one on the other in accord with the abstract principles defining the rational properties of the organization. Hierarchy by position is a constitutive feature. It pertains to the overall demand that all segments of the organization make sense in terms of the stated goals of the organization. If a segment makes sense—that is, if it fits into the overall plan or purposes of the organization—we say it possesses the property of **accountability**. Official reasons for its existence can be readily expressed and they are generally acceptable to higher levels of responsibility within the organization, the executive or officer charged with ultimate accountability.

We can easily understand how the bureaucracy demonstrates secondary forms of social interaction. Yet, as we describe its ideal features, we begin to suspect that a neat distinction between this form and the primary is impossible. We have stressed before how social life should be seen as dynamic and unfolding in character. Secondary and primary forms contrast in provocative ways; each counterpoints the other. In everyday life, whenever people actually try to act in the presence of others, conflicts emerge; the form in which much of this conflict takes place is called the mixed form.

MIXED FORMS: EMERGING CONFLICTS

The study of work groups in industrial and formal settings has reaffirmed the importance and pervasiveness of primary form. Although considerable debate has been generated over this issue, investigators who have attempted to view the performances of workers in terms of incentives and rational matters only, soon discovered such factors themselves took on meaning within the context of primary or informal groups created by the workers; for instance, an efficiency rating achieved by a ship at war for the accuracy of its shelling may not be a totally valid indicator of the gunnery practices of that ship.

Altheide and Johnson (1980) describe the practice of gundecking in the United States Navy. **Gundecking** refers to the practice of falsifying, by writing up official reports as if requirements had been met but without

Although everywhere in a formal organization one can find informality, on certain occasions the formality of interactional style is obvious and overwhelming. Notice how clean the conference table is.

actually having carried out the required procedures. For example, one could gundeck the daily reports on the night before an inspection. The authors contend that gundecking cannot be fully understood as merely a matter of dishonesty. In fact, it is often the case that the practice of gundecking is built into the normal operations of a ship. For example, although the formal requirements of tests for sonar equipment conflict with those for tests of full engine capacities, navy regulations suggest that both tests should be conducted at the same time. However, because engines running fullout make so much noise that accurate sonar readings are impossible, the tests are routinely done at separate times and reported as if they were done according to regulations. Likewise, the battle efficiency of a ship (a ratio of rounds fired to target hits) depends on a series of complicated decisions made among the spotter and the ship's gunnery personnel. To avoid having to average so-called "lost rounds" (shells that the spotter never saw explode), ship personnel would classify these shells under the category "target of opportunity" to indicate that indeed the round had fallen on target (Altheide and Johnson 1980, 217).

The relationship between primary and secondary form can be exceedingly complex. Another example comes from Gouldner's research of a wildcat strike, a strike not authorized by a union. He studied a mining operation (the General Gysum Company) and discovered that a major cause of a wildcat strike among the miners could be traced to the workers' reaction to any management policy which ignored pre-existing informal group relations (Gouldner 1954). Miners had developed a procedure among themselves for making judgments about what counted as "a good day's work." This procedure was grounded in an understanding between foreman and miners. They had a tacit agreement that there is a certain amount of work to be done in a day. That amount of work had to satisfy the minimal demands of the "boys at the top," in other words, an amount of work that would keep the bosses off their foreman's back, and hence him off of theirs. The agreement took the following form: we, the workers, will do the necessary work, if you, the foreman, do not ride us too hard, allow us to pace ourselves with frequent breaks and, perhaps most importantly, tolerate the informality of our attitudes toward work. Gouldner called this mode of interpreting work the **"indulgency pattern"** (Gouldner 1954, 18–23).

The indulgency pattern defined a satisfactory work day and allowed strong friendships to develop among the workers and between the workers and the foreman. With the untimely death of their trusted foreman, the workers clamored for one of their own to replace him. They wanted to be able to continue the indulgency pattern and realized that a new foreman would have to be trained. They feared a green foreman would require them to work at dangerously fast rates. Upper level management policies prevailed and an outsider, from the above-ground processing plant, was appointed foreman. Predictably, he went by the rules, formalizing work breaks, demanding maximum efficiency and being generally intolerant of informality between himself and the miners; in short, he behaved in a manner inconsistent with the indulgency pattern. So intense was the workers' reaction to this violation of their primary form that the conflict exploded into a strike which was eventually resolved by management contractually agreeing to portions of the old indulgency pattern, like work breaks and work quotas. However, the settlement resulted in a curious formalization of the primary form which undermined the nature of the work group itself. We can say that the resolution of the strike explicated the tacit knowledge expressing formally what was properly merely understood, and relieved the men of their social obligations to each other and to their foreman. One did not need to become an accepted member of the group in order to understand work arrangements since these arrangements were now a matter of formally applying the contract agreements.

In each example of a mixed form, either primary or secondary form dominates. The goals of the company may be subverted by friendship relationships among the workers, with their ways of interpreting work winning out, if only temporarily, over the rational procedures of the company. In the navy, rational requirements and incentives get renegotiated in such ways that gunnery targets are redefined, or the work habits

Norms are being built from the activities of these men.   It is from activities such as taking a break or merely talking that informal groups emerge within the more formal structures of organizations.

and attitudes of enlisted personnel can co-exist with those of the regulations.   The settlement of the wildcat strike that Gouldner documents had the effect of transforming the tacit meanings of social life into a contract. In this case, the goals of the company were fostered by promoting a fleeting experience of primary group membership.

The mixed form is either an arena or a mask for conflict.   One can always be fired or laid off from "King Fast Foods" if the sales of hot dogs drops or the price of wieners rises.   These reasons for termination do not necessarily create a crisis of the self, but expulsion from a friendship circle, or breaking up with a lover, or being rejected by a parent goes to the heart of the self.   The investment of selfhood in secondary group forms can only lead to problems for the person and for the organization.   A lifelong, loyal employee of an oil company suddenly finds his accounting section has been replaced by automated, modernized procedures; he is without a job and feels deprived of the reason for his social existence.   Or, there is the other extreme, the chameleon who anxiously ponders in moments of solitude what he really stands for, what his life is all about.

Jackall (1977) studied the pressures to conform people sense in a commercial, bureaucratic work situation.   He discovered bank employees not only were aware of pressure to shape their behavior and demeanor according to standards of dress and appearance, but they also recognized that these standards vary in proportion to contact with the public. Hence, tellers and loan officers who have the most contact with the public must dress most conservatively and conform most closely to bank rules. The consequence of all this pressure is a kind of alienation, a detached cynicism about oneself and one's relationship to the organization. Jackall identifies this alienation as a kind of **self-artificiality**, a consciousness on the part of employees of inauthentic role performance. A payroll clerk's remarks during an interview illustrate this feeling:

How do I see myself at work? Well, I wouldn't associate with me given a choice. Tie, suit, sports coat. Everthing geared toward doing what somebody else wants (Jackall 1977, 283).

Standardized public faces are an integral part of secondary form interaction. In the bank, workers experienced this conformance to organization demands as partially negotiable. Their response was to "dissemble" themselves, "both to do their jobs and get along at the office"; most felt uneasy about this alienation but saw no alternatives to such "internal detachment from external behavior" (Jackall 1977, 285). Jackall found a few employees who

resolved the problem by agreeing with Goffman (1961) that, in a bureaucratic world, the ability to manipulate whatever public face a situation demands is not only a necessary means of survival but may even be considered a personal virtue.

In such extreme cases, we see the victory of secondary form over primary. More frequently, adaptations to conflicts take on the shape of chameleon conformity and a very strongly felt sense of self-alienation.

Alienation between self and the group is a consequence of conflict created by mixed group forms. Alienation refers to a separation between self and others, a fundamental failure to achieve reciprocity thinking. It occurs whenever the features of the self oppose those of the other. Thus, alienation results from tacit, informal, and deep commitment to a secondary group form, like that of the faithful clerk for the oil company. It also develops when a rational stance is taken toward the primary group as we saw in the wildcat strike. In the primary relationship, there is a merger between self and group. The person's identity and, most crucially, the principles of organization and the expression of that identity are rooted within the character of the group form. A person, in effect, becomes a member of the group—a regular at the Oasis Bar or a half of a couple. The relationship between selfhood and group membership functions smoothly.

In the secondary form, the reliance on the rational grounds of exchange is not necessarily alienating, at least not in a fundamental sense, for the secondary form presupposes the primary. The shallow commitment that

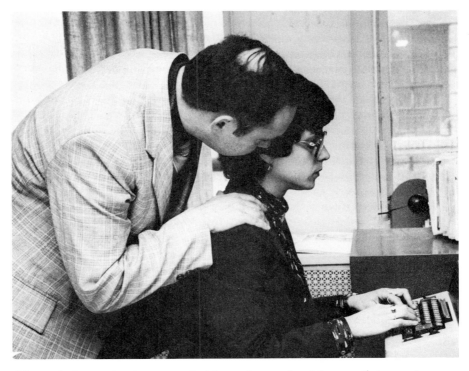

Often, a business setting becomes a mixed form where people act in ways that are not ordinarily appropriate to a formal group. Clearly, the consequences of mixing forms can be quite problematic.

the bureaucracy demands of the individual is not conducive to stability in the organization of the self. This is true because the bases of the secondary form thrive on change such as technological innovation. On the other hand, the primary form resists change; each modification calls for a renegotiation of the tacit group supports. Thus, the alienating consequences of the secondary form derive from either the individual's investment of self in the form, or the absence of a primary grounding in the individual prior to contact with the secondary form. Of course, the latter results in an investment of self in the form, but the first consequence differs from the second in that a person may rebel against his primary past experiences or at least confront them without forsaking them altogether. The secondary form forsakes, the primary embraces the self.

Although strains and conflicts may emerge from the mixed form, the mixed group form may be a part of the "way things are" (Dayton 1957). The consequences of mixed forms in groups are variable. In some instances, a primary form may be at cross purposes with the secondary. The literature is rife with examples. Many sociologists refer to this phenomenon as bureaucracy's other face (Blau 1961). In still other cases, primary forms within a formal organization may inadvertently further the rational goals of the organization.   For example, friendship ties among executives might influence one of them against accepting a position with better remuneration in a competitive firm.   Our point, however, aims at the essentials of group form.   One must distinguish between the consequences of forms and the forms themselves.   It is the nature of forms and their interrelationships that generates opposite forces, fostering conflict.   We can summarize as follows: formality is out of place in the primary form; informality is out of place in the secondary.   The butcher who serves his favorite customers first and, in return, they remember him on his birthday with a special gift, is a reciprocal arrangement not permitted in self-service supermarkets.   The person who experiences mixtures of forms in everyday life must go through a difficult and taxing interpretation of the meanings of conflict.   These meanings, then, become the definitions of the situations out of which are created the realities of lived-through consequences.

SUMMARY

Social interaction may be characterized according to three interrelated components: background knowledge, communicative skills, and emotional dimensions.   In a person's lifetime various amounts and degrees of skill in these three components are acquired.   The process of acquisition, known as socialization, produces consequences in the individual which we call the social self.

Groups require interaction between self and others.   These interactions exhibit typical forms which can be depicted using the same three components of social interaction.   Each group type (primary, secondary and mixed) predisposes a self-other relationship.   These relationships, in turn, either synthesize or antagonize the identities of self and others implicated in a given social encounter.

EXERCISES ON GROUPS

1. One way to appreciate the power of groups is to recall, in our own life experiences, the groups that influenced you.   Professor Spradley devised a technique for doing this.   He suggested that you focus on a period of your life, for instance ages eleven to thirteen, and begin by writing down the names of your friends.   Then arrange these names into activity groupings. You should discover that you interacted with some kids only for certain activities while others appear in all of our groupings.   Finally, think about who among these friends and acquaintances exerted control over you and whom you could control.   This exercise should provide you with vivid illustrations of reference groups.

2. Homans' theory suggests that people you interact with are people you should like.   List names of people you know fairly well.   Then, rank these names in an order which reflects how well you like them.   Look at the

results of this exercise and see if Homans' theory works. If it does not, think of why not. Often, we may interact with family members whom we do not especially like. Does Homans' theory of group dynamics help explain the problems arising from such interaction?

3. All of us have had experiences in a secondary group. If you were a member of a scouting association, or a church youth group, or even if you attended a summer camp, you have probably experienced the problems of mixed group forms. To document these problems, think about the ways in which what you and your friends actually did in these groups differed from what you were supposed to do. Write a few examples. These will make exciting topics for discussion, and they should dramatically show the problems of mixed forms.

KEY CONCEPTS

Form and content
Primary group
Secondary group
Hawthorne effect
Activity, interaction, sentiments, and norms
Love-couple
Friendship
Family
Expressive
Instrumental
Gemeinschaft and Gesellschaft
Rational forms
Formal
Impersonal
Technical
Ideal of merit
Hierarchical
Accountability
Gundecking
Indulgency pattern
Self-artificiality

SUGGESTED READINGS

Entertaining and informative reading is not hard to find on the topic of groups. Beginning with Homans' classic *The Human Group* up to more recent books like Altheide and Johnson's *Bureaucratic Propaganda,* the idea of group form has been a major explanatory device in social science. We select three sources for their readability and their appeal. First, Davis tells us how to understand what we might ordinarily think of as traits of personality in terms of interactive styles within social organizational contexts. From him we learn the social meanings of "obnoxious and nice." Next, E.E. LeMasters describes the group forms that are manifest in a working class tavern and how these reflect some fundamental social changes taking place in the organization of society. Finally, in a provocative article, Jackall relates the effects of social form on presentations of self among employees of a bank.

Jackall, Robert. "The Control of Public Faces in a Commercial Bureaucratic Work Situation." *Urban Life* 6, no. 3 (1977): 277–302.

Davis, Murray S., and Cathrine J. Schmidt. "The Obnoxious and the Nice." *Socimetry* 40, no. 3 (1977): 201–13.

LeMasters, E.E. *Blue-Collar Aristocratics: Life Styles At a Working-Class Tavern.* Madison: University of Wisconsin Press, 1975.

Chapter Six

Language and Social Life

OUTLINE

Language and
Social Life

*On the early morning shift at the County Hospital two residents con-
verse as they walk down the hall toward the rooms of their patients.
"Did you buff that gomere?" "Sure thing, I buffed her, and they
turfed her to urology, but she bounced back to me!" "Well, they
must think she is LOL in NAD. Tell you what, see if you can turf her
to some slurper, buff her as an interesting ortho, maybe that'll turf'er."
"She's a tough one, but I'll give it a try."*

*In a special variety of language, these doctors are talking about a
difficult to treat, female patient ("gomere"). They want to transfer
responsibility for her to another branch of the hospital (turf her). They
attempted to transfer her to urology by modifying her chart (buffing it)
to request urine tests, but the doctors in urology sent her back
(bounced her). They thought she was just a little old lady in no
apparent distress (LOL in NAD). One resident suggests to the other
changing her chart to make her seem like she has an interesting bone
problem (ortho) in hopes that an ambitious, upwardly mobile doctor
(slurper) will accept her as a patient.*

I N the approach taken in this book, great stress is placed on the traditional definition of Homo Sapiens, people as thinking beings. The position
is developed that all social interaction is, to a degree, cognitive. Without
the human capacity to imagine thought, feelings, and actions outside of the
realm of immediate experience, society would not exist. The previous
chapters showed how consciousness and its consequences result in the
building and maintaining of social worlds and self-identities. Although I

132

have already discussed language as a part of the general socialization process, the role language plays in the construction of our social environment has not been clarified.

WHAT IS LANGUAGE?

One of the truly revolutionary developments of the twentieth century has been the way in which scholars have come to think of language. Traditionally, languages were studied so that they could be read and spoken, and a person who studied languages was presumed to know many of them. So taken-for-granted was the fact that people have language and that they are different from one another, that it took several decades of research and argument to convince the academic world that language could be studied formally. The formal, scientific study of language, is, of course, now known as the discipline of linguistics.

Beginning with Roger Brown's 1965 social psychology textbook, however, it became increasingly clear that social psychology could not address questions of the symbolic nature of social life without learning a little of the advancements made by linguistics. He showed that linguistics can help us understand social life. Since language is a principal medium for social life, to the extent that it influences the outcomes and qualitative nature of social life, a full appreciation of social life calls attention to the medium itself.

This line of reasoning requires caution. Social psychologists do not want to be in the position of saying something like, "you can understand how a carpenter builds a house by studying the tools he uses to build it," but, it is obvious that a complete appreciation of carpentry is not possible without understanding its tools. Keeping this analogy of the house builder in mind as we move through the rudiments of language study, it is especially important to recognize that tools themselves, even though they were invented to enable the accomplishment of tasks, influence workers' decisions about what can be built and about what the finished product should look like. As media analyst Marshall McLuhan once remarked about understanding human communication, it is often crucial to know that the medium may be the message (McLuhan 1964).

Human language is more than verbal behavior. The founding father of linguistics, Ferdinand de Saussure, made a distinction between behavior and conception with respect to language. He pointed out particular performances of any given language (**speech**) make sense only in their relation to more general principles and rules of performance (**language**). He showed that similar or even identical performances could have quite different meanings. The significance of something said derives from the place that the saying has in an abstract system.

We can better grasp this distinction by working with an example. Take the sentence "flying airplanes can be dangerous." This sentence can be uttered twice in exactly the same way and still have at least two different meanings. It can mean the act of piloting an airplane may result in injury or even death, or that the object, an airplane in flight, can be dangerous if, for instance, it were to strike another object or a person. Ambiguity is a universal feature of speech. The sentence is ambiguous because there are at least two different sets of rules for deciding what has been said. A person who hears the sentence has to decide what is said according to how he or she understands the abstract systems of meanings called language. An ambiguous sentence is one for which there are two or more ways to decide what has been said (Lyons 1974).

When we discuss language, then, we are discussing a fundamental feature of human life, namely, the interpretive capacity of human beings. Language can be thought of as a highly developed system of rules for the interpretation and production of meaningful performances. Language is a concept which refers to the organization of meanings according to a very specific set of rules for encoding (sending) and decoding (receiving) messages.

A formal study of a language describes the rules by which messages are encoded and decoded. Generally, these rules break down into three categories. There are rules in any language for deciding which among the great variety of human sounds and motions are to count as language sounds or motions. For instance, in a spoken language, there is the difference between a pause, an extraneous noise like clearing one's throat, and a speech sound. We know that the sounds that make sense in one language do not in another. In Middle Eastern languages, certain guttural sounds, when produced out of context, sound impolite to a speaker of Western languages. Among deaf people, a brush at a worrisome fly in the midst of a flurry of sign language does not necessarily have language significance.

The formal study of language has taught us that it is not possible to understand a language by linking the performances of a person to effects from his or her environment. Rather, the most fruitful approach is to link behavior to a community of people who understand and use rules. All language has rules for distinguishing those segments or portions of behavior which belong to the language from those that do not. These rules are generally referred to as **phonological** or sound rules. The smallest segments or components of a language, usually units of sound, are called **phonemes**, and this first class of rules operates on this basic level.

In American Sign Language, which is based on motions not sounds, there are three basic phonemes. The shape of the hand, the direction of movement, and the portion of body indicated. Hence, an open hand (five-finger shape) placed on a signer's forehead means "father" while the same handshape moved to the chin means "mother". The same hand configuration on the chin accompanied with slight movements of the fingers means "dirty." In a spoken language, a slight difference in how a sound is articulated, whether, for instance, the vocal cords vibrate or not, will be the

Linguistic research has demonstrated that language does not need to be spoken to be a fully developed form of communication. For this woman, language is on her hands.

difference between two words, such as /pet/ and /let/. People learn to hear or to see different words because they know the units of their language.

All languages also have rules for combining the basic segments permitted by the phonological rules. In American Sign Language, for example, if two hands move at the same time to signify a meaning, the hands must assume the same shape. These kinds of rules are **morphological** or word rules. They operate to produce what most of us recognize as words, although in the formal analysis of language, a **morpheme** and a word are not the same thing.

Finally, all languages have rules to allow their users to put together strings of words into expressions that others can interpret as meaning something. These rules are generally referred to as **transformational** or sentence rules. They generate sentences out of the basic components of a given language. Through the use of these rules we know that *"The Road Warrior* is an exciting movie" is a sentence, and "a is *Warrior The Road"* is not.

Linguistics, perhaps better than any other discipline, demonstrates that the study of behavior—what people do—must be supplemented by how they interpret these doings. Language is the most obvious example of what turns out to be a fundamental feature of humanity. Language is an arbitrary system for interpreting behaviors defined according to how they relate to each other within an abstract system of rules shared by groups of people. It is a cognitive facility, a learning experience common to a group of people, and a way of making a social environment. It is a system defined as real, and therefore, real in its consequences.

HOW HUMAN IS IT?

Great commotion resulted from the studies conducted by the Gardners in the late 1960s. They attempted to teach a chimp to use a human language. There are two separate reasons that this attempt was not dismissed outright by the social psychological community of researchers. First, the modern linguistic attitude made possible the discovery of Sign Language. We have already noted that the communicative systems used by deaf people in various parts of the world, although quite distinctive from one another, can be described formally as language. This breakthrough—the discovery that human languages need not be grounded in sounds—opened new and exciting research vistas for linguists and social psychologists. The linguist could do comparative analysis between spoken and signed language. He or she could dig deeper into the search for the distinguishing features of human language. Visual language was seen as a rich source of data from which much could be discovered about the amazing ways humans build and use communicative systems. Until this research on signs, most linguists defined language as a sound system.

Secondly, the Gardners, and other scientists stimulated by their research, were not seen as merely latter day Dr. Dolittles because the same linguists who had insisted on the spoken feature as definitive of human language had drawn sharp distinctions between animal and human communicative systems. Animals communicate, humans talk. This was a dictum in the study of language. Although major strides had been made in discovering how animals and insects communicate, most social psychologists either ignored this research or used it to show the validity of the sharp demarcation they insisted on between nonhuman and human communication.

The Gardners' work was conducted at the right time. They were able to say that all previous efforts to teach animals human-like communicative systems failed not because of the intrinsic inability of the particular species, nor because of the intrinsic nature of language, but because these animals simply lacked speech-producing anatomy. In other words, chimps may be smart enough to learn language if a language suited to their abilities could be found. First they asked if sign language is a true language. Yes, answered some linguists. Then they questioned whether it possesses the formal features that demarcate animals from humans. Again the answer was yes.

The Gardners knew that chimps have remarkable manual dexterity and might be able to learn signs. If sign language is human, and we can teach chimps to sign, then the validity of the distinction between human and nonhuman communication must be re-examined. Such a re-examination might call into question some of the fundamental differences between psychological and sociological versions of social psychology.

The Gardners began the arduous task of training a chimp named Washoe to sign. They began to report their findings in the 1960s. They listed a sizable vocabulary for Washoe. They produced films documenting her progress as she learned to say "open the door," ask for water and generally make gestures that her human companions could agree were appropriate and meaningful enough to be called signs.

Almost everybody from scholars to interested readers of popular magazines took note. Had the Gardners talked to the animals? Maybe not exactly. They didn't learn chimpanzee, but it appeared that they were making unique contact with another species. Many other researchers followed in their path: the Premacks' chimp Sahra learned to use plastic discs to communicate, and signing chimps and gorillas were to be found in many university research labs.

Does this research mean we have to rethink the qualitative bent of social psychology? The reply consists of several interrelated points. First, one of the reasons for the spectacular success of this kind of research is that it builds on very *human* dreams and imaginations. For humans, animals represent ideal creatures in a world free of human problems. Somehow, we believe that if we contact animals, we will learn something about ourselves in our natural state. Regardless of the scientific merit of this kind of research, it is appealing because it seems to offer a connection between a corrupt human world and an idyllic natural one. In short, such animal research plays on a basic symbolism in Western society.

Second, we have to note that an important feature of human language is that it is made by and for humans. In every case, research on chimps involves humans teaching chimps how to communicate in a humanly designed system. The chimps did not invent the systems, nor do they need it to maintain themselves.

Third, the problem of species-specific behaviors remains at the heart of this research. That is, the very best chimp signer, the most proficient gorilla lecturer, operates under limitations of intellect that make its accomplishments noteworthy only in comparisons with others of its species. In other words, gorillas and chimps are no match for the average four-year-old human. We are still left with the vast difference between the layered duplicity and creativity of human talk, and the simple structure of the learned sign vocabulary of nonhumans. Research on signing chimps deserves a place in social psychological literature, not because it informs us about humans and their language, but because it tells us about the ingenuity of human researchers and the capacity for training that some animals actually possess.

When we seek to understand human language, it may be that the crucial questions are not necessarily the formal ones, as important as they may be. Instead, we should inquire what is important about humans having a language. The answer to that question is another: "What do humans do with their languages?"

THE THINGS PEOPLE DO WITH LANGUAGE

As it turns out, the tool of human invention most significant for the social construction of reality is language, for it is with language, through its performances, that people get things done. Obviously, language functions as an instrument for coordinating complex work, but of more relevance to our purposes are the less tangible but equally important social functions of language.

The word **function** carries many connotations. It has a mathematical meaning, meanings in biology, and a variety of meanings in social sciences. The particular sense in which we use the word is to denote the results of identifiable usage of language.

We usually associate language with national or ethnic groups. We talk about the organization of language performances by groupings of people as the language of that group. Italian, English, German, and Hindi each refer to both political and cultural phenomena. These languages are shared by all members of such groups, providing the basis for communication in daily life. But within these political and cultural groupings, there is a remarkable variety of language performances. Even small groups tend to develop special languages, ones that are clearly derived from the national language but which include special terms and meanings. The discovery of the widespread existence of special ways to use a language led students of language to coin a term, the **argot**. Argots are sub-languages organized by members of social groups engaged in activities that mark them off from other groups. The way they use language is an important part of their group.

We can illustrate how language functions by examining in detail a special group of youngsters in American society who call themselves "BMXers." BMX means bicycle motocross. In recent years, literally thousands of young people have been participating in recreational and competitive riding and racing of BMX bicycles. BMXers speak of "endos" when their bike flips over forward either by accident while racing or as a part of a skilled trick maneuver. They suffer a "medical" when they hurt themselves in accidents. But why do BMXers, or other members of sub-groups in complex societies develop special argots? Is the national language not a sufficient means of expression? The answer to this question lies in what the language does. Like most languages, argots reflect the special needs found in the social world of their speakers. For BMXers, this means that the argot must permit them to name and talk about special technical aspects of their sport. It must also meet social needs such as enhancing a sense of group membership, and permitting involvement with others such as business people, parents, and new recruits, while allowing insiders the advantage of remaining special and elite.

These men do not seem to be saying much at all, but their dress, appearance, and facial expressions tell rather complete stories about them. Can you pick a winner from among the men in the front row?

BMXers usually range in age from four to their early twenties; however, most are boys between the ages of seven and fifteen. For these boys, their bicycle is often their most precious possession. It is the object of their participation in economic life. They figure out ways to get money for parts; they learn to work on the machines and most importantly, to ride them with style. Modeled after motorcycle motocross, BMX has become organized at national and international levels. Races are sponsored virtually every weekend all across the nation. Like motorcyclists, BMXers race over dirt tracks laid out with jumps, sharp turns, and bumps. The sale of special BMX bicycles, competition clothing, and racing accessories has become a multi-million-dollar business influencing styles of dress and the values of young people all across America.

We can refer to BMX as a social world. Participants in BMX share knowledge about bicycles, equipment, riding techniques and all the other activities that make up their sphere of interest. As in all such groups, they use language to communicate with each other about these things, but unlike members of the general public, they use a special argot to do so. When BMXers talk about racing, they use phrases such as "wire the start," "get the hole shot," "wipe out," "get medical," and "cross up." They may say that they "dusted the pack," or "swooped" a competitor at the "zookers." They may complain that they "tweaked" something, "slipped" a pedal, or perhaps worst of all, were "cherry-picked."

Presumably BMXers could say these things in standard American English. They could say that "they got a fast start out of the gate and had the lead into the first turn" (hole shot), or that "they fell off their bike and got hurt" (a medical trash). They could note that "they broke a piece of equipment" (tweaked it), or that "they lost a race because an older boy lied about his age in order to race in a younger age category (got cherry-picked). But they don't; they insist on using their specialized way of communicating. They need specialized vocabularies to name things. Many of the things they want to name, they believe, are difficult to name. A perfectly tuned bike—one that rolls with ease, pedals well, and has that "great feel"—is said to be "dialed-in." There are well over fifty different types of frames for the component BMX bikes. Each has its own name. Features of tracks (whoopdeedoos), attitudes (rad), and other aspects of BMX have corresponding words in the BMX argot.

In addition to its communicative functions, language, including argots such as BMX talk, functions to increase a sense of group identification, mark group boundaries, and instill group pride. The need for special groups is especially acute for children and adolescents in the modern society. Many scholars have suggested that the rise of peer group culture in our complex society is at least a partial adaptation to changes in traditional institutions. For example, families relocate often, reorganize when both parents obtain jobs, and divide when parents are divorced. As children find it more and more difficult to feel part of a family group, they turn to other young people who are also uprooted. They form such groups as BMX which are often organized in a formal way by aging members and other adults.

BMX language is an efficient way to mark boundaries of the group. To an outsider, words, like "zookers," "whoopdeedoos," and "ant hills" are a part of a foreign language. On the other hand, when a BMXer advises a fellow racer that a "berm" on a particular track is a place where "you can get medical," not only is he telling his friends that the turn is dangerous, he is also reaffirming a sense of membership by speaking a shared insider's language. Consider this conversation between two young racers, Jim and John:

JIM: Hey, you chasing points? (Are you racing as often as possible to pile up points toward your year-end standings in your district?)

JOHN: Nah, but I'm goin' to the triple pointer. (I am going to the upcoming race which awards triple points for first, second, third and fourth place finishes).

JIM: That's a real rad track. You can wire the starts but you'll bum out on the berms. There's an awesome European there you can really get medical on. (The track is very good. You can get fast starts there. But some of the turns are dangerous).

Using the argot gives these two racers a shared feeling of mutual experience and belonging. It permits them to compare their sense of being special and test their degree of involvement in BMX. At the same time, a non-BMXer listening to Jim and John talk would be reminded of his alienation from their group, although he might be impressed by the insider knowledge of the speakers.

Another important function of language is that it allows a group to deal with outsiders. In the case of BMX, a highly commercialized scene, insiders must recruit new members or at least encourage the purchase of BMX items and bikes. Therefore, the language must sound exotic enough to be attractive to potential BMXers, and at the same time, be specialized enough to enhance the sense of group membership. Linguistically, BMX argot accomplishes this by building up vocabulary which is nevertheless used according to grammatical forms that are widely distributed in society (English). There are many such argots that serve a dual function of attracting members and demarcating membership into **core** and **marginal**. A BMXer can talk some BMX to his father for the purposes of influencing

The highly specialized activity of BMX racing is the basis for the development of an argot. BMXers speak in specialized ways in order to describe more accurately the technical aspects of their activity, and to accomplish the social ends of group membership which are special action and special talk.

what the father will give him on a birthday. The BMXer must know enough of the argot to order parts and to stay up with the fashions in clothing and equipment. Yet, true insiders, those who initiate and refine the terms of the argot itself, still feel secure with their place in the world of BMX.

Sometimes the way an argot functions to tie insider and outsider together is quite subtle and difficult to appreciate. In his study of a halfway house, Wieder (1975) discovered that the inmates communicated with each other and understood their experiences in prison and prison-like settings according to a **code** which here means beliefs that support an argot. In the inmate code, the men would speak of not "sniveling," (not trying to ingratiate oneself with the authorities). The code also required that inmates not tell authorities about the activities of other inmates (do not "squeal") and that they obey the norms of inmate life (stay in line).

Wieder understood the actions of inmates according to his understanding of the code. He saw the reluctance of inmates to participate in activities encouraged by the staff as instances of code conformity. However, as he began to pay closer attention to the situations in which inmates talked the code, he found out that more was happening. In one instance, a staff member requested that an inmate organize a pool tournament to which the inmate replied, "You know I don't snivel." This remark did not seem to make sense according to the code. Inmates liked to play pool and the activity was not generally seen as "official." The inmate's reply did not seem relevant to the code.

Wieder began to notice other instances in which inmates talked in code appropriate language in situations where it did not seem necessary or called for. By interviewing the inmates and observing what was happening in the halfway house, Wieder learned that the inmates knew that staff knew about the code. They knew that the staff generally honored the code unless it led to serious violation of the rules. Staff people thought that if they forced an inmate to violate the code, they could actually be endangering the well-being of the man. Inmates knew that staff thought this way.

Whenever the staff would request of an inmate that he do something which he did not want to do, one way to get out of the task was to say that the activities would violate the code. However, the inmate could say this outright since that would force the staff to admit to the power of the code. Hence, the inmate would **tell the code**. This meant that he would use code words and phrases to create the impression that what was requested was, indeed, code-relevant when, in fact, it was not. In this fashion, inmates exercised considerable control over the staff. Telling the code could cover up the real motivations of inmates which often were to get out of the halfway house as fast as possible. By telling the code, inmates could hide from the staff a number of practices which, if discovered, could even lead to a return to prison. For example, in order to obtain a release from the halfway house, an inmate needed to have a place of residence and a full-time job. Recently released inmates would write to

This official looking representative of a professional sport seems to be in the "hot seat". Perhaps, he is explaining about some violent stick-swinging incident in which a player was seriously injured. Do you think he might be doing a little code telling?

officials at the house with false offers of jobs, from false addresses to help their buddies out of the "joint." These practices could be covered by telling the code. For example, if a staff member questioned an inmate about the stationery on which a supposedly official letter was written, the inmate could avoid giving a response by pointing out that other inmates might think he was "trying to get close to staff."

We see that argots are associated with special groups within larger, more complex societies. They function to name the special cultural categories that make up the knowledge and social reality of the group, and they permit precise and economical conversation among group members, giving them a sense of sharing common interests and experiences while setting them apart from outsiders. They signal commitment, elite status, and by their unintelligibility, create an attractive and mysterious aura about group members. Finally, they function as a cover for the pursuit of both individually defined and group interests.

MOTIVE TALK

A few decades ago, C. Wright Mills (1948) suggested that the words people use to describe purposes and intentions contain all the information we need to assess their motives for various actions. He referred to such talk as a

vocabulary of motives. Building on this idea that "talk is the fundamental material of human relations," Scott and Lyman (1968) proposed that basic questions of social analysis could be answered by looking at a particular kind of talk which they called **accounts**. An account, they wrote, "is a linguistic device employed whenever an action is subjected to valuative inquiry" (Scott and Lyman 1968, 46). It is a statement made by a person to explain unanticipated or untoward behavior. In short, it is talk which is intended to reveal reasons why a person did something they were not supposed to.

By examining this type of talk, we can see more clearly what kinds of assumptions ground social life, how a particular kind of thinking operates as a foundation for social order. Scott and Lyman examined transcripts containing examples of such talk from a variety of different sources. They used published materials, tapes from interviews conducted for their own research purposes, and generally looked at talk occurring within a wide array of different situations of everyday life. They classified accounts into two types: **excuses** and **justifications**. Excuses they defined as "socially approved vocabularies for mitigating or relieving responsibility when conduct is questioned." There are at least four kinds of excuses: appeal to accidents, appeal to defeasibility, appeal to biological drives, and scapegoating.

Justifications are accounts in which "one accepts reponsibility for the act in question, but denies the pejorative quality associated with it." There are at least four ways to justify an untoward action: denial of injury, denial of victim, condemnation of condemners, and appeal to loyalties.

We will illustrate each instance of motive talk and suggest what function it can perform in the "shoring up" of the "timbers of fractured sociation."

When a person tries to talk their way out of unpleasant consequences or the negative responses that might come from others, he or she aims to disassociate themselves from the meanings of their actions. In one situation I might say, "Sure, that gravy does seem to have spoiled my shirt, but the ladle simply slipped from my hand," an account which points to some recognized hazards in the environment, some understandable incapacity of the body. Blaming some feature of simply being human arranges what everybody knows (commonsense knowledge) in such a way that the consequences of action are not linked to the intentions of the actor. Pointing out how "clumsy" an act was—that, for instance, one missed an appointment because of a memory lapse—means that the act under question was simply "by accident." Children may employ this device, in a kind of overkill, when they claim that everything which gets them in trouble with adults is "by accident."

When one appeals to defeasibility, he or she arranges commonsense knowledge according to assumptions people make about the mental elements that make up the world. We are talking about ordinary understandings of "knowledge and will." One can defend oneself against an accusation by saying "I didn't know . . ." or "I can't help it . . ."

"Why did you make her cry?" asks the accuser. The presentational strategies in reply to this question allow several modes of defeating the central claim implied in the question, namely, that the actor intended with full knowledge to make the lady weep. However, men ordinarily impute to one another some measure of foresight for their actions so that a simple denial of intent may not be believed if it appears that the consequence of the action in question was indeed what another person might expect and therefore what the actor intended [so, we may resort to several simple and complex devices] . . . I did not know that I would make her cry by what I did . . . I knew matters were serious, but I did not know that telling her would make her weep (Scott and Lyman 1968, 49).

We can also excuse ourselves by pointing to features of what is understood in our culture about the "fatalistic" or "natural aspects" of life. "Boys will be boys," he's just "feeling his oats" and the like, are statements that attribute qualities or meanings to acts based on an understanding of nature. Scott and Lyman use an example from research literature about beliefs that first and second generation Italian men have about their sexual appetites. They believe that they are naturally motivated toward sexual aggressiveness and that this aggressiveness can become an uncontrollable impulse. Similar beliefs are widespread in Latin-American cultures.

In American culture, there are many manifestations of fatalistic thinking, for example, homosexual preferences are often thought of as "natural," as are differences between the behaviors and tastes of boys and girls. All manner of accounts can be built upon assumptions about the validity of such thinking.

Scapegoating is a form of thinking in which a "person will allege that his behavior is a response to the behavior or attitude of another" (Scott and Lyman 1968, 50). By pointing out that one's untoward actions were not directly one's own, that is, that they were the result of some characteristic or trait of another person, one can dissociate or excuse oneself from the negative consequences of his or her actions. For example, in Oscar Lewis's research on Latin-American cultures, we read of how a Mexican girl who was constantly in trouble blamed her tendency to fight on the nature of other girls, or the young Mexican boy who scapegoats by explaining how it was a girl's fault that he got into trouble for showing off on his bicycle.

Justifications are socially approved vocabularies that neutralize an act or its consequences when one or both are called into question. In contrast with an excuse, a justification asserts that the consequences of the act were, in fact, positive or, at least, not as they appear.

A person can attempt to justify an act by saying that it was permissible because no one was injured—hence the exchange, "Did you set off that firecracker under the gasoline can?"; "Yes, but there was no fire." Or, another way to use this device is to suggest that the person allegedly injured can not really be hurt by such action. A younger brother says of an accident on the Fourth of July, "He got in the way when I was lighting my firecracker. Sure, the punk burned him, but you know how tough he is. He's not hurt."

In denial of the victim, one argues that the injury to another resulting from one's actions was somehow deserved. Members of certain groups, "whitey," "rednecks," or "pimps," occupy a social status so low, so despicable (according to the one arguing) that they are legitimate targets for attack. A policeman making an arrest may feel less restrained by his training and the law which prohibits him from handling the suspect roughly when he is dealing with a particularly odious criminal. In other words, cops may rough up certain criminals and not others. When questioned by authorities about this brutality, they may reply, "He was just street scum."

In condemning a condemner, one simply points out that others do these or worse acts and "these others are either not caught, not punished, or even praised" (Scott and Lyman 1968, 51). In appealing to loyalties, one says one's actions were "permissible or even right because they served the interests of another to whom he owes an unbreakable allegiance or affection." We are all aware of this justification which has been used to "make seem right" some of the world's most hideous crimes, like the executions of Jews by the Nazis.

Accounts may assume a variety of forms. Scott and Lyman illustrate some of these. What is important in their analysis of the account is not so much whether they have correctly identified the full range of types of accounts, but the point they make that talking in a certain way can be understood as a device for accomplishing desired social ends. They show how a successful account, or one that is **honored**, is one that is consistent with the background knowledge of the group into which it is offered, and one that is balanced with the gravity or severity of the alleged action. They make a distinction between an illegitimate and unreasonable account to further illuminate this point:

An account is treated as illegitimate when the gravity of the event exceeds that of the account, or when it is offered in a circle where its vocabulary of motives is unaccepatable . . . An account is deemed unreasonable when the stated grounds for actions cannot be "normalized" in terms of the background expectancies of what "everybody knows."

Further, they show that the question of the effectiveness of a verbal device depends also on how well the account is performed. Using the work of Joos, they identify five styles of discourse: **intimate, casual, consultative, formal,** and **frozen.** These styles amount to different ways of presenting information. They differ in vocabulary and grammar, but, most importantly, they rest on different social bases.

In the intimate style, one uses specialized words and phrases to communicate whole ideas or emotional states. This is the language of the couple, the restricted code, which is virtually unintelligible to another not intimately familiar with the person talking. The casual style is similar to the intimate but usually involves larger numbers of speakers. This is the language of the peer group. Most argots are used in a casual way. Consultative style is "that verbal form ordinarily employed when the amount of knowledge available to one of the interactants is unknown or problematic to the others." It conveys an air of "technicality." In the formal style, there is an audience too large to permit one-to-one exchange. A speaker, therefore, adopts a presentational style to "hold the attention" of his audience. Goffman (1981) refers to this form of talk as the "lecture."

Finally, the frozen style is an extreme form of the formal style used by those who are simultaneously required to interact and yet to remain social strangers. The communication between pilot and control tower is in this frozen style; likewise, the talk of CBers is largely managed by a frozen style that allows the impression of community without either the intimate or casual contact required in face-to-face interaction.

Obviously, an account must be proffered in an appropriate style. A father's account of why he is late to pick up his daughter from her dance lessons must be formulated one way for the ten-year-old daughter and yet another for the mother who waits for them at home.

FATHER: I'm sorry honey, I had some stuff to do at the office. Hope you didn't get too bored waiting?

DAUGHTER: It's OK daddy; I just practiced with the next class.

or

FATHER: Sorry, honey, we were running late on that monthly report and the computer was down for half the day.

MOTHER: Well, you should have called or made other arrangements.

FATHER: I know, I'm sorry. What's for dinner?

Human talk is very complex and can not be fully understood on formal grounds alone. In the social psychology of language, we must also look at the functions of talk, that is, what is accomplished by it. This often requires that we look at both sides of communication, at the reasons people have for communicating and the relationships they have with one another. One final illustration of the human way of communicating involves looking at how people use a sense of time in their talk. Among the many ways they do this, perhaps the clearest is the practice of disclaiming.

Everyday life is full of potentially embarrassing situations. There are serious and trivial departures from role obligations and downright troublesome occasions in which an aspect of one's selfhood is revealed at the wrong time, in the wrong situation, or to the wrong people. All of us have experienced these unpleasantries. As we gain more experience in less than desirable interactions with others, we learn to recognize cues as to what might happen, what a person might do or say if we pursue a certain line of conversation or course of action.

Just as accounts can shore up a fractured relationship, there are ways of talking which can "ward off and defeat in advance doubts and negative typifications which might result from intended conduct" (Hewitt and Stokes 1975, 3). These verbal devices are called **disclaimers**. When we use a disclaimer, we know that something we are about to say or do might offend, embarrass, or even incite conflict. Yet, we must say what is on our mind. Unlike the account which works to mend the results of untoward deeds, the disclaimer looks into the future. When we use a disclaimer, we imagine an interactive occasion. Disclaiming involves a form of "if . . . then" thinking. If I say that my wife's new dress is too revealing for the formal party we are attending, then she will feel that I have insulted her judgment and taste. I know, nevertheless, that if she wears the dress, I will be embarrassed, even if she is the hit of the party. Therefore, I must say something about the dress, and, at the same time, avoid any remarks that she might take as critical. This is a real interactive problem.

Hewitt and Stokes inventory some of the available solutions to this problem. First, I could **hedge**, which means that I could preface my remarks by impugning my own identity. I could say something that tells her that I am really not all that concerned about it (my identity is not really at stake in the matter). I am not fully, unalterably opposed to her wearing the dress, but still I have an opinion about it. When I hedge, I also communicate a sense of openness to compromise as well as my understanding that other people's reactions to the dress might be negative, and hence, call into question the impressions that I think she wishes to give. I know that she wants to appear stylish, not brazen.

So to hedge, I say, "I'm no expert on fashion, but . . ." or, "You know how I think everything you wear is sexy, but this dress . . ." or "It's just my first reaction to the dress, but . . .". If it works, she may save me my embarrassment—or even hers, were she to have to deal with unwanted advances from males at the party—by changing to a more conservative dress, for instance.

I could also used a device Hewitt and Stokes refer to as **credentialing**. To credential, I must know that what I say will offend her, but I remain strongly committed to saying it. I must establish myself as a person with a particular identity to which I am strongly committed. "You know I am no jealous husband, but . . ."; "I have never lead you astray before, so hear me out". When I attribute a credential to myself, I establish myself as someone who knows what he is saying. "You know I'm a social psychologist of everyday life, and I can tell you that dress will make you look like a hussy."

I could use another device, the **sin license**. This device wards off my wife's undesired response toward me by recognizing that I know full well what I say to her will be seen as boorish and none of my business, but I do not care how she will react. I simply must have my say. "I realize you might think I'm criticizing your taste in clothes, but . . ." Or, "I know we have independent lives and what you do is your business, but this dress is just too . . ." "Sure, I'm going to break a rule of our relationship, but . . ."

I could also use a **cognitive disclaimer**—that is, I could point out something peculiar about the way I see the world, my empirical grasp of the world, that might account for what I am about to say. "This may seem strange to you . . .", "Don't react right away to what I'm going to say." "I know this sounds crazy, but I think that dress will make you look . . ." By demonstrating through advance knowledge that a negative consequence might result from an action, I can show the purpose for my action, an action that otherwise might be interpreted as without purpose, or as "reflecting a loss of cognitive control" (Hewitt and Stokes 1975, 5).

Finally, if I assume that my wife and I have a common purpose to pursue at the party, I can **appeal for a suspension of judgment**. "Don't get me wrong, but . . ." "Hear me out before you explode . . ." What I have to do is show that her actions (wearing the dress) might negatively affect our common goal, which is to appear as a happily married couple.

There are, of course, many different ways in which people can respond to accounts and disclaimers. An account can be honored and a disclaimer can be heeded. A person can get themselves excused and manage to avoid imagined, unpleasant circumstances. Disclaimers succeed when they seem reasonably valid. If they smooth interaction, they succeed in one sense. They facilitate interaction and allow things to go on in spite of obvious differences of opinion. Much of this interactional work depends upon reading clues in interaction. My wife sees that I am really concerned about her, even if I seem childish to her. There is a constant signaling and a finesse in interactive sequences whereby we can tell each other what kind of person we want to be seen as for a particular exchange. Disclaiming is one powerful way of signaling identity.

In the case of the failure of an account or a disclaimer, the identity a person seeks to establish is simply not accepted by the other. The person becomes an irresponsible juvenile who always tries to get out of the mess he makes, or is cast in another identity by those with more authority than he has.

Language is the medium through which identities are exchanged, negotiated, and changed. These functions go beyond the formal properties of language and turn out to be the truly human distinctiveness of communication.

FORMS OF TALKING

In his last book, Erving Goffman dealt in detail with the social organization of talk. He developed a social psychological approach to everyday conversation by stressing the importance of "**ritualization**," (by which he meant the movements, looks, and vocal sounds we make as an unintended by-product of speaking and listening), "**participation framework**," (which refers to the full range of potential listeners and speakers for a given instance of talking), and "**embedding**," (which means messages that are carried in our sayings over, above, and within the strictly formal or linguistic content).

He illustrated how all these social dimensions operate in the form of talk we recognize as the lecture. When we walk into a classroom, or even when we hear a friend speak about a favorite subject, we know when we are about to be lectured. All of us have learned that this particular way of talking is not so much a matter of grammar and vocabulary, but has more to do with the social organization of what is said.

Goffman defines a lecture according to its social dimensions. A lecture is an institutionalized "holding of the floor" to present a "text." Even if no actual written text exists, the speaker presents material in such a way that the impression of the existence of such a "text" is maintained. The primary intention of a lecturer is to "format" a text.

Formating does not require of those in the participation frame that they be engrossed in the presentation. Those of us who listen to a lecture need not, and know that we need not, be fully attentive to what is being said. We can think of our own text, interpret what is happening idiosyncratically, simply daydream, or go blank. This contrasts markedly with other activities which require engrossment. Think of where your attention is while playing a video game; without engrossment in the game, your quarter loses its entertainment value quickly.

In the lecture, the person who makes the text come to life is also the same person who is assumed to have authored the text and is the principal of the occasion. Other presentational formats are quite different. Actors are not necessarily authors, newscasters do not make the news in a literal sense, and one person is not supposed to dominate a conversation—we do not normally chit-chat to focus on a single person as a source of information.

A lecture can not just be given. Indeed, lectures are "celebrative occasions." They are usually the main business at hand, but other things commonly happen along with lectures, such as a luncheon or the "giving of an award." Some event, educational, patriotic, or even entertainment, is being highlighted with the collective intention of communicating the message that what is happening is worthwhile, indeed, worth an organized happening.

Formal organization is a prerequisite to giving a lecture. The college, university, civic group, or political party provides the platform on which the lecturer stands and derives some identity. Organizations, thus, foster a star system. They seek out lecturers who give off a good impression. Of course, the interests of the lecturer and those of the organization need not be identical, but the lecturer must have something to offer the organization.

Lectures are social as well as linguistic phenomena. They can be defined according to their social features, and most importantly, we can analyze the lecture by describing how the social meanings of it are achieved.

Goffman lists ways in which a speaker "animates words." By this, he means the devices available to make one's speaking appear to be alive, energetic, and personal; these are memorization, reading aloud, and fresh talk. Lectures often depend upon a fresh talk illusion, but the person must not be seen too distinctively from the content. The form of the lecture must be maintained or else one is left with "the box and the cake", or too much of self and not enough of the occasion.

Memorization means simply to commit to memory what is to be said. This device allows the speaker to give off the impression of a person "who knows the material." If, however, one never glances at notes, he might appear to be merely "talking off the top of his head." This impression would violate the form of the lecture transforming it into something less formal and perhaps something seen by the audience as less important; consider, for example, how many students stop taking notes when the lecturer looks up from the prepared text to offer an aside or a further explanation of a point.

This tendency to display too much of oneself can be counteracted by reading aloud, verbally holding up the text for all to see. By reading from a text, all are reminded of the organizational features of the presentation. Too much reading, of course, hollows the performance of any element of self, and the presenter runs the risk of becoming unanimated.

By digressing, or telling a story, the speaker can enhance the image of giving off fresh talk, new materials, things never said before. Goffman writes of the image of talking freshly:

There is irony here. There are moments in a lecture when the speaker seems most alive to the ambience of the occasion and is largely ready with wit and extemporaneous response to show how fully he has mobilized his spirit and mind for the moment at hand. Yet these inspired moments will often be ones to most suspect. For during them the speaker is quite likely to be delivering something he memorized some time ago, having happened upon an utterance that fits so well that he cannot resist reusing it in that particular slot whenever he gives the talk in question (Goffman 1981, 178).

Goffman continues his analysis of lecturing by discussing how the lecturer aligns himself with the underlying identities of the occasion. This process he calls "footing." Most of these devices have to do with the work that goes on prior to the performance, the advertising or announcing of the lecture, its sponsorship, the actual printing of the text in its entirety or in sketched forms. He also points out how footings can be accomplished during the actual delivery of the lecture by making tongue-in-cheek remarks, using sarcasm, changing styles, using props, or making parenthetical remarks.

Under Goffman's treatment, we learn to appreciate how talking carries with it a host of social meanings, and how a person works with the forms to achieve a desired effect. One can break a form to give off an impression.   For example, a lecturer can discard his notes in order to speak face-to-face about matters of grave importance.   In Goffman's view, talk is an accommodative social form in which the business of impression management is carried out.

FORMS OF CONVERSATIONS

We have been discussing forms with respect to specific situations of talk. However, in everyday life, we often encounter situations in which several forms are used at the same time.   When this happens, there may be some interesting interaction among the forms.   To help understand the complicated organization of talk, we can set down some basic observations.   We have learned that talk is shaped by the interests of groups, and that the shapes that talk assumes can be called argots.   We have also discovered that members of groups talk one way among themselves and another whenever they converse with those outside their group.   By identifying assumptions that people make about each other with regard to their membership in a particular group, we can describe forms of conversations. To make this practice seem less abstract, let's follow an example throughout the various forms.

Running has become a part of American leisure life.   Millions of people wearing expensive running clothes and shoes jog or run through parks and on roadways.   Many participate in organized competition.   For some people, this form of exercise becomes an important part of their selfhood and major portions of their social life are taken up in actual running.   Even larger portions are occupied with talking about running.   When people talk about any topic, they express more than the facts.   Any fisherman knows the importance of being able to discuss fishing with another fisherman; likewise, the runner has to learn to talk about running.   As a conversationalist, he or she must be sensitive to two considerations.

First, one's conversational partner is seen as naive about, indifferent to, hostile toward, or a believer in the system of knowledge from which the meanings of a particular activity derive.   There is a runner's code, for example, which holds that running is fun, that it is good for you, that it makes you a better person and gives you a sense of well being, that it makes competitive sense, it hurts, and that it requires specialized knowledge of equipment and training routines.   Whenever one talks running, then, he or she must assess whether or not the other person listening believes in running.

Second, whether the conversationalists may reasonably expect accuracy in the comments about the topic sets another condition.   Some forms of talk do not necessarily require truth.   Greetings are good examples of these.   One responds "fine, thank you" to "how are you" even if, in truth, he or she is quite miserable.

Within these distinctions talk about a wide range of topics can be assessed according to its relevance to and consequences for the runner's code itself.   Oftentimes lying can operate as an important device for building or reinforcing belief systems that underly an activity.

Nomic Talk

In **nomic talk** both the sender and the receiver can expect of each other truthful statements.   (See Figure 6.1.) If one runner asks another how far he ran, the other can respond, "Did 23 in under three.   Felt good.   Little pain in my knee.   Not bad."   He will be understood as telling, more or less accurately, the actual miles run, and he will be seen as relating information about his physical condition.   A fellow runner might reply, "Great, man.   I just can't get up that high.   Maybe next month.   I'm building.   Got 58 last week."

What is important to understanding this conversational exchange is the context or background assumptions that each party makes about the other. Neither will criticize the other's assessment of mileage; they both know their "miles" are approximations, probably never to be measured.   Both view each other as supportive of the values of running and as sharing individually defined but collectively meaningful goals.   By being honest about what they can do, how they train, and what the effects of training are, they build or buttress norms in the running world.

		Receiver's Membership	
		Within Code	Outside of Code
Sender's Claims to Accuracy	Relevant	Nomic Talk	Truth Telling
	Irrelevant	Ritualized Lying	Code Telling

Figure 6.1 Matrix for Code Talk   (from Nash 1980)

Nomic talk requires trust. It is a confiding talk in which persons assume of each other reciprocal, unambiguous identities (Henslin 1972; Garfinkel 1963; Berger and Kellner, 1964). Not only do nomic talkers make assumptions about their respective intentions and about their membership in a collective grouping, but they also could put the credibility of their membership in jeopardy by telling the truth. For example, a runner who admits to less than demanding training could be interpreted to mean that he does not believe in the runner's code; at least, he could be seen as inappropriately casual in his attitude towards running. In nomic talk, each party knows the danger. Each must regard the underlying identities as unproblematic. Talk can take place honestly between equal members of a social world.

Two persons whose identities are mutually recognizable and whose reciprocal understandings communicate a claim to accuracy, can, by being truthful with each other, build standards for the realistic evaluations of performances as a scene member. In the running scene, if running long distances really does hurt, really does enervate and result in irritability and the inability to function normally, then honesty without calling into question the code's validity is important to the very survival of the code.

Ritualized Lying

HOWARD: How far did'ja go?

FRED: About 10.

HOWARD: How's your time?

FRED: Around 6:30 per.

HOWARD: Hey!

Fred ran 7.9 miles as measured by the odometer in his VW Dasher and according to his Accutron's sweep second hand that distance was covered in fifty-nine minutes. Howard, however, does not challenge Fred, nor does he even respond with suspicion. In fact, he acknowledges this performance as a laudable accomplishment. The question to be addressed here is why such lying among runners is not only possible, but even condoned.

The answer depends upon a discussion of the function of the form of talk rather than the content, or what is literally said. In this example, since both persons know each other to be serious about running, the question of the validity of running never comes up. Within the context of this potentially nomic situation, lying can take place.

Ritualized lying signals that code relevant talk is talking place. The opening question, "How far did'ja go?" is intended less as a request for accurate information than as a signal for a desire to "talk running." "About 10" is an appropriate remark because it is a sufficiently long distance to convey a serious attitude, and, yet it is not so long that it calls into question the speaker's mastery of running knowledge. Further, the answer conforms to a structure of talk about running: it is a straightforward utterance, interpretable as relevant to the code, hence, "about 10" instead of "just around the neighborhood."

The answers are testable according to the code and one's participation within it. "Six-thirty for 10," although a notable accomplishment, is a reasonable response. It is certainly possible for someone with Fred's record, in spite of his recent lack of training, to run at that pace. In other words, "6:30 for 10" is (according to the reputation of this runner) quite understandable. Had Fred said, by contrast, "5:38 for 10," the limits of the ritualized lie would have been strained, indicating either that Fred was not knowledgeable enough to lie appropriately, or that he was, perhaps, uninitiated to the custom. Of course, too slow a time, such as "10:00 for 10," would also be unreasonable, since Fred's record would suggest that such a slow pace signals physical or mental trouble. Specifically, "trouble" would mean either an incapability to apply the code or a corresponding doubt about maintaining identity in light of insufficient seriousness or reverence toward the code. The code cannot be regarded flippantly in ritualized lying. Lying allows the negotiation of expectations towards and grounds for actual performance. A runner, or any member of a code-governed activity, can understate or overstate his or her preparation either to make a poor performance acceptable or to enhance the dramatic effect of an outstanding performance. Among runners, a profitable situation for gathering examples of ritualized lying is the conversation just before the start of a race.

To overstate one's performance indicates at least symbolic affirmation of status as a member. Understatement can also indicate location in the organization of an activity, like the organization of races on weekends for amateur runners. By underplaying one's commitment and actual preparation, the goals of accomplishment can be kept in perspective; the goals can remain attainable and one can claim a degree of loyalty to the code appropriate to specific conversational exchanges.

Ritualized lying may also take the form of an appeal (Scott and Lyman 1968). While not eschewing the code, a runner can refer to information pertinent to his or her particular state in an effort to suspend the code. Thus, a runner with a known back problem can appeal to an injury to account for a short mileage week, or a slow performance at a weekend racing event. A runner who has an unusual philosophy toward training—such as doing all speed work at short distance—can lie ritually: "I'm not doin' much. Probably can't stay with you at the Grapeyard 15k," or "you know me—I never really train."

There are many types of appeals that members of scenes can use to account for their performances. Any one of these appeals can be fashioned into a lie if it can be spoken in such a way that the person's commitment to the scene is upheld, and the code itself is exercised.

Code Telling

We have already seen how **code telling** operates in the halfway house among inmates who wish to pursue their individual interests under the cover of their loyalty to a code. A type of code telling can take place in virtually any scene. Code telling is the intentional, selective presentation of information about a norm-governed set of activities, with the intention of impressing on the receiver the validity of a paticular identity. In running, this means overstating pain, training rigor, joy, and knowledge—in short, all the aspects of the code. Such lying sets the identities of runner and nonrunner apart allowing both to distinguish themselves on the one hand as participants in an action, and on the other, as outside interpreters of the scene.

Understating can also function in this fashion. However, here the claims for the distinctiveness of running accomplishments silence potential criticism with the consequence of leaving the code intact or unscathed. Telling, then, protects the code while preserving the identity of the speaker.

Truth Telling

FRED: Are you going to run the Boston this year?

HOWARD: No. I'm really not getting much out of running. Marathons hurt me too much. Last time I ran one, I suffered so much that I got mad at the kids and my wife over nothing. My whole week was shot—just not worth it anymore.

Telling the truth is, of all the forms of conversation, the least likely to be employed because such talk does not serve any function in the scene. It can be interpreted only according to standards of validity outside the norms of the scene. Persons talking in the capacity of expert, or appealing to common sense can tell the truth. Thus, scientists can try to investigate the modes that runners use to endure pain, assuming that physiological stresses must indicate an inward state subjectively known as pain; or, dropouts from the running world—those disenchanted with the crass commercialization of running, for instance—may decide to go public and use common sense or expert knowledge, rather than code knowledge, to assess their past involvements. They reinterpret their heavy training as the result of an addiction or the compulsive nature of runners' personalities. They say they had an exaggerated view of the importance of running in maintaining good health.

The truthfulness of messages, in terms of social functions, cannot be discussed independently from the conditioning contexts of the conversation. Thus, when runners respond to questions concerning the evaluation of performances and the revelation of attitudes towards the act of running, these responses are conditioned by the form of conversation evoked. It is only when speech is in terms not relevant to the code, and when there are motivations for establishing accuracy for the content of the talk unrelated to scene activities, that "truthful" assertions as a form can be said to operate.

SUMMARY

This chapter discussed the role of language in social life. It outlined how language can formally be conceived of as a system for deciding what constitutes meaningful statements. The formal study of language expands the social psychologist's understandings of the power available to humans for building and maintaining social worlds.

Even though animals can be taught to use human communicative systems, such as the sign language of deaf people, only people rely heavily on language as a tool for accomplishing social ends. People use language in specialized ways to meet the unique needs they have as group members. We have referred to these specialized performances of language as argots. Argots seem to proliferate in modern, complex societies, and they serve many and sometimes quite complicated functions.

The way language is used can shore up fractured social relationships as in the case of giving accounts, and using language in a particular way can warrant off undesirable consequences as in the case of offering disclaimers.

By examining the social organization of talk, we can appreciate that it is often more important for the social psychologist to understand the way that something is said and the social context within which it is said than to simply understand the language. The skillful use of language is a distinctively human feature which results in complex organizations for even the most routine and ordinary occasions of everyday life.

EXERCISES FOR UNDERSTANDING TALKING

1. Alfred Schutz wrote that the words we use in everyday life, our vernaculars, are "mirrors of social reality." He meant the way people actually talk, the words and phrases they naturally employ in routine communication reflect the assumptions and values they use to build social relationships. Hence, if we wish to understand social life, we must start with the vernaculars of everyday life. Select a particular activity you frequently engage in. This can be anything from watching television with others, to working on automobiles, to playing fantasy games. Collect a list of at least ten slang words or terms that pertain to the activity. Define the terms using standard English. Then, see if this translation exercise helps you understand something about the social world of the activity? For example, in hospitals doctors, nurses, and other staff people refer to patients who are beyond help as *gomers* . The fact that this word is a part of the working vocabulary of hospital staff reflects a consistent view of patients by the staff.

2. We identified four forms of talk: nomic talk, truth, code telling, and ritualized lying. Illustrate each of these for the slang system you described above. Recall how we did this for the activity of running.

3. Accounts and disclaimers play an important part in the establishment and maintenance of social order. When order is threatened, these ways of talk come into play. From your own experiences, give examples of each of various types of accounts and disclaimers.

KEY CONCEPTS

Speech and language
Phonological rules
Phonemes
Morphological rules
Morphemes
Transformational rules
Functions
Argots
Core and marginal membership
Code
Tell the code
Vocabulary of motives
Accounts
Excuses and justifications
Honored accounts
Intimate, casual, consultative, formal, and frozen discourse
Disclaimers
Hedge
Credentialing
Sin license
Cognitive disclaimer
Appeal for a suspension of judgment
Ritualization
Participation framework
Embedding
Nomic talk
Ritualized lying
Code telling
Telling the truth

SUGGESTED READINGS

The topic of language in society and the social psychology of language is an area of increasing research. For this chapter, we recommend readings that focus of the precise ways in which talk functions: the first is a classic by Scott and Lyman. Their paper entitled "Accounts" started a wave of research which attends closely to language in social context. Next, the article by Gordon exemplifies Schutz's assertion that vernaculars reflect social reality. However, as Gordon shows these realities may not also be what they appear. Finally, Schwalbe provides the reader with a complete conceptualization of langauge from a social psychological point of view.

Gordon, David Paul. "Hospital Slang for Patients: Crocks, Gomers, Gorks and Others." *Language in Society* 12, No. 2 (1983): 173–185.

Schwalbe, Michael L. "Language and the Self: An Expanded View from a Symbolic Interactionist Perspective." *Symbolic Interaction* 6, No. 2 (1983): 120–135.

Scott, Marvin, and Stanford Lyman. "Accounts." *American Sociological Review* 33, No. 1 (1968): 46–62.

Chapter Seven

Deviancy: The Meanings of Being Different

OUTLINE

Deviancy: The Meanings of Being Different

A deaf man walks into a drug store. It is the first time he has been inside this store, and he is in a strange neighborhood of the big eastern city where he lives. He wants to buy a pack of cigarettes. He walks to the counter and speaks in his best voice, "Salems, please." The woman behind the counter looks puzzled. He repeats his request. She bends down and comes up with the pack. He is relieved. He knows that he can pronounce "Salem" better than his favorite brand, "Chesterfield". He turns and walks outside. A man runs past him, almost knocking him over. Then, he feels a burning sensation in his side as he falls to the sidewalk.

Dateline June 9, 1982: "A deaf-mute was shot and fatally wounded today when he stepped into a policeman's line of fire. The policeman was in pursuit of a robbery suspect, and had shouted several warnings while firing his pistol into the air. Just as he fired at the fleeing man, the deaf man walked out of a nearby drug store into the line of fire. An investigation of the shooting incident is scheduled but the chief of police is quoted as saying, "It was just an unfortunate accident."

M EMBERS of society learn to think of certain ways of acting as acceptable and ordinary and others as unacceptable and deviant. Much of social psychological research is devoted to understanding the processes through which these distinctions are made.

Early research demonstrated that social pressures to conform are very strong. Two such studies are now regarded as classic. The first took advantage of a feature of human perception to show how other people's judgments can influence one's own: when placed in a darkened room and asked to stare at a pinpoint of light, most people will perceive that the light moved when, in fact, it remained stationary; this phenomenon is called the **autokinetic effect**.

Sherif (1948) placed people in a darkened room. All but one had been instructed to make their judgments of the light's movement within a specified range. In other words, they were confederates. In repeated experiments, naive subjects shaped their estimations of motion according to those of the confederates. If three persons said that the light moved four inches to each side, the naive person would use this information to make his own estimation. In situations where judgments of the length of motion were large the subject's estimations were significantly larger than in those where confederates said the movement was small.

Similarly, Asch (1952) confronted people with ordinary tasks of perception like judging the longest or shortest of three lines, and found that persons could be influenced to say that a line was the longest or shortest even if they knew better. They were influenced to ignore their better judgment in situations in which actors, straight-faced and apparently quite sincere, said that a short line was actually a long one. Again, most people prefer conformity to confrontation.

These experimental studies do not tell us much about why people conform, but they do show how effective pressures to conform can be. In everyday life, we see much conformity, as when young boys buy expensive BMX bikes (bicycles designed for off-the-road racing) because their friends have them. We observe wave after wave of fads and fashions in clothing, music, and conversation. Yet, we also know that there is considerable deviation even among members of the same group. No two friendship pins are exactly alike, and a boy has no difficulty in telling his bike from others in the neighborhood.

We also know that what some people regard as acceptable others do not. Further, acceptability is not synonymous with legality, and within a given society, ideas about acceptability and appropriateness of action are expressed organizationally as groups of outsiders and insiders.

There is, then, a sense in which, like the self and society, **conformity** and **deviancy** are two sides of the same coin. We can understand this relationship more fully by looking at what it means to be different.

What we learn first is that it is not a particular act itself which is unacceptable but the meanings attributed to that act. Becker (1963, 9) writes:

Deviancy is not a quality of the act a person commits, but rather a consequence of the application by others of rules and sanctions to an 'offender.' The deviant is one to whom the label has successfully been applied; deviant behavior is behavior that people so label.

Who is on the outside and who is inside is largely a matter of which group in society can make its labels or meanings the dominant ones. For instance, the acceptability of homosexuality has become a subject for open debate. As gays "come out" (that is publicly acknowledge their identities as "deviants") they attempt to refute the negative or stigmatizing meanings that "straights" (heterosexuals) have attributed to them. In this way, some of them hope to remove the discriminatory consequences of being so labeled.

SOCIETAL MEANINGS OF DEVIANCY

Every society provides to its members ways of thinking about what is normal and appropriate. These systems of widely distributed knowledge we have referred to as **institutions**, or **societal meanings**.

Although no single individual or group is ever completely "**normal**", there are generally understood criteria which we learn from childhood throughout life, and which we use to judge both our own appearances and actions and those of others. As members of society we assume that certain physical, moral, and mental states are "normal."

In modern society, physical normality is understood in terms of what Manning and Fabrega (1973, 283) call the disembodied self. They write:

In modern society, man has adopted the language of the machine to describe his body. This reversal, wherein man sees himself in terms of the external world rather than seeing the external world as a reflection of himself, is the representative formula for expressing the present situation of modern man.

The body is defined biologically. This does not mean that everybody in society can correctly identify anatomy, cell structure, and other physiological facts, but they learn that such identifications are possible, and they tend to use a lay version of biology to understand departures from the "normal body machine." For example, the body has parts named organs and they are organized into systems, like the respiratory and circulatory systems. People believe the body works unless external or internal causes interfere (germs and diseases). They trust that the senses are universal. Everybody feels, sees, hears, touches, and tastes. In this natural attitude, disease is universal, and its distribution and causes are knowable (Manning and Fabrega 1973, 255).

In varying degrees of completeness and detail, members of society come to think of the body machine. We judge the problems of our bodies as breakdowns or malfunctions requiring intervention by a body mechanic, for example a physician. A person who cannot hear, see, move, or control his or her body in the ordinary fashion may be ascribed a deviant role in society.

Whenever we ascribe meanings to other persons where those meanings attribute to them an undesirable set of traits (thinking of them as a "homo," for example) which, in turn, become the basis for our interactions with them, we say such persons are stigmatized. A **stigma** is a literal or figurative symbol that a person, group, or kind of action departs negatively from the general expectations we have about what is normal.

Often, departures from normality have a moral dimension. Stigma, then, may mean much more than a malfunction of the body. It may be taken to mean that the stigmatized person has done something wrong. Stigma may be a moral cross which a person must bear. Spastic slobbering may be taken to mean that the spastic is an unclean person; the so-called noises that a deaf person makes in the effort to speak may be interpreted as a lack of grace or as stupidity; a blind person's groping posture might mean his or her loss of autonomy.

As members of society we learn what is normal in very general terms. We make assumptions about what other people can do, how they think and feel based on our knowledge of what it means to be normal. Finally, we attribute mental and moral states to others according to their conformity to our standards. The results of these judgments under certain conditions is the ascription of a label.

General and Specific Contexts of Deviancy

The meanings of social life are highly situational. People do not merely apply societally given meanings. They use them according to the particular situations in which they find themselves. Hence, although all members of society know what normality is in a vague sense, when they make specific judgments about themselves and others, immediate and practical consequences are important. Growing up with deaf parents, having a mentally retarded child, becoming involved in the intimate life of a criminal or an alcoholic, are all experiences that shape the specific judgments we make about what is normal. Often in dramatic ways, the first-person accounts of people who have been labeled deviant reveal to us the ordinary character of their lives. A deaf man writes of the need to be recognized as a whole person; a death row criminal touches our hearts relating his sufferings and repentance.

What is normal takes on a more delimited meaning when we begin to describe the social context of deviance. In fact, we discover that a person who becomes labeled deviant may be seeking social approval which we would regard as normal under other circumstances; yet, the practical contexts of his life-world provide to him meanings that are at odds with those of the institutions of society.

For example, Carl Werthman (1969) writes that in the youth gangs he studied several values seem all important: "coolness," "action," "risk taking," "smarts," and one's "rep." In order to gain the esteem of fellow gang members, one must display "cool." This means that in situations of tension and conflict, looseness, relaxation, and presence of mind are maintained. Threats from a rival gang are met in "coolness" when the member can continue with his display of bravado and control in spite of real danger and fear. "Smarts" refers to knowing how to use cool. To be "smart" means to know when to fight, with what weapons, and how to handle the weapons. The "smart" man knows when to make a challenge and how to control his temper. Young gang members may actually seek out danger in order to display "cool." These boys are said to be "on the make," "coming up," or "looking for trouble," and should be avoided since they do not yet possess "smarts." To actually fight such a boy would be too great a risk to the older boy's established "rep" (reputation).

In this setting, to acquire esteem and loyalty a gang member may have to violate the law: to show cool he must confront the police; to display loyalty to friends, he may risk parole violation by association with "known criminals"; or to gain a "rep" in the gang he must challenge and fight a member of another gang, or one of his own gang who attempts to take over his position.

Suttles (1969) portrays a similar situation for ghetto drug users. He points out that heroin users are at the top in the drug world since it is widely known that heroin addiction is a very expensive habit and, hence, requires the most skill at hustling (getting money for buying drugs). A heroin user may even suffer the pains of early withdrawal in order to remain "righteous" (to use only heroin). He will associate only with other heroin users, who understand the "true" meaning of the "flash" or "call" (the sedated state that comes after an injection of heroin), or being "on the nod" (the relaxation and sleepy state that heroin produces). To maintain status in the world of drug users, in order not to drop to the level of a "garbage junkie" (one who will use any and anybody's drugs), the addict must make connections, often in the world of crime. He pimps for whores, engages in petty theft, and even deals himself to stay the "righteous dude."

Problematic Relationships between General and Specific Contexts

We can understand that there may be conflict between societal meanings for deviancy and the specific meanings of acceptable behavior for certain groups. The practical matters of living in poverty, for example, within a society that values success and defines your life situation as failure may set up circumstances in which a person becomes deviant (Merton 1957, 161–194). A consequence of being a good member of a bad group can be that an individual becomes a deviant.

Returning to the description of gang life, we learn that members often challenge each other by becoming "smart." They may purposefully say things to insult or demonstrate a superior attitude towards other people. Such a display of "being smart" means that one's place in the gang is being challenged; sometimes these challenges assume the form of rituals of verbal insult. Among young blacks, this practice is known as "sounding," "**signifying**," or "playing the dozens," and often involves sexually vulgar language. One member will, for instance, remark in rhymed couplets:

I fucked your mother on top of the piano

When she came out she was singin' "The Star Spangled Banner."

To which another may retort:

Iron is iron and steel don't rust

But your mamma got a pussy like a Greyhound bus.

(from Labov 1974, 86).

In this fashion, verbal superiority and coolness are established.

A teacher in a black school who is unaware of the meanings of the boy's contests or defiant of their way of life may inadvertently issue a challenge in what he regards as the routine discharge of teaching responsibility. Of course, it is the boy's response to the challenge that is out of place in the school and may be the very act or simply another in a long series of instances which labels him a trouble maker or a behavioral problem.

Werthman (1969) relates a story told by a gang member in which a teacher's demeanor was interpreted as "getting smart", hence, challenging the young boy. The boy explained that he played it cool and put up with the teacher until the opportunity to get even arose. A verbal duel came first.

TEACHER: You two shut up, or I'll throw you out on your ear!

GANG MEMBER: The best thing you can do is ask me to leave and don't tell me. You'll get your damn ass kicked off if you keep messin'.

A short while later the boy walked out of class, went out in the yard to play basketball; he walked back into the school with the ball and passed the classroom door. Upon seeing the teacher with his back turned, the boy threw the ball at the teacher hitting him on the back. The boy exclaimed, "I hit him with the ball. Got him. I didn't miss. Threw it hard too. Real hard!" (Werthman 1969, 625).

THE POLICE AND THE DEVIANT

The police occupy a strategic position in the relationship between the world of the deviant and the societal meanings of moral normality. They symbolize the contact between the acceptable and the unacceptable, and although they deal with specific instances of deviancy, they represent the general role of social control agent. In the course of their becoming policemen, they learn a great deal about outsiders and their worlds. Yet, their job is to represent societal moral order. On occasion, the line between "good cop" and "bad cop" becomes blurred as the policeman who is simply "doing his job" allows the guilty to go free or arrests the innocent. The policeman contacts the criminal world in an intimate way and this affords him the opportunity to "go on the take" or become "bad."

From this unique vantage point, the enforcers of moral order serve as labeling agents. As Aaron Cicourel (1968) suggested, it is the police, probation officers, and judges who transform gang boys into "delinquents." Becoming a deviant may, therefore, be looked upon as an organizational rather than a legal process "since the criteria used to contact, categorize, and dispose of boys often has little to do with breaking the law itself" (Werthman 1969, 626).

The patrolman faces another interesting problem. His solution of it has a great deal to do with the labeling of deviancy. He must make judgments about the "**moral character**" of a person from appearances alone (Sacks 1972). He does this basically by becoming a specialist at being suspicious.

Strength in symbols. We understand the process of deviancy in terms of who has the power to apply labels. The police often function as moral judges in the process of deciding which types of social action should be labeled as deviant. The power in this labeling process is symbolic.

He uses a principle of thinking called the **incongruity procedure** in which he looks for small details or larger features of the social scenery which somehow do not fit in. A man dressed as a postman in a high crime area of town may be stopped and questioned since the policeman does not know him as the regular route man. The policeman knows that the postal uniform is a perfect front for "running numbers." Provocatively dressed women in front of all night convenience stores may mean "trouble with hookers." So, the policeman comes to see gang members as potential trouble makers. He may want "to give them a break" and help them "get straight," but he has lost the capability to interact in an ordinary way. He cannot accept their intentions at face value; he does not suspend his knowledge of their background as he deals with them in routine questioning. Instead, he keeps his eye on them, watching for the first sign of trouble.

The police, then, are **moral judges** in modern society. It is they whose unique role as enforcers may create the criminal. It is they who hold great discretionary power in the definition of deviance.

This position of morality judge gives the police power to "normalize crime" as well as repress it. Sudnow (1965) points out that police and other legal officials come to think of crimes as typical. They understand a particular act according to whether or not it is like others. They accept categories of crime as normal and often plea-bargain and settle offenses by placing them within the knowledge system of what is a greater or lesser offense. In this system an offense is considered normal if it fits with what the police know about how that particular crime is ordinarily committed, under what circumstances, and by whom. A charge of burglary can be settled through a guilty plea to the lesser offense, such as petty theft, if the burglary in question was considered normal—was committed in accord with the official's understanding of typical burglaries. The specifics of typical burglaries will vary from police department to police department, from precinct to precinct. In one area a type of burglary may be perpetrated by young blacks who fence to organized professionals in order to earn money for personal use—even to support their families. In another region, youths with good families may break into a house "just for the fun of it." Judgments about the circumstances of crime are important to settlement. The policeman's intentions to get a "criminal off the street" or to "give a good kid a second chance" may be the determining factor in whether or not an actual arrest is made.

What becomes deviant and how it is defined is often the result of complex relationship between societal meanings and contextually specific meanings for actions. The deviant possesses knowledge and interactional skills in both meaning systems. He or she is a member of society as well as of a peer group or gang. What distinguishes the plural life-world of the deviant from those of regular citizens is the antagonism between the two. Deviants are caught in a bind between what they know about normality in general and what they know about acceptable attitudes and actions within their specific worlds. When these relationships result in the label of deviant for the total life-world of the person or group, as in the case of the transformation from gang member to delinquent, we have observed the creation of "discredited, virtual social identity" (Goffman 1963). After that process has been completed, the identity itself is a stigma.

THE ORGANIZATION OF DEVIANCY: THE WORLDS OF OUTSIDERS

The socialization process introduces people to both general and specific ways of interpreting experiences. When there is consistency between these, the person will most likely not become deviant. However, inconsistent and conflicting meanings for societal and group life offer the conditions for deviation. Becoming a deviant involves several steps and some rather common experiences. In fact, there are rituals and ceremonies that mark a person's entrance into a deviant life or identity.

After a person has been attributed a discrediting identity, the first step towards becoming deviant is the **degradation ritual** (Goffman 1963; Garfinkel 1967). In a degradation ritual, a person's change in social status is publicly acknowledged. Further, there is an advance warning of the possible loss of self-creditability. A jail sentence functions as such a ceremony, as does a psychiatric diagnosis of mental illness, or even a medical diagnosis of cancer. In all these practices, a person is placed outside the everyday moral order and defined as a threat to that order. The accuser must be defined as morally superior and evokes moral values of normality which then must be accepted by the degraded person. The successful degradation ceremony forces the person to accept his new status. This is one way in which the scales are tipped in favor of the deviant lifestyle.

Another ritual is **initiation**. Here, a person undergoes some rite of passage which marks entrance into a group or to a new status in a group. A gang member achieves "cool" by "rippin' off" a car, or a boy's first arrest by the police functions to cement his membership in a gang. The person becomes publicly initiated into a new way of life. If that way of life is deviant according to societal meanings, the person adopts deviant life meanings as the dominant ones for his or her life. A ceremony may be negative, as with the degradation ritual, or positive, as in the case of the initiation. Either way the person enters, in more or less complete fashion, the life-world of the deviant.

There are three types of deviant life-worlds: *physical, mental,* and *moral.* The physical deviant is ascribed a stigma and must live life under the stigma. The mental deviant achieves a stigma and often becomes a career patient; and, the moral deviant chooses a life of crime or a life in the vagueness between legality and illegality.

The Physical Deviant

Generally, there are two types of physical deviants: 1) those born with a deficiency like deafness, blindness, or mental retardation; and, 2) those who have lost their normality by becoming blind, deaf, or paraplegic.

Social dimensions are invariably associated with physical stigmata. Deaf people, for instance, live much of their lives in the company of other deaf people. Together they make up a vital social organization known as the deaf community which revolves around their unique means of communication, sign language. Although not all hearing-impaired people join this community, most do by early adulthood, either through associations they make in special education programs or in state-supported residential schools. Also, a small number of deaf people live in families in which all of the members are deaf. Learning the language of the signs opens associations with other people and enriches the lives of the deaf. However, they live in a four-sense world, and "normals" or hearing people assume that deaf people experience less of the world around them. The stigma of deafness, which is made visible to all by their language, consists of assumptions that other people make about them, assumptions that deaf people are less capable, less responsive and suffer from a "lack of maturi-ty" (see Jacob 1974 and Higgins 1980). Of course, these assumptions can become the basis for decisions about the educational potential of deaf children, and, finally, employment and career opportunities of deaf adults.

In both negative and positive ways, the stigma of deafness is reflected in the social organization of the deaf community. The community gives to deaf people a strong sense of belonging, a sense which can buffer an individual against some of the stresses and strains of everyday life. For example, G. Becker (1981) writes that the deaf community helps the aging deaf person deal with isolation and depression. Yet, this very community isolates the deaf person from larger society, thereby depriving him or her of opportunities to acquire "success."

In more subtle fashion, the stigma of deafness reflects itself in the attitudes that deaf people can have about their own language. Although attitudes are now changing, particularly among younger deaf people, there is still the tendency for deaf people to devalue signs and emphasize the value of speech. For example, many deaf parents want their hearing-impaired children to be "oral," which means to learn to speak and lip-read. However, they must use signs in everyday life to communicate with their children, so they manage to neutralize the stigma of deafness by devaluing their native language and overemphasizing the power of Standard English. Accordingly, their children learn two things: the importance of "proper" language and the meanings of being a physical deviant. An illustration of such dual meanings in the action of a stigmatized person is the practice of some deaf people who wear hearing aids even though the devices really do not aid them in distinquishing or producing speech sounds. The hearing aid is a symbol standing for the normality of hearing and speaking.

When people engage in deviant behaviors and are caught, actions are taken to establish boundaries between what they did and what is legal or right. This young man is caught between two policemen. In this picture, we can actually see the separation of the deviant from the rest of society.

Physical deviants may possess extensive technical and social knowledge about how to manage their "spoiled identities." The organization of this knowledge into life-worlds is the result of constant efforts to either achieve normality or mask an actual social identity. It is only with those who share the condition, or who already know about it, that ordinary social interaction can take place. The physical deviant must learn to manage his or her stigma. Successful management of stigma may mean passing as a normal person. For example, a victim of a mastectomy may use a prosthesis to cover the actual contours of her body. With a physical stigma, failure to pass may mean life in a degraded condition, holding a job for which one is overtrained or being denied access to opportunities which presume normality.

The second type of deviant, those who have lost normality, occupies a different place within the life-world of those with spoiled identities. They have been normal and know the experiences of the insider. They must master a new set of meanings for their physical appearances. It is they who often become politically active, demanding that the stigma of being handicapped not only be made illegal but actually be removed through accommodative legislation. For example, people with adventitious hearing losses may never become members of the deaf community. They may resist taking up any behavior that they see as embodying the stigma of their handicap, like using the sign language, or as in the case of a blind person, carrying a red-tipped cane.

Often the strain of the struggle with stereotypical thinking about handicaps is accompanied by acute mental distress which can place the individual under a double stigma.

The Mental Deviant

Laing (1969), Szasz (1961), and many others have written that mental illness is often the end result of complex interactions in which behavior, although not intrinsically ill, becomes so interpreted. Laing believes social situations become defined as "something is wrong" by members and outside agencies like social workers, physicians, and psychiatrists. Within a given situation, it may be true no one knows what is happening. The task of social interaction is to "discover the situation" and unravel the chains of events that interlock the members' self-identities. In the case of families, members may collude to practice mental illness. When their practices attract the attention of outside agencies, the members, or one of them, run the risk of becoming a mental deviant. Out of the social situations of family life emerge ways of deviant thinking. (Laing 1969, 89).

Another example of how social contexts can exacerbate and even create the deviant role comes from literature on the **sick role**. Mechanic (1966) describes a process through which people learn to recognize illness behavior. When a person begins to do erratic things, he or she exhibits symptoms we associate with abnormal and temporary conditions. Then, the people who make up his or her immediate social network treat the person as if he or she were ill—that is, in ways they understand as appropriate for dealing with an ill person. Consequently, the ill person is not held responsible for his or her incapacity. After that, the ill person is not allowed to make decisions, or care for him- or herself. Second, he or she is exempted from usual role or task obligations, such as parental supervision, housework, and job responsibilities. Third, the person demonstrates through attitude and behavior that he or she desires to leave the sick role; he or she is expected to talk about getting better, getting his or her head together, breaking the habit, or licking the disease. But, and lastly, the ill person is obliged to seek and comply with technically competent experts.

Alcoholics, junkies, mental patients, and others may assume this role. So widespread is this interpretation in our society that Mechanic suggests that the sick role or "illness behavior" functions as a form or outline for many particular deviations. Since we are referring to interpretations of diseases and not actual illnesses, our concern is with understanding how

Physical differences are often assigned social meanings in society. This young man is engaged in a very ordinary work activity, but his appearance calls to mind our ideas of normality. Using Goffman's terms, in what sense would you say this is a picture of social stigma?

people impute to others certain traits and characteristics, and how these imputations, in turn, affect social interactions.

The Moral Deviant

In this form of deviancy, the stigma derives from a violation of a prevailing moral standard. Such a stigma is earned through some act or series of actions. These violations are often organized. Some authors (Lindesmith, Strauss, and Denzin 1975) suggest that groups constitute "deviant worlds" or "deviant communities." The moral deviant belongs to social circles where the practices are acceptable within those circles, but are unacceptable in larger society. Criminals are moral deviants. The criminal world consists of 1) **conventional criminals**, 2) **white-collar criminals**, and, 3) **racketeers**. The degrees of moral deviation vary from type to type. Conventional criminals may be either professional or amateur. Violent crimes like murder, rape, and assault are not typically committed as occupational activities. However, some members of society do become skillful at violence and threats. Hit men and guns for hire are appropriate examples. Others learn skills such as picking pockets, shoplifting, safe-cracking, or stealing and stripping cars.

Conventional criminals are morally stigmatized even though, according to their relative world view, they see themselves as completely ordinary or even superior to other members of society. In fact, they may regard their way of life as exciting compared to what they imagine as the dull, routine world of everybody else (Sutter 1969).

White-collar crime consists of offenses committed in the course of conducting a legitimate occupation or business. Such enterprises as "kickbacks," "payoffs," "cover-ups," "embezzlement," and "corruption" are so widespread and seemingly such an integral part of ordinary business affairs that Douglas and Johnson write of "**official deviancy.**"

They use the term to refer to crimes or moral offenses among the high officials of society, elected and appointed persons of power. They include moral offenses taking place in federal or state governments, higher education, regulatory and planning agencies, and even in police departments. Although much white-collar crime happens at lower levels and its practice may result in only small and shortlived pangs of conscience, we can speak of a morality of the job. For high-level jobs, a moral element may be an important aspect of the job itself. Douglas writes:

> The primary reason why the public is so outraged [at offenses] is precisely because we do have higher standards for government officials. Each act of deviance which has been transferred from the private sphere to the government by the welfare state revolution has increased our degree of moral outrage over that one deviant act (Douglas 1981, 403).

The racketeer lives and works in a domain of underworld business: gambling, prostitution, and fencing of contraband goods are examples of underworld activities that serve the respectable world. Klockars (1974) details the life of a man he calls Vincent Swaggi. Vincent spent a lifetime in the world of crime. He learned hustling skills as a child growing up in a large city, and he later established himself in the business of fencing. He had a store for a legitimate front and developed elaborate social and business connections in the "legit" and criminal worlds. Klockars' book has Vincent relating in vivid detail how to run the store, how to possess stolen goods without danger of identification, how to make a drop, and other practices and procedures for running a fencing operation. Vincent actually saw himself as a conventional person:

> The way I look at it, I'm a businessman. Sure I buy hot stuff, but I never stole nothin' in my life. Some driver brings me a couple of cartons, though, I ain't gonna turn him away. If I don't buy it, somebody else will. So what's the difference. I might as well make money with him instead of somebody else. (Klockars 1974, 139)

In the classic study of the professional thief, Sutherland shows that some criminals do contact the legitimate society and use their acquaintances with bondsmen, politicians, and lawyers; however, they are suspicious of all legitimate people. The professional thief believes:

> Whoever is not with him is against him. Any noncriminal individual not personally known . . . is a possible danger . . . because of this the professional thief lives largely in a world of his own and is rather completely isolated from general society. The majority of them do not care to contact society except professionally (Sutherland 1935, 166).

So, the world of the criminal has a definite organization. It requires special skills and knowledge, has occupational specialization, and networks of interpersonal involvements. There are divisions of labor within the underworld of crime and conceptions of membership as well as degrees of shared moral stigma.

Another type of moral deviant is the person whose behavior is stigmatized primarily on moral, not legal grounds. Groups such as homosexuals, traffickers in pornography, and massage parlor employees make up this category of moral deviants. In this kind of deviancy, the line between legal and illegal is blurred and constantly changing. Acts that fall into this category clearly demonstrate that deviancy results from the imputation of a moral stigma. People who engage in stigmatizable acts are discredited and acquire a moral character. When people with similar characters congregate and develop particular norms for their social organization, we speak of deviant worlds. To be sure, we use the word "moral" in a relative way. What is moral depends on the social context and some acts, like homosexuality and white-collar crime, are so widespread that the interpretation of their morality becomes very difficult to establish. Further, the worlds we describe are, from the vantage point of society, immoral and, hence, we could refer to "immoral character" and "immoral worlds." But we have learned that relationships between general and specific meanings of morality are dynamic and the label of deviancy can be fixed, removed, or altered.

An idea that is central to understanding deviancy is the career. The worlds we depict are organized around the idea of a **moral** or **immoral career**. A person who occupies a place in a deviant world has a career as a deviant.

Goffman summarizes the interrelated aspects of a career (1961, 127–128). He writes that various worlds offer different career avenues. These are marked by entrances and accesses. A person's movement through these avenues is controlled, and there are clear phases and levels of involvement. Just as a person must meet recruitment, educational, and socialization criteria to become a physician, nurse, or a policeman, so a person becomes a deviant by contacting the worlds of deviance, entering those worlds, and passing through them. Sometimes the avenues and entrances are quite specifically defined and can be described as a funnel which leads to conversion to a deviant perspective.

For example, Lofland and Stark (1965, 874) account for conversions to an obscure millenarian cult in terms of a model that describes a funneling

Some forms of deviancy carry moral messages.   What are the moral messages we receive from this picture of street people passing the bottle?

of social experiences towards more and more exclusive involvements with the cult members and their world view. The authors depict a sequence of occurrences from a general tension coming from a life of disappointment or failures in marriage or job, to religious problem-solving perspectives, to a self-identity as a "religious seeker," to an encounter with the cult itself. All this leads to emotional ties with cult members. These interactions tend to focus all social attachments on the cult's activities and finally result in the person becoming a "deployable agent" to recruit for the cult. All the while the person's image of himself, the skills at interaction which he acquires, and the biography his life assumes shape him into a full-fledged member of the deviant world.

Some careers are deviant while others are normal or ordinary. Although, as in the case of the professional fence, the line between these careers may be fine, from the perspective of societal knowledge (what everybody knows), everybody, including the deviant, knows the difference.

A social psychological understanding of deviancy requires a description of the organization of deviancy. Such descriptions, in turn, lead to the classification of patterns or forms of actions, thoughts and feelings that are stigmatized in some fashion. Persons who enter the deviant world assume identities and careers that result in characteristic thinking on their part which, in turn, helps to create and maintain those worlds.

CONSCIOUSNESS OF BEING DIFFERENT

How does a person who has been labeled a deviant think? How does this thinking relate to the construction of social worlds of deviancy? Some sociologists who study this aspect of deviancy use the term **secondary deviation** to distinquish between the societal label and the individual thought processes that result from that labeling (Lemert 1967, 7; 40–60).

We can think of secondary deviation as the individual's conceptions of and reaction to the label "deviant." Generally, an individual's consciousness of the meanings of being different reflects both the general meanings of deviancy and the specific version of it that pertain to a group. However, the interpretations that persons make of the stigma they bear varies greatly according to life circumstances such as the degree of involvement they have with the particular world of deviancy and their understanding of their overall place in society.

The Passive Deviant

One adaptation to stigma is to simply accept it according to its general meaning. Here, a person thinks of himself in stereotypical fashion, that is in terms generally understood in society. For example, a homosexual accepts that he cannot control his sexual impulses and, hence, feels he should not be allowed to teach small children since such an opportunity could lead to an "immoral offense" which he wishes to avoid. Whereas this particular example becomes less applicable as the meanings of homosexuality are more particularized and people learn that the general notions do not apply with much accuracy to specific individuals, there remain situations in everyday life where stereotypical understandings define situations as real.

For example, a deaf man acquiesces to a lifetime of low-paying jobs because he believes he is language deficient, that his native language is less than complete and that he surely is so immature that he cannot be entrusted with the responsibility of a high-paying job. Or, a criminal knows that he will return to a life of crime once he is freed from jail simply because, in his mind, that is all "he is fit for."

In passive interpretations, the person labeled as deviant will take on the general meanings of deviancy as the way he thinks about himself. This does not mean that deviants like the discrediting connotations of their stigma, nor that they necessarily devalue their station in life. They simply think as they think others think. A subtle part of this adaptation has to do with the consequences which a deviant experiences from passive responses to labels.

Deaf people, for example, may elect to join a community of their peers in which they can enjoy spontaneous and ordinary communication with their kind. The young boy becomes a gang member so that he can gain stature and esteem in the eyes of his fellows. In return for this refuge from the larger world, the person bears the stigma of being a deaf-mute, or a juvenile delinquent. It is almost as if we are describing a trade off or barter situation in which a person receives the rewards of being like others as long as he realizes that the others whom he is like are not totally acceptable to society. In return for being strange, in exchange for calling into question the ready-made accounts or normality that our society offers us, the person finds the opportunity to retreat from confrontation with the larger society. By accepting a discredited or spoiled identity, conceptions of normality in general for the non-stigmatized can remain unaltered and the "able" person can function in society without firsthand knowledge of what it is like to be stigmatized. Whenever contacts are made between the stigmatized and the normal, as long as the deviant retreats into the pre-defined meanings of his label, he may co-exist with normals.

The Active Deviant

More often contacts between the normal and the deviant are not simply a matter of the deviant's retreat. Instead, there is an active confrontation which entails three kinds of thinking, or forms of consciousness. The deviant who assumes a posture of actively confronting the meanings of being different may 1) attempt to normalize others' imputed interpretations of him and, in doing so, refute or deny the stigma by demonstrating that he is really not deviant, 2) accept the label but reject the negative interpretations of it by offering an entirely different version of his actions, or 3) formulate a counter-stigma theory in which he typically directs his assaults at the very basis of society, namely the taken-for-granted assumptions about what is normal.

Normalization In this process, a person tries to avoid having a stigma placed on his or her actions or identity. A deaf person tries very hard to "speak normally," by wearing expensive hearing aids and attending lip-reading classes to become like everybody else. An amputee exercises and practices diligently to master the use of an artificial limb. In both of these examples, it is not so important that the deaf person actually learns to speak "normally," nor that the artificial limb really allows normal movement. Rather, a stigma-avoiding strategy is being used. The goal of normalization is to **pass**, which means to so successfully mask the discreditable trait that no one recognizes it. In interaction, the person who passes does not demand of others a special knowledge of communicative systems or an appreciation of the difficulties of life without normal movement.

Many forms of deviancy depend on established links with the normal world. The oldest profession in the world is perhaps the best illustration of this linkage.

Not all efforts to pass are successful. But our focus is on the intentions and assumptions that ground social life. Efforts to approximate the ideal of normality by those who know or think that their condition, if discovered, would lead to discrediting are directed at becoming, or at least appearing to be, normal. Many studies of alcoholics and drug users show that sometimes the relatives of a heavy drinker or drug user will interpret his drunkenness or altered behavior as normal—in light of the pressure of job or an illness—they, and perhaps, the deviant himself, can be said to apply the interpretations of the meanings of routine life beyond their limits. A husband may see his wife's drinking as "normal," given the boredom of housewifery and the stresses of child care.

However, other people who use more widely distributed and agreed upon meanings do not concur about the normality of these kinds of behaviors. An employer may be forced to ask an employee to seek counseling, a husband comes to see that he has an alcoholic wife. Both the deviant and those who make up his or her immediate social context must learn to see their respective behaviors as others see them. In the case of current treatments of drinking problems, the deviant and those affected learn to shift their thinking about drinking from a practice of harmless fun to a symptom of a deadly disease.

We see that normalization can refer both to efforts of a person to avoid revealing his stigmatizable trait and to accounts of an already detected character flaw. Crucial to active deviancy of this type is a clear conception of normality which is used to interpret an aberrant trait or behavior, or which is used to mask a condition. The deviant in either predicament knows what is normal and acts on the basis of that knowledge. The "closet queen," so long the stereotype of the male homosexual, exemplifies one form of this adaptation. This type of homosexual hides his identity behind ordinary role performances. He avoids stigma by managing any discrepancy between his identity as a normal, heterosexual, and as an abnormal, homosexual.

Similar processes operate with the heavy drinker. In the early stages of alcoholism, the alcoholic works hard to perform job and even family roles. In spite of his drinking, accompanied by blackouts and failures to perform the social responsibilities of family and job, he continues to think of his social activities as normal. He must become deviant, i.e., acknowledge his problem, and then become normal again through the removal of the discrediting conditions of heavy drinking. He must say he is a "drunk" and "dryout" and "stay sober."

Neutralization Another active response to the stigma of deviancy involves accepting the label but re-interpreting its meanings. The new meanings, ones that the person accused of some discrediting act attempts to assign to the act, neutralize the label.

Vincent Swaggi relates his autobiography as a professional fence in an apologetic tone: Of course, his actions were illegal; sure, his best friends and business associates were criminals; but, in Vincent's view, his work gave him a measure of respectability. Klockars (1974) thinks Vincent was able to maintain an air of respectability as an impression, an effect of his mannerism and style. Vincent saw himself as a businessman "who never stole anything." In his opinion, clear distinctions could be made between "thieves" and "receivers" and "thieves" and "drivers."

See Carl, what you gotta understand is when I say "driver," I don't mean "thief." I don't consider a driver a thief. To me, a thief is somebody who goes into a house and takes a TV set and the wife's jewelry an' maybe ends up killin' somebody before he's through. An' for what? So some nothin' fence will steal the second-hand shit he takes? To me that kind a guy is the scum of the earth.... Now the driver, he's different. A driver's a workin' man. He gets an overload [on his delivery truck] now an' then or maybe he clips a carton or two [boxes of wares]. He brings it to me. He makes a few bucks so he can go out on a Friday night or maybe buy his wife a new coat. To me a thief an' a driver is two entirely different things (Klockars 1974, 140).

Vincent was also certain that "If I don't buy it [the stolen goods], somebody else will,"; besides, "he does not cause the goods to be stolen," and no one is hurt by his transactions. He sees himself as a part of the legitimate business structure. He "helps out" a large corporation by more equitably distributing their goods. All in all, Vincent thought he was a "pretty decent guy."

Sykes and Matza (1959) suggest that deviants often employ "techniques of neutralization." They enumerate four:

1. Denial of harm—little or no real harm has been done.
2. Denial of the victim—the victim provoked the action and got what was coming to him.
3. Attacking the accuser—the police are corrupt, brutal and unfair and laws are unjust.
4. Invoking other or higher loyalties—that of loyalties to one's fellow gang members, for example.

Others, like Scott and Lyman (1968) and Hewitt and Stokes (1975), have expanded these conceptions into a general notion of "motive talk." These authors point to processes whereby one's intentions for an untoward action, committed or anticipated, can be displayed in such a way that the display restores a sense of social order. This concept was discussed earlier in chapter six. Within the context of understanding deviancy, neutralization implies that the sense of guilt and the ideology of the deviant world used to recount this guilt indicate that the deviant is committed to the values he violates. Knowing normality and knowingly violating the rules of routine social life entails both accepting stigma and normality.

Merton's (1957) analysis of innovation describes this predicament. The deviant knows and accepts the societally defined goals, but invents new ways to achieve them. For instance, Vincent knows about legitimate ways to achieve success, but thinking them unavailable to him, he innovates. His longings for success lead him to the deviant world. He actively confronts the negative connotations that society places on his life activities while acknowledging the stigma of them. Neutralization techniques allow for membership in a deviant world by reinforcing societal meanings through the violation.

Counter-Stigma When deviants begin not only to refute and deny the negative connotations of the labels they bear, but also to question and attack societal meanings for these labels, we are dealing with the final process of the active responses to stigma. To attempt to approximate normality or to neutralize the effects of the label through use of an ideology grounded in a deviant world does not require of the deviant a vocal and deliberate frontal assault on society's foundations. In fact, we have learned that the two types of active responses do require the deviant to embrace some measure of the meanings of legitimacy. This is not so for the counterattacking deviant.

Of course, any deviant must be able to recognize normality and, hence, his putative departure from it, but he does not accept the meanings of his condition. He wishes to formulate new meanings and replaces the societally given ones with those from his own alternative world view. This deviant then campaigns, demands, rebels, and organizes to establish a new version of the meanings of his particular condition. He or she formulates a **counter-stigma** theory.

A counter-stigma theory is both ideology and practice. It offers alternative meanings for the person's condition which conflict with those available in the larger society. It prescribes courses of action which are often political and confrontational. For example, many physically handicapped people lecture, write, and proselytize. They want those responsible directly for the labels they bear, physicians, psychologists, employers, and even those indirectly responsible to know the truth about their conditions. They want the societal meanings modified to include "whole social persons." They want definitions of an "able-bodied" person to be based on a new set of criteria. Blindness does not necessarily mean dependency; deafness does not mean lack of intelligence; bodily impairments do not require social restrictions. These people want others to know what they themselves know but cannot get accepted generally—that they consider themselves full human beings. A counter-stigma theory requires action,

The vision of judgment. Recently, the labels of deviancy have become more open to negotiation and people understand the requirements for appropriate appearance and actions in more specific ways. A blind judge is a symbol of this recent development. Can you think of any objections people might have to a blind person making important decisions in a court of law?

and so we see political action by the handicapped—picketing, lobbying, and, in the late 1970s occupying for weeks a portion of a government building in San Francisco. They demand full equality in the social world and symbolic, if not literal, removal of their stigma. Such effects, they argue, will be consequences of legal action and tough enforcement by government agencies. Counter-stigma theory gives meaning to confrontational strategies and can serve as the foundation for wholly different ways to decide what is normal in society.

A paraplegic related the following story of his encounter with a **"labeling agent"**:

I had been working down at the state capital trying to make legislators understand that we must have public access to buildings. I spent a lot of time getting appointments, doing research, mostly on my own. A friend of mine helped me get into the building because there was no way for me to get inside. Well, I had been parking up close to the building in a loading zone—after all they were "loadin' " me. Over a period of weeks I collected quite a few tickets. I refused to go to court. Finally, there was a final summons to appear in court. Well, I called them up and told them to come get me. They did. A patrolman came to my house. I went with him. When we arrived at the court house we faced that long flight of stairs up into the building. The policeman started to pick me up from the wheelchair and carry me in. I said, "if you drop me I'll sue the state, you and the judge." I demanded that the judge see me. Well, after a long argument, the policeman left me in my chair at the bottom of the flight and the judge met with me there! He left his chambers to see me on the street! I guess I got my point across. He dropped the charges on the tickets.

In recent years many moral deviants have also adopted a rebellious stance toward the meanings of their labels. Homosexuals contend that the civil rights movement and its consequences must apply to them. Their stigma is discriminatory, they say. Public gayness disqualifies them from jobs in many parts of the nation. They attack the stereotypes of themselves as child molesters and as bad security risks. They reaffirm the naturalism of homosexuality through reconstructing a history of it. They point out that some great men were homosexual, that other cultures accept the practice as normal, and some suggest a biological or body chemistry cause that is as "natural" as heterosexuality. Of course, militant factions of the deviant world of gayness illustrate the counter-stigma response.

The counter-stigma theory aims to change society, not the deviant. Its goal is the total alteration of the general meanings of normality. The counter-stigma theory is, in this sense, revolutionary. Normalization and neutralization are defensive postures, the former, conformist and latter, innovative. Thinking counter to a stigma focuses on grand changes and is, hence, rebellious in nature.

SUMMARY

Deviancy as a meaning of social interaction is understood as a result of the definitions of situations people are able to enforce. Generally, this perspective is know as labeling theory. There are both general and specific meanings for being different in society. The concept of stigma covers the interactive aspects of deviancy. Problems often emerge from attempts to define what is and is not acceptable. Studies of the relationships between police and deviants teach us a great deal about the judgments and control of judgments which may produce a social deviant.

There are outsider worlds made up of deviants and those who deal with them. This chapter described these worlds and offered a scheme for classifying deviants according to the primary meanings imputed to them. There are physical, mental and moral deviants. Within each type there are several possible reactions to the label of deviant. These reactions are depicted as active and passive. The processses through which people attempt to give meaning to their situations of life as deviants are discussed as normalization, neutralization, and the counter-stigma reaction. Generally, the matters of being deviant are concerned with the acquisition of identities, attempts to avoid these identities, and, once acquired for better or worse, their management.

EXERCISES FOR UNDERSTANDING DEVIANCY

1. With a few friends, go to a restaurant where you have never eaten before. Select a place where you can be reasonably sure no one will recognize you. Go through the entire evening without speaking. You can gesture, point or otherwise figure out how to order your meal, request water, etc. just so long as neither you nor any other member of your group speak. After you leave the restaurant, sit down and record everything that happened to you and how you felt during the experience.

Another exercise for those of you who are shy persons is to watch a popular television program without the sound. Do this exercise with at least three other people. After you finish watching without taking notes, try to reconstruct the story. Compare your version of what happened with the others in your group. Did you all have similar versions? If not, how do they differ? If you have access to a video recorder, it is a great idea to record the program you watched so you can listen to it after you have completed discussing what you think happened with the others doing this exercise. You should be surprised at what you missed and the variation in the versions of what happened. This exercise should help you grasp a little of the experience of being an outsider.

2. In the course of a typical day, as you go about the routines of living in the dormitory, attending class, record all the words and phrases you overhear which seem to label another person (examples of some common ones are "you queer," "jerk," and the like). Of course, the precise expressions will vary a great deal from place to place and time to time. Still, you should have no trouble hearing a few dozen or so on an active day.

Rank these words according to what you think is their power to label and what kind of deviancy they connote (physical, mental, or moral). Also make notes about the situations in which you heard or used these labeling terms. This exercise should help you appreciate how prevalent these attempts to distinguish insiders, from outsiders are in everyday life.

3. Imagine you have been caught with an "excessive" amount of a controlled substance on your person. You are about to acquire an identity of a deviant. According to your reading of this chapter, what can you do about it? In other words, what devices are available for managing the label of "deviant." We listed the neutralization techniques and there are many others which you can deduce from our discussion of the meanings of being different.

KEY CONCEPTS

Autokinetic effect
Conformity
Deviancy
Institutions
Societal meanings
Normal
Stigma
Signifying
Moral character
Incongruity procedure
Moral judge
Degradation ritual
Ritual of initiation
Sick role
Conventional criminals
White-collar criminals
Racketeers
Official deviancy
Moral or immoral career
Secondary deviation
Pass
Counter-stigma
Labeling agent

SUGGESTED READINGS

Some fascinating reading awaits the student of deviancy. The version of social psychology we have introduced in this text is rich and detailed on the meanings of being different. By now, we see that the very concept of deviancy requires an appreciation of situational meanings and of the practical consequences of interaction. Of course, we learned in chapter two that these principles are basic to social psychology. We recommend three readings: two books and an article. Douglas, Rasmussen, and Flanagan document the meanings of being naked in public in their book, *The Nude Beach.* Although action at the beach does change, the authors have described an interesting phenomenon (being naked in front of strangers) which calls into question and thereby illuminates some fundamental ideas we have about the association between behavior and appearances of the human body.

Howard S. Becker whose name is virtually synonymous with the social psychological study of deviancy wrote a provocative article which has become a standard on the process of acquiring the identity of a marijuana user. In a related piece of research, the Alders document the extent to which the use of this drug has "filtered" throughout society while still retaining a deviant status.

Alder, Patricia, and Peter Alder. "Tinydopers: A Case Study of Deviant Socialization." *Symbolic Interaction* 1, No. 2 (1978): 90–105.

Becker, Howard S. "Becoming a Marijuana User." *American Journal of Sociology* 59 (November 1953): 235–242.

Douglas, Jack, and Paul K. Rasmussen with Carol Ann Flanagan. *The Nude Beach.* Beverly Hills, Ca.: Sage, 1977.

Chapter Eight

Inequality in Interaction

Inequality in Interaction

He drove up riding low to the road in his new baby blue Porsche with leather interior. Although he was dressed much like the other teenagers—he wore camping shorts, a brightly colored loose-fitting shirt, his right earlobe glinting with the gold of a miniature lighting bolt—all the others at the dance knew this boy came from a wealthy background. It was not just the Porsche. Everybody knew about Shawn and his family before he got the Porsche on his eighteenth birthday. Some resented him and openly criticized him—even making jokes about his silver spoon and his tough life. They wished they had his wealth, imagining what they would do differently. Even his friends felt a sense of injustice about the Porsche.

But this night they all went to see a movie—one of those new ones about "break dancing." The one they saw was about the natural and authentic character of street dancing. The story was simple, its point clear enough. The rich and artsy folks, members of the Los Angeles high society, simply could not match the energy and creative drive of the street dancers. In the end, the street dancers were up on stage in a big production number, a part of the "high society" they tried to criticize and change. Shawn dresses street-wise, but drives a Porche.

I N everyday life, people make comparisons between themselves and others. Often people support each other in these comparisons. They congratulate, compliment, and make remarks about "good fortune." Clearly, some comparisons reflect mutual respect and admiration. Other comparisons are critical, and can be quite profound in their effect on the way actual everyday life is conducted. These are the comparisons which make the difference between admissions to a prestigious university, or promotion to a better job. The business of evaluating each other is central to social life. In this chapter, we are interested in how people's judgments of one another become the basis for distributing rewards in society. The practical consequences of evaluative comparisons are of utmost importance for understanding the meanings of inequality.

THE MEANINGS OF INEQUALITY

One of the first observations is that people may feel superior in one aspect of their lives but inferior in others. A rich man may value what he thinks of as the freedom and spirit of the vagabond, while the vagabond envies the money of the rich man. A housewife longs for the feelings of accomplishment she believes the career woman possesses, while a mother combining a career and child rearing sometimes wishes for the relief of having just one job. As students of social interaction, we need ways of talking more precisely about these comparisons of everyday life.

Alfred Schutz wrote that society is composed of **systems of relevancy** within which comparisons are appropriate and meaningful (1971, 226–229). The meanings of commonsense ideas about equality are bounded by society, organizations, and individual circumstances. Within the different systems of activities there are rules for comparison.

In the game of baseball, for example, a pitcher may have a fast ball unequaled among his peers. To say, however, that the pitcher is a better athlete than a star running back for a football team has little meaning for either the pitcher or the running back. One activity is, for practical purposes, irrelevant to the other. It is only in terms of some overarching system like that of exercise physiology that such a comparison might become appropriate; hence, comparisons have meaning within larger contexts. These contexts define the relevance of actions, thoughts, or feelings to be compared.

Spradley and McCurdy (1975, 77–78) develop the idea of systems of pertinent comparisons when they discuss the **domain**. A domain is defined as any major subsystem of a group's acquired knowledge. For example, although they focus exclusively on knowledge and its role in the culture of a group, we extend their idea to include comparisons that members of society make. In one of Spradley's studies, he examines the domain of the urban tramp. He describes how tramps organize their knowledge of themselves into categories which they then use to make judgments about each other's character and about such practical matters as how to spend the night in a new city or how to find transportation. For example, tramps classify themselves as "mission stiffs," "rubber tramps," "airedales," and "dings." Each type of tramp can be recognized according to distinguishing characteristics. A "mission stiff" survives by going to skid row missions where he must "take a nose dive," a reference to bowing one's head in prayer. In exchange for praying, the tramp can count on a warm place to sleep and a hot meal. "Rubber tramps" travel from place to place in old cars. "Airedales" walk the railroad tracks from town to town carrying their belongings in bedrolls over their backs. A "ding" is a professional panhandler or beggar (Spradley 1970).

In addition to categorizing each other, tramps also rank the various styles of their lives. For example, independence and freedom are highly valued. The rubber tramp's car allows him to avoid the degrading "ear banging" and the "nose dives" that the mission stiff routinely endures in order to "make a flop" (find a place to sleep the night). The rubber tramp can always sleep in his car while the mission stiff must listen to a sermon and pray in order to stay the night in the warm, dry mission.

Evaluations are made within a domain, or a system of relevant things. Ball (1976) offers an analysis of the meanings and social consequences of failure in professional athletics. He suggests the social organization of sports serves as a context which gives "failure" its meaning. Baseball, with its major-minor league divisions, allows a player to be "cooled out." Ball writes, "In baseball failures may follow you, and you them, up and down the major-minor hierarchy" (1976, 735).

Tramps live in their own domain. Although that domain is clearly in the lower ranks of inequality in society, within it status distinctions exist. Do you detect any clues from the appearances of these two men about what kinds of tramps they may be?

In football, with its single league organization, "failures may face you." The football player who does not make the grade often feels that he loses his very existence. In terms of his status as a football player, this is literally what happens to him. (Part of the appeal of a successful new football league might be the hope for resurrection it offers ex-players.) The baseball player simply changes status or position within the institutionalized organization of the game. Tramps, likewise, may change their identity from mission stiff to rubber tramp or vice versa and gain or lose independence and, hence, status, as a tramp. Where a person's identity comes from, the domains that impart meaning to his or her life, has a great deal to do with the quality of participation in society.

When social psychologists use the phrase **stratification system**, they usually refer to the standards employed by members of domains to rank actions, thoughts, and feelings within both a particular domain and across several domains, for not only do tramps and pitchers rank themselves, but they can also be ranked by outsiders according to their identities as members of their respective domains. Professional baseball pitchers enjoy considerably higher status or rankings than tramps, in spite of an occasional proclamation to the contrary by disgruntled fans.

The comparisons people make of one another can be understood according to processes they follow in forming judgments within, among, and across domains. Some evaluations result from competition for the same reward. Professional athletes vie for a starting position on the first team and as large a cut of the team's budget for player's salaries as possible. Within corporations, unions compete with management for their share in the distribution of profits. Unions may wish to have corporate earnings committed to pension funds to support its members in their retirement while management wishes to plow back earnings into research and development to ensure future markets.

Competition both within and between domains occurs whenever a single and limited resource is available for reward. Further, competition for these limited resources, whether they be tangible, like money, or intangible, like esteem, takes place according to taken-for-granted notions that some people deserve greater rewards than others. A pitcher with a history of success deserves more money and better treatment than a newcomer of unproven ability and performance; a manager deserves more than a laborer and an administrator more than a teacher. Although elements of all the processes of comparisons may be involved in any instance of unequal reward, we say **competition** occurs whenever a single resource is the goal of two parties. The possession of the resource by one excludes its possession by the other, and the means of achieving the resource are the same for both parties.

Exploitation describes the situation of interaction in which one party controls the "rules" for access to rewards while the second party is kept naive or helpless with regard to access. Much of the stratification system of American society rests on this process. For example, an electronics industry may move its assembly plant across the border to Mexico so that it can use cheaper labor. The absence of organized labor, low standards of living, and large numbers of unemployed and unskilled workers affords a business an opportunity to "exploit" Mexican workers. Such a practice is exploitative because (1) Mexican workers do not receive pay in proportion to the earnings of the products, and the company earns a larger profit by using Mexican labor, and (2) the workers are either naive about the size of their pay check in comparison to the market value of the products or powerless to do anything about it. Another example is the widely known fact that women are paid less than men for the same kinds of jobs. Women are exploited whenever they are not allowed to compete under the same conditions as men for economic rewards. Some sociologists (Davis and Moore 1945, 52) refer to this type of comparison as **invidious**. The social distance between men and women becomes institutionalized in differential pay scales. Women, in increasing numbers, consider this practice unfair. It is their awareness that rules of fair competition have been violated which leads them to a sense of "distributive injustice."

The view from the bottom. In some societies blind and deaf people begging on the street are a common sight. Think about the contrast between this picture and the one of the blind judge in Chapter 7. What do the pictures of these two blind men say about the society to which both men belong?

The third process, **accommodation**, describes situations of interaction in which parties within or in different domains take each other into account in the actual distribution of rewards. This does not mean rewards are equally shared. Instead, rewards are distributed according to clear conceptions of social identities and relationships among these identities. Large businesses accommodate each other by informally recognizing marketing territories. A Midwestern CB manufacturer, for instance, may refrain from advertising in the South because they concede that territory to another company.

Of course, one company may decide to compete for another's territory thereby openly challenging, or competing with, the other company on its home turf. But as long as both maintain the integrity of their respective territories there is an accommodative process.

We can illustrate an instance of an accommodative process resulting in territorial boundaries by looking at some research on weekend, long-distance runners (Nash 1979). A race sponsored and organized by an association of distance runners draws people of varied abilities and aspirations. Observations of these events reveal that territories develop in the course of racing. These territories represent the various levels of self-involvement in the running scene as well as actual running ability. Elite runners are encouraged to line up near the front of the pack at the starting line. As races draw larger and larger numbers of participants, these informal practices become formalized and racers are lined up by reputation which they establish on entry forms by stating what their best time is for past races. There are some runners who are committed to running in ways which involve their very sense of selfhood, even though they may have limited talent as runners. Categories are set aside so that these people can compete with each other. These categories include age and sex groupings as well as informal distinctions among joggers and beginning runners. During a race of substantial size (one hundred or more participants) an interactional ecology will emerge in which various participants accommodate each other. The pattern looks like that seen in Figure 8.1.

There may be considerable overlapping of the territories, and over time a runner may change identity as well as location within the ecology of the races he or she enters. A jogger may become a runner, or a runner become elite. But the distribution of rewards (prizes, compliments, and feelings of accomplishment) is roughly in accord with these categories within the domain of distance running. The informal system of feeling good about one's performance also depends on participants having an identity like those described and being aware of the presence of others. For example, a jogger may derive self-satisfaction from participating in a race with a class runner, or a class runner feels good about his "off his personal record" performance by acknowledging that his presence in the race stimulated greater participation in and status for the race as an event in the runner's world. Most importantly, runners derive a sense of satisfaction from

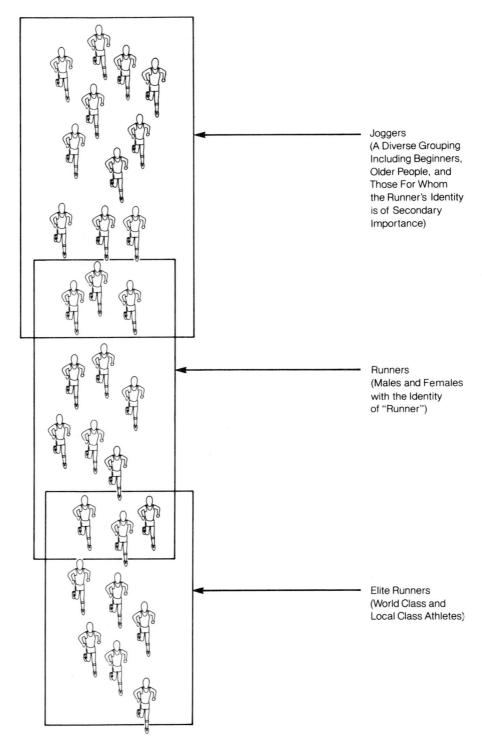

Joggers
(A Diverse Grouping
Including Beginners,
Older People, and
Those For Whom
the Runner's Identity
is of Secondary
Importance)

Runners
(Males and Females
with the Identity
of "Runner")

Elite Runners
(World Class and
Local Class Athletes)

Figure 8.1. Territories of a Footrace

participation in the race according to their tacit recognition of others' assessments of their abilities and aspirations. A runner who finishes a ten-mile race in sight of the elite runners feels good about his or her showing. To be sure, the reward that accrues to the actual winner of the race may be greater in both psychological and monetary value. However, few elite runners would want to ban others from participation or exploit them by not allowing rewards by classification or level of participation. The only exception to this generalization is the recent practice of inviting small groups of elite racers for special record-setting attempts. A marathon in the summer of 1983 was held in Amsterdam on a "fast layout" for the purpose of bringing together the best distance runners in the world. The race may have been a media success (it was aired on ABC's *Wide World of Sports*), but there were no records set and judging from the small crowds of people who turned out to see the race, this "elite" race did not qualify as an eventful occasion, like the Boston Marathon, or the Bay-to-Breakers race in San Francisco.

As W. Lloyd Warner (1949) noted some years ago, even money must be translated into social respectability and reputation before its possession converts into social ranking. It is common among sociologists to draw a distinction between comparisons and rankings made on the basis of money and wealth alone (**class**) and those formulated from socially grounded meaning systems or domains of comparisons (**status**). Social psychologists usually focus their investigations on subjective or status-based comparisons.

Inequality Given by Society

It can be difficult to describe how different areas of social life may be ranked by members of society. Some may place their families first, others their work, still others their religion. There are even some for whom leisure time activities are all important. Still, there are some identifiable themes at the societal level which are evident whenever inequality characterizes interaction. In other words, within the commonsense knowledge systems out of which thoughts, feelings, and actions are generated, there are certain themes that the members of society use to establish the relative rankings of performance they regard as belonging together.

Ralph Linton (1936) drew a distinction between rankings of persons and organizations and the societally meaningful actions depending on the attribution of rank. He observed that rank was attributed in two ways. First, some rankings are acquired from the very organization of society, such as birth into wealth or nobility. Second, other rankings may be earned; a person or group may do something or follow a course of action that, if successful, will increase their rank. Linton called the first kind of rank **ascribed** and the second, **achieved**.

THE PROCESSES OF ASCRIBED AND ACHIEVED INEQUALITY

In almost every area of living, the meanings of social life have become increasingly individualized. Peter Berger (1979) has depicted the modern experience as a transformation from fate to choice. Particularly in modern American society, the range of individual choices has become vast and profound. One chooses careers, whether to marry, whether to have children, and even in some cases, how to have children. In modern society, persons are known by what they do rather than who they are. Put in a social psychological way, people are increasingly held personally accountable for their performances. Conversely, less and less of what people do can be taken uncritically as simply "the way things are." Competition emerges as the principal criterion for distributing rewards unequally under these circumstances.

Competition

Members of modern society typically believe that through motivation, initiative, and hard work, a person may achieve rewards. In addition, as in the phenomenon of distributive justice, most people adhere to a set of judgments about exactly how reward should be proportionate to achievement. The young woman of limited financial means may achieve her station in life by hard work. She waits tables to earn money for tuition. She studies harder and more diligently than other students. She performs well in school and accumulates a record of A's and B's. Her subsequent admission to medical school is "deserved," we say. And her eventual status as a doctor, Linton would call an achieved status. An achieved rank can be interpreted as having been accomplished, and is highly valued in American society.

Accomplishment may result through competition, exploitation, or accommodation, and the relative ranking of the accomplishment is not necessarily proportionate to "fairness". In the case of the female medical student, we can illustrate how the high ranking of her accomplishments might have derived from each of the processes.

Accomplishment through competition assumes equal opportunity or access to the arena of potential achievement. If all students could support themselves by working after class hours, if all students were ambitious enough to exercise their capabilities fully under such stress, and if all students followed the same ground rules for achieving, then a limited access to medical school would seem fully justifiable. We could say all students desiring entrance to the medical profession had the same opportunities. The difference shows up in those who have the energy, diligence, and perseverance to become physicians. The high rewards and rankings

The upward climb.   Upward mobility is a prevalent motivating force among the members of modern society.   This man projects an image of a willingness to work hard to achieve success.

accruing to physicians can be accounted for in terms of the competitive process operating in the selection, education, and retention of physicians.

This line of thinking extends even to the folk wisdom of being "first with the most," and "being at the right place at the right time."   The valve for the aerosol spray can surely would have had diminished marketability had it been invented after public alarm over the depletion of the earth's ozone layer.   Being able to judge these chance factors and having good timing seem to be a legitimate part of the meanings of accomplishment. Competition does not eliminate fortune, it merely distributes it in a random fashion (cf. Callois, 1961).

Exploitation

In an exploitive relationship, someone is assured accomplishment.   The process is set up so that one actor uses the other in an instrumental way. The energies of the exploited person are spent in the direction of accomplishing the aims of the exploiter. Edwin Schur (1976) convincingly argues that certain aspects of the "awareness movement" often exploit women. He reasons the problems of sexism are institutional in America. Women occupy ascribed positions in which they are dominated by men. In the language of social psychology, this means that commonsense knowledge systems function to assign women to work of a submissive and denigrating nature; typical of this are attitudes and statements such as "everybody knows" that married women do not need high salaries, are not really committed to their careers, and so on. Although Schur (1976, 143–144) points out that political action has been effective in attacking sexism in American society, much work remains if true equality is to be established. The complete eradication of societal sexism will require assaults on all fronts of discrimination: economic, family, political, religious, and educational. If women are taught to accept themselves and, in the bargain, full responsibility for their fates, they may enrich their personal lives, but societal discrimination will continue unaffected. Mainly, he contends, women who participate in awareness and consciousness-raising experiences are essentially still trying to conform to the movie star image of what will be pleasing to men, indirectly upholding the idea that how women look and feel is more important than what they do (1976, 133). If women acquiesce in their ascribed status, and they do this with a false idea that they are being fulfilled, liberated, and made equal to men, they have been exploited by the gurus of consciousness. As Schur puts it, "Being in touch with one's feelings and natural surroundings may help, but it can never be a substitute for [social] efforts" (1976, 144). An outcome is that women who experience serious disadvantages of inequality (working-class, and minority race women, for example) discover their middle-class sisters claiming that they need only accept full responsibility for and awareness of their lot and it can be improved. Indeed, exploited persons are often very much aware of their life situations. They are ready for concrete changes in the organization of society, changes which will lead to a more competitive position for them so they can share the rewards society has to offer.

Our example of the aspiring physician further illustrates the exploitive process. If after this pre-med student achieves a laudable record, she runs into a panel of interviewers at the medical school who believe women will not make good physicians because they will inevitably drop out to start a family, she is being exploited. Not only is the woman denied entrance to medical school, but typifications of her have been used to justify the existing order of things. We all recognize that such blatant examples of this type of discrimination are becoming less frequent in society, particularly at medical schools. But exploitation and the operations of typifications can be subtle. It can have to do with acquiring social identities and ideas about how various identities ought to relate. A man's work is typically regarded as more important than a woman's and, as Schur demonstrates, a middle-class way of life may serve as the standard for the whole society.

Accommodation

Accommodation is the process of making the meanings of accomplishment relative. In this process, social identities are not equalized, nor are identities used for the purposes of another person. Instead, people recognize identities and their relationships, and take them as the basis of the interaction. At the societal level, accommodations are marked by the kinds of relationships among groups in which social identities and meanings are preserved.

For example, in American society, law requires that handicapped individuals be accommodated as much as possible in the society of "normal people." In any relationship, societal knowledge may lead to a stigmatization. Under legal mandate, this same knowledge is to be put to different use. Everybody knows the paraplegic cannot climb stairs, and when this fact becomes the basis for job discrimination or permanent assignment of low-paying employment, we can say the paraplegic is being exploited. Likewise, we know competition between a "normal" person and a paraplegic is not possible in a physical sense. Nevertheless, we wish equality of opportunity to pertain in certain domains, like access to public buildings. So, we modify existing systems to accommodate the handicapped person. For the blind, we provide readers, special tape recordings that condense speeches and lectures into shortened forms for rapid listening. For the deaf, interpreting services must be provided. Or, for blacks, women, and Chicanos whose identities have handicapped them in competitive processes, quota systems operate to "correct" the injustice of past comparisons.

Although accommodative processes are overshadowed by competition and exploitation in modern society, there are still many examples of interactive exchanges, from individual to societal, which are essentially accommodative. Merton's (1963, 71–82) well-known analysis of "political machines" showed that newly arrived emigrant groups achieved rapid access to power by being accommodated within existing political systems. In return for "block voting," key positions like precinct captain were awarded to members of ethnic groups. In this way, Italian-Americans and others gained power without having been thoroughly assimilated into American society.

Of course, the versions people have of how inequality is accomplished can change. The same practice which seems to be accommodative under one set of circumstances, we may judge as exploitive from a slight different vantage point: yesterday's accommodation becomes today's exploitation. The processes we depict are the results of how people interpret and make comparisons which have immediate and practical consequences for them. It is how those involved in the action see things that count. W. I. Thomas taught us to appreciate this general insight about such matters being "real in the minds of people."

Returning to Merton's research, we recall he demonstrated that political bossism of many of America's largest cities during the 1920s and through the 1940s could be seen as both exploitive and accommodative. In the first

Social processes are never fully one type or another. Hence, some people may be accommodated to the competitive process. When processes of comparison are mixed, special interactive devices develop to ensure that fair judgments of performance can be made. Can you think of one such device to judge this professional woman's performance?

instance, newly arrived Poles, Italians, and Czechs were exploited when they were forced to vote for the boss. Their ignorance and naivete left them vulnerable to the powerful political machines then ruling the cities of America. However, there were positive, latent consequences of such exploitations. The newcomers acquired access, albeit illegally, to the system of power. By serving as lackeys and political "boys", the emigrants gained power and economic resources enabling them to move out of their disadvantaged life situations. Some analysts point out parallels between the experiences of earlier arrivals to big cities and those of contemporary urban blacks. The powerful machines which were integrated into the very organization of the city itself no longer exist. In their place are amorphous bureaucratic organizations, isolating adaptive practices such as sharing and community building, and even the formation of street gangs. All of these ways to "stay alive" have the effect not of integrating recent arrivals into the whole structure of the city, but of permanently isolating them from it (cf. Stack 1974).

THE ORGANIZATION OF INEQUALITY IN INTERACTION

Daily, members of society compare and use forms according to how they understand the composition of society. Sometimes such uses can be dramatically tied to the perpetuation of societal inequality. Perhaps the most notable instance is what we have come to call the "cycle of poverty" (Williams 1970, 1–10).

The adage, "the rich get richer and the poor get poorer," contains some sociological truth, at least insofar as it applies to the poor. Sometimes groups of people learn to act and think in ways which do not conform to broader societal meanings. Further, we have seen that even in modern society people have ascribed statuses. From early socialization experiences within the context of ascribed social environments, people form deeply held self-concepts and acquire a variety of interactional skills. However, if the opportunities for learning that we experience provide us with selves and competencies which are not highly ranked, then a social dilemma emerges. The more competent we become within our particular social world, the more we risk displaying behaviors which may be disapproved and may even be the legitimate bases for discrimination. Even though we may be enhancing our survival within the practical demands of our everyday lives, we are acquiring habits and skills which disadvantage us in the general society.

We can understand this dilemma more clearly by referring to how competitive selections are made for high-paying jobs in our society. Entry into most high-paying jobs requires that a person have a credential of some sort. Typically, this credential takes the form of a college degree. However, the cost of acquiring this credential may be very high. If a person is born into a poor family, it is unlikely that he or she will be able to afford the most impressive credentials, like a degree from an "ivy league" college. Instead, he or she will apply his or her talents to the aspirations, goals, and opportunities available. To be sure, scholarship funds, government loans, and other programs have been designed to "accommodate" the disadvantages of an ascribed position. But current research has revealed that the cycle of disadvantage in modern society entails more than simply being in the wrong place and at the wrong time. Important social psychological mechanisms result in discrimination. These mechanisms turn out to be primarily communicative.

Different ascribed positions within American society are associated with identifiable linguistic and communicative expressions. Blacks in urban American use a version of English that is unique. So pervasive is this version of English that many linguists refer to nonstandard Black English as a variety of American English (Dillard 1966; Baratz 1970; Labov 1972). Although Black English has its own rules of tensing and inflecting verbs, for expressing possession, and so on, its use is often taken to mean that the person so talking is "illiterate," "uneducated," or perhaps even worse, "unsocialized". Hence, people may be known, not only by the company they keep, but by the way they communicate. From a linguistic point of view, there is no reason that any version of a language should be taken as superior to any other. Any language may exist in multiple varieties and any one of these varieties, intrinsically, can serve as a carrier of all the information necessary for complex learning and social experiences.

In practice, as a sociolinguist notes (Labov 1972), comparisons among the varieties of a language are made by members of speech communities and often these comparisons are invidious. A well-educated, successful black engineer knows that his chances for that new job he wants will be diminished if he speaks Black English, or displays his childhood skills at playing the "dozens." Since our engineer friend is already successful, he probably knows Standard English as well as Black English. People who have mastered more than one variety of their language are in a position to **code switch**. This means that a speaker can change varieties of language performance to fit what he thinks is the appropriate form of talking. To a certain extent, we all know different varieties of our language and do switch manners of communicating. Whenever status meanings accompany the variety, as they often do, code switching skills may be necessary for establishing and controlling unequal relationships in interactive encounters.

But what of the black man whose economic position and life experiences precluded learning Standard English? He may well be a bright, articulate and capable person. These qualities, however, may go unnoticed when they are entrapped within the vernacular of the urban poor. William Labov (1970) has shown that, indeed, Standard English in its middle-class usages may mask the display of logical thinking in verbiage, while nonstandard Black English leads itself to tightly reasoned and efficient storytelling. Labov's tongue-in-cheek treatment of the differences between the speech of a gang leader named Larry, and that of a educated middle-class black man, Charles, asserts that no form of language ensures lucidity and clear reasoning. Indeed, in this case Larry, while using the nonstandard variety, follows an intricate line of reasoning. On the other hand, Charles constructs a simple and logically flawed argument while conversing in the idiom of textbooks and lecturers.

As Labov writes:

Our work in the speech community makes it painfully obvious that in many ways working-class speakers are more effective narrators, reasoners, and debaters than many middle-class speakers who temporize, qualify, and lose their argument in a mass of irrelevant detail (1970, 167).

Whereas this may be true, in the minds of most white and many black Americans, speech like the following means that the speaker lacks higher qualities of intellect and character: "He'd be white, man," and "Cause the average whitey out here got everything, you dig? and the nigger ain't got shit, y'know? Y'unnerstan'? So—um—in order for that to happen, you know it ain't no black God that' donin that bullshit" (Labov 1970, 167). Such a manner of speaking ranks low among employers, of course. Its use may become the grounds for discrimination resulting in inequality which is best described as exploitive. For those whose speaking competencies restrict them to a form of communication which carries with it a low social rank, the chances of ever breaking the very conditions resulting in the initial inequality seem locked in the habits of speech.

When it comes to linguistic variety and the choices of which to use for which situation of everyday life, our society is not very accommodative. Most institutional channels of competition (save professional sports) assume competency in Standard English. However, as we have learned, not all members of society possess equal linguistic backgrounds, and they may well have unevenly distributed communicative skills.

Many everyday interactive situations can be classified according to whether they require people to be equally matched in skills, or to possess skills for interaction in different forms of talk. Hence, we can distinguish talk among equals and talk among unequals, as was mentioned in chapter six. Some of the detailed devices and processes of interaction are referred to as **modal** and **cross-modal communications.**

Consider two people of different ranks talking to each other; each is aware of the differences in their social rankings. An erudite scholar and a "semi-literate" janitor meet on the elevator on the campus of large, prestigious university. The scholar wishes to be friendly, but he assesses the man next to him on the basis of his appearance and judges him of low verbal skill and limited intellect. He speaks to him in a manner which he assumes is understandable. The janitor, likewise, enjoys chit-chat with the professor and puts on his best speech. Each will be performing within a form assumed to be the other's. The scholar's mode of communicating is Standard English and perhaps a professional jargon; the janitor's is a nonstandard variety (he may know several of these). In cross-modal communication the janitor or the professor, or both, must attempt to speak as they believe the other speaks.

We can portray the interactional dynamics of situations like this one in Figure 8.2 by thinking of a sender and a receiver of messages and then imagining that each has a visibly different social rank. We will visualize a circumstance in which to describe the form of talking which might take place.

Even though we are focusing on cross-modal comparisons, many evaluative comparisons are possible within a mode. For example, Professor Smith really never did think much of Professor Jones' writing and may proceed to tell him so. Smith may rebut, become angry, or refuse to dignify the criticism with further remarks. Whatever happens, it will happen expressively within a linguistic form: Standard English.

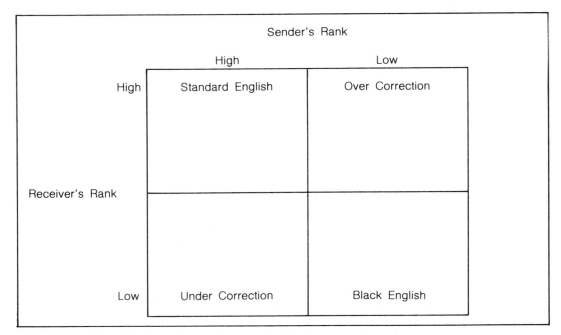

Figure 8.2 The Relationship between Social Class and Language
(Adapted from Bernstein 1966; Labov 1966; Grimshaw 1966)

Likewise, janitors tend to speak vernaculars of their social position, and within the vernacular many important comparisons do go on. A person may be a good conversationalist (Kockman, 1969), tell a good story or joke (Labov, 1970), or be an outstanding listener (Labov, 1971). But within the rankings, people assume of each other equal backgrounds. As Gold's (1952) study indicates, janitors rank and model comparisons among themselves. They may even see themselves as of higher rank than their tenants, as was the case in the study Gold conducted where janitors were generally better paid than the tenants in the apartment building they maintained. These janitors had definite ideas about tenants, and they were acutely aware of the ideas tenants had about them. In the flat (floor of an apartment building) Gold studied, janitors upgraded their services as professionals and were resentful of tenants who treated them as inferiors. Tenants tried to degrade janitors by forcing them to wait for personally convenient times to perform requested services and by blaming them for poor equipment and other general unpleasantries they attributed to their dwellings. This all happened in spite of the fact that these janitors often earned more money than the white-collar tenants they served. However, these janitors seemed to accept among themselves a "public" definition of their work and duty. They experienced relative financial success but remained low in status in their own evaluations as well as those of their significant others.

The presence of an increasing number of black executives in American businesses can be interpreted as the result of a shift from accommodative and exploitative relationships between black and white people to competitive ones.

By looking at instances of cross-modal interaction, we can better understand the mechanisms of inequality in society. A janitor may actually make more money than the tenants he serves; a street person may display elan and cunning that the social worker completely misses; a student may posssess greater knowledge about the subject of the day's lecture than the teacher. But matters of comparisons are masked by the distortions created and perpetuated by maintaining an **impression of rank**.

Within modes, competition and more or less accurate readings of the societal selves of others can be made. Here, reciprocity thinking works to allow interaction to proceed according to the knowledge about and rankings of the competencies people mutually attribute to each other. However, if the societal rankings preclude practical testing of ideas about the other person, then ranked inequalities are continued into the present and interaction and communications become distorted (cf. Habermas 1971). If we act on the basis of misinformation about the other, any possibility of finding out what the other person meant becomes remote, and neither party understands the other. If one party possesses a higher ranking than the other at the beginning of the interaction, or if he can control the meanings which make a difference to the interactional outcome, distorted communication simply plays out pre-existing social inequalities.

For example, Gold points out that professionalization of janitorial services conflicts with the societally given meanings of clean and dirty work (179). No matter what the janitor says, if he can be identified as a janitor by his speech or appearance, he assumes a subordinate position in interaction. Efforts by those who realize that such identification will invariably distort their intentions and interests have been referred to as **hypercorrections** (Labov 1973).

Hyper or over-corrective responses occur whenever a lower-ranked sender tries to communicate in the "hyper" forms of the high-ranked receiver of the message. Labov (1973) demonstrates that lower-status New Yorkers were aware that they omitted the *r* sound from such words as *guard* (thereby pronouncing *god* and *guard* the same). When they were asked to be formal, or otherwise were led to believe they were on equal rank with the interviewer, who was middle class in appearance and seemed to be highly educated, they inserted the *r* sound much more frequently in words where they thought it might belong than did their middle-class counterparts. Another common instance of overcorrection occurs when students attempt to use words they think will make them sound "intellectual." Unfortunately, some do not know how to pronounce (or spell) them properly. Another good example is the use of elaborate "incorrect" grammatical inflections on verbs to create the impression of being educated; perhaps, the most common example of the overcorrective use of a grammatical construction is the use of I as the pronoun form in formal speech. A person who might ordinarily say, "Him and me went down to the store," will say, when trying to sound important or formal, "Him and I went down to the store," or even more commonly "She went with him and I."

People's motivations for the use of these linguistic devices reveal the inequalities they wish to avoid and the very ones we want to describe. The lower-ranked speaker knows that the higher cannot speak his vernacular. He knows that even if he can be understood, using his ordinary talking form will identify his social rank. This does not mean that he will just be ranked as a black, for instance, but that as a speaker, he tacitly recognizes that such an identification means *inequality.* To avoid what he rightly perceives as the consequences of being so typed, he attempts to assume the higher status form. However, since he is not fully competent in that form, he errs in ways which, nevertheless, mark him according to his position in society. Although overcorrection does not avoid distorted communication, it does reveal the societal meanings that underly the communications. In this instance, forms function to perpetuate inequality.

The higher ranked sender's efforts to converse with the lower often unmask the inequality of this situation through the form of **undercorrec-**

tion, or simplification (Grimshaw 1966, 202). Here the higher-ranked party imagines he knows the appropriate form of the lower speaker. Since he does not really know it, as he invariably believes it to be simple, unsophisticated, and easily mastered. Then he proceeds out of a motivation to be understood as an ordinary person to reveal his ignorance and social rank by speaking. A professor will gloss distinctions among cleaning solvents to make a point to the janitor that the smell in his office is offensive thereby establishing his ignorance and inadvertently his possible disdain for such trivial knowledge. A white woman will "come on hip" to build a rapport with a black man, painfully revealing her dilettantism in keeping cool (Lyman and Scott 1970, 145). At times, the lower-ranked person may chide or outright rebuke the higher. "You honky, y'can't rap like nothin'," or, "Hell, doc, you don't know nothin about cleaners." But in terms of the systems of given rankings of social status, the outcome of the antagonism is irrelevant. The professor still has higher rank than the janitor and the white higher than the black even though at the interpersonal level appearances give off the opposite impressions.

Undercorrection, like overcorrection, does not create equal conditions for communications. Instead it highlights inequalities as these are given in the readymade meanings of rank (cf. Cicourel 1975). To anyone interested in describing social meanings, cross-ranked communications serve as strategic events for the uncovering of meanings people attribute to their part in social interactions. And, like it or not, inequality is an ever present feature of the meanings of interaction in society.

CONSCIOUSNESS OF THE UNEQUAL OTHER

Possibly, the most important part of any formula which explains interactions is how we think of others. We should not be surprised to learn, then, that one's consciousness of the other person conforms to societally distributed meanings of inequality. This section of the chapter will relate how high rank can be vicariously experienced by assuming the imagined consciousness of the higher ranked person; that people have conceptions of the entire ranking system for society; and that these conceptions of others tie in with processes of competition, exploitation, and accommodation.

Forms as Implied Rankings

Forms embody implicit rankings. This means that people have, organized and readily at hand, ways to interpret the merit and value of other people and their activities. The make and model of a particular automobile carries with it a hidden rank. To many, a Cadillac symbolizes "excellence and success." These are attributes of the car as a form, and a person can assume these same attributes by owning and operating the car. We do not mean Cadillacs actually excel other cars in craftsmanship and engineering.

"Real" facts about cars are only tangentially related to their symbolic value. Of course, a rattling, smoke-belching, rusted hulk of a Caddy retains little of its former meanings. But even in this case, some of the social meanings of the car remain. A person may buy the old "clunker" simply because it is a Caddy. The person's own station in life becomes secondary to his vicariously experiencing the "joys of Cadillac ownership". The car may cost him more than a compact; he may be forced to pay higher taxes and maintenance costs; and, he may actually divert funds from food and housing to "keep the beast runnin'." But for the joyful moments of driving around town, cruising the street in search of action, "the man has his wheels."

The form, the car in this case, in-and-of-itself carries the rankings of inequality. Previous meanings of the car are residuals that penetrate the meanings of the immediate and present. Hence, the particular adornments of the Caddy, like the special grille, bug-eyed headlights and leopard skin seats, stamp the former meanings with the personal and class meanings of the present owner. Both sets of meanings function to establish an image of rank through the recognition of the societal system and immediate high rank within the values of the community. Thus, both general overall low rankings and the specific high ranking are simultaneously communicated. In short, ranking is displayed through the exhibition of taste according to the immediate social context. Although we may observe that many different makes of cars are favorites among urban blacks, and certainly many own plain compact cars, it is the big car which carries societally and subculturally relevant meanings.

Big old cars, color television sets, and other affordable symbols of success may be found among the possessions of the poor. Theirs is not an effort at overthrowing the systems of inequality in society. Instead, they want a piece of the pie either literally or, more often figuratively. Lyrics of the theme song of the popular television program, "The Jefferson's," express this sentiment, "I finally got a piece of the pie." And as recent surveys of urban looting and civil disorder indicate, widespread unemployment and discrimination seem to foster an acquiescence which does not provide motivation to get rewards of society, for instance to loot when the opportunity arises. Rather, people who have jobs that they do not regard as fulfilling and who receive pay they regard as unfairly low, those who subscribe to societally given meanings of success, but whose efforts have been thwarted in ways they see as invidious and exploitive, are the ones who seize the opportunities to loot during a blackout or a riot. (see National Advisory Commission of Civil Disorders 1968).

Such unusual circumstances as the 1977 blackout in New York city afford some people the chance to have what they believe they should always have had or could have had if ascribed a different status in life. "If I had been born with a silver spoon, I would have all those things. So what's the big deal a 'poor boy' like me taking some honky color TV?" Such actions, in part, are motivated by vicarious assumptions of high rank through possessing the available things that symbolize success and thus escaping from current life conditions.

Every action has a formal meaning. Many aspects of social life require that persons assume a formal rank from another person. Usually we are encouraged to assume a higher form. Car manufacturers have, of course, catered to and perhaps fostered this tendency with regard to purchasing their wares. They offer luxury packages for all cars regardless of their sticker price. To be sure such "marginal differentiation" allows the purchasers to feel that she or he is getting economy and class while providing greater profit for the manufacturers and dealers (Reisman 1950). Nevertheless, our point here is that our conceptions of luxury and high rank are embodied in arbitrary forms that we all learn about and use. The luxury compact does not seem a contradiction to most of us. This is not the same thing as saying that all people share the same interpretation of the forms. We have seen that a person's life-world is class and status bound, and that within each station of the system of inequality, the people there have distinctive ways of viewing themselves and the other people of society.

How Society Stacks Up

Immediacy, practicality, and **similarity** are the three considerations running through the relative conceptions of the systems of inequality which condition interactions among members of society. Immediacy refers to the degree to which people believe their own personal life-worlds are directly and particularly implicated in a stratified society. Practicality has to do with how people interpret the outcomes of the actions of others as having consequences to their own interests. And, similarity hinges on the perceived closeness among life-worlds. People's conceptions of how society stacks up revolve around their beliefs as to how these matters affect them in their present life circumstances, what the consequences of these effects are, and who else may be involved.

If you ask people to identify where they fall within the stratification system of their society, most will say that they are middle or working class (Centers 1949; Converse 1959). They apparently wish to emphasize they are no better or worse than the next guy. But if you can be specific about social context for comparisons, you discover that people have elaborate ways of conceiving of each other in terms of the general arrangements of society. An anthropologist, Lloyd Warner, and his many associates, studied the comparisons people make of each other within many communities across America. These investigations revealed specific ways in which we make comparisons among what we think are the domains of society.

For example, people with low earnings, or those who experience frequent periods of unemployment, tend to see the stratification of society from their point of view. (See Figure 8.3.) They make few distinctions among those who are much more successful, but they make many fine comparisons among those whom they see as close to themselves in circumstances.   They refer to people who have steady jobs, own their own homes, as the "way ups" or "high society," or "snobs."   It makes little difference to these people what style a house is, in what part of town it is located (other than being on the right or wrong side of the tracks), or the occupations these people pursue.   All that matters is that, for the moment of comparison, these differences have no consequences for, or similarity to, their own life circumstances.

However, among those whose station they see as close to theirs, they often draw careful lines: to have a job or not makes a difference; after that, what kind of job it is matters.   To be uptown or downtown makes a difference, just as it does to live in a flat or an apartment.   To have a dry flop, not a wet one, among tramps is a mark of status.   Davis, Gardner and Gardner (1941) illustrated the relative nature of comparisons.   They found that people draw finer and finer distinctions as the people with whom they are comparing themselves become more immediate, practical, and similar to themselves.

Likewise, from the top looking down, we find the same considerations of others operating.   (See Figure 8.4.)   Little regard is given to differences such as the status markings between a bricklayer and a sod carrier, or a

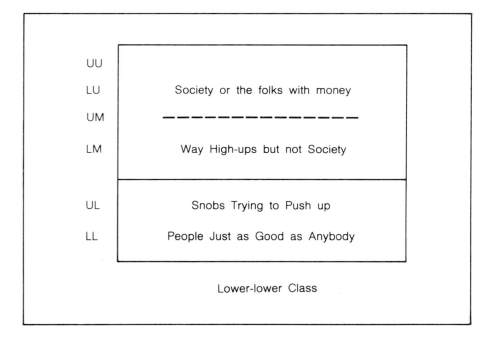

Figure 8.3 View from the Bottom Up   (Davis, Gardner and Gardner, 1941)

——————— = Sharp class differentiation

. . . . = Indefinite class differentiation

postman with his own route and an assistant letter carrier. However, great attention may be given to such considerations as the reputation of the school in which one's children are enrolled, the labels of clothing, the cut of a suit and, perhaps most importantly, the source of one's income—is money "old" or "new"?; does one know how to display wealth?

Warner (1960) discusses the differences between the new rich with their larger homes, ostentatious luxury cars and self-indulgent spending habits, and the old rich who are subdued and refined in the display of their societal good fortune. Just as the poor make distinctions among themselves which the rich lump together, the rich make comparisons among themselves, the bases of which are unknown to the poor. From Davis' and the Gardners' work, we can draw an illustration of how the rich in a southern town saw the order of their society.

Relationships among People of Different Rank

We can see, then, that people interact on the basis of their conceptions of each other. When this principle is applied to interactions between people of different rankings, an interesting insight emerges. People know more about those who are similar to them than they know about those remote

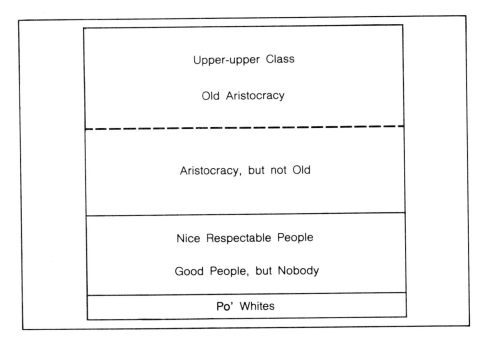

Figure 8.4 View from the Top Down   (Davis, Gardner and Gardner 1941)

————— = Sharp class differentiation
- - - - - - - = Indefinite class differentiation

from them in terms of rank. Within a domain, interaction requires of people that they know a lot about each other and assume a common knowledge system. This is especially true if the relationships are conflictual and antagonistic. You must know your enemy well.

However, when interactions take place across rank, each party is interacting on the basis of what one thinks he or she knows about the other. This means that it is one's own relative conceptions which ground the interaction. Hence, as in the discussion of forms, a person really interacts with the conception he or she has of the other and this may be quite different from the conception the other has of himself or herself. Distortions of meanings and intentions, and misunderstandings of reality highlight interactions of this sort.

A welfare worker may simply want to provide support and warmth to a client while the client interprets the worker's actions as forward, nosey, and officious. On the other side of this interaction, the client may be looking for help and instead receives inquiries as to his or her eligibility for help (Zimmerman 1974). A rich person is shocked at the ungrateful attitude of a domestic servant, or a maid sees the loose change about the house as part of her tip and is "surprised" at her dismissal. We have no way of knowing how many conflicts are rooted in these kinds of distorted communications. We can only guess the number is considerable. Understanding the difficulties of cross-ranked communications, however, leads to another discovery: if competition depends on rendering all aspects of social life irrelevant, save those specific to an immediate goal, and if ranking increases relevant differences (generalizing about those outside of the rank and differentiating among those within it), competition across rankings must be very difficult to accomplish.

Since parties to the exchange do not share the same perspectives, inter-rank interactions are almost always exploitive. Each party must find ways to use the other. This is so because people who occupy different ranks have different access to reward. The rich man will not become poor to understand poverty. Nor will the social worker become a client to experience "depersonalization." The essence of ranking itself is inequality. Equality is a within-domain prerequiste for communication. That is, it is an ideal from which distinctions are made. Within the domain of status inequality is a given. The dominate party has what the dominated party wants. Staff and the police have freedom, the inmates and the tramps want it. The rich have money and the poor want it. The business person wants profit and the consumer wants lower costs. Therefore, it is the strategies for "getting what one can" which characterize stratified interacting in modern society.

In today's world, we have committed ourselves to competitive inequality. However, there is a paradox in our intentions. The more such competition becomes a reality, the less stratified the society should become since, presumably, everybody is "good at something." However, the meanings of inequality are embedded within the stratified society. The

"Quality care is our career". These nurses are on strike to raise the status of their jobs. While they do not share equal status with the physicians with whom they work, their absence from their hospital jobs underscores how essential they are to health-care services. What does the act of going on strike tell us about the relative status of being a member of the nursing profession?

very system that established inequality precludes the possibility for "competitively established equality." To compete requires a leveling of life experiences. Professional football players compete; they dominate lesser players. A con-man exploits his mark, and computer-dating salespeople become wealthy while their clients still search for the ideal mate. Friends can communicate, and teachers can lecture. Women can understand each other, and blacks are brothers and sisters. Social identities come, in part, from "places" within a preconstituted social system. We work out the meanings of interaction. The circumstances of this work vary from those conducive to understanding, cooperation, and competition to those that promote misunderstanding and exploitation.

Can there be a social order which differentiates according to ability and promotes fair competition? Can there be a society without exploitation? This question has produced a continuous debate. On the one side are those who claim stratified systems are necessary to any social organization, and hence, a society of equals is an impossibility (Davis and Moore 1945).

On the other side of the question are those who criticize the systems of inequality for creating artificial and unnecessarily invidious comparisons among various members of society (Tumin 1957). True to our descriptive charge, we can say only that modern American society rests on rather strong ideas of fairness and competition. However, when we look at how rewards are actually distributed, we can not help but notice the inequality. Accommodative relationships have been consistently rejected by our legal system as well as by those who have been accommodated in the past, minorities and women provide the clearest example of this reaction. However, past accommodations to minorities were mixed in the sense that exploitive processes also operated. A profound problem of our social order is how to allow competition and still preserve complexity and richness in the knowledge and action systems that we created by living within a stratified society.

SUMMARY

This chapter dealt with the questions of inequality in social interaction. Through a descriptive approach which appreciates the relative nature of comparisons, the importance of the concept of domain was discussed. The meanings of inequality were analyzed according to three social processes: competition, exploitation, and accommodation. We learned how comparisons may be thought of as invidious, and how people understand their relative position in social worlds in terms of principles of comparison. Finally, mechanisms of discrimination were illustrated and shown as resulting from the different socialization experiences of people variously located in society.

The deeply rooted existence of inequality is dramatically revealed in exchanges between persons of different rank, and in situations where rank seems incongruently arranged. It is important to recognize the roots of inequality in order to function most efficiently in society and continue to negotiate a more reasonable social order.

People understand themselves as members of ranked systems of activities. The sense they make of this ranges from a competitive, through an accommodative to an exploitive version of what happens. We conclude that people transform their rankings into forms of interaction. These forms function to place them, in the judgments of others and of themselves, in larger social contexts which they, in turn, make sense of. Inequality, at least for the time being, is an essential meaning of social life, or, as it were, a fact of life.

EXERCISES FOR UNDERSTANDING
INEQUALITY IN INTERACTION

1. Most all of us, male or female, has had experiences in organized sports. Donald Ball analyzed "failure" in sports in terms of the social organization of the sport. Hence, failure in baseball means something quite different from failure in football. Recall an experience in your life where you "failed" to achieve a goal in sports. What happened to you? What were the circumstances of your failure and how did you make sense of it? Relate your account of what the failure meant in the organization of the activity itself. The contemporary writer Michael Novak once remarked that one of the most important lessons of sports is to learn to lose. If you think about what he might of meant by this, you can get some ideas about the relationship between failure and the organization of competitive activities.

2. In an exercise for chapter four, you listed friends you had in the past and ranked them in order of their influence on your early sense of selfhood and identity. Go back to that material. See if you can rank the groups of names into some kind of status arrangement. State what the criteria are from saying why there is a rank, and expand this exercise to a description of what the status world of this period of life was like. For example, many high school students rank their fellow students into status hierarchies. My own experience was with "sosies" and "greasers," or Southsiders and Northsiders. These designations reflected an entire social status system.

3. On most college campuses, there are observable differences in the physical surroundings, equipment, and other accoutrements of academic departments. Visit at least three academic departments on your campus, and take notes on the environs. Pay attention to details like the conditions of walls, floors, and carpets; note whether there is art work and expensive equipment. Visit one department in the division of physical sciences, one representing the social sciences, and one in the humanities. Can you tell anything about the system of inequality from these observations?

KEY CONCEPTS

Systems of relevancy
Domains
Stratification system
Competition
Exploitation
Invidious comparison
Accommodation
Class
Status
Ascribed and achieved inequality
Code switching
Modal and cross-modal communications
Impression of rank
Hypercorrection
Undercorrection
Immediacy, practicality, and similarity

SUGGESTED READINGS

In sociology proper, there are technical and varied theoretical books on stratification. This text stresses the meanings of inequality from the viewpoint of the people who experience it. Hence, I suggest three readings which artfully and accurately convey a sense of lived-through experience of inequality. In his widely respected book, *You Owe Yourself a Drunk*, Spradley describes the complicated and often misunderstood world of the tramp. Carol Stack, in her controversial book, *All Our Kin*, ties the social organization of life, particularly family life, to the interactional strategies necessary to cope with being at the bottom of the status system in American society. Last, Wolf offers an entertaining and descriptive account of the "lower class" practice of car customizing in his highly successful book *The Kandy-Kolored, Tangerine-Flake, Streamlined Baby*.

Spradley, James P. *You Owe Yourself a Drunk: An Ethnography of Urban Nomads*. Boston: Little Brown, 1970.

Stack, Carol. *All Our Kin*. New York: Harper and Row, 1974.

Wolfe, Tom. *The Kandy-Kolored, Tangerine-Flake, Streamlined Baby*. New York: Farrar, Straus and Giroux, 1965.

Chapter Nine

Gender and Sexual Identity

OUTLINE

BIOLOGICAL BASIS FOR SEXUAL IDENTITY

GENDER DIFFERENCES IN PLAY

GENDER DISPLAYS
Talking Like a Woman

SEXISM AND LANGUAGE
Mothers and Daughters

MALES AND FEMALES TOGETHER
Power in Dating Relationships
Messages of the Body

HOW DO I LOVE THEE?

SUMMARY

EXERCISES IN UNDERSTANDING THE MEANINGS OF GENDER

KEY CONCEPTS

SUGGESTED READINGS

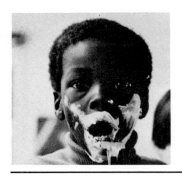

Gender and
Sexual Identity

A popular television situation comedy, "One Day at a Time," recently aired a program dealing with the home delivery of a baby. The mother, Julie, was portrayed as trendy, wanting to try the latest techniques to bring an infant into the world in the most peaceful fashion possible. Although she was not able to deliver "underwater," she did experience the joys of uncomplicated, home delivery. Among the characters in the program is a macho janitor named Schneider, who has some rather old-fashioned, stereotypical ideas which clash in episode after episode, as he encounters the new world of single parents, independent women, and sexual equality.

In this particular show, he enters the room shortly after Julie gives birth. Julie's husband, who is in bed with her, her sister, her sister's husband, and Julie's mother and grandmother fill the small bedroom. All are jubilant and tranquil as they feel a close emotional bond with the beginning of a new life. Schneider's voice is heard asking, "Is it a girl or a boy?" No one replies. He repeats his question with more urgency. Finally, as if to silence this voice of practicality and to satisfy the demands of convention, Julie's mother answers, "It's a girl."

As this example suggests, **sexual identity** is perhaps the primary attribute of the self. This conclusion is supported by a fascinating exercise in which a researcher dressed a research assistant in a green bag. The bag reached from head to toe and completely concealed the assistant. There were holes in the bag through which she could see. The bag sat in a classroom during a regular class, and moved about the halls of the classroom building between classes.   The researcher and the bag assistant were attempting to expose the basic assumptions people make about each other.   In interviews with those who had encountered the bag, and through observing the reactions of people to it, the researcher and her assistant found that a primary concern of those who tried to contact the bag was not so much what it was, or what was going on, but what *sex* was it? Much of what we have learned about how to get along with each other depends on the assignment of sexual identity (Nelson and Jorgensen 1975).

In the modern world, the meanings of sexual identity have become ambiguous, and there may be a rather remarkable amount of negotiation possible about what it means to be a male or female.   Still, sharp differences exist even if they are regarded as vestiges of more traditional ways of deciding the meanings of personhood.   That Julie's baby is healthy, wanted, and loved overshadows, in her modern mind, the classification of "boy" or "girl".

This chapter describes the ways in which people acquire identities associated with biological sex.   I will stress the arbitrary features of these processes in an attempt to understand what it means to have a "gender."

BIOLOGICAL BASIS FOR SEXUAL IDENTITY

Although there are obvious and important physical differences between sexes, a biological argument is inadequate to explain these differences.   In fact, whenever scholars and laymen have attempted to tie specific behaviors to a biological basis, they end up with weak connections.   Even health statistics, which have shown females to be somewhat resistant to certain illnesses, and hence to have longer life expectancies, change with the social roles women play.   The most dramatic indication of the association between sex and health is the rapid and alarming increase in the rate of lung cancer for women (US Health Statistics 1978).   Thirty years ago, relatively few women died of this disease.   Now, although their rate of death is still below those of males, with more women smoking at earlier ages, the chances of a woman dying of lung cancer are fast approaching those of a man.   These grim statistics as well as those for heart diseases, strokes, and rising crime rates, (especially for violent crimes for women offenders) clearly show that social influences operate equally on both sexes.

A recent study provides very strong evidence for this conclusion.   It indicates smoking is the principal factor for the differential in life expectancies for males and females.   A study in Erie, Pa. of people who died between 1972 and 1974 found that men who had never smoked and who did not die violently (by homicide, suicide, or accident) had roughly the same life expectancies as women.   The researchers conclude:

when...women who have smoked as much as men reach the later decades of life...our study suggests that their lives will be shortened as much as men's and that the present differences in longevity between men and women will disappear (Quoted in the *St. Paul Dispatch,* August 11, 1983).

It turns out *social* influences affect almost every aspect of what we think of as **sex-related behaviors**. The early research of Margaret Mead on sex-related behaviors showed that aggression, power, and carelessness (male traits in our culture) were found as typical traits for females in some cultures. There seems to be little, if any, direct link between the content of action and sex. Throughout this text it has been stressed how the meanings of behavior derive from culture and society rather from any intrinsic physical feature of an act. The opening example of the incident with the heart attack victim in Mexico City is one such example.

However strong the evidence against biologically determined behaviors, every known society marks the differences between males and females socially. The early anthropologist George Peter Murdock cataloged activities in societies around the world and found that those activities which required leaving the home were typically male while those which were either conducted in the home or close to it were female.

Murdock's data (exemplified in Table 9.1) are quite valuable for showing both patterns of sexually divided tasks and the rich diversity of what males and females do. However, his data depict pre-modern societies which, to a great extent, no longer exist. When we turn our attention to modern society, we see that such divisions of labor by sex do still exist (secretaries and nurses vs. construction workers and university presidents), but there is an undeniable trend in modern society to increase the choices that individuals have, especially in occupations they wish to pursue. As Berger (1979) writes, the extension of choice has reached sexuality itself:

Thus even sexuality can now be experienced as an arena of individual choices. All one has to do to grasp the dramatic change this entails is to try and explain to, say, an Indonesian—even a Western-educated intellectual—what Americans mean when they speak of "sexual life-styles"! The outcome of such an effort is likely to be not disapproval or revulsion but puzzlement if not sheer incomprehension (Berger, 1979: 16).

Human sexuality varies considerably from culture to culture and within the options of choice exercised by members of modern society. Human sex is fixed by biology, but even the boundaries of biology can be modified by modern medical technology. Gender seems not so much a given set of biological conditions but "the socially constructed identities bestowed and presented through sexual appearance" (Weigert 1983, 239).

Having said all of this, we must be emphatic about not drawing the conclusion that people can literally decide their gender. Some notable cases like Agnes, whom Garfinkel (1967) studied, seem to warrant that conclusion. She came to the University of California Los Angeles Medical Center during the 1960s and, though biologically a male, convinced physicians that she deserved a sex-change operation. She accomplished this largely through a selective retelling of her childhood experiences, focusing on how she functioned socially as a female, even though she actually had male genitalia. Subsequent investigation revealed she had some help from

Table 9.1 Number of Societies and Sex of Person Performing Selected Activities

Activities	Men's Work	Either Sex	Women's Work
Hunting	179	0	0
Trapping Small Animals	141	4	3
Herding	46	4	5
Fishing	132	19	7
Preparing and Planting Soil	54	33	57
Tending and Harvesting Crops	25	35	83
Cooking	6	9	186
Basket Making	28	10	88
Weaving	21	2	73
Making and Repairing Clothing	15	8	194

Adapted from G. P. Murdock, "Comparable Data on the Division of Labor by Sex," *Social Forces* (1935): 551–553.

medical science and from a friend. It seems her mother purchased female hormones for her which she took to enhance her female appearance.

Agnes is clearly an extreme illustration. Few of us exercise this degree of control over our sexual identity. Rather the effects of socialization, of years of experience as a member of one or the other sex, promote in most of us an uncritical acceptance of our appearance and environment as "naturally" male or female.

Although women are gaining fuller and more complete participation in all aspects of life in modern society, this does not mean gender differences will become insignificant. By reviewing some of the literature which documents precisely how gender differences show up in situations of everyday life, we can more fully appreciate their significance.

First we will look at research on the play of children; then, we will discuss the differences in the display of emotions by females and males in American society. Finally, we will discover the subtle but profound differences in speaking performances of men and women.

GENDER DIFFERENCES IN PLAY

One of the most reliable ways to find out about something is to watch it happen. If we are interested in the differences between girls and boys in modern society, a powerful way to document these differences is by observing their natural occurrence. Janet Lever (1976; 1978) conducted a research project which consisted primarily of simply watching children play. She focused on a group of fifth graders, aged ten to eleven, in a Connecticut town. In addition to watching them play, she interviewed

Many of the ideas we have about appropriate gender behaviors are learned early in life and are strong and enduring. What meanings of manhood is this boy learning while he searches for his idol?

them, administered a semi-structured questionnaire, and kept daily diaries of the children's play activities. She wanted to show what children do when they are relatively uninhibited by adults or other figures of authority. Like many of the early social psychologists, she chose "play" as the arena for her observations.

By developing elaborate categories for classifying the content and organization of the children's play, she noticed differences between the girls and the boys. Her findings can be summarized as six generalizations: first, boys play outdoors far more than girls; second, although both boys and girls play alone about the same amount of time, when they were involved in social play boys more often played in large groups; third, boys' play occurs in more age-heterogeneous groups, meaning that they play in groups composed of older and younger boys while girls preferred groups of girls their own age; fourth, girls more often play in predominantly male games than boys play in girls' games, an example being that girls play baseball more than boys play jacks; fifth, boys play competitive games more often than girls; and sixth, boys' games last longer than do girls'.

Lever's study shows girls are more imaginative and interested in other people being involved in their play than boys are, and boys, indeed, are more rough-and-tumble. These findings do not imply that boys are "by nature" more active than girls. In fact, most social psychologists believe such differences in play reflect the definitions of self which the children learn from parents and the wider social worlds in which they participate.

Kohlberg (1969) theorizes that children form an image based on what they have observed and have been told about what it means to be a boy or girl. Those features which are most visible and easiest to understand make up the child's viewpoint. A child's gender role conceptions are sketches—oversimplified, exaggerated and stereotyped. Their play reflects these ideas even if they are not totally accurate. Kohlberg illustrates by relating a story about one of the girls he studied. She was a four-year-old girl, who insisted that only boys become doctors, even though her own mother was a physician.

The notion that the child's understanding of his or her social world shapes concepts of gender is known as **self-socialization.** According to the exponents of this theory, there is a critical period for acquiring a sense of gender. By age six, some argue, a child's gender identity is already fixed and provides an organizing focus for social interaction. Allan Katcher (1955) reports that four- or five-year-olds cannot assemble dolls by sex anatomically, but they know the categories of "boy" and "girl" exist and can identify with their own gender category.

The essential portion of Kohlberg's theory differs from an exchange perspective which suggests society rewards children for "sexually meaning-ful" behaviors. Kohlberg believes, instead, that self-attribution comes first—hence the thought sequence, "I am a boy, therefore, I want to do boy things, therefore, the opportunity to do boy things (and to gain approval for them) is rewarding."

An exhaustive survey of the literature dealing with sex differences seems to support the self-socialization explanation. Maccoby and Jacklin (1975) conclude that available data seem to fit with the theory. They cite, for example, research which demonstrates children are not directly affected by the behavior of their parents. A boy will choose to play with cars and trucks even though he may see his mother drive a truck. Girls play hopscotch and jacks even though they do not see their mothers doing so.

GENDER DISPLAYS

Males and females present themselves to others in fundamentally different ways. Goffman (1979) show us how we can understand the differences between the sexes by turning our attention to what he calls "**gender displays**," by which he means a behavior rooted in an emotional motivation. We have already learned society encourages different types of play for the sexes. Aggressiveness, assertiveness, and activity seem to us to be masculine. Likewise, we recognize the impression of nurture, of emotional sensitivity, and of domesticity in the female. The question Goffman raises concerns whether there are differences in how the details of everyday life are arranged by gender. He answers affirmatively and chooses to support his response by looking at the **display**. A display is an action that is simplified, even stereotyped, so that it can be recognized through almost any social context. The "smile," the "leer," the "seductive posture" are all examples of displays. A display communicates an emotional message to the person witnessing it. A gender display refers to "culturally established correlates of sex" which are "conventionalized portrayals of these correlates" (Goffman 1979, 1).

By analyzing advertisements from magazines and television, Goffman hopes to uncover the gender displays which are certainly there for the unmasking. He documents "the feminine touch," the "ritualization of subordination," and other meanings tacit in advertising. He observes that a woman's hands are seen just barely touching, holding or caressing—never grasping, manipulating or shaping. Men instruct women in these pictures of interactions between the sexes. Women recline more than men. The head or the eye of a man may be averted by some object or occurrence

These women seem to be doing a good job of holding this man's attention. Research on conversations between males and females indicates that this is often not the case. What conditions at the beach might result in the suspension of the ordinary rules of talk?

while female attention is usually on the man she is with. Women are shown as "drifting" mentally from the scene in which they are set while males are more physically in touch with their surroundings. Finally, women, more than men, are pictured at the kind of psychological loss or remove from a social situation such that one gets the impression they could not act.

Goffman's contribution in this analysis "is the continuous, ever-deepening connection he makes between our image of women and the behavior of children" (Gornick 1979, viii). According to his analysis, women are linked to children if not through the sense of family, then through the posture and attitudes that they are supposed to assume. The female display connotes "play," a lack of "seriousness," and a strong sense of the leisure and emotional context of private lives. Goffman does not argue that advertisements *cause* these displays in women, nor that the real world is accurately depicted in advertisements. However, he does write:

Although the pictures shown here cannot be taken as representative of gender behavior in real life...one can probably make a significant negative statement about them, namely, that as *pictures* they are not perceived as peculiar and unnatural (Goffman 1979, 27).

In everyday life, we see these displays. That is why we know them in advertisements, and this is why those advertisements are effective and appealing to most of us. Women are typified as being able to cope with emotions but not to suppress them. The playthings of girls are not as mechanical, as manipulable as are those of boys. While at the same time, dolls for girls show the pleasurable side of ordinary life, but the fantastic creatures of outer space, the monsters of war and of galactic adventure are for boys.

A major part of gender learning, then, is learning how to present oneself in interactive exchanges. In American society, males are taught to control and master their surroundings, even if only in imagination. Females, on the other hand, are taught to invest in emotions and interpersonal relationships. Such differential socialization results in varying rates of interest in the objects and happenings of the social world. Boys tend to occupy themselves with their bicycles, exciting play, or more recently, the family computer. Girls, while also interested in bicycles and computers, are focused on friendships, matters of reputation, and the displays of these concerns.

A recent study of video games and arcades produced results which support these generalizations. Not only do males play these games more than girls, male games predominate in the video world (Kaplan 1983). Games appealing to boys are Defender, Joust, NATO Command and Zaxxon, games with violent themes and requiring a great deal of concentration and practice. Defender, for example, has five separate controls. Older games like Asteroids also have stick controls (joy sticks) and several buttons to control fire and movement of the space vehicle. Games like

Roads to manhood. Why do you suppose that racing games are so popular among young boys?

Zaxxon have graphics which offer the illusion of a third dimension. In order to play well, the player must learn to see depth in the graphics. At one point in the flight of the craft, the pilot must maneuver his craft through a hole in a wall. Although there are aids to "seeing" the opening, a player must accumulate considerable experience at the game in order to fly effortlessly through the openings in the walls.

On the other hand, games which have themes of everyday life, chase-and-run games, like Pac Man, Frogger, and Ms Pac Man do not require as much engrossment with the game and do seem to have a greater appeal for female players. Although these generalizations may seem strong, Kaplan reports the results of a survey he conducted with 430 male and female college students. He found that women acknowledged their lower level of skill as compared to male players, and his findings revealed, as other observational studies have shown, that at arcades, although girls are present and playing, it is the boys who amass top scores and who are engrossed in the difficult games that invariably have military and space themes.

To find out why this sex difference exists, Kaplan conducted another survey. He speculated that perhaps females saw arcades as undesirable places, and because of this interpretation simply avoided them. His data did not support this conclusion. In fact, he discovered that females gave arcades a generally favorable evaluation seeing them as relatively safe places to go for having fun. He accounted for the strikingly significant male presence in the video world in terms of differential socialization. Females thought the males were simply being "macho" while playing the games. On the other hand, "females were seen as being more interested in activities conventionally defined as being appropriate to females" (Kaplan 1983, 98); hence, females saw males' intense involvement in play as "wasteful." They repeatedly said they preferred shopping to playing video games in mall arcades. According to this study, we would not be far off the mark by saying that boys go to arcades to play, and the girls go there to meet boys.

It appears that even in the 1980s among college students, some stereotypical ideas about gender still operate to explain differences in behavior. Men are seen as game-oriented, interested in science and machines, and relatively unconcerned with what others think about them. Women are defined as more conventional, focused on social relationships, and less apt to become engrossed in a world as artificial and plastic as the video arcade.

Although the names of the games will surely change, and those whose business it is to predict, create, and sell to the youthful consumer will work hard to extend the appeal of video games, the differentiation of emotions and activities by sex seems to be deeply ingrained in American society. Changes occur and opportunities for educational and professional development broaden, but these social trends do not seem to signal the demise of gender.

We return to a point made by Goffman. Women are associated with children in American society in ways that run deep into the meanings of self. Goffman means more than just the association of women and children in commonsense thinking. He exposes very subtle processes and comparisons that go on in both same sex and cross-sex interactions.

Talking like a Woman

In some provocative, exploratory research, West and Zimmerman (1975; 1977) present evidence from their study of the naturally occurring talk of men and women showing how the speech behaviors of the females they studied resemble that of children talking with adults.

Of course, they do not mean women literally talk like children. Instead, they show certain features of conversations to be like those of adult-child interactions. They examine interruptions, turn taking, the length of silences, and intonation patterns.

When men and women converse, generally men interrupt more than women. Likewise, the degree to which a man will arrange his comments so that they overlap those of a woman is greater than that for women.

Women remain silent for longer interludes in cross-sex conversations than men. Finally, there is a definite "female" habit of raising one's voice at the end of an exclamation. When making an assertion, one usually drops the tone of one's voice at the end of it. It is possible, of course, to speak the assertion as if it were a question. Hence, one can say, "I told you that paper was incorrectly punctuated!" Or, "I told you that paper was incorrectly punctuated?"

In another research project by Fishman (1979) tape recorders were placed in the apartments of three couples. The couples were aware of the recorders and could control when they operated. After several weeks, Fishman was able to collect a considerable body of ordinary conversations between men and women. She found women asked questions nearly three times as often as men, and they used the question as a device to ensure continued talk. "Know what?" and "Do you know what?" were common forms used by women to open conversations. They used this type of attention-getting device twice as often as men.

Women also tended to use conversational fillers such as "yeah," and "huh" more frequently than men. From these data, it appears they used

Cross-gender conversations are often intimate in style. However, even in a conversation this close and this personal, misunderstandings can develop because of differing conversational skills. Can you imagine some of the ways in which this couple might misunderstand each other?

these methods of talking in two ways: first, they used them at the end of the man's statement to discourage interaction, and second, they punctuated conversations at pauses to encourage more talk. Whereas women's short responses tended to come *during* the man's turn at talk, men's short responses marked *the end* of the woman's turn. Fishman believes these data illustrate the kind of work that women must do in cross-sex interactions. Women, she argues, must do *extra* work to ensure that topics of their choice get talked about. Without this effort, women's interests become subordinated to those of the men they are with. The parallel to the position children occupy with adults is obvious.

Although Fishman and West and Zimmerman report preliminary results often based on less than representative samplings, their findings are quite interesting and provocative. Generally, they describe **asymmetrical conversations**, and they take this situation to be a reflection of unequal power relationships. At this point, we might conclude that we are simply looking at male dominance. Certainly, such dominance does show up in many relationships. However, gender differentiation can be very subtle, and its consequences need not be intentional. A man may be following what he unreflexively regards as his usual manner of speaking, while a female may likewise follow her conceptions of what makes for ordinary talking. The practical results, what the conversation brings to both parties, may be something else.

Handel (1982) offers an alternative interpretation of the data on cross-sex conversations. He examines West and Zimmerman's data and finds that what appears to be a one-sided exchange between a man and a woman may not be as asymmetrical as one might think. Men do interrupt women, but this does not mean they will be successful in changing the topic of talk. In fact, the very same data we just reviewed indicate that the interrupted topic was typically *reintroduced* later in the conversation by the female. It seems, then, that men and women react differently to interruptions. Men, when interrupted, tend to move on to new topics. Women, on the other hand, are much more persistent, reintroducing their topic in conversation when the opportunity arises.

Handel suggests that these studies demonstrate that conversational style is an important way in which men and women differ, and that styles can become a central medium for getting what one wants. However, he points out there are many unresolved questions about the asymmetry of talking between males and females. He writes, "it is not clear whether women acquiesce in the abridgment of their rights relative to men's" (Handel 1982, 144). What we may be observing are very different rules for conversing, the implementation of both the male and female versions:

Suppose, now that men and women define the word "enough" differently as it applies to various qualities of talk. If men, on average, preferred less talk than women and if men and women applied the two conversation-limiting norms without attention to the sex of others in the conversation, all the observed phenomenon would occur. Women would tend to talk more than men would prefer.   That should lead to less frequent encouragement by men to continue, more interruptions by men, and less frequent follow-ups by men on proposed topics. Men would tend to talk less than women prefer.   That should lead to fewer interruptions by women, to more frequent encouragement by women to continue, to more frequent follow-ups by women on proposed topics, and to the reintroduction by women of interrupted topics.   Also, since these quantitative preferences are linked to gender, conversations between people of the same sex ought to display less asymmetry.   People would still interrupt one another but would do so approximately equally (Handel 1982, 145).

What is significant for us in Handel's explanation is the proposition about how following rules which are quite functional in one situation can produce unintended results in another.   Handel tells us how simply "doing what comes natural" can create interactive situations characterized by gender inequality.

We have emphasized throughout this book the primary role consciousness and active thought play in social life.   Now, it might appear we are saying something else; however, that is not the case.   While it is true that asymmetrical conversational situations are the unintentional consequences of following rules, this does not imply "mindless" sexist practices.   What Handel suggests has to do with minds at work, minds molded from the different gender worlds because the learning experiences of males and females reflect many subtle and tacit differences in their socialization.

Something as seemingly trivial as how a man and woman talk to each other can embody years of habits and, indeed, actual skills—skills which differ by gender learning.

The question to which we can now turn is to what extent merely being a man or woman has consequences reinforcing gender and sexual identity. Whenever we describe practices so wide-spread in society they are taken for granted, and so uncritically a part of ordinary life that people simply do not recognize their results, we are dealing with what many social scientists refer to as **institutionalized practices**.   We have already learned how institutions can be conceived as ready-made formulas for the solution of the problems of everyday life.   Now we want to examine the degree to which these solutions create other sets of problems.   The issue at hand is **sexist language**, and what its use means to both men and women.

SEXISM AND LANGUAGE

Language acts as a social mirror.   It reflects the images and common sense thinking of the members of society.   Adams and Ware (1979) outline what they believe are the images of women implicit in the English language. These images, of course, represent centuries of language use in which the practicalities of everyday life work their way into the very fabric of language.

Words used to refer to women are apparently "sexually weighted."   In particular, nouns seem to impart a strong sexual imagery to women.   For example, consider the noun pair *master-mistress.* Both of these words refer to someone who possesses or has power over someone or something else, as in "He is the master of his fate," or "She is the mistress of a great fortune." Still, in the vernacular, only the word *mistress* acquired a sexual connotation. "Tom is Jane's master" does not imply sexuality while surely "Jane is Tom's mistress" does.

In a recent study of slang, one researcher (Schultz 1975) found over five hundred synonyms for prostitute but only sixty-five for the masculine sexual term whoremonger. Indeed, the latter term seems outdated and strange while the former is as contemporary as "gnarly." There are literally thousands of phrases and words that describe women in sexually derogatory ways in English. Nothing like this number exists for describing male sexuality.

Schultz (1975) traced changes in the meaning of words which were once neutral in sexual meanings but have come to have negative sexual meanings for women. Some of her examples are hussy (an old English word which meant "female head of the household"), spinster (which originally meant someone who operated a spinning wheel), broad (which referred to a young woman), and tart and bibby (once terms of endearment, according to Schultz).

In another study, Adams and Ware (1979) suggest the quite excessive vocabulary available to English speakers for denigrating women's sexuality mirrors society's institutionalized sexism. Although there may be other interpretations of this imbalance in slang terms for male and female sexuality, it does point to the existence of typifications, widely distributed in society. These typifications can not cause sexist behavior, but they may serve as the basis for actual interactive encounters. This means, of course, that whatever built-in tendencies there are at the start of an encounter between men and women become apparent in practical outcomes.

Adams and Ware also suggest the English language trivializes women. We have already explicated some of the meanings of the association of women with children. Now we build on those observations by noting that children, while certainly essential to society, are assigned trivial roles. Women suffer a kind of guilt by association. For instance, calling adult females "girls" has a trivializing effect; girls are small, immature, and irresponsible. In fact, Adams and Ware argue that it is only in matters of marriage and a few female-dominated professions where female terms are primary. Whenever males do participate in these female domains, we see the unusual linguistic practice of modifying with a male term, hence male nurse, or male mid-wife.

Peter Trudgill, a English sociolinguist, has researched yet another way in which males differ from females in both their language performances and their attitudes toward language. He found that women are much more concerned with the proper use of English than their male counterparts. Regardless of socio-economic status, women speak in ways that come closer to correct speech. Specifically, Trudgill looked at such common language mistakes as the use of the double negative, nonstandard pronunciations of words, and the use of slang.

In middle-class families, the mother will typically function as the keeper of proper speech. She will correct the sentences of her children, making sure "don't" doesn't show up where "doesn't" should. Fathers, however, have more lenient attitudes toward the latest teenage vernacular, and seem more comfortable with jargon terms introduced into everyday life.

Trudgill provides strong support for observations about the female concern for correct speaking. He conducted a study of Norwich English (a form of British English) and found that indeed women did use the more prestigious and more nearly standard form of their language to a much greater degree than did the men. However, when he measured their actual speaking performances, he discovered that, in fact, women did use nonstandard forms of talking and did depart from the standard in their own talk.

This poses an interesting question. Were the women aware of their departures from the standards? He asked them, and found they were less accurate judges of their actual speech behaviors than were their male counterparts. In other words, they perceived their own speech in terms of the norms they were aiming for, not the ones they actually followed; hence, they consistently under-reported their use of slang, double negatives and other nonstandard usages, and over-reported their use of "correct" pronunciation, subject-verb and pronominal agreements. Males, on the other hand, seemed to be rather good judges of the extent to which their speech was or was not "correct."

Trudgill (1974) interprets these findings according to the social context of gender. Women, he contends, identify with the main institutions of society (family, church and community), while men seek a sense of who they are through their involvement in the world of work and friends. The pub, the shipping dock, the male world of leisure and work are all removed from the home, church, and community. The male derives his sense of self from the small worlds in which he lives, worlds which to him are clearly not integrated with the ongoing concerns of the larger institutions of society. Of course, vernaculars are created and used in such small worlds. Slang and other nonstandard ways of talking give men a strong sense of "class" identity. His female counterpart is largely excluded from his small worlds. She identifies with what she understands as the basic institutions of society. Ironically, women seem to anchor judgments of their performances in the very institutions which perpetuate sexism.

Social psychologists who study language usages do not suggest that language causes sexism. They also avoid the simple linkage between thought and language that some early thinkers like Benjamin Whorf (1956) expounded. It is not so much how we talk that perpetuates sexism. If we use language in an uncritical fashion, simply applying formulas as we find them, then the consequences of our actions might favor one person's definitions of the situation over another on the basis of gender alone. Patterned language performances are data which tell us about the relationship between society and self. The remarkable and subtle gender differences in language use are properly seen as reflections of changing and often confused versions of the meanings of gender.

Mothers and Daughters

How we experience various stages of life as well as our relationships with others is conditioned by the larger society of which we are a part. Any given social relationship, then, must be seen in its larger context. When discussing gender and its significance, a major portion of our task is to see how the societal definitions of gender have an effect on the actual lives of people.

In our society, middle age seems to be a particularly stressful time for women. Pauline Bart (1979) wondered about whether this was true in other cultures. She examined anthropological evidence and discovered "in each culture there is a favored stage of the life cycle of a woman" (1979, 246). In many societies, women actually enjoy higher status during the middle period of their lives. However, in almost every case, a woman's prestige in her middle years was bound-up in the meanings of kinship for her society. Bart summaries her finding in the form of a chart (Table 9.2) which she uses to discuss the life experiences of a middle-class, American, Jewish mother who suffers as a long-distance mother.

Table 9.2   Status Change Due to Age

Raised Status in Middle Age	Lowered Status in Middle Age
Strong tie to parents, siblings and other kin	Marital tie stronger than tie to nuclear family
Extended-family system	Nuclear-family system
Reproduction important	Sex an end itself
Strong mother-child relationship reciprocal in later life	Weak maternal bond, adult-oriented culture
Institutionalized grandmother role	Noninstitutionalized grandmother role, grandmother role unimportant
Institutionalized mother-in-law role	Noninstitutionalized mother-in-law role, mother-in-law does not train daughter-in-law
Extensive menstrual taboos	Minimal menstrual taboos
Matrilocal, patrilocal or duolocal residence pattern	Residence pattern that isolates women from kin and grown children
Age valued over youth	Youth valued over age

Source: Pauline Bart, "The Loneliness of the Long-Distance Mother," in Jo Freeman (ed.) *Women: A Feminist Perspective,* Mayfield Publishing Company, 1979.

Table 9.2 condenses basic societal meanings. It summarizes the materials given to individuals with which they begin the arduous processes of making sense out of the life situations in which they find themselves. Certainly, some people are more creative than others in using interpretive materials. Bart interviewed twenty women who were not very successful in how they applied the "stocks-of-knowledge" available to them. They were all in mental hospitals having been put there because of their inability to deal with their lowered status as mothers and women. These women expressed themselves through depression and physical disorders. One, Sara, told her story.

Sara saw herself as a martyr to her children who did not reciprocate for the "sacrifices" she made as their mother. She tied her impressive list of physical ailments to how difficult her life was as a mother. She was divorced and resentful of the freedom and lack of responsibility she imagined her former husband to have. She felt her past accomplishments as a Jewish mother had failed her. Much of her frustration and confusion focused on her daughter who, in her mind, had abandoned her to a cruel and cold medical profession.

Bart links Sara's case to a larger study she conducted on the social and psychological profiles of middle-aged women who experience medical and psychological trouble. She discovered that Sara was typical. Many of the women she studied had had successful husbands; and their children, by conventional account, had succeeded. Their sons had "good" jobs, and their daughters "good" marriages. Not only this, but they seemed to have daughters who continued some version of a mother-daughter relationship through phone calls and visits. What was wrong; why did an apparently valued life course turn sour, ending in divorce and tragic hospitalization?

In her explanation, Bart stresses the strong sense of loss these women feel. Psychologically, they did not think their children owed them anything, but they nevertheless felt resentment. Socially, they felt they had nothing to live for.

Bart draws on Durkheim who explained how societies which foster an extensive sense of individualism (**egoism**) and which are undergoing rather rapid social change (**anomie**) can produce life situations that provoke a strong sense of loss. Although not everyone responds the same way to relatively uniform social pressures, if these pressures are generally present in society, they will show up in disproportionate numbers among persons subject to them. This is precisely what Bart observed. Women who had performed well and derived a sense of self from their roles as mothers discovered they had little else when they reached the phase of life where mothering skills were devalued in favor of skills of independency and individualism.

Although there must be similar experiences of social loss with the decreased importance of roles of fatherhood, most men have built relationships outside of the family in ways that earlier generations of women did

The solitude of gender. The consequences of gender roles are often unexpected. Perhaps, this is a picture of a long-distance mother.

not. As Durkheim would have said, the male is buffered from the impact of the loss of one role by his involvement in many others. In fact, the very middle-age period which turns out to be so stressful for the tradition-al woman is often a productive and rewarding period for the male.

MALES AND FEMALES TOGETHER

In the last section of this chapter, we want to look at the dynamics of gender interactions. Many situations of everyday life require that gender identities be suppressed; at least, one is not always supposed to interact with a member of the opposite sex in ways which highlight the sexual meanings which are so basic to social life. It is curious that in modern society with its emphasis on individual choice, in work and public places interaction is supposed to be gender neutral. The adaptive capacity we have acquired through socialization allows most of us to bracket, on occasion, the years of gender learning we have accumulated and treat each other similarly regardless of sex. To see how remarkable such an accom-plishment is, we need only review how deeply ingrained gender discrimi-nation is in the common happenings of everyday life.

Power in Dating Relationships

Over the past several decades, the dating practices of young people in modern societies have changed dramatically. A short twenty years ago, males asked females for dates. Thus, the male decided what the couple would do on the date. He usually mentioned these activities in his invitation: "Would you like to go to the prom with me?" The customs of chivalry were somewhat alive in America in the 1950s. Boys opened doors for girls; they even walked around parked automobiles to perform this ritual. Most importantly, except for the occasional role reversal of the Sadie Hawkins Day, the male controlled the general outline of the date's activities. Of course, females were hardly without power. They used subtle interactive devices to get what they wanted, and were usually advised by their mothers to carry "mad money" which could be used to get home or call for help if one's date were to become so obnoxious that there was simply no recourse to "going one's own way," or if the trouble they encountered was beyond the young male's ability to cope. There can be little disputing the generalization that "traditional" dating was quite sexist by today's standards and that these practices, while still quite familiar in our society, have undergone thorough change.

In a recent survey study of the dating practices of college-age students, Peplau (1979) reports overwhelming numbers of both males and females endorsed egalitarian ideals in male/female relationships. On the other hand, when these same students were asked to what degree they believed they had achieved an equal-power relationship in their experiences with the opposite sex, fewer than half replied they had achieved this ideal. A closer examination of these students' attitudes revealed there was a considerable variation among their views of power in a dating relationship. By asking them questions about whose career, a husband's or a wife's, should have more importance in a marriage or who should do most of the driving on a family vacation Peplau was able to classify the students into traditional, moderate, and liberal categories regarding sex-role attitudes. She discovered that sex-role attitudes often have an important impact on the balance of power in dating relationships, but the effect is often not straightforward. It depends upon the "imbalance of involvement and resources" which describes the relationship the couple has. Generally, the person who is least involved or interested in a relationship will have greater influence.

Sociologist, Willard Waller (1951 as revised by Reuben Hill) calls this the **principle of least interest**. For these data, where the man was least involved, it was most common for the man to have more power. Similarly, when the woman was least involved, nearly half the couples reported that the woman had greater power. Among the many factors which influenced the power a person has in an intimate relationship were physical attractiveness, social skills, prestige or money. Among these physical attractiveness was quite important.

Some forms of play in society are related to gender identities.   Here a young woman uses a playful ploy to get a drink of pop from a youmg man in a very masculine posture.   What would your reaction be if you were the young man caught in the middle?

It seems that old, traditional male dominancy patterns in dating have changed among college-age students, but this does not mean that equality actually characterizes modern couples.   Instead, we find some "old-fashioned" ideas persist, and some new, individual ways to wield power have emerged.

A study of door-opening shows us how sex role changes can result in some fascinating new ways of negotiating the ordinary problems of male-female interactions.   Walum (1974) followed Goffman's lead and looked at the rituals of everyday life to see if how they are conducted tells us anything about changing sex roles.   She chose a little interaction ritual with which we are all familiar—that one which happens when a man and a woman approach a door at the same time.   Of course, the etiquette of past generations is clear about how to handle this situation: the male opens the door for the female.   Today with increased awareness of the "meanings" of daily rituals, as more and more women interpret the message of "passivity" in having doors opened for them, there may emerge what Goffman calls

deference-confrontation. This happens when the ideology of a ritual (in this case its patriarchical meanings) is no longer taken for granted. Where the ritual used to smooth interaction, it now highlights confrontation and places a premium on skills of negotiation.

Walum (1974) asked college students to keep journals documenting their experiences at doors. She analyzed these and discovered that this simple **door-opening ceremony** did contain informative materials. For example, some students, both males and females, reported a great deal of confusion about what they should do at the door. Some said they would try to time their approach to the door so that they would arrive clearly ahead or behind the member of the opposite sex. This maneuver avoided confrontation. When they did arrive simultaneously, some women reported the man would simply stare at them with a puzzled look on his face. Still others used a strategy Walum referred to as "testing." Here, the man would wait to see what the female expected of him. In one case, a woman reported that she simply asked the man to open the door for her, to which he replied, "I didn't know that girls still liked for boys to do that?" The woman answered, "Well, I'm not in Women's Lib."

In another case, Walum suggests that some males may have ulterior motives. A male student wrote in his journal:

It's almost like discovering a third sex to deal with liberated women. In the past I would make advances to my date almost as a matter of course. Now, I must "discover" if my date is sexually traditional or not before I decide on the conduct of our date. I can't just open doors and light cigarettes and expect to score (Walum 1974, 508).

According to Walum, there are three other typical reactions to the changing door ceremony: the **humanitarian**, the **defender**, and the **rebel**. The humanitarian is perhaps most consistent with what has been described as modern ways. These people see opening doors for each other as matters of necessity and consideration. They point out that a male should not "circle" a door to wait for a female, but neither should a female wait at the door for the male to open it. There are problems with this strategy, however. If a male acts in a way he regards as simply being considerate, some women may mistake his motives as sexist. If a female opens a door for a male who has his hands full of books, she may be seen as too forceful, and aggressive. Despite these problems, many males and females seem intent upon being humanitarian.

Defenders recognize social change but want no part of it. They go out of their way to act in ways that conform to the old etiquette; a male will walk faster to "beat" a female to the door, or a female will wait pensively at a door for a male to open it. Finally, rebels seem to know that change is taking place, but do not want to be associated with any possible new meanings; hence, they just act rudely. They seem to take pleasure in their sacrilege of the ceremony. A woman, for instance, reports that she purposely opened the door for a date whom she knew wanted to open it for her; "I never wanted to go out with him anyway, Ha!" she reported. Or in another instance, a male may gleefully not open doors for his date; one such student said: "I don't want to serve them just because they are women. If they had their heads screwed on right they wouldn't trade doing laundry for me lighting their cigarettes."

Walum interprets her findings as showing that we are now in a time of change and normlessness about relationships between sexes. If social order is dependent on the enactment of routines in daily life, and these seemingly insignificant acts carry the morality of society, then we may be in for a period of anomie with regard to male-female interactions. As patriarchal meanings become less dominant in interactions between the sexes, new substantive change in rules may emerge. Walum suggests that the new rules might require us to redefine some basic assumptions that ground routines. New rules might even bring "efficacy and joy" she writes.

Messages of the Body

Walum's research obviously examines nonverbal communication. When a man and woman confront each other in front of a door, they communicate through posture and gesture. In our society, we do a great deal of nonverbal communicating which is gender-related. The attitude of the body in the way men and women walk, throw a ball, or carry their arms, and even the very presence of our bodies have male and female meanings. Earlier in this chapter we learned how advertisements use these matters of gender to convey commercial messages. Now we turn to some clever research which attempts to describe precisely what the minute details of gender messages are.

John Spiegel and Pavel Machotka (1974) put together an unusual book which combines knowledge of great art with the experimental vigor of social psychology. Some of the great art works of western civilization reflect and may even have become standards for the assessment of messages of the body. What is it about a painting, a statue, or a photograph that tells the story? In an effort to be precise in their answer to this question, the authors developed what could be called **somatic categories**. They used various labels for the postures of bodies (approaching, contacting, manipulating), and they looked at the exact parts of the body that are accented in various messages, such as arms extended or the body rotated. They used elaborate schemes for classifying these messages of the body.

What is important is the application to which they put their schemes. After they explored famous art works and described them in terms of their schemes, Spiegel and Machotka then turned to the question of male-female encounters. They asked if it is possible to characterize certain postures of the body as female and others as male. To test this notion they used several techniques, among them showing students at an eastern university drawings depicting males and females together in various poses. Some of the drawings, for instance, showed a male figure standing with arms at his side; others, a female reclining with outstreched arms. There were seventy different sketches in all. Their colleague, Paul Williams, followed their investigations with a similar project. This time, however, the students were asked to set up small wooden manikins in various poses which they were asked to describe. Hence, they set up aggressive encounters between males and females, warm and cold encounters, encounters with the male receiving and the female receiving. Again, this project was quite exhaustive and yielded many comparisons. We can summarize the major findings of these two research projects as follows:

1. Female figures who extended their arms and torsos into the space in front of them were judged as erotic, active, aggressive, and determined.
2. Male figures who were seen as advancing received the most active evaluations, while male figures seen as retreating received the most passive evaluations.
3. All the female figures with outstretched arms were seen as action-initiating. When their legs pointed away from the man, all these qualities were accentuated.
4. When interpreting the nonverbal messages of these figures, men seem to have a tendency to project more than the women into the future and to see the interaction at an imagined subsequent time.
5. When instructed to set up manikin poses which were task-oriented, males and females differed little. However, when instructed to assess an inner motivation or state of mind in setting up the poses, men and women differed in the way they posed the manikins. It was the men who made strong male figures and weak passive females. Women, on the other hand, stressed themes of sharing and made their females more resisting in aggressive encounters. There were also significant differences in the way men and women used space, men made far encounters "calculating" while women saw calculation taking place in close encounters.

What this reseach demonstrates is that in ambiguous communicative settings, like the ones the researchers contrived, or like the one Walum describes at doors, people are presented with a challenge. This challenge is to figure out what is happening. They do this in the only way they know how, by reading into the situation what they expect. In the case of gender differences, we see that even highly educated people who espouse ideologies of equality and humanitarianism still must depend on the differential learning they have accumulated. In our society this learning is separated by gender differences.

A valid question is, if men and women are so vastly and subtly different, how do they ever get together for long-lasting relationships? Of course, in traditional societies, this question is not very relevant because the differences between men and women are ritualized and ceremonialized; men and women do not have to construct relationships with each other since that is already accomplished by the sharp sex roles that determine divisions of labor. In modern societies however, rituals are confused and people are indeed left to their own resources.

When a man and a woman build a relationship in modern society they are supposed to do so without regard to what we called in an earlier chapter "ascribed" status. As Berger and Kellner (1974) put it, the couple symbolically and socially build a new world in which they will live. Marriage and living together are the mechanisms for the construction of reality in modern society. What is the common bond which holds new relationships together? What is strong enough to bond persons of different backgrounds, interests, and learning experiences into a new social union? The answer is, of course, that "many splendored thing" called love. Love, or as we shall see, our interpretation of it, turns out to be, if not a particularly strong bonding agent, at least one that has significant practical consequences.

HOW DO I LOVE THEE?

The social psychologist does not attempt to define love. That task is best left to philosophers, theologians, and poets. What social psychology can do is depict the situations of interaction under which people believe they are in love. Judith Katz (1976) reviewed the literature on this topic and concluded that love situations are ones characterized by absorbing attention given to one another, by intimacy and thorough knowledge of one another, and by generosity and sacrifice. People who are absorbed in one another, who know each other well and who give and sacrifice for each other often say that they are in love.

Katz surmises that three conditions seem necessary for the perception that one person loves another. First, for a behavior to be taken as indicating love it must be perceived as initiated by the loving person. Second, it must fulfill a present desire of the loved person, and third it must appear to be motivated solely by the desire to please the loved one, with no intended benefit to the one trying to show love—that is, the act should appear selfless.

There are problems in the **perceptions of love**. When a man wants to show a woman that he loves her, he must know enough about her to avoid having to ask. For example, a man knows that his wife's birthday is soon approaching, he can not remember the exact date. He has forgotten to record it and does not know where to find it out. In order to plan the party he, with good intentions, wished to throw for her, he must ask her when her birthday is. Now he has violated the first condition of love; he has to ask which means that he really did not know, which means that perhaps he really does not love her.

Or, consider a second serious matter. He remembers the birthday but once again gives her a blouse that is too big and in her least favorite color. Katz suggests that we think of this problematic situation as "Now you ask?" or "A purple bow tie!" Or finally, there is the problem of simply being too much alike. Suppose the husband remembers his wife's birthday and gives her a present. However, if the present seems too much like something *he* wants, then the present loses its power to communicate love. Imagine as an example that the husband gives his wife a speed boat, or a new color television. Although these items might be desired, they do not carry the message of love because they seem too self-serving.

Katz points out that there is a real double-bind in the conditions of love. First, in order to know what to give to a person, how to behave toward them, one must know them well. In the process of getting to know another person, it is quite often the case that people discover they have similar likes and dislikes. The more compatible a couple is the more difficult it is to demonstrate love, since everything that is done can be seen by the other as self-serving. Simply, all this means that the conditions for the perception of love are contradictory and self-defeating. So how is it that couples love each other? Katz's answer is that at least one of the couple must believe in love itself. Love, she writes, is like an hypothesis; one must believe it is true to test it. Some people are skeptics, simply not believing in love, while others see love everywhere.

Love, it turns out, is like faith. You have it or you do not. It is, of course, not necessary to perceive love all of the time to know someone loves you. It is only necessary to see it enough. Katz concluded that what we usually call "loving" relationships, even those enduring over long periods of time, actually involve few instances of meeting the three conditions of love. Instead, such relationships are surrounded by enough ambiguity for one or both loving persons to see love.

SUMMARY

In this chapter we have stressed how the most important meanings of being defined as a member of one sex or the other are primarily social in nature. This does not mean gender differences have little impact on the interactions of society and self; instead, it is the subtle differences in the learning and socialization experiences of the different genders that have profound and unintended consequences in everyday life. From the playground where we learned about the assertive, aggressive play of boys and the associative and cross-gender play of girls, to the talk of couples where we discovered the devices of interruptions in turn taking used by males and the counter devices to get attention used by females, we outlined how gender identity influences the meanings of social life.

Some gender identities are built into the basic institutions of society, like language and courtship. In this regard, we reviewed sexism in the English language and the changes that have occurred in dating practices as well as the ceremonies of everyday life like opening doors for others. Although dating practices have surely changed in recent decades, there are still striking gender differences in the exercise of power in these intimate relationships. At both the nonverbal and the verbal levels of interaction, gender identities make a difference. Postures have gender meaning; nonassertive, demure poses seem to be feminine while outreaching and intruding stances of the body are masculine. We learned how gender displays are often used in advertisements to associate a product with one gender or the other.

Finally, the very act of constructing intimate, love relationships depends, it turns out, on differences in the way the world looks from the male or female vantage point. In our society, the search for love seems closely associated with how people have learned to perceive the motivations of others. In American society, there are clear differences between males and females in these ways of seeing the world.

EXERCISES IN UNDERSTANDING THE MEANINGS OF GENDER

1. Most of us have opportunities to observe children at play. Recreational centers are good sites for observations, and, many of you may actually work with or care for children in the course of your daily life. Of course, when you observe children, you must be careful not to alarm them, or other adults who may be supervising them. If you choose to do this exercise, please use good judgment and simply watch the children in an unobtrusive fashion. Some researchers have discovered that they can observe children simply by taking advantage of the routines in their lives. On a warm spring day, when you are at home on spring vacation, for example, you may find that just sitting in your front yard, or on your front step, you will be able to see a great deal of the activities of children.

Make notes on the activities of the children you watch. Record details about their kinds of play, whether or not they are supervised, their age and sex. After you have collected several pages of notes, compare your findings with those of Levers. Did you find something different, or are similar patterns present in your data?

2. Select at least four popular and recent magazines at the local book store or get these magazines from your home. It is not a difficult task to find magazines people do not want anymore. Find three examples of gender displays from the advertisement sources, cut them out, record date and name of magazine. Then, write a brief account of why you regard these as illustrations of such displays. You might also check to see if the nonverbal communication used in the posing of the models is consistent with the research findings of Spiegel and Machotka which we summarized in the chapter.

3. Try to become conscious of whether you use any of the devices which characterize male and female conversational practices, such as interruption patterns or raising inflections. Recall conversations you have had recently with a member of the opposite sex about your same age. Document these practices in either your own or your partner's talk. Once you become practiced at recognizing these devices, try using the ones appropriate for the opposite when the opportunity comes up and record what kind of reaction you receive.

4. Repeat Walum's research on your campus. Keep a journal for several days of the experiences you have at doors with the opposite sex. Have things changed much since Walum did her research in the mid-seventies?

KEY CONCEPTS

Sexual identity
Sex-related behaviors
Self-socialization
Gender displays
Display
Asymmetrical conversations
Institutionalized practices
Sexism in language
Egoism and anomie
Principle of least interest
Deference-confrontation
Door-opening ceremony
Humanitarian, defender, and rebel
Somatic categories
Perception of love

SUGGESTED READINGS

There is rich and growing literature in the social psychology of gender. In fact, because this area of research was neglected for so long and has now been recognized as of utmost importance, keeping up with the publications is no small task. I recommend pieces that cover contemporary concerns and illustrate the version of social psychology developed in this text.

First, the delightful book by James P. Spradley and Brenda Mann, *The Cocktail Waitress: Women's Work in a Man's World* , gives the reader a real sense of the world as experienced by women in this occupation. Also, for the adventuresome reader, two other sources are highly recommended: Robin Lakoff's book on the language of women was the first and is still a very important book on the social significance of gender difference in speech; and, Young's article "Throwing Like a Girl" is strong statement of the effects of perceiving and experiencing the world through gender interpretations.

Lakoff, Robin. *Language and Women's Place.* New York: Harper and Row, 1975.

Spradley, James P., and Brenda Mann. *The Cocktail Waitress: Women's Work in a Man's World.* New York: Wiley, 1975.

Young, Iris Marion. "Throwing Like a Girl: A Phenomenology of Feminine Body Comportment, Motility and Spatiality." *Human Studies* 3, No. 2 (1980): 137–156.

Chapter Ten

Aggression: The Meanings of Violence

OUTLINE

Aggression:
The Meanings of Violence

*Two huge men, one black and the other white, face each other.
They are virtually naked, circling in a ring surrounded by thousands of
people. Television cameras pan on the ring as they jab at each other
with gloved fists. Suddenly, one of the muscular, finely trained men
thrusts his fist forward at the head of the other man. The blow lands
squarely on the other's jaw. Those close to the ring can hear the
impact. Microphones mounted ring-side pick up the sound and millions of people in their living rooms hear the powerful strike. The
man's head snaps back, his knees stiffen and he falls to the canvas
floor of the ring. The fans roar with approval. They are energized
with excitement.*

*Three days later, in a local bar two men who watched the champi-
onship prize fight on television, and who used to fight a little themselves as kids, have a few beers. They start to discuss the fight, and
for no apparent reason their disagreements over who should have won
the fight increase. Soon they are shouting at each. One invites the
other to "come outside" to settle the matter. The two men leave the
bar for the back alley. There they brawl. Out of shape, highly agitated, and intoxicated they flail at each other. One man picks up a
brick fallen from a dilapidated building near-by and strikes the other in
the head with it. The fight is over. The fallen man does not move,
blood trickles from his nose and ears. The other man runs away in
fear and panic.*

WHAT causes aggression and the "base" emotions of humans is a central
question of many philosophical and religious belief systems. It is

also a matter of grave practical concern. For the social psychologist, aggression appears to be so general a characteristic of the human condition that it demands explanation. There are several approaches to explaining aggression, its nature, and causes. One suggests that aggression is natural, that it is an intrinsic feature of the human animal. Those who follow this track, like the famous Konrad Lorenz (1963), draw parallels between animal and human behavior.

It is well known that aggression has considerable adaptive value in nature. Most animals fight to establish and defend territory. In almost every instance, however, animals do not kill members of their own species. Their aggression and violence is constrained by learning and instinct. Lorenz and others argue that humans are likewise instinctively given to violent and aggressive behavior. However, because the social realities they have constructed are so elaborate and so persuasive, whatever instinctive controls *Homo sapiens* might have once had are covered by layers of civilization. The trouble is, whenever civilization or societal controls become weak, the unbridled violent side of humans can express itself. According to Lornez, humans have lost the fully developed, self-regulating instincts of aggression. This places the control of aggression squarely in the social arena which Lorenz apparently distrusts. This line of reasoning is very similar to Freudian theories in which it is also said that human beings are naturally animalistic. The Freudians also look to social control in the form of customs and habits to regulate the "base" nature of humans.

Most social psychologists think Lorenz's explanation as well as the Freudian theories are too simplistic because they do not fully appreciate the role that social reality and meanings can play in aggression. While human beings are probably encoded to react in aggressive ways, there is no compelling evidence that there is a direct link between social meanings of aggression and biological conditions or genetic dispositions.

Explanations which enjoy more favor in the scholarly community include the remaining two approaches to aggression: the **frustration-aggression hypothesis**, and a variety of social learning theories. We will briefly survey each of these and then move to a discussion of the meanings of aggression and violence in several different social contexts.

Some years ago Dollard, Miller, and Sears (1939) proposed an explanation for aggression which tied destructive and violent behavior to the experience of frustration. Through both laboratory studies and in studies of racial relationships in southern towns, they refined their theory. According to them, frustration arises from interference with the satisfaction of some need, either biological or social. The result of such frustration, so the theory goes, is anger, and in the expression of anger, the person is rewarded if only by a general reduction of the tension he or she experiences. For some years, this was the predominant view among social psychologists. More recently, however, critics reasoned that whenever persons experience frustration, they may respond with new or added efforts to realize their goal, substitute a new goal, abandon the goal, or become apathetic. In short, they do not necessarily become aggressive.

To account for the variation in responses to frustration, social psychologists expanded the theory to include differential social learning. It was at this point that the influences of the social environment became important to the explanation of aggression. Generally, researchers compiled evidence showing that people *learn* to act aggressively. When violence and aggression were seen as learned, attention shifted to the settings in which the learning took place.

It has been stressed repeatedly how such a shift is apt to produce an incomplete understanding of social phenomena unless environment is seen as symbolic social interaction. Perhaps nowhere is this incompleteness better illustrated than in the study of violence. Typically, there have been two approaches to explaining how violent and aggressive behavior are acquired. The first focuses on the early socialization experiences of children. For example, Gelles (1974) and Strauss (1973) identify "violent families." Their research shows that some families use aggressive and even violent modes to interact with each other. A mother reports she "blistered" the small behind of her four-year-old daughter to teach her not to run into the street. Couples report they love each other dearly, but fight frequently. Some even use implements like the proverbial rolling pin in the acting out of their violent relationships. Generally, these studies conclude with a description of historical or habitual uses of violence, like hitting and punching, as means of communication and control in the complex and often subtle reciprocal relationships that make up families.

Unfortunately, according to these same studies, persons socialized in such families often continue to use the same or similar child-rearing techniques and modes of dealing with frustration as adults. It is as if the social learning of violence is passed on from adult to child by a social code that values nonverbal, tacit, and emotive communicative modes over verbal, explicit, and rational ones.

One other common way to explain violence is to sketch a connection between individual behavior and the larger societal context. Most studies of this kind bring children into a laboratory setting and subject them to stimuli which are designed to induce violence. Some researchers have shown video tapes of prize fights, battles, or fight scenes from movies to children who are then given the opportunities to act out any violent urges they receive from the stimuli (cf. Phillips 1983).

These studies, which in general concern the effect of media on behavior, yield consistent results. Subjects imitate violence under the following conditions: (1) when violence is portrayed in a positive way; (2) when those who perpetrate the acts are rewarded, and they seem to have fun or are excited in the acts; (3) when the acts seem real and justified, and (4) whenever the perpetrator is not criticized and is presented as intending to injure his victims. Children, in research situations, strike a doll in the room with them, and they respond to measures of their emotional stages in more aggressive ways than they did before they saw the stimuli (Comstock 1977).

DEFINITIONS OF AGGRESSION

Thinking about aggression presupposes we know what it is. In the literature and theories we have reviewed violence means everything from striking an inflated doll, to a well-timed body check, or a sharp left jab, to the intentional taking of another person's life. In a sense, we understand, or think we do, what each of these meanings of aggressions is about; however, when attempting to be specific about a definition of aggression we usually come up with a general gloss of a variety of behaviors.

Lorenz (1963) defines aggression as a "fighting instinct." He analyzes attack behaviors, displays of emotions, and the energetic defense of territory. Dollard, Miller, and Sears (1939) seem to consider any behavior that results from frustration as aggression from a well-formed obscene phrase to a fist in a stranger's face. On the other hand, experimenters demand such specific definitions of aggression and violence that what they are referring to is limited to the circumstances of their own studies.

Let's look at typical textbook definitions of violence and aggression. First, **violence** is generally understood as an instance of aggression. Violent acts are acts where a person intends to injure another (either physically, emotionally, or mentally). Throughout all attempts to understand violence, one must assume that **aggression** is an energetic effort to do harm. Violence and aggression are bound together in such a way that we sense something wrong, unusual, or even aberrant has occurred. In the average study, aggression seems to have something to do with motivation and commission, while violence refers to the outcome of the action—outcomes which can be tied to actual harm or intent to harm.

Although this way of thinking about violence and aggression seems to have a kind of face validity, we must consider it inadequate for two reasons: it does not force us to look critically at the ideas we have about desirable behavior and interpersonal relationships, and it covers a multiple of acts which occur routinely in the course of everyday life which also meet the criteria of aggressive and violent behavior. Gelles (1974, 24–27) makes this point when he describes some of the methodological difficulties in defining violence in his study of families. He acknowledges the great variation existing among meanings of, for example, members of a family striking one another. Striking can range from a blow delivered in anger by a mother across the face of her child who accidentally spilled milk on the newly carpeted living room floor to a stinging slap in the intimacy of a marital embrace.

Definitions serve as devices with which analysts can talk to each other. Reading Gelles, for instance, we discover that he is willing to include, as violence, incidents of corporal punishment and other violent exchanges between members of a family even if these acts are not consensually understood as harmful, or intended to do damage. He does this for the sake of getting on with the analysis of violence and its prevalence in the

American family. Although Gelles is sensitive to the role of context in relation to the meanings of violence, he believes strongly in the harmful features of what he defines as violence.

The fact that meanings vary according to situations is given in our approach; this means that no general assessments of violence can be valid without careful descriptions of the contexts within which so-called violent acts take place. Still, we recognize that people within a given culture may well have a commonsense consensus about what a violent act is. However, the precise meanings of a particular "violent" act are frequently the result of decisions made by the people for the special purposes of the given situation, and further, the decisions and interpretations of what counts as a violent act can be quite different even among the same people from place to place and time to time. A technical way of expressing this concept is to say that the meanings of violence are, to a degree, ad hoc and, above all, highly situational.

Gregory Bateson (1972) wrote of a visit he made to a zoo. There he observed monkeys at play. Their play appeared to him to be quite aggressive, as they wrestled, punched, and rolled with each other. He reports he had little trouble and the monkeys seemed to have no trouble at all deciding when the boundaries of play had been crossed and play was transformed into fighting. Play, he argued, always communicates a paradox: It is both serious and trivial, aggressive and passive. This is seen regularly in children's play. My son, an eight-year-old boy, plays on the front yard with his friend from across the street on a warm summer's day. They wrestle with each other. One calls out in loud voice, "I'm Mad Dog Smith and I'm goin' body slam ya!" He attempts to lift his friend in the air. With difficulty, he manages to get his friend's struggling body off the ground. He whirls quickly and falls on top of his friend. There is second of silence. Then the boy on the bottom cries out in apparent pain and anger. He pushes my son off of him and stands up, fists clinched and arms pumping punch after punch mostly into the air. One finds my son's face. I must stop writing and intervene. Their play has stopped.

Commenting on the subtle shifts that seem to make the difference between fighting and playing, Bateson (1972) noted the role of gestures and bodily communications in conveying messages that something has changed. He suggested that the way we can understand these transformations is to see not the behavior itself but the importance of the behavior as derived from the basic way in which the experiences are organized. Goffman, following Bateson and others, carries this analysis further and offers the idea of a **frame**, which is a way of organizing experiences. For example, we can think of a "kidding" or "puttin' on" frame—if a person you are taking to recognizes and accepts this frame, you can say to them, "You are real ugly today, man," without insulting him. Bateson used an ingenuous visual device (Figure 10.1) to illustrate the idea of a frame.

Everyday life, he contended, is understood as organized according to typical experiences. There is "play" and there is "fighting." In play, things are not as they seem: in fighting, they are precisely what they seem.

Violence can be keyed. This means that the impressions given off by an act do not strictly convey the message of violence. A keyed act communicates several messages at once. What features of this picture would lead to the conclusion that these men are not really fighting?

More importantly, with increasing skill at social life people learn to "key" framed experiences. **Keying** means the changing of the tone, intention, or presentation of experiences. Play frames activities. Play can be reframed as fighting, or fighting can be framed as play. In short, how an activity is understood depends on how that activity is framed and on the transformation the frame goes through. This basic insight turns out to be crucial to understanding violence and aggression.

In order to understand how people understand activities as aggressive or violent, we must recall earlier discussions in which we depicted the nature of everyday life in modern society. Such words as *negotiation, situated,* and *layered* remind us of the problematic character of everyday life. Nowhere are the processes of attributing meaning more fundamental than in the decision and subsequent actions that derive from formulating an action as *violent.*

These basic insights of social psychology can be illustrated by examining some situations of violence across widely different activities. From

All statements within this

frame are untrue.

I love you

I hate you

Figure 10.1 Frame   (From Bateson 1972, 184)

rape, to hockey, to the families in which members physically hit each other, we will see how acts are framed, keyed, and often understood from very different vantage points by those who take part in the acts.

SITUATIONS OF VIOLENCE

A sociological truism guides our view of social psychology: there are no intrinsic social meanings. We have repeatedly demonstrated how the meanings of social acts must be seen as constructed. Now we add some information about what the construction is like. Goffman's idea of frame is very important in this task as is his elaboration of that idea, the *key* .

A sexual act can be interpreted as a sensitive and intimate expression of a loving relationship. The same act under different situational conditions, becomes a vile, deplorable crime. The meanings of sexual intercourse are complex and layered in our society. The more room there is for negotiating the meanings of an act, the more confusing and less clear-cut are decisions about what really happens both for those engaged in the act and from the point of view of those who, for various reasons, must make an assessment about the social significance of the act. Imagine, as Scott and Lyman (1967) suggest, how silly it seems to ask a husband and a wife why they have sexual intercourse. It makes more sense to ask of them why they do not. However, there are many other circumstances of everyday life in which questions to the effect "Why do you have sexual intercourse?" seem quite appropriate. The most obvious concerns an issue which has had monumental significance throughout human history: what is rape? We will approach that question by asking another which social psychology can more properly answer, "How do people make decisions about the commission of rape?"

To provide at least a partial answer to this question of the meaning of a violent, aggressive act (rape), Shotland and Goodstein (1983) conducted an experimental study of how rape is perceived in dating situations. They discovered that cultural assumptions and previously acquired attitudes about women influence decisions about whether or not particular actions should be called rape.

They conducted their experiment by first reviewing existing literature. The most obvious finding they uncovered is that it is often difficult for policemen, jurors, and people not directly implicated in the act to say that, indeed, a woman had been raped. They identified what they called **"acquaintance rape,"** a term referring to situations in which a woman is said to have been raped by someone she knows. In other words, these cases involve allegations that an "acquaintance" of the woman has raped her.

The confusion, they reason, about whether or not a rape has been committed comes from cultural assumptions which govern sexual activity among dating couples. These assumptions often suggest that women conceal their genuine interest in sex in subtle and symbolic ways, and that males in particular hold this belief. In addition, cultural beliefs about the dating situation hold that a woman is expected to resist a man's advances at least in the beginning stages of a sexual encounter. These beliefs are further confounded by the widespread judgment among males of society that women enjoy being dominated.

Certainly, no great leap of imagination is required to appreciate that these beliefs, when operating together, might result in confusion about the meanings of sexual acts. It was to sort out how these beliefs might operate that Shotland and Goodstein devised their experiment.

Stories depicting an intimate sexual encounter were read by 287 students in a undergraduate psychology course at a major state university. About an equal number of men and women read the stories. Each story was selectively written for different groups of these students. Some read a version in which the male in the story became aggressive in spite of the verbal protest of his date. Other stories varied how much and when the woman protested. In each version, the story ended with the couple engaged in sexual intercourse.

By arranging accounts of the sexual encounter in this fashion, the researchers were able to classify the depicted scene according to whether the male was forceful, and how forceful he was, such as when, in the necking process, the female protested. They also measured the student's perceptions of the roles of women in general. They grouped students according to how egalitarian their attitudes were and according to how they judged the principals in the story: the female for her desire to have sex, the amount and kind of protest she gave to the male (from verbal to physical protest), and the male for the amount of force he used.

Their findings clearly demonstrate how cultural beliefs can influence a judgment about whether rape has occurred. They found, for example, that in the story where the woman protested late and was seen as desiring sex, a

Many researchers believe that the meanings of rape and perhaps the reasons for the act itself are the consequences of some widely shared cultural beliefs about the nature of sex. Can you list at least two of these beliefs and show how they might become a motivation for a rapist?

male's forceful sex act was likely to be seen as rape, but the female was more likely to be blamed for what happened to her. The man in the story, on the other hand, was more likely to be seen as violent and the incident more likely to be seen as rape when there was more force, and more and earlier protest. These differences generally held for both male and female students who judged the accounts.

This study leaves us with an interesting observation which helps inform us about the framing of violence and aggression in our society. Whether a female is seen as desiring sex and judgments about the male's aggressive pursuit of his goal of coitus seem to be important considerations in making a decision that the crime of acquaintance rape had occurred. We seem warranted in concluding that the cultural beliefs people have about female sexuality and male aggressiveness confound clarity about the meanings of intimate acts. As Shotland and Goodstein write:

We believe our results have important practical significance . . . it appears that people are reluctant to label these scenarios as rape, although they will admit that the male's behavior was wrong and the woman had a right to expect the male to cease his advances (1983, 231).

The authors of this research concluded by calling for stronger and more flexible rape laws which would better fit the actual situations under which a woman may be forced to engage in sex. Their project also underscores our point about violence in modern society. In spite of some very strong and widely shared feelings about the sex act and its meanings, the decisions people make about violent and aggressive acts are indeed, highly complex and situational. This means that many of us may well agree in general yet have a great deal of trouble agreeing about the specific meanings of particular acts. We want to treat this problem as a matter of the organization of social experience.

As Goffman showed us, the meanings that we see in everyday life derive from presuppositions, states of mind, beliefs, values, and moods that we surmise as characteristic of the other person. To impute a violent motive to another person is not only disquieting, but it is problematic as well. Since the meanings of social life are **layered, laminated**, and made to seem to be something they are not, (Berger, 1979, refers to this aspect of social meanings as a "doublefloor", as in a magic act), it is no wonder we are somewhat troubled by our inability to achieve consensus about violent and aggressive actions.

By shifting our attention to how people make decisions, we can at least understand the dimensions of the problem. Not only this, but we can also show how decisions made about the violent nature of acts are always couched in a larger social context. We want to understand that much of the violence that occurs is the result of incomplete understanding, mistakes, and unskillful actions.

HOW VIOLENCE IS LEARNED: A CASE OF THE KIDS AND THE PROS

Early on a Sunday morning, cars begin to arrive at the ice arena. Eleven and twelve-year-old boys emerge from the cars. They carry bags stuffed with equipment, and sticks over which are draped pairs of skates. They are silent, but friendly as they greet one another and head for the dressing room for final preparations. They put on skates and helmets and "hit the ice" just as the Zamboni finishes its cleaning. The boys circle on the ice, warming up and taking "shots on goal."

The game begins and the action is fast and wild. At one point in the game, the puck glides to a stop in the corner at the opposite end of the ice. Two boys chase after it. They arrive at the same time both lunging for the puck with their sticks. They collide with a violent impact. There is a groan from the crowd. One boy goes down but quickly recovers while the other controls the puck and begins skating toward the opponent's goal to the cheers of his teammates, parents, and friends.

Hockey is known as a violent game. The movie, *Slap Shot*, portrayed it as cross between street brawling and sport. Perhaps the comedian, Rodney Dangerfield, expressed it best with his joke, "Yesterday I was watching a fight and a hockey game broke out."

The professional sport of hockey has dealt openly with the issues of violence. Law suits, brawls involving fans and players, and the exposes of journalists have focused public attention on hockey as a violent sport. Coaches, players, and owners are sensitive to questions about fighting and they are seriously concerned with the image of the game.

In the past twenty years, programs in youth hockey have proliferated, especially in eastern and midwestern cities. Children as young as six years old are now playing organized hockey. Critics point to the violence of pro hockey, and caution parents and organizers about the deleterious effects of hockey on children. Generally, they argue about the contribution hockey makes to the already violent world. Why add an aspect of sanctioned experience to the images of fast cars and fighting which the children see on television? they suggest. Defenders of hockey, and youth sports in general, counter with claims about the teaching of character, the value of competition, and the power of sports to keep children—particularly energetic young boys—"out of trouble."

There seems to be validity to both claims. Young hockey players are not generally as deeply involved with drugs nor identified as trouble makers as are other students (Vas 1982). Still, most of these claims are made by parents and coaches and there is little empirical evidence to suggest that involvement in sports does much more than extenuate behaviors already learned by the participants. That the environment in which children grow to maturity is laced with violent images can not be doubted. But the crucial question here is the same one we encountered in our treatment of the effects of media, only now we are concerned about the actual experience of violence. A few years ago, at the end of an important high school game in eastern Massachusetts, a riot occurred. Several students were injured. The riot took place the night after the infamous North Stars vs. Bruins brawl, a hockey game which set a record 406 minutes in penalties. The question we ask is inevitable: what is the impact of violent models of professional hockey on young players?

Nash and Lerner (1981) conducted a study attempting to assess the impact of a professional model for hockey on violence in youth hockey. They went about their study by gathering two kinds of information. First, they wanted to describe the way professionals, who supposedly are the model, think about fights and other violent aspects of their game; second, they wanted to learn how youthful players think about these same matters.

To answer the first set of concerns, Lerner observed professional hockey games over a month period. He was able to secure a press pass which allowed him into the locker rooms of the respective teams after the games. While observing the games, he took notes of the circumstances of fights.

While these boys are surely encouraging a violent act, they are also helping to organize and impart meanings to such acts. Goffman would have said they are framing violence. What does it mean to say that this is a picture of framed violence?

He jotted down what was happening just before, during, and after the fight. After the game while star players were being interviewed by media representatives, Lerner talked to the men who had been involved in the fights. He discovered that the players were, by and large, willing to discuss what happened. More importantly, this approach provided a convenient entry to questions about fighting, a subject most players do not frankly discuss with press people. In other words, the professional players were quite willing to discuss specific fights, even though they were unwilling to discuss the topic of fighting.

From this data base, the researchers sketched a pro version of the meanings of hockey violence:

1. Players do not regard hockey as a particularly violent game. They play with "force," using terms like "aggressive," "playing with authority," "hot," or "a run on" to describe a particular of play. They did not describe hockey using the word violent.
2. Players have well-developed conceptions of themselves and their fellow players in terms of their dispositions to fight or play aggressively. There

are essentially four types of players: *enforcers*, whose purpose it is to intimidate and fight; *stickers*, who use their sticks to intimidate but rarely fight; *temperamental players*, a category that applies to most players indicating that under the "right" circumstances any hockey player will fight; and the *passive players* who avoid fights at all costs and rely on skill and speed to play the game.

3. Fighting is regarded as a "natural consequence" of a fast and forceful game where collisions are inevitable and clashes of intention are part of the organization of competition. Players are not particularly bothered by the possibility of a "fight" during a game (Nash and Lerner 1981, 231–234).

It seems professional hockey players espouse a version of violence that presupposes a system of knowledge about the game. Briefly, this regards intimidation as a strategy of play. This makes fights unavoidable. Players know that fans like to watch fights. Fights add excitement to the game. They punctuate the rhythm of the game, and focus attention on the game in way that even a goal does not. A fight erupts, stops play, and requires the attention of all participants on the ice and in the boxes. Still, most players consider fighting not to be a part of "good hockey." They regard those who fight habitually as "bad" players.

Yet there is a resignation about fighting in hockey; fights are "bad," but necessary. They must not be eliminated for fear that in the void left behind something even more violent, like the increased use of sticks to intimidate, would take their place. Fights, therefore, must be controlled.

From these data, it seems fighting is for the most part controlled. A player says, "Fighting is no real problem now like it was in the past. The referees pretty much control it now." It has been controlled, not eliminated, through the **ritualization of the fight** itself. A ritualized fight is less a life and body threatening activity and more of an aggressive display, what Goffman would call a keying. However, fights are real and emotions genuine. The hockey fight is not staged in the sense of a professional wrestling match. It is, however, governed by sets of well-understood norms: fighting is with fists, not sticks; fighting generally takes place without gloves, on the ice, in the presence of referees, and as a consequence of something that happened in the course of the game.

In professional hockey the expression of force to achieve an end is ritualized. This ritual appeals to fans, adds excitement and an element of spontaneity to the game as well as serving to release tensions that derive from a highly competitive activity.

The interpretation by professional hockey players of violence in general and fighting in particular is complex and only partially described here. However, it should be clear that the interpretation of violence in professional hockey is built around contradictory tenets regarding the undesirability and the necessity of fighting. In the game, the role of intimidation is legitimized. The complex interpretation of violence allows fine distinctions between "good" and "cheap" play. The ritual of the fight itself functions as an outlet for players' tensions and frustrations in the expression of an aggressive display.

A father who was heavily involved in a young hockey program in a northern state related the following story. The story illustrates the particular, and even bizarre ways, young hockey players have of interpreting their particpation in the game.

After the last game of the regular season, during the thirty-minute ride home, I asked the three boys in my car what they had received penalties for. The first boy replied that he slashed at a boy who punched him. The second said that he had "held" to prevent a "breakaway." I turned to the third boy who had been involved in a fight and I asked him what his penalty was for. "It was for violence," he said.

Not only are young hockey players aware of issues of violence, they use their understanding of the pros as a model for interpreting their own participation in the game. However, it is important to note that it is their version of what the pros do that serves as their guideline. They see the slap shot as "pro," and the boy who can raise the puck in a straight, hard line "on net" enjoys their esteem. Coaches insist that games are won with the well-aimed wrist shot; and, they criticize the boy who sets up for the slap shot. Still during a game whenever a player "fires a cannon," the coach and players alike react with approval.

The boys' version of "good" hockey contrasts with the pros'; but the effects of the pro model can be identified. These effects are indirect, and they are filtered through vantage points of the youthful hockey player. Nash and Lerner (1981) suggest these effects can be appreciated by observing contrasts and similarities between the pro and the youth versions of the game.

First, there is a contrast: the boys regard hockey as fun. It is the playing that matters, not the fact of winning or losing. Whenever a coach does not encourage the explicit goal of winning, the talk of the boys focuses on fair distribution of playing time, or on requests for "extended ice time." To play and play a lot is the prime objective of the young players. The appeal of hockey is its action. A puck in the corner affords the opportunity to kick, flail, elbow, push, and collide with the other boys. Such legitimate situations are exceedingly rare in the everyday world of the middle-class preadolescent. As boys find themselves closely supervised at school and at home as adults work systematically to control violence in virtually all aspects of life, there are precious few places where "boys can be boys." As long as a boy "makes an effort" for the puck, he can openly and in a supportive environment exhibit aggressive behavior. For the boy in youth hockey, this is fun on its grandest scale.

Second, boys do not believe they will be injured while playing or fighting the game of hockey. Like their pro counterparts, kids as well as their parents and the coaches espouse the belief that "no one really gets hurt." "Hockey is not like football," a father said, "there are no serious injuries."

Of course—and this is precisely the point—one can question what is a "serious injury." In virtually every game Nash and Lerner observed, at least one boy "went down on the ice"; this means that he was injured sufficiently to stop the game. Apparently, these "hits" do not count as injuries. In the language of hockey boys "shake it off," "rebound," or "skate it out." Very rarely will a boy, down on the ice, be out of the game. Instead, he gets his breath back and waits for the pain to stop from a blow to the stomach or a stick to the neck. Going down and rising to the applause of parents and other spectators is part of the game.

Third, the discipline required to play "hard or aggressively" is within the range of ability for most boys. What this means is the rules which referees evoke, the judgments coaches and parents must make about the appropriateness of "aggression" during the game take into account the levels of skill and the motivations of the players. Only when sticks get too high, elbows too loose, or checks too late are penalties called. The line between a "great" check and the offense of "charging" is fine indeed, and the overly aggressive player will receive penalties. Hockey sanctions mistakes, and this aspect of hockey is well understood by the boys who play the game.

The **code** that players must abide by, as they interpret it, consists of six interrelated tenets:

1. Play hard.
2. Skate fast.
3. Do not complain about ice time or the position the coach wants you to play.
4. Control your emotions, and express them appropriately through aggressive play.
5. Do not give "cheap" shots unless in retaliation.
6. Play hockey in kind, clean for clean, cheap for cheap.

In hockey, fighting and getting penalties are not necessarily "bad." Youthful players understand "good" and "bad" hockey by way of a two-dimensional interpretive process. The two dimensions, often used simultaneously, are **simplification** and **accentuation**. These processes have been identified as a part of the developmental stages through which general thinking moves (cf. Furth, 1980).

Simplification occurs whenever a boy pares down the complexities of adult models into interpretations he can remember. Boys think about hockey in relatively simple terms. The code they use is oriented toward the coach and becomes simple through repetition. In the simplified version the boy uses, mistakes can be made, and interpretations of an act may be different from those a pro would make. For example, a boy may confuse "hustle" with "staying in position"—in an effort to please the coach, he may skate too fast and find himself on the wrong section of the rink.

Accentuation entails a purposeful exaggeration of certain themes in the meanings of hockey violence as well as the emotive expression of these themes. A team member may come to think of being ready for a "hard check" as the salient feature of the game, contrasted with being in position. Accentuation seems to function in the management of identity, as in looking "tough" or being "big on the ice." This dimension is emotive and is articulated through personifying which means establishing a presence on the team through making his personality visible to others. An example of this would include the custom of "sticks in the air" after each goal a team makes; pros do this as well but not with the zeal exhibited by the boys.

The game of hockey and a description of how children model their play after the pros tells us that modeling is never a direct imitative process. Boys interpret hockey in accord with a preadolescent understanding (cf. Furth 1980). They simplify and accentuate themes of available adult models in terms of their own needs and social relationships. The pro model is the model for youth hockey; still, hockey becomes an opportunity for learning an aggressive display. By virtue of the organization of the game itself, interaction with coaches, parents and most importantly, their fellow players, the boys learn the meanings of **situational violence**. The boys learn the time, place, and the form for aggression. The formal character of hockey equipment, travel, pre and postgame rituals of handshaking, line changes, and other game procedures allow for the learning of the right time to be aggressive and by implication of the wrong time. Fights and penalties, when they occur, help to define the "proper" channels of aggression by demonstrating to the youthful participant the boundaries within which aggression is supposed to take place.

Studies such as this one of how boys learn to play aggressive hockey highlight an important point about aggression and violence in general. Situational meanings ascribed to an action are of primary social psychological importance. Now we will shift our attention back to more serious forms of violence and develop a view of their meaning which focuses on the socialization and the institutionalization of violence.

THE VIOLENT HOME

We have already suggested that violence and aggression are learned responses which vary greatly from situation to situation. We have seen how people involved in a violent situation can attribute different meanings to it, and we have reviewed how membership in groups and the place of groups in the larger society effect the attribution of action as violent. Whereas society may actually encourage some types of violence (such as the ritual display of aggression in hockey and other sports), other perhaps even less physically violent acts are regarded as serious and discouraged. Recently, public attention has been directed to a particular kind of this behavior, family violence.

Perhaps the most important social psychological research done on violence in the home is the work of Gelles and his associates (Gelles 1974; Strauss 1973). These authors used interview techniques in conjunction with surveys to assess the extent and kind of violence existing in American homes. The most general conclusion drawn from these studies is that violence is a part of the organization of family life. However, such a statement does not mean that all parents are brutal and insensitive toward their children, rather, as Gelles suggests, there are many methods of violence (slapping, punching, hitting with a hard object) and there are different meanings attached to violent incidents by family members. What is of primary importance is how the family members account for incidents or sequences of violent acts (Gelles 1974, 57). Some forms of violence are regarded as "normal." These are cases where the use of force to achieve some end is interpreted as routine, normative and even as necessary. Hence, almost one-fifth of all Americans approve of slapping one's spouse on appropriate occasions.

Gelles uncovered several forms of **normal violence**. He found that husband-wife violence was sometimes thought of, especially by wives, as somehow deserved. Wives would report that their husbands struck them because of their badgering or nagging. Another form Gelles refers to as "I

In society, some types of aggression are sanctioned and legitimate. Identify some of the symbols of legitimate aggression in this picture. What is it about these symbols that tells you that the aggression they represent is legitimate?

tried to knock her to her senses" which apparently has to do with helping one's spouse control emotions and gain and maintain composure. Hence, one husband reported that he slaps his wife on the arm to "help her get a hold of herself." This happens infrequently, he said, like when the children get hurt, and his wife "loses control of herself."

Another common form of normal violence is embodied in the remarks of several parents in the study, "kids need to be hit." This belief seems to be quite widespread in American society. Some of us may know it as the adage, "Spare the rod, spoil the child." The belief amounts to an institutionalized use of force to achieve control over the behavior of children. The most common expressions of this violence are slapping, pinching, jerking, and spanking.

Gelles shows how violence is built into the family system. However, this does not mean all families are pathologically violent. Borrowing a concept proposed by Strauss (1973, 115), Gelles refers to situations in which disputes over the proper use of violence create additional or **secondary violence**. A father might spank his young son. His wife, in turn, might criticize him for this approach to discipline; an argument ensues which ends in a fight. This is so called secondary violence.

There is also a type of violence which Gelles calls **volcanic violence**. This occurs when:

the offender has reached the end of the line—has run out of patience as the result of externally caused stress such as losing a job, frustration at being unable to communicate with his spouse, or victim-induced frustration (where the victim badgers the offender until he can take no more). Volcanic violence is illegitimate violence that is explained as rising from the buildup of stress and frustration...the offender "erupts" into violence (Gelles 74, 174).

Others types of family violence include alcohol-related violence; protective-reactive violence (here a spouse strikes the other to stop an anticipated attack); one-way violence (usually a husband assaulting a passive wife); and sex-related violence (jealousy).

Common themes of meaning for the persons involved run through these violent acts: whether or not the violence is interpreted as legitimate or illegitimate; and, whether it is **expressive** (spontaneous and emotional), or **instrumental** (used to achieve an end). Under the expressive and instrumental meanings of violence, there is the question of whether the violence was or was not seen as **victim-precipitated**.

Gelles interviewed members of eighty families. He sought out families with a reputation for violence traceable through their contacts with agencies set up to help violent families and through records of police calls to their homes because of fights and other domestic problems. He found that the incidents of violence even among these "problem" families included a goodly number of legitimate uses of violence. In other words, not all the incidences of aggression (pushing, slapping, etc.) differed substantially from what might be found in the "average" American family. Certainly, these families are not representative of American families, but the meanings which those most intimately involved in violence attribute to these actions help us understand the extent to which violence may be institutionalized as a part of family life.   Studying these families and distinguishing between the kinds of acts which "got them into trouble" and those which did not may help us recognize general rules used by society to draw the line between "ordinary" and "extraordinary" violence.

These families volunteered to tell their stories, and they were aware that their experiences were, at least in part, outside the norms which govern the expression of force in families.   If we can be confident that violence is a normatively governed, framed experience in families, and if we are correct in the importance of situational meanings for violence, then why do the members of some families go over the boundaries, breaking the frames of the organization of aggression, and taking part in excessive violence?

One conclusion we can draw is that **out of frame** or excessively violent acts are at least partly the result of different levels of competencies at interaction among the participants.   A person who acts in ways that are consistently improper might simply not know what he is doing, or, from another point of view, the competencies he has acquired might be unbalanced in favor of violent means of solving problems.

Gelles offers a comprehensive model of family violence which includes all these factors.   He stresses that an adequate explanation must account for the situational and societal meanings of acts.   He writes about societal factors (like position in society), the stress one experiences daily (like unemployment and financial problems), the self-identities of people, the actual structure of families, and the way in which members of the family see themselves as belonging to society.   He also investigates the socialization of the members of families, whether or not they themselves were victims of violence as children, the vitality of the norms governing both expressive and instrumental uses of violence, and the specific norms and values of the community to which the family belongs.   Finally, he studies the interpretations that actual experiences receive in routine life courses (situational factors).   All of these factors interact to result in violence.

Gelles (1974, 188–190) summarizes his model in propositional form.   He writes:

1. Violence is a response to a particular structural and situational stimulus.
2. Stress is differentially distributed in social structures.
3. Exposure to and experience with violence as a child teaches the child that violence is a response to structural and situational stimuli.
4. Individuals in different social positions are differentially exposed both to learning situations of violence as a child and to structural and situational stimuli for which violence is a response as an adult.
5. Individuals will use violence towards family members differently as a result of learning experience and structural causal factors that lead to violence.

Gelles teaches us that violence is both a part of normal life and an aberration.   It becomes an aberration whenever its meanings no longer make sense to the people who are intimately involved in the situation or to others who notice it can call it into question.

ANGER: ONE OF SEVEN DEADLY SINS

Before the development of modern social sciences, the matters we are discussing in this chapter were often thought of as sins, weaknesses in moral character. Among the sins which were said to be "deadly" is anger. In anger, persons show their base nature. In the defense of their lost sense of self, they may act without the civil constraints which make social order possible.

In a fascinating book, called *The Seven Deadly Sins,* Stanford Lyman reintroduces a way of thinking about aggression (anger and its manifestations) as sin. Although he does not wish to dismantle all the knowledge social scientists have amassed about the violent and base ways in which humans sometimes behave, he does wish to recover a sense of freedom and responsibility for people who express themselves in anger. He notes that the way in which social theory explains aggression and anger relieves humans of responsibility to choose between good and evil. The very terms "good" and "evil," he notes, have been pushed out of the vocabulary of social science. Whether we anchor aggression in the psychological nature of humans, tie it to the frustrations of living in a complex world of contradictory demands, or draw parallels between the animal world and the human, the effect of this reasoning is to shift the focus away from the individual.

Lyman, however, points to recent developments in sociological theory which once again allow us to address the questions of freedom and choice. Even though structural and situational factors may be said to cause violence, there is still the issue of how much the burden for anger must be laid at the feet of the individual.

Lyman argues that the fundamental cause of anger is damage to or **loss of self-esteem**. He continues:

Modern societies provide a remarkable number of institutional degradation ceremonies that unintentionally or by design deprive individuals and groups of their sense of personal and moral worth as well. Sending people to social death while leaving them physically alive is a dangerous move, since, like Achilles, they might strike out in enraged fury. (Lyman 1977, 124).

Lyman develops a meaning for the causes of anger around the concept of territory. In modern society, life seems to be a continual challenge to the sense people have of their territories, both public and private. Anger seems to be very much a matter of display. Its counterpart, aggression, follows the unsuccessful communication of self and territorial integrity. Hence, in the modern society, figurative anger becomes a matter of drama.

Lyman is saying that complexity and increased problematics in everyday life have transformed the arena of defense of territory and self. It is no longer a matter of a straightforward issue like the integrity of the home. In a nonmodern context of stability and literality of territory, the weak character without a sense of worth is indeed existing in a life of sin. But in modernity, the whole matter of self-worth becomes figurative, a dramatic enactment. In order to survive socially, one must learn to stake claims and defend them with symbols in interaction. With the increased difficulty of performances comes more and more risk of failure and subsequent loss of self-worth. The tasks to be learned are necessary before anger can be expressed mockingly, as by the professional wrestler, or so that rage can be called out for the purposes at hand, such as the football player before the game. When these complex learning tasks have been mastered, then:

> The mock anger of the professional wrestler that everybody who knows the game takes to be only pretense is a source of fun in a harmless and "fixed" encounter. The contrived anger of the businessman, who has rehearsed his part and knows just when and how to explode in rage, is recognized as a useful and sometimes effective tactic in ongoing commercial relationships. But the spontaneous uncontrolled rage of the truly angry person is often taken as a weakness, a defect in character, and, in the older parlance, a sin. (Lyman 1974, 134).

Lyman contends that in modern society, it is no easy task to develop a sense of self-esteem. There is a great significance placed on the ability to "act," and the performances of everyday life are given on a constantly changing stage. The irony of explaining aggression, violence, and anger in modern society is that the very society which fosters a sense of loss of freedom and responsibility and thereby creates conditions for the expression of anger and aggression also forces the truly angry person to carry the greatest burden, a sense of worthlessness.

THE MOST ANGRY OF US ALL: THE UNDERCLASS

Our description of anger, violence, and aggression has stressed how these phenomena vary with situation and structure. Now, we address a related question: what happens to people in their dealings with others when they are locked into a particular location in society? Certainly, violent and criminal acts are committed by persons located throughout the strata of society. In fact, the violence of the privileged classes make for sensational news, successful television programs, and best selling novels.

However, we are becoming increasingly aware of the skewed distribution of violence in our society. It appears, as Gelles notes in his account of conjugal violence, that most violence takes place among persons who occupy the lower rankings of society. It has long been accepted that social class is clearly associated with violent crimes. Recently, we have come to understand that this relationship is not a simple socio-economic one, nor is it merely a result of temporary conditions under which some people must live before they are fully assimilated into American society.

In a provocative book, Ken Auletta (1982) identifies what he calls the American **underclass**. This category of people is mostly poor, mostly ethnically and racially stigmatized, and mostly outside of the mainstream experiences of American society. Of course, not all members of the underclass are violent. In fact Auletta is careful to show the diversity of the category. He suggests it consists of four types of people: the **passive poor**, the **hostile street criminal**, the **hustler**, and the **traumatized** (drunks, drifters, homeless "bag ladies" and released mental patients).

Two of Auletta's points are pertinent to our treatment of the meanings of aggression. First, evidence is growing to indicate that members of the underclass are responsible for a large amount of the serious, out-of-frame violence—the kind that shocks and leaves the ordinary citizen with a strong sense of puzzlement. Auletta is referring to the senseless crimes that make headlines, like the apparently random beating and raping of elderly women.

Auletta cites evidence which indicates the magnitude of the problem. He writes about a study conducted in Philadelphia by Marvin Wolfgang which zeroed in on 1,862 offenders. Wolfgang found that this group constituted fifty-four percent of those considered delinquent and committed eighty-four percent of Philadelphia crimes. These chronic offenders included a subgroup of persons who had been arrested five or more times. This relatively small group, it turns out, was responsible for fifty-two percent of all offenses and eighty-three percent of the serious crimes listed on the FBI index.

Secondly, according to Auletta, not only do members of the underclass act violently, they also are becoming a permanent feature of American social structure. If he is correct, the sketch he offers of the profiles of violence in America is much like that of the novelist, Anthony Burgess, whose *Clock Work Orange* society fostered senseless violence.

Our approach to social psychology forces us to be careful with terms like "senseless." These acts appear senseless to most ordinary citizens. However, from the point of view of those who commit them, they have meaning. To be sure, that meaning is vastly out of frame. Auletta makes a unique contribution to our understanding of "sinful" violence in society by showing us how to understand the roots of meanings so badly misaligned with the majority rules for making sense out of everyday life.

We can debate about what is really learned in youth hockey, or whether the violence on television is a significant factor in causing homicides, but we repeatedly end up with a single observation: what counts as a case of violence involves judgments about the meanings of aggressive acts. Many acts of aggression in everyday life have institutionalized meaning. The organization of society seems to reflect human efforts to deal with aggression, not to eliminate it. For the most part, the social control of aggression is accomplished through the teaching of interactional competencies, ways of display, and techniques to reach ends.

As society has become vastly complex, there are varieties of competencies which people can acquire. Most of these are adaptive, that is, they help people deal with the practical problems of everyday life. However,

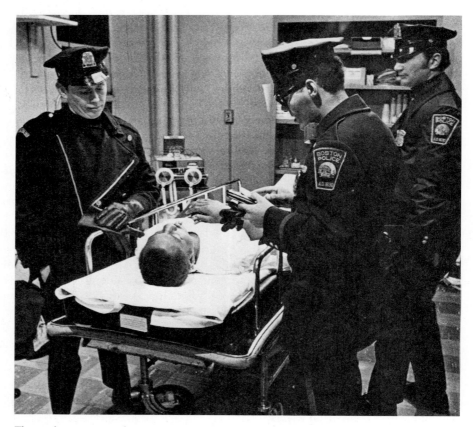

These policemen are making sense out of a violent act by reconstructing the circumstances of this man's death. What are the social functions of such an accounting for violence?

for some people the very skills which help them survive within their particular social worlds lead to serious trouble whenever they contact larger more encompassing social worlds. Hence, although most people are socially competent, the senses in which a person may be "competent" are relative to situations of social life. When we compare the relative "competencies" people possess, some members of society are, in a very real way, deficient in social skills. At first the term "deficiency" was used timidly, but now Auletta uses it with more confidence to describe the interactional skills of the members of the underclass. The basic lessons of life in mainstream society, which include the framing of aggressive acts, the keying of anger, and above all, the mastery of **situational propriety**, are lost on the underclasses. As one sociologist suggests, the "focal concerns" of lower-class members set them up to be out of the mainstream (Miller 1958, 5–19).

The violence they manifest does not mean they have no interactional competencies. It does mean, however, that their skills for building social relationships serve them as poorly in larger society as they serve them well in their own place in society; street survival skills do not transform well into adaptive competencies in larger society.

It is difficult to imagine the anger at the loss of self-esteem which comes from learning that "playing the dozens" well does not mean much to a prospective employer or from learning that the comfort from retreating from a problem home environment into the security of membership in a street culture is of no practical value at school. The male and the female member of the underclass lives with a constant institutionalized reminder of his or her lack of self-worth. The underworld teaches useless skills and inappropriate attitudes as necessary for survival in the immediate realities of everyday life. To get through the day in the underclass, with or without money, one must assume identities that are at odds with the values and attitudes used more generally to build the social worlds of everyday life. This is the dangerous move of sending people to a social death while leaving them alive that Lyman wrote of as a prescription for anger.

SUMMARY

In this chapter, we discussed aggression and violence as topics of research for social psychology. We discovered that aggression is a ubiquitous feature of everyday life. In some cases, aggression seems to be supported by society. There are some very powerful influences on the lives of people in modern society which foster aggression and even violence. Sports represents one of these influences, media violence another.

In order to understand both the ubiquitous and the problematic character of aggression, we stressed the description of the attribution of meanings to acts. There are legitimate and illegitimate instances of aggression and violence in society, and the process of assigning a meaning to an act is complicated. People work with cultural belief systems, but they often modify these to fit their location in society. Furthermore, they learn to frame action so that the impressions given off by an action can be controlled, to a degree, through processes of keying or "playing" with the organization of the experiences of aggression.

Families may be the schools of violence, and the intensity and problematic character of family violence is specific to the interactional patterns that develop within families. Since families may be relatively isolated in American society (there is little direct supervision of what goes on in the family home), these patterns can become quite esoteric. Still, studies of violence in sports and in the home show the organized nature of most violence and aggression.

This chapter concluded by following Lyman's version of the cause of violence, the loss of self-esteem. A society which systematically promotes such feelings among a selected grouping of its members (the underclasses) may well be creating the very problems it seeks to control. Skilled interaction is a hallmark of human existence, however, the kinds of skills acquired and the ends to which these skills are applied vary with the location people have in society.

Most importantly, we have tried to demonstrate how the increased complexity of organized social experiences brings about multiple meanings which are open to varied interpretations. The successful management of violence and aggression, therefore, becomes a matter of socialization.

EXERCISES IN THE MEANINGS OF VIOLENCE

1. Visit a professional wrestling match. It is best to actually attend one of these performances, but if you are pressed for money, you can always tune in "All Star Wrestling" on the television. Describe what happens and record your reactions to the show. Can you identify frames for the violence you observed, keys, or other ways in which the violence of the wrestlers was staged?

2. Working in groups of four for this exercise, make up three, fictional cases of what you consider "child abuse." Make up the cases so that you can rank them from "obviously" abusive or only mildly so. After each of you has four cases prepared, read your examples to each other. See if you all agree on the ranking of the severity of the cases. What particular acts do all of you agree on as abusive? Which acts provoke the most disagreement?

3. Draw a map of your campus and show which areas of it "make you anxious" when you have to walk there. Show areas where you feel safe. You might also think of the campus as composed of areas which are warm and friendly and cold and threatening. Share these maps in a group and see if there are differences in how each of you drew your maps. Be sensitive of male/female differences in sense of danger, and see if you can identify territories of potential violence.

KEY CONCEPTS

Frustration-aggression hypothesis
Violence
Aggression
Frame
Keying
Acquaintance rape
Layered and laminated meanings
Ritualization of the fight
Hockey code
Simplification
Accentuation
Situational violence

Normal violence
Secondary violence
Volcanic violence
Expressive violence
Instrumental violence
Victim-precipitated violence
Out of frame
Loss of self-esteem
Underclass
Passive poor
Hostile street criminal
Hustler
Traumatized
Situational propriety

SUGGESTED READINGS

This chapter draws on the perspectives of a number of researchers and theorists. To recommend any source over another introduces a bias, hence, I used the criteria of ease in reading and comprehension for the books as well as how informative and insightful they may be. Of course, the serious student may want to explore the materials used in this chapter according to his or her own interests.

Gelles' work meets these criteria. We have already discussed his major findings, but the reader will discover much more in the book and will be rewarded with his rich and lucid descriptions of what actually happens in some families. Sipes uses anthropological methods of cross-cultural research to test whether or not sports functions as a control for aggression. His controversial conclusion is they do not. Finally, the novelist S.E. Hinton captures the experiences of violence in the lives of teenagers in her powerful book *Rumble Fish.* Although many of you may have read this book as a junior high or high school student, rereading it as a description of youthful experiences in violence in a modern society can give you a new appreciation for the book.

Gelles, Richard. *The Violent Home.* Beverly Hills, Ca.: Sage, 1974.

Hinton, S. E. *Rumble Fish.* New York: Dell, 1974.

Sipes, Richard Grey. "Sports as a Control for Aggression." In *Sports in Contemporary Society.* 2nd ed., edited by D. Stanley Eitzen. New York: St. Martins' Press, 1984.

Chapter Eleven

Collective Behavior

Collective Behavior

It is 1957 in Selma, Alabama. Three black men walk into a coffee shop on a downtown street. They take seats at the counter. There is tension in the air. The waitress ignores the men as she serves white men who sit nervously at both ends of the counter. Soon a crowd gathers outside the shop and people peer inside. The white customers finish their coffee quickly, pay their bills, and join the spectators outside. Excitement becomes electric talk among those watching the three black men who seem strangely still, staring almost trance-like at the wall behind the counter. Racists slurs become louder as the spectators grow in number until finally, several young white men rush the three black men, wrestle them to the floor, shouting insults and kicking at them. The sound of sirens grows closer, and the white men disperse, leaving the injured black men lying on the floor attended to by a sympathetic observer.

T HIS vignette describes a kind of action which social psychologists refer to as **collective behavior**. Collective behavior includes a wide range of phenomena from rumors and gossip to organized efforts of large numbers of people trying to change societal values (social movements). Most typically, collective behavior studies are about crowds, riots, responses to natural disasters, and the organized action of people against other people or against what they regard as their established social worlds.

Although there are many ways to define collective behavior, most definitions emphasize that such social actions have elements of spontaneity and significance to them. A collective behavior, then, is one that appears novel, as an innovative response to some set of social conditions, but one which is so out of the ordinary that it is not covered directly by the institutions of society. Hence, although acts of collective behavior may or may not be illegal, they are not necessarily "deviant." Certainly, most collective responses are of short duration, and do not have a lasting effect on established social order. Still, when conditions are just right, collective responses can alter social order. Turner writes of one kind of collective behavior, social movements: "Social movements are great stirrings that rattle and threaten the institutional order, attracting adherents whose motivations are diverse and producing manifold effects in society" (1983, 175).

Anytime a sociologist deals with such a diverse range of actual experiences, there is danger of losing sight of the focus of the subject. Building on the earlier thinking of Blumer, John Lofland (1981) offers a scheme for bringing coherence to the study of collective behavior. He suggests that there is a sense in which all collective behavior manifests a form, like a typical social organization, even though this organization is largely "extra-institutional" (Lofland 1981, 414).

According to Lofland, collective behaviors vary along dimensions defined by **dominant emotions** and **organizational forms**. A great many emotions may be expressed within a social movement, but in most cases, there is a primary feeling associated with the movement, "the publicly expressed feeling perceived by the participants and observers as most prominent" (Lofland 1981, 414).

Lofland, again following the work of Turner and Blumer, stresses how variation and gradation are invariably present in any instance of collective behavior. He feels it is important to identity the definitive sentiments of people who are caught up in the behavior and the means by which they organize their actions.

We will follow Lofland's classification of forms of collective behavior, but in no way will these examples depict all forms of collective behavior. In fact, we will not even cover all the possibilities in Lofland's scheme, however, the examples selected are representative and dramatic.

CROWDS

Everyone has at one time or another, been a part of a **crowd**. Most of the time, this amounts to an inconvenient or, at worst, mildly irritating experience. And perhaps most significantly, this experience is usually ordinary, routine, and even boring. On occasion, however, something happens that sends fear throughout a crowd. Rumors travel among those present that something terrible has happened. The most dramatic illustrations of this kind of collective behavior are the several tragic cases when a crowd of people in a nightclub or at a theater learn that a fire has broken out near them. People who were enjoying themselves in an atmosphere of relaxation and entertainment instantly shift to behaviors they believe will assure their survival. Of course, their collective actions taken in fear can have the opposite effect as they rush the doors, disregarding the elemental rules of turn taking that would make orderly escape possible.

Panic is a fear-based response to a situation that is perceived of as beyond hope, a collective expression of fear. On the sociological level, it means a loss of trust in the routine, a sense that something so extraordinary is going on that the problem-solving methods of everyday life simply do not apply. As Lofland points out, not much contemporary research exists on panic. However, he suggests that some guidelines can be drawn for an understanding of the social psychological significance of the concept.

Panic may well follow different patterns. It may develop in sequences from frustration and excitation to expressions of panic. There can, however, be great variation in the expression of panic; for instance, *escape* panic, as with people who believe they are trapped in a burning building, may be quite different in its expression from *acquisitive* panic in which a crowd tries to gain something like in an attempt to take over a building, or secure a territory, or obtain a Cabbage Patch Kid for a Christmas toy (Brown 1954, 859).

Panic is also a reaction to the breakdown of social organization. Crowds are, of course, minimally organized. No one is in charge, and there is no taken-for-granted routine in a crowd. Of course, though crowds may be described as orderly, we usually mean by this that the people who make up the crowd behave in accordance with internalized standards of "good public conduct." The design of a public space, such as

These cute dolls were the objects of acquisitive panic a few years ago and they remain popular gift items. How would you explain the crowd panic that occurred among people waiting in lines to buy Cabbage Patch Kids?

a baseball or football stadium, for example, compensates for the lack of internal social organization in crowds by imposing physical restraints, such as the turnstile (cf. Goffman 1971).

Terror is another expressed form of crowd fear. Moviemakers have long been aware of ways to evoke a sense of terror in their audience. They take an ordinary scene, a setting everybody takes for granted (a kitchen, a suburban living room, a summer camp); then, they suddenly violate our assumptions by showing something totally unexpected. The result evokes sheer terror.

In the movie *Friday the Thirteenth,* there is a scene which illustrates what we mean. A young woman goes to the refrigerator, opens the door and discovers the head of her mother posed like leftover meatloaf. As she stands shrieking, immobilized by terror, she is knifed in the temple. In another scene, a crisis seems to pass after the killer has been "done away with." As the actors rest relaxed in an ordinary living room, a grotesque figure crashes through the picture window. Terror is called forth in the audience by a shocking interruption of everyday life.

Movies like *Friday the Thirteenth* fabricate terror, but several sociologists (Goffman 1971 and Lefebrve 1971) have related terror to the particular social organization of public life in modern society and the overbearing need to impose order on a disorderly public.

Henri Lefebrve (1971) shows how the overall organization of society operates against the achievement of clarity about one's location in society. Routine life is constantly challenged by planned change which is necessary for modern economy. A consequence of the contradictions built into modern society is organization into vastly different classes (compare the middle classes with the underclasses). Because of the differences literally created by society, repression is the only remaining effective means of control.

A repressive society maintains order through persuasion and compulsion. The first mode is primarily communicative and the second, legal. According to Lefebrve, "over-repressiveness" produces a terrorist society, where the threat of violence is ever present. However, we are not referring just to overt violence against individuals or groups, but to violence that intrudes on everyday life.

There is irony to life in modern society, according to Lefebrve. Whereas everyday life may be devoid of festival, style, and art, and its linguistic forms hollow, a "zero point of language," people are still preoccupied with communication and meaning. Terrorist society "is obsessed with dialogue, communication, participation, integration and coherence, all the things it misses" (Lefebrve 1971, 185).

We can conclude that citizens in modern society learn to assume a cynical attitude about others and about any hope they have for a permanently valid interpretation of the nature of their social existence. They work to establish order in the small worlds over which they believe they have some control (Luckmann 1974). These small worlds, however, are built on networks of interaction which may be either stretched thin over

Many social movements are grounded in strong beliefs. These beliefs are expressed in ways appropriate to the movement's goals and style. Imagine that you are a reporter for a newspaper and your assignment is to write a narrative caption for this picture. What are these people doing and saying? What features in the picture allow you to reach your conclusions?

relatively large numbers of people of disparate backgrounds (as in the case of crowds) or consist of a few people bound together in closely knit, emotional associations. Either way, the breadth of change and uncertainty in the larger social world renders these small worlds exceedingly fragile leaving us vulnerable to modern forms of collective behavior.

Angry Crowds

Whereas many instances of collective behavior in modern society derive from terror, there are many others which grow out of a sense of violated distributive justice. We have already discussed the social psychological consequences of inequality. Now we expand on those insights. For instance, a riot may be a systematic, collective way of expressing hostility. Wright (1978) studied the riots in the Watts area of Los Angeles in the late 1960s. His data refute the impression many lay people have of riots, namely that they are unorganized, irrational, and uncontrollable expressions of hostility.

Instead, he discovered rioters used rather systematic means to identify what they regarded as proper targets for hostility. His field notes read:

As I was making a right turn on the street where the action was centered, several Negro youths ran up to my car. They said, "Turn your inside lights on,

Blood, so we can see who it is." . . . Large numbers of men and women and children were gathered on both sides of the street with bricks and other objects in their hands. Just up the street was a car which had been upturned and set afire. . . . A car came roaring down the street. The crowd yelled: "Whitey! Get him!" . . . Bricks, stones and pipes, hurled from both sides of the street, dented both sides of the car. The front windshield was smashed. The car speeded up and kept going until it was out of the area. . . . The people around, watching the man being beaten, kept yelling: "Beat the _____ _____. Teach him to keep his ass out of Watts." (Wright 1978, 47).

Wright's point is that whether or not we see this kind of behavior as acceptable, it *is* based on judgments and it *does* involve symbolic meaning. Wright suggests that we view these types of "irrational" actions as "situationally rational."

Frustration may well fire crowd hostility. Black citizens in Watts, in undesirable living conditions, expressed their hostility toward whites who, according to the black interpretation of the social world, were responsible for those living conditions. Less global but still powerful examples of crowd hostility can be found within leisure time pursuits, for instance among football fans. A cameraman for NFL games in a major midwestern city gave the following account of crowd hostility:

Let me tell you it was a zoo out there. The camera I worked was the sideline camera. At the old Met, the camera blocked the view of people who had paid fairly big bucks for those seats. Well, when the Vikes were behind, or there was some important play going on, I'd catch hell from the fans. I didn't mind much 'til they started throwing things . . . first paper, then bottles and finally full cans of beer. I started wearing a football helmet, and once I had to have a police escort to get off the field after the game.

The nasty side of collective behavior is related to both individual and social experiences, and neither experience can be appreciated without the other.

Joyful Crowds

The literature on collective behavior generally focuses on the darker side of social life. However, there are many instances of collective behavior which are far from gloomy. These include a range of phenomena from the sacred to the profane, from festivals to excited crowds. In a recent article, Lofland (1982) outlines the important considerations in the understanding of the **joy crowd**.

He instructs the reader to think of joy crowds in terms of five dimensions:

1. The level of psychobiological arousal of crowd members.
2. The proportion of minority to majority members displaying this level of involvement.
3. The social definition of the nature, meaning, and import of the arousal.

4. The degree to which joy crowds are institutionalized.

5. The duration of the arousal (Lofland 1982, 357–58).

Among the examples of joyous crowds Lofland discusses are sacred crowds. This includes "ecstatic upheavals" such as the Vailala Madness reported by Goodman (1974, 232). This famous event occurred in 1919 in the then British territory of Papua (New Guinea). Members of villages began to behave "hysterically." Their heads were said to "go around", and they "twisted" their bodies, fell to the ground, and spoke "unintelligible exclamations". These manifestations of extreme joy were interpreted by members of the villages as meaning that the ancestors of the village were about to return in cargo-laden ships. There were several phases to the excitement. Generally, these followed a pattern of arousal, climax, plateau, and resumption of routine life.

Lofland continues to demonstrate the variation among sacred joy crowds by discussing **ecstatic conventions**, which refer to the practice in some societies of "harnessing" crowd energy into regularized occasions.

Some collective gatherings celebrate special accomplishments. In this picture there are many clues as to what is being celebrated, but as with collective behaviors, the messages are open to differing interpretations. Think of at least three plausible reasons for a football team to stroll down a residential street.

There are devices in the organization of crowds which can stir up such religious "effervescence." These include singing, swaying of bodies, piercing cries, and chants. These manifestations are typically short-lived, but they may give rise to more enduring forms.

The ecstatic congregation exists in American society among fundamentalist religious groups. Hardly anyone who attends such a service can avoid the feelings of emotional arousal. Of course, there are degrees in the permanency of these crowds. A permanent form is the stable congregation, and a temporary one is the euphoric mood. There are regular conventions in some groups for arousing excitement. Preachers conducting revivals travel circuits attempting to evoke high levels of joy in audiences. Lofland also identifies "reverent congregations" which can be observed at festivals, sometimes involving vast numbers of believers crowding together to celebrate some occasion like a miracle.

Such sacred crowds contrast with the profane. These latter can be reveling crowds like those typical of a New Orlean's Mardi Gras, or even the wild excitement of *Rocky Horror Picture Show* audiences. Of course, celebrations of World Series or Super Bowl victories can result in reveling crowds. There is also a sense in which we can talk about the excited crowd, one anticipating the arrival of a celebrity, or as is often the custom on campuses of northern colleges, the gathering of students for snowball fights after the first big snow of the year.

Lofland offers us a program for thinking about the rich and wide-ranging variations accompanying the collective expression of joy. Some leaders of social movements are, indeed, masters of arousal, playing to the joy potential in a crowd with their rhetoric. By using familiar cultural beliefs, they can create, even in the midst of modern society, occasions of collective celebration. However, the meanings we attribute to these occasions are fluid. A joy crowd can transform into a hostile crowd with astonishing suddenness. The president of a major university recently commended the crowd behavior of football fans after an important game. He said it was true the coach of his team was pelted with eggs and several football players were drenched with liquor by excited fans, but he added, "this was the best-behaved crowd we have had in several years."

MASS COLLECTIVE BEHAVIOR

Sociologists often use the term **mass** in discussions of collective behavior. Several years ago, William Kornhauser (1959) attempted to give a precise definition to this term. He distinguished among several meanings for the word "mass." His theory distinguishes between people who lead and have power (**elites**) and those who react or follow (**nonelites**). Further, he defines mass in terms of **availability** and **accessibility**. He means by these two latter terms the degree to which people in control of a given occasion can be influenced by those they control (accessibility) and the degree to which people in control can influence those they control (availability). He defines a mass society, for example, as being characterized by both high availability and high accessibility. You can think of this distinction in terms of the flow of information: in a mass society, information flows from a highly accessible elite to a highly available audience. This way of thinking of mass society generalizes to understanding some types of collective behavior.

Max Weber, in his classic discussion of **charisma**, suggested that organizations which grow around charismatic leaders are better defined the closer one gets to the center of power. An inner circle almost always surrounds the leader. As one moves into the outer circles of the movement, one finds less well-defined units until you reach the masses. Masses are primarily audiences, loosely defined categories of people who are perceived as having homogeneous feelings, thoughts, or reactions to some topic or state of affairs.

Kornhauser's (1959) model helps us appreciate the exchanges taking place between leaders and followers. These exchanges may be imbalanced in favor of the elite, but they are not completely one-sided. Consider a typical fall afternoon at a football game. The people in the stadium, physically present, occupying space are a crowd, while the audience at home watching or listening to the game through the media of TV or radio are a mass. Although masses cannot directly affect the content of the game whereas the crowd can (think of the home field advantage), the mass can be described as having a symbolic territory and as being a social reality.

In an intriguing article, Zurcher (1983) details how a football game can be seen as an elaborate and skillful production designed to evoke appropriate emotions both in participants and spectators. If a game does not succeed as "staged emotions," if for instance, it is interpreted as "boring" by the mass audience, then television ratings are low and a network or station may cancel the future broadcast of football games. With the stakes so high, we can easily see how the audience can affect production, and, likewise, we can grasp the necessity for the production of an exciting event (games which elicit the emotions of fans). Football, both at the professional and college levels, can be accurately described as the deliberate staging of a performance complete with audience warm-ups, props, costumes, and well-rehearsed performers.

Mass Fear

Returning to the dark side of collective behavior, we can look at fear as a mass phenomenon. **Mass fears** may be connected to possibilities of environmental and social disasters, or to widely publicized trends which people believe will change their lives irrevocably. Since the flow of information to the masses is asymmetrical (high accessibility and high availability), the study of the content and style of news and other types of public information is of vital importance in understanding mass fear (Lofland 1981, 421–27).

We can distinguish two kinds of mass fear derived from information people receive about events outside their personal social world. First, there is an immediate and often short-lived fear associated with disaster. Whenever members of a community first hear of a disaster, like the explosion at the Texas City Oil Refinery in the 1950s, a sense of fear rapidly spreads over the community and beyond. The fear is more intense, of course, among those who feel closest to the site of the disaster. Relatives of men who worked in the refinery reported the eerie feelings they experienced when they heard of the disaster. Disasters of this type, however, affect relatively small numbers of people. Most people simply hear about the disaster. The fear evoked by news of a disaster fades in immediacy as it is filtered through personal relationships. Ironically, our everyday routines transform the "terrifying" news which has become a common part of our knowledge of world and community events into impersonal information. Mass fear begins from mass sources, radio, television, or newspapers, but it is absorbed into existing social structures. A report of a disaster, for example, becomes something to be fearful of according to how people interpret that event as relevant to their everyday lives. If the event is relevant, it may have involved them in personal tragedy; if it is seen as irrelevant, people simply have more information about the tragic nature of life in society.

Studies of how communities react to natural disasters generally indicate that the initial reaction of mass fear is a transitional stage leading to a redefinition of ordinary life. The first redefinition has to do with formulating "rescue" operations into routines. Rescue work may consist of actually clearing debris and helping people relocate after a violent storm; or, it may consist of emotional and social rescue, as in the case of giving comfort and performing other remedial tasks necessary for victims to "pick-up" the pieces of personal and public life.

In his study of the Texas City disaster, Killian (1952) showed the significance of multiple group memberships in the handling of fear. He reported that persons experience extreme role conflict in connection with disasters. For example, foremen who were home at the time they heard about the explosion at the refinery, were caught between a sense of obligation they felt to their friends at the refinery who might need their help and the needs of their families. Generally, the resolution of this dilemma paralleled a description of the ordering of role obligations. Although this ordering could vary from person to person, it seemed to reflect an internal organization. People ordered their reactions to the disaster in ways consistent with their self-concepts. Most men, therefore, looked after their families first, then proceeded with their jobs. If they had been at the refinery at the time of the blast, their first concerns were to inform family members of their safety. If they were "off duty," they first "ordered" their family affairs (located their off-spring and spouses) and then headed for the refinery.

Again, following Lofland, we note how vast the variations of mass fear can be. Some disasters can be prepared for, as in the case of hurricanes and, more recently, with the advent of sophisticated radar equipment, even tornados. Earthquakes are still random from the perspective of everyday life. When we look at the meanings of mass fear, we discover that disasters which seem random, yet are perceived as immediate, elicit the strongest fears. Rarely occurring phenomena, like major earthquakes, can be pushed from everyday consciousness, as can remote disasters like terrorism in the Middle East.

Actual disasters, on the other hand, call for mobilizing what people know about solving problems, and activating links between their home territory and larger societal domains. A good way to think about the process which underlies how people make sense of disasters is to remember a generalization: *Action reinforces existing and potential symbolic links between victims and their larger social environments, while fear without action, heightens the vulnerability of social structure by increasing the distance between what people think they know and what they actually know.*

Several studies illustrate this principle. Truly "massive" disasters, like tornados and floods, may have far-reaching effects on the social life of victims. Erickson (1979) studied a flood at Buffalo Creek and concluded that the disaster destroyed the community and social networks within it. He characterized the residents of the town as apathetic and powerless. However, as they began to react to their loss, they transformed the tragedy into a symbolic starting point for a new sense of community, the process involved was a kind of storytelling about the meanings of the flood for the community.

On the other hand, fears for which no corresponding courses of action are available, often reach proportions out of scale to the probability of actual disaster. Lofland (1981) refers to such fears as "false." An illustration of **false fear** includes Orson Welles' famous 1938 radio broadcast, "War of the Worlds." This story of the invasion of the earth by Martians evoked mass fear in the audience when dramatically performed as a newscast. Audiences tuning in for parts of the broadcast (and recently alarmed by on-the-spot coverage of the real tragedy, the crash of the airship *Hindenburg*) believed the space invasion to be real.

Of course, there is a sense in which false fears reflect real fears. In 1938 people were fearful of an invasion and of the war that eventually involved the United States. Any fear may be based on some actual threat not fully articulated by the person who believes a rumor or who even experiences a "phantom" or imagined physical symptom as was the case when workers at a clothing factory "suffered what purported to be insect bites" in the summer of 1962 (Kerckhoff and Back 1968).

Studies of such false fears (Cantril 1947) provides a model for describing how people deal with information they do not fully understand. Some treat it as an immediate personal threat, and may experience an imagined physical symptom. Extreme reactions of this kind of audience, in the case of the invasion from Mars, included actual preparation for the invasion (we might include survivalists in this category). Other listeners simply became confused and alarmed, gradually realizing the true nature of the broadcast as they continued to listen to the program. While most people have learned to distinguish the everyday or the imaginative from the news-worthy, this is not always an easy task.

Mass Hostility

Crowd hostility has been extensively studied. At first, it is difficult to imagine hostility in a mass form. We have a point of reference for the image of the "angry crowd." The mass, however, is amorphous. Masses can not act in concert since they are primarily merely audiences. Crowds act. Masses react. Although there are few empirical studies of the distribution of feelings of hostility, we can cite observations and experiences which indicate how powerful this form of collective behavior can be.

Anyone who has driven in a large city is familiar with one manifestation of **mass hostility**. Several years ago, Walt Disney produced a cartoon about the average American driver. The cartoon began with a tranquil scene showing a well-mannered Goofy preparing for an automobile trip. He is the picture of patience and forbearance as he copes with the frustrations of bags which do not close, and children who do not cooperate. However, as soon as he gets behind the wheel of the car, he transforms into a hideous monster. His face contorts into a hog's as he battles other drivers for dominion of the roadway; flames roar from his nostrils as his hostility emotes on the screen.

It is easier to honk a horn at another car than it is to insult a person face-to-face, because there is something isolating about the vehicular shell which surrounds a driver. The metal and the glass seem to insulate one driver from another in the same way that rituals of exchange, little niceties of greetings, and turn taking, smooth out differences of backgrounds and intentions. But the objects of traffic are not people, and to many of us, it is easy to treat a car as a proper target of hostility.

Mass hostility which leads people to treat each other as objects may well be associated with specific features of modern life. For example, Phillip's (1983) research indicates that suicide rates are tied to reports of certain kinds of media events, like presidential elections, prize fights, and suicides of prominent people. This association might well be linked to increased or decreased levels of mass hostility. Likewise the studies by Smelser (1963) and Spilerman (1976) indicate how dramatic events of disorder in black ghettos are clustered following equally dramatic mass events. Of course, the riots and increases in individual violence which followed the assassination of Dr. Martin Luther King illustrate this kind of phenomenon.

Although it is difficult to measure and usually benign in its effects, mass hostility can be felt. In American cities which have National Football League teams, hostility may be expressed by football fans. Males whose hometown team has suffered a particularly disappointing loss may bring hostility to work with them on Monday morning. This hostility is typically channeled into productive activities, or it may become a factor in a person's mode of dealing with the world. Fans report being depressed, or feeling "out of sorts" after such a loss. On the other hand, they may be "high" on a "sweet victory" for several days. A mass experience like extreme disappointment with a professional sports team can affect a pervasive mood among members of a community.

Such pervasive moods play a part in the statistical relationships Phillips and others report. In their most malignant forms, these moods can target groups for vilification and even punishment. Irwin (1980) documents "swastika epidemics" in American prisons where mass hostility erupts in individual acts of anti-Semitism and vandalism. And as Spilerman asserts, "there is considerable evidence that skyjackings, prison riots, bomb threats and aggressive crimes of other sorts have been spread by television and other mass media" (Spilerman 1976, 790).

Hostility is a concept which refers to individual emotion. In its collective form, it can be expressed in varying degrees of organization. It can be tightly packaged into personalities, it may be the bond of solidarity which holds a crowd together, or it can be a generally distributed feeling collectively experienced but not expressed. Mass hostility is typically diffused through a thousand horn honks and angry verbal exchanges. It flows without focus and without symbolic import in the "keyed" playing of the roles of everyday life. Still, on occasion, it can reach a highly organized level of mass expression.

Mass Joy

The most common forms of **mass joy** are crazes, fashion, and fads. A craze evokes in its participants high arousal levels, but it does not often sustain them. A good example of this was the Hula Hoop craze; for a while, it seemed that the whole nation was twirling circles of plastic around their waists in frenzied but pointless activity.

At times a craze can grasp the attention of large numbers of people. A recent illustration of a craze is the rather systematic and energetic "yearning for yesterday" which we call **nostalgia** (Davis 1979). It is everywhere: art deco candle holders, artists of the 1930s, and certainly movies like *Raiders of the Lost Arc* evoke "tones" and "feelings" of the bygone days. From "puttin' on the Ritz" to a yearning for a return to the days when gangs were noble, without drugs or confusion (a theme which runs through the film *Rumble Fish*), citizens of modern society consume versions of the past in ways designed to comfort and impart meaning to the present.

Davis shows us how nostalgia as a social phenomenon serves collective ends. By reconstructing what the past was like, we can sharpen and define meanings in the present which we want to make important. We may know the simplicity of yesterday is lost, but through nostalgia, we can express a yearning for its return.

Everyday life in modern society, we have learned, is full of problems associated with the business of interacting with strangers. We must negotiate our own sense of belonging in society, rather than rely on tradition to locate us in society. No wonder, as Davis suggests, nostalgia has its greatest appeal during times of transition both in the society and in the life cycle of the individual. The strong nostalgia craze which we witnessed during the 1970s was due in part to a convergence of real changes in the society and the coming of age of millions of Americans. A yearning for the past which can take on proportions of a craze represents the efforts of a generation of people to make sense out of the past during times when the continuity between past and present is difficult to see.

Although most of this yearning is put into practice in acts of consuming (tickets to movies, records, clothes), it also serves wider social ends. Davis carefully defines the phenomenon of "generational nostalgia" as the construction of a version of the past by persons who collectively experience rapid social change at critical junctures in their life cycles. Seen in this light:

...nostalgic sentiment partakes of one of the great dialectical processes of Western civilization: the ceaseless tension of change vs. stability, innovation vs. reaffirmation, new vs. old, utopia vs. golden age. Its role in this dialectic is that of a brake, to be sure, since little in contemporary life seems capable of arresting the march of modern technology and rational organization. Nonetheless it is, perhaps, enough of a break to cause some individuals and peoples to look before they knowingly leap (Davis 1979, 116).

Fashions and Fads

A **fashion** is a "pleasurable mass involvement which participants define as important but not critical and in which people are variously engaged depending on the particular fashion" (Lofland 1981, 442). Fashions influence the meanings of objects and activities as diverse as the shape of collars on a dress shirt to life styles. Fashion is clearly influenced by the institutions of society. The fashion industry, for example, may make available to the consumer the "latest" in clothing. Certainly, the influence between this institutional production of fashion and the spontaneous emergence of fashion is mutual. Styles of clothing which were once thought of as exclusively "hippie" are now part of the standard apparel of the "well-dressed" urbanite. Blue jeans are the best example of this. Since the advent of designer jeans, we have exchanged the conscious rebellion of blue-jean-clad teenagers in the mid-sixties for the designer label across the derriere.

We can appreciate the social psychological significance of **fads** and fashions by tracing their origins. If we can locate in a social context the fashions of dress, like Ocean Pacific clothes, pierced ears, blue jeans, long or short hair, then we have yet another way to describe the ways in which society and self interrelate at the collective level.

THE SCENE AS AN ACTIVITY SYSTEM

John Irwin has developed concepts for understanding some specific types of collective behavior. His ideas also have added greatly to our appreciation of how some seemingly trivial fads and crazes can influence the very normative structures of society.   His idea is simple, yet profound in implication.

He begins by noting the major changes that have taken place in society. The most significant for collective behavior, he suggests, is the fact that individuals have increased leisure time and have more expendable income. Whereas the workplace used to be the primary arena in which persons established their adult identities, in contemporary society more and more people find themselves employed in jobs which they regard as boring, routine and, most importantly, as unfulfilling.   Although a strong case can certainly be made that work in industrial society has always been mostly menial, what is different now, Irwin contends, is the relative pay people receive for work—they have more money left over after purchasing basics—and, the fact that they simply spend fewer hours at the job.   The arena in which people derive a sense of self has shifted from work to play. Along with the shift have come several other changes.

According to Irwin, people are self-consciously aware of the degree to which they are "on stage" in everyday life, and they have learned how to participate in small activity systems in ways which allow them to think of themselves as doing important things.   Even if the systems of activity they operate in are purely recreational, they have learned to interpret their activities as relevant to their self-concepts.   Irwin calls these systems **scenes**.

Scenes are urban, leisure-oriented, and youthful.   They are the territories within which action is sought.   They operate to provide people excitement and a sense of doing something out of the ordinary.   The picture of scenes Irwin portrays shows loosely organized bands of people coming together around shared interests, engaged in "finding where the action is."   He discusses how people learn to "plug into" scenes, how they establish levels of involvements in scenes and how they move from scene to scene in search of new action.   He stresses how all this scene activity is conducted self-consciously, and how even participating in criminal scenes can be transitory, staged, and essentially for fun.

Irwin offers a theory of scenes which give us insights into the nature of life in modern society.   Contemporary lifestyles, crazes, and fads must be seen, he suggests, neither as passing temporary deviations from normal life or as revolutionary social movements.   His view of youthful actors playing in their chosen arenas takes into account both the transitory and the genuinely influential aspects of modern scenes.

A scene activity represents learning how to make and to maintain contacts and mutual interests, and how to behave in ways which, at the same time, serve individual and social ends.   Irwin traces the emergence of the scene to pre-World War II California. In a sense, scenes began out of the efforts of large numbers of idled young men to find things to do on the beaches of southern California.   Just as the economic recovery from the Great Depression was moving forward, beach bums began to inhabit the shores.   They simply "hung out," talked, and combed the beaches in search of action and shells. Some of the more athletic men began to surf on heavy redwood boards. The war broke up these aggregates. But after the war, some of the men returned to the beach. This time some of them had skills in aircraft technologies which they put to work in the design of lighter and better surf boards. After the war, there were gradually more and more people on the beach. California boomed, and by the late 1940s and early 1950s, a large enough number of people had interest in and skills for a single activity that the first "grand scene" emerged. This scene was what we now know as the "surfin' scene".

By carefully describing the history of surfing, Irwin develops a model for understanding the life phases of any scene. According to Irwin, scenes past through separate stages. First is the **articulation stage**. During this stage, relatively small numbers of people come together around a single activity. They spend many hours talking about and doing the activity. An outcome of all this action is the emergence of norms and values for scene conduct. These often include beliefs about the worth of the action (usually defined in contrast to what are imagined as mainstream values) and strong ideas about the "proper" conduct of action. The norms of a scene are formulated during the articulation phase, and people who may later become heros and leaders of the scene find they are in the center of a new world.

The second phase in the "natural history" of scenes is the **golden age**. During this phase, most of the basic norms governing proper activities have been formulated. Leaders emerge. They are charismatic types who happened to have been involved in the formation of the scene. They find themselves in the center of action, serving new members as references for the mastery of norms and appropriate action.

Third is the period of **expansion**. Expansion is not inevitable in the growth of scenes. It does occur, however, whenever a scene attracts national attention. Surfing, hippies, running and a variety of other scenes have gone through expansion. During this period the informal character of the norms of the scene are stretched to the breaking point. There are simply too many people participating in the activity for the old ways to function.

Also, a related problem of control appears. In the articulation and golden age of a scene, leaders can look over the core action. They can literally be in the territories of action. Their presence helps to reinforce the particular versions of meanings for what is going on. Drug "trips" can be managed; the ultimate wave can be discussed in terms of the latest experiences of core members, and the "best" run ever can be judged by those who know and respect each other's competencies at running. When strangers, first timers, and the generally uninitiated flood the territory (the beaches, the Haight-Ashbury district of San Francisco, and the roadways of city parks), scenes change. They confront the mainstream values of society squarely, and they must accommodate themselves to pressures from within their ranks and from without.

From the vantage of scene members, expansion means a corruption of the norms and purity of action. A consequence of expansion is, then, the spoiling of the scene. This happens as the direct result of institutional social control, like the police breaking up hippie "crash pads" with drug raids, the enforcing of no trespassing laws so that surfers are driven off the best beaches, and, of course, clashes between runners and motorists in which attempts by communities are made to license runners and restrict them to certain roadways.

Corruption forces the scene to be more conventional, "to clean up its act." A scene may well survive corruption. When it does it enters **stagnation.** Stagnation is a stage in which there are remnants of the old norms (a flavor of the "good old days"), but the scene has come under control of the more widely distributed control mechanisms of society. What is gained in respectability is lost in distinctiveness. Whereas the scene used to be a source for the derivation of self-esteem and a sense of uniqueness, now scene involvement has become routine and businesslike. Although many "diehards" and even latecomers may sustain a scene for long periods of time, the magic of the stages of articulation and the golden age is lost. Irwin suggests that by the time a scene stagnates, most of the original members are into something else.

Irwin substantiates his model with detailed documentation of surfing and hippies. Although the relative length and intensity of the phases varies, each of these two scenes went through the full cycle of the natural history. Irwin calls these two scenes **grand scenes**. By this he means they reached a level of popularity in which they involved literally hundreds of thousands of people. The label grand scene suggests "special dimensions and unique histories," and that, at one time, these scenes were exciting and appealing in ways which reached far beyond the actual people participating in surfing or living as hippies. According to Irwin, these scenes not only elicited attention from society, but they also altered convention. Surfing as a scene continues to be a major influence in clothing styles and musical tastes in America. Likewise, attitudes toward leisure, work, and the search for meaning in personal life are "hip" in origin.

To appreciate how pervasive the values and norms of surfing have become, we need only watch television where surfing can still appear as a theme in a beer commercial. A well known surfer, speaking from a surfer bar, beer in hand, expresses the opinion that he might get a job and quit all this "beach life." His friends cease their reveling and quietly turn their attention to him. There is a long pause. Then, he replies "Naw", to the joyous relief of his friends.

Irwin's thesis that the work place has lost much of its power for imparting self-meanings seems quite plausible, as does his idea that profound social change, beyond that of clothing and hair styles, can derive from essentially leisure time activities. Irwin teaches us how seemingly trivial items of collective behavior can be a part of a process of change affecting even the core values and attitudes of members of society.

FROM SCENE TO SOCIAL MOVEMENT

Irwin's theory of scenes pertains to particular kinds of societies, those with relatively high degrees of affluence for large numbers of its members. A scene is a modern **social movement**.

The study of social movements concerns collective responses to some conditions or needs which become organized toward specific goals. Social movements are goal directed. They are comprised of people, sometimes from disparate backgrounds, who are banded together around a common cause. The history of social change in western societies is often a history of the impact of powerful social movements.

Social movements can be focused on a remarkable range of topics, concerns, and perceived problems. Currently, we are familiar with various ecological movements, some designed to save the American eagle, others, the whales, and still others, the whole world itself. Of course, anti-abortion movements can be quite strong as can causes like freedom for political prisoners. It is apparent that movements know no limits of topics or political persuasions. However, even though movements can concern an amazingly wide array of issues, they do all have a typical form.

We will discuss two social movements to illustrate this form: First we will examine how people bound together by religious beliefs about the necessity to save the world became a significant social force in the life of many American young people; secondly, we will study an important social movement which "changed the face of the world."

From the late 1950s through the middle 1960s, John Lofland studied what was then an obscure religious cult. It happened that this cult later gained national attention because of the extreme techniques members used to assure conformity among its members and because of the conflicts it had with the conventional culture.

During the course of the study, Lofland, first with Stark and then alone, worked on a model of the **conversion process**. He offers a detailed description of the conditions, both psychological and social, which are necessary for an individual to experience a conversion (a radical alteration of worldview and social being). The people whom Lofland observed were not only "joining a cult"; they were being transformed in what appeared to be a rather fundamental way. People who had been functioning as graduate students in a state university suddenly, or so it seemed, expressed a belief in the immediate end of the world. Their whole lives were absorbed in the belief, and they became members of (and in some cases proselytizers for) the Divine Precepts, also known as "A Complete New Age Revelation." Such dramatic transformations are not very common, and Lofland sought a thorough understanding of how a collective movement like the Divine Precepts cult appealed to, recruited, and transformed the lives of ordinary people.

He explored the backgrounds of people who had become cult members. In some cases, he actually watched them convert to the Divine Precepts.

Participation in some collective movements results in conversion experiences where people acquire new identities. Sometimes these identities are strong and enduring and seem to encompass all other identities that the member of the movement might have.

After years of documenting these transformations, he advanced a model which explains the conversion process. Although Lofland offers this model to account for his observations of the DP (Divine Precepts) cult, it clearly has implications for understanding how certain beliefs and emotional dispositions already existing among people can be organized to effect significant changes in the lives of those who convert as well as the lives of those who must deal with the converts.

Before a person becomes a candidate for conversion, he or she must have first experienced "enduring acutely felt tensions." These tensions are usually felt in personal ways; they may entail the death of a loved one, a tragic event in one's own life, or the life of a close friend. Secondly, without exception, the converts to the DP cult experienced these tensions within a religious, problem-solving perspective. Not all DP converts had been devoutly religious before their conversion. In fact, many were living outside of any conventional church. They did, however, tend to evaluate their problems religiously. Hence, they saw their problems as resulting from past "sins," and they saw God as punishing or as rewarding their "earthly" deeds.

The third dynamic in the conversion process required a shift in self-concept. Instead of seeing themselves as people suffering at the hands of fate, DP cult members saw themselves as seeking the truth about their own predicaments. As Lofland puts it, they become "religious seekers." While they still were not full cult converts at this point, they typically learned of the Divine Precepts. In their general quest of religious insights, they were exposed to the beliefs of the cult. This happened sometimes through chance (they just happened across a pamphlet), or they ran into a cult member who explained DP to them.

Fourth, the encounter with the DP beliefs and with DP believers became a turning point in the convert's life. Soon the bulk of their waking hours, topics of conversation and thoughts were exclusively about the Divine Precepts. This process can be thought of as an immersion in the social world of the believers. Although at this stage, converts are still not full cult members, they are undergoing what was referred to in a early chapter as extreme secondary socialization. Simply talking and thinking in DP terms, however, is not sufficient for complete conversion. At this stage the crucial experience seems to be an emotional one.

Sentiments, or in Lofland's words, "affective bonds," emerged out of hours of interaction with cult members. In some cases, these bonds pre-existed, that is, they were established previously, even in a secular context. But most often, these emotional ties were fresh and strong. Since the topic of talk and thought at this point was almost exclusively the Divine Precepts and related matters, cult ties began to supplant extra-cult friend-ships and social relationships. Lofland refers to this stage as one in which "extra-cult attachments are low or neutralized" (Lofland 1980, 8).

Finally, the indication that full conversion had been accomplished was when a person became a "deployable agent," trustworthy enough to go into the world of unbelievers and represent the Divine Precepts. This stage entailed intensive interaction among "true believers". These "agents" served as symbols for the cult itself. They ultimately became proselytizers for Divine Precepts.

Lofland's work tells us that collective behaviors can become all encom-passing for some people. As we know, on occasion, such movements can generate considerable interest among the representatives of conventional culture. However, it is important to understand that Lofland is depicting a **funneling process** of recruitment. At the first stage the criterion is minimal; it applies to many, perhaps all members of society. We have all experienced tension and problems in our everyday life; the next stage narrows the opening of the funnel. Now, the movement draws only from those who see these ordinary problems in an extraordinary way (sacred meanings for secular events). Each successive stage narrows the opening even more until only a few are selected as converts.

Social movements often recruit in such a funneling process. Hence, they build on as broad a base as possible to groom a few core members. Although a social movement may involve relatively few core members, it can exert a disproportionate influence on society if it uses themes of common experiences. This is exactly what the DP cult members were able to accomplish, until the formal social control institutions of society (courts, churches and families) operated to conventionalize the cult. Faced with the overwhelming power of the institutions of society, most social move-ments, including the DP cult, adapt. Adaptation is achieved in several ways. A movement can retreat from confrontation. When this happens, the core goals of a movement may be redefined. For a millennial cult like the Divine Precepts, this may mean changing their beliefs about the necessity to save the world. They may have to be content with maintaining themselves within more modest goals (like simply being ready themselves for the end or the second coming of Christ). Cult members may become more conventional themselves, or, as is often the case, a cult may simply fade away when its techniques to neutralize extra-movement contact weaken and its members drift back into the mainstream of social life.

Adaptations reflect the power of convention. Most movements, even grand scenes, fall short of their expressed ends. Society remains secular in spite of literally thousands of hours of human effort on the part of believers to transform it into something more Godlike. Ironically, scenes which are not true movements may have much more lasting effects on society than true movements which have explicitly defined goals for social change. Overall society is more "hip" in 1984 that it was in 1964.

Davis (1967) argued this point several years ago in an intriguing article entitled "Why All of Us May Be Hippies Someday". In this article, he contends that the values and norms which emerged from the hippie scene had their roots in changes already taking place in society, such as the shift from work to leisure or changes in traditional social structure. Hippies offered middle-class society an alternative way of living. The hippies represented an extreme, even distorted alternative; nevertheless, what they offered was understandable by the very standards the middle class sought to maintain. Although the whole idea of hippies now seems quaint, their legacy remains. They made explicit the effects of social change in personal life. Davis was right, it appears; we are hippies in our relaxed attitudes about personal relationships, drug use, egoism and the individuation of experience. As a social movement, hippies influenced attitudes and styles of life in profound, if indirect, ways.

Under special conditions social movements can exert pressures on society which result in direct major change, even in the very structure of that society itself. Perhaps, no other single social movement had more profound impact on the fate of a single nation, or of the world, for that matter, than the National Socialist Party, known as the Nazi party.

The usual way of explaining the appeal of Nazism has been to trace its ideological inflexibility to corresponding inflexibilities in the personalities of those involved in the movement (Adorno, et. al. 1950). According to this theory, people learn to be intolerant of differences among people, and because of their own "retarded" psycho-social development, are generally hostile and rigid in outlook. The classic study illustrating this approach is Theodor Adorno's (1950). He and his associates conducted extensive interviews with large numbers of people in California. They inquired about the childhood experiences of these people, located them in the socio-economic scheme of the times and developed measures of their willingness to accept change and tolerate differences among other people. Out of their research emerged the notion of the **authoritarian personality**. Authoritarian people seemed to have experienced repressive socialization as children and seemed to share a collective sense of frustration. According to the researchers, these people are potential recruits for totalitarian social movements, the prototype being Nazism.

When applied to understanding social movements, the authoritarian personality hypothesis seems to offer a reasonable explanation. People recruited in totalitarian movements are people who share repressive socialization experiences. These people represent reservoirs of potential support to social movements. Sparked by a charismatic leader, they can supply the force necessary to effect major changes, particularly in democratic governments.

However, Rudolf Heberle (1951) offered an alternative account. He argued that one must not be misled by oversimplifying "psychoanalytic explanations." Further, his own personal experiences lead him to write:

> This writer has known quite a large number of men and a few women who joined the Nazi Party before 1933 or soon after the seizure of power. In most of these cases he finds strong indications of frustration-disappointments in careers, conflicts or frictions in marriage, absence of or unsatisfactory nature of sexual relation, and so forth. But, he also remembers similar types among members of a middle-of-the-road liberal club in Germany. After 1933, when the "bandwagon effect" came into play, the proportion of frustrated individuals among the members of the N.S.D.A.P. [Nazi's] must have decreased to approximately the average proportion in the nation. The more extreme cases of Hilter, Hess, Goebbels, Streicher, Ley and many minor figures in the Nazi hierarchy are now well known. Hitler's notorious craziness and the large number of crackpots among the early Nazis were one reason why the movement in the beginning was not taken seriously by most of its opponents (Heberle 1951, 110).

Heberle's studies indicated how one must look to the interaction of psychological and sociological factors to appreciate the complexity of social movements. Although it may have been true that Nazi leaders were frustrated individuals, this was apparently not necessarily true of the ordinary citizens who supported them or acquiesced to their power. Heberle emphasized the role of social structure in assessing the strength the party had in its rise to power. According to his research, where social stratification was not pronounced, where a village community was well integrated, the Marxists tended to be weak, the conservatives only temporarily strong, the liberal parties strong and relatively constant during the earlier years, and the N.S.D.A.P. and its forerunners very strong towards the end of the period. On the other hand, in areas of Germany where there were sharp differences of wealth and class, the Marxists were strong, the conservatives also strong and comparatively constant, the liberals weak, the Nazis late in coming to predominance. Family farm areas with little stratification offered the best chances for the Nazism, the poorest for the Marxists.

Other things being equal, he concluded, the chances for the extreme parties were better the more specialized and therefore more sensitive to business cycles the farms were. The tempo of change from liberalism to Nazism was slower in areas of diversified farming and well-to-do farmers than in specialized areas of less wealthy farmers. Lastly, in areas where the rural upper strata (farmers or landlords) had been politically active for a long time, new parties could less easily gain a foothold than in areas where no broad politically trained stratum existed. Where class consciousness among rural laborers was still in its infancy, political radicalism was more likely to develop than in areas where labor had been organized politically in unions for a considerable time (Heberle 1951, 232–33).

Heberle teaches us how an account of a social movement must deal with society and self. Information about the social organization of the society, community, and the national political climate within which the movement develops is as important as the "readiness" of people to join a movement, and as the charisma of a leader. The coincidences necessary for a social movement of the magnitude of Nazism are rare. It happened, of course, and it could again, but Heberle's data describe a set of circumstances closely bound up with the transition from rural, traditional society to urban, industrial society. In modern society, the closest we see to the sweeping reinterpretation of basic values and norms of society that the Nazis effected in Germany may well be the grand scene.

SUMMARY

Sociologically, collective behavior refers to the extraordinary, nonroutine occurrences of everyday life. We have related the importance of collective behaviors by placing them within the larger context of social organization. We have concluded by stressing how describing an organization underscores the concept of group forms. Wright expresses the reasoning embodied in this concept. Group forms are "the collective configurations or patterns which emerge out of crowd members' distribution in space" (Wright 1978, 12). These patterns, in turn, result primarily from the nonverbal interactive mechanism for coordinating and carrying out collective activities. The identification of forms is easier, the smaller and the more contained the collective phenomenon is. The idea of form, however, generalizes to all collective behavior, as Lofland's scheme demonstrates. Crowds can be angry or joyful; mass collective behavior involves fear, hostility, and joy; and finally, fashions and fads reflect emergent meanings of groups trying to find some pleasurable mass involvement in society. Whether we are studying a riot, a fad, or the creation of a political party, we are examining how people communicate their emotions collectively and how they organize these communications.

When we study collective behaviors, we are, in a dramatic way, studying social change. Consistent with our view of modern society as encouraging a complex, multiple social self, we see how collective behaviors in modern society are likewise apt to be complex and multiple. Although this does not necessarily mean that a single collective phenomenon is less important in modern society, it is less likely to alter basic societal trends, as Irwin says of the scene. On the other hand, the collective behaviors of citizens of modern society turn out to be very rich and colorful, involving even fundamental skills of interaction. Everyday life has become, according to Irwin, more scenelike. This means among other things, that participation in collective behaviors may become routine through the staging of excitement. In short, as is true with many configurations of social meanings in modern society, the distinctions between meanings become blurred. An accurate description of the attitudes of many people in modern society may well be that they routinely expect "to find out where the action is."

EXERCISES IN SEEING COLLECTIVE BEHAVIORS

1. Go to your school library or to the local city library. Select a month at least ten years ago and ask the librarian to help you find the newspapers for that month. You will probably work with microfilm or some facsimile. Go through the daily papers for each day of the month and read the front page. Record all events which you believe are instances of collective behavior. Classify all the instances according to Lofland's scheme. Look for dominant emotions and see if there is enough information in the account to guess at the organizational form of the instances.

2. Next time you are at an event where several hundred people are present, like a sports contest or a rock concert, take notes on the mood of the crowd. Describe the seating or gathering arrangements of the people, how they get in and out of the building or grounds and other details of the occurrence. After you return home, read your notes and see if you can detect mood changes throughout the course of the event. If you can, tie these emotional cycles to what the crowd is doing. You should have an interesting data basis from which to discuss the emergent forms of collective behavior for this particular event. For this exercise, crowds are better than more organized gatherings like audiences at a theater.

3. Recall your junior high school days. List the fads and fashions which were important for you and your group. These should include such details as the kinds of clothes you wore, the labels you wanted (the way you showed you didn't care about labels), hair styles, and shoes. Which of these fashions do you still follow? Can you think of reasons why some of these behaviors have persisted and others not? Look for "extra-institutional" practices which have become more institutionalized with time. Use Irwin's model of the natural history of a scene as a guide.

KEY CONCEPTS

Collective behavior
Dominant emotions
Organizational forms
Crowds
Panic
Terror
Joy crowds
Ecstatic conventions
Mass
Elites
Nonelites
Availability
Accessibility
Charisma
Mass fears
False fear
Mass hostility
Mass joy
Nostalgia
Fashions
Fads
Scenes
Articulation stage
Golden age
Expansion
Corruption
Stagnation
Grand scenes
Social movement
Conversion process
Funneling process
Authoritarian personality

SUGGESTED READINGS

Lofland's and Stark's account of the conversion process has become a standard article of understanding the ways in which social movements attract, hold, and convert new members. Sam Wright's book *Crowds and Riots* presents the reader with a very useful approach to understanding the idea of the group form. He graphically illustrates his approach with maps and accounts of a variety of different kinds of crowds and riots. The book is a great way to see the action of collective behavior recorded on the printed page. Lastly, from a textbook which has been a standard, Turner and Killian's *Collective Behavior*, second edition, I recommend their last chapter entitled "Social Functions of Collective Behavior." In this chapter, they discuss how collective behaviors contribute both to stability and change in the total structure of society.

Lofland, John, and Rodney Stark. "Becoming a World Saver: A Theory of Conversion to a Deviant Perspective." *American Sociological Review* 30 (Dec. 1965): 862–875.

Turner, Ralph H., and Lewis Killian. *Collective Behavior* 2nd ed. Englewood Cliffs, N.J.: Prentice-Hall, 1972.

Wright, Sam. *Crowds and Riots: A Study of Social Organization.* Beverly Hills: Sage Publications, 1978.

Chapter Twelve

Life in Public Places

OUTLINE

Life in Public Places

A lone figure walks down a dark street. It is 3:00 A.M. in a large eastern city. The street narrows into a passage which moves the pedestrian under a skywalk. The figure quickens his pace as he sees the narrow passage ahead. Then he pauses, looks around, and spots a lone figure on the other side of the passage. His heart races as he resumes walking, this time more deliberately with measured steps, his hands in a forced relaxed posture, an attitude of readiness to run. As he comes closer to the passage, he walks faster until he is there. For a split second while he is sheltered from the dim rays of the street lamp, he feels vulnerable. As he emerges into the street light, he sees the other figure moving away, he walks on more slowly, just a few more blocks to go.

L IFE with strangers and the problems of establishing grounds of trust sufficient to permit minimal social order is nowhere more readily observable than in what social psychologists call **public behavior**. Relations in public are a special case of collective behavior. Although they are not strictly outside of institutional meanings for social life, they are also not completely spontaneous, or emergent. We all learn how to navigate city streets, avoid traffic, cross streets, and recognize danger. Of course, the special problems of public relations derive from the short-term nature of interaction with strangers, an interaction intended to serve limited functions and which exposes the person to public scrutiny.

Since the work of Goffman (1971), public life is no longer overlooked as a subject of analysis. In fact, Goffman demonstrated how the very foundations of social order in modern, urban social life are revealed in the encounters between strangers in public places. As the scope and influence of private life diminishes, public life becomes the arena of crucial importance in matters of social control. Since people must rely on appearances in order to know each others' intentions and motivations, we can learn a great deal about how people interact by looking closely at what they do in public. Goffman stresses the importance of describing in detail how appearances are organized and how the accomplishment and management of organization takes place. Through understanding public life, we move closer to a comprehensive understanding of the relationship between society and self.

Matters of organization can be discussed by using the concept of **form**. When we discussed group forms, we learned how a set of mutual activities among people results in a relatively coherent set of rules for how to conduct that activity. For example, Irwin described the proper rules for dress and behavior among surfers. Homans referred to these rules as **norms**. Although norms derive from stable places (where the activity happens), once they have been formed and people learn to practice them, there is a sense in which they travel. As we move about in the territories of everyday life, we bring with us the norms and rules we regard as appropriate. These rules function both to define places where the rules apply and to define appropriate activities in those places.

The senses of place and the ways in which people attempt to use place are called **territoriality**. Lyman and Scott suggest that territory in its social sense can assume several forms: public, home, interactional, and body. Each of these is significant to an understanding of how people define and accomplish sense of place in the presence of strangers, in locations of varying degrees of freedom.

Public territories are "those areas where the individual has freedom of access, but not necessarily of action" (Lyman and Scott 1970, 91). In these areas, there is general agreement among most who enter that the laws of society apply. Hence, in a public territory one expects to be observed, and one recognizes that there may well be people present who have legitimate claim to enforce the rules. Also, in these territories certain categories of persons are accorded limited access and restricted activity. As Lyman and Scott point out, children are not expected to play in the park after midnight.

Contrasting with public territory is the **home territory**, a place of intimate, private life. There can be wide ranges of variation in the usages of private spaces. Persons generally feel free to arrange this space as they see fit. They have a sense of degree of autonomy in the home territory.

Other territories are mobile and are not associated with physical surroundings but with the form and content of the social life that takes place within them. They are called **interactional territories**. These areas are where "social gathering may occur." Of course, they have implied boundaries, but these boundaries are much more fragile than those of either home or public territory.

Finally, there is the space of and around the **body**. Goffman has been particularly explicit about the shape and functions of body space. He

Human interactive work can have a dramatic effect when it shapes the natural environment to convey its messages. In this picture we clearly see a territory of wealth.

writes that these spaces vary in different human cultures. The body may become a vehicle, it may be enclosed within a sheathe, occupy a stall, or be composed of parts that vary in terms of their accessibility to others. For instance in a crowded elevator, we may touch elbows but not stomachs.

The question of the meanings of social life in public, then becomes one of describing how people understand place and how they negotiate appropriate uses of places. People accomplish the locations of social life in terms of all four types of territories; however, in public there is a tension between the ways people have habitually come to think of their power to define territory and the fixity of public places with their markers. Public places are organized into zones, large and small, which explicitly tell us appropriate use (thirty minute parking zone, for example). Public places are often so thoroughly organized that each portion of the territory has a predefined use. On the other hand, by virtue of "normal" socialization, people have a sense of home and privacy. In the public domain, this sense of territory can be restricted, intruded on or violated.

HOME IN PUBLIC PLACES

Every night a world created, complete with furniture friends made and enemies established . . . At first the families were timid in the building and tumbling of worlds, but gradually the techniques of building worlds became their technique. Then the leaders emerged, then laws were made, the codes came into being. And as the worlds moved westward, they were more complete and better furnished, for their builders were more experienced in building them.

John Steinbeck, *THE GRAPES OF WRATH*

The sense of home is so well entrenched in our commonsense understanding of the meanings of social life that home and family are often thought of together. Families defend their home territories by enclosing them, erecting fences, and installing elaborate security systems. But what happens to "home," how is it defined and defended when the family moves about? As Steinbeck suggests, families migrating from the Dust Bowl states in the 1930s learned to take their homes with them.

A kind of migration that gives us information about the definition and defense of temporary territory takes place today during vacations. In the summer millions of families take camping trips. They prepare themselves to move from site to site, establishing and re-establishing a "home" at each site. Of course, modern campers are not poverty-stricken and they return to their "real" homes; however, campers share a common problem, the

Markers of the boundaries of home are sometimes less than subtle. Here the meanings and functions of the picket fence are obvious and overbearing. Even if the fence were not there, would you still see the house as marked territory?

solution to which gives us basic insights into how humans define and defend home territory within public domains.

The Marking of Home

The sight of a recreational vehicle, a car-towing trailer, a camper bus, or a pick-up truck outfitted with a house-like enclosure has become a familiar part of the landscape of America. All this equipment has one purpose— camping out. Certainly, the phrase *camping out* can mean many kinds of activities, from jockeying for a parking place on a level plot of paved real estate with electrical hookups to backpacking into the wilderness. Whether in tent or Winnebago, camping out requires solutions to two interrelated problems: (1) how to transform a public place into home territory and (2) how to successfully communicate this transformation to others.

The principal device through which a public territory is defined and defended as a home is the **marker** (Goffman 1971, 41–44). A marker is an object which communicates territorial boundary. It may consist of odds and ends, like ropes, tires and pieces of camping equipment, but the effectiveness of the messages that markers send will depend upon how the people who put them down use commonsense knowledge about the meanings of "homes."

Markings are not always physical. Can you identify territories of interaction among the people in this picture? Make a list of all the ways that interactive territories are marked in this classroom.

Nash (1982) conducted a study to observe marking phenomena. He camped out in five Western states in national and state forests over two summers, limiting himself to areas designated for camping—with facilities such as toilets and sometimes electricity. He gathered observations by walking or driving through the campgrounds, noting cases when people temporarily left their sites, and, on occasions, interviewing them about the ways they saved their places.

Obviously, when a recreational vehicle fills a numbered site where white boundary posts stake out the corners of the lot, there is little trouble in getting the message that the site is taken. With tents or trailers the campers are free to drive around, since the camping equipment marks the site. However, the more completely outfitted the "rig," the more self-contained the vehicle used for overnight sleeping, the more difficult becomes the problem of marking the site when temporarily vacating it. When a family drives out to fish a local lake, or simply to see the country, they take their home with them. Therefore, it is necessary to mark the site if they intend to return there for the night.

Types of Markers

Seemingly any object can serve as a marker. A list of the items used to mark includes children's toys, a spare tire, sack signs, garbage bags and cans, empty and full six-packs of beer, and a set of longhorns from a steer used by a couple from Texas to save a site. A simple listing of objects will not reveal how these items function as markers, instead the common meanings they possess must be discovered. For instance, a spare tire left behind in the middle of the parking space for a site related a strong message: "We're comin' back!" Whereas, a garbage bag and an empty six-pack left in the middle of the parking space function as weak markers which seem to say, "We may have found another place: if you need it, you might get away with taking it."

It appears that messages a marker can convey derive from the relationship between the item itself and generally understood camper's knowledge. Any item can serve as a marker if it can enter into an interpretable relationship with features of camper knowledge. The first task to understanding the message, therefore, is to describe the camper's knowledge of sites and their features.

Nash describes seven components of meaning which function as background for marker messages. Table 12.1 presents the components and their dimensions. The first component, scarcity, refers to perceived difficulty in getting a site which depends on two interrelated situations: whether the sites are managed by attendants who issue sites to campers, and whether there is crowding. The second component has to do with spatial requirements of equipment, and the third component with the physical layout of the sites themselves—whether their boundaries are predefined, and what their location is relative to other sites. The fourth component relates to the perceived risk of loss in leaving behind an item—

Can the item used as a marker be easily stolen? Also included here is a judgment about the personal or impersonal nature of the item. A shovel might be seen as impersonal while a sleeping bag is personal. The fifth component refers to whether or not a written message, either and sentence like "This site is taken," or a single word like "taken" is used. (One camper used a paper plate and wrote on it "taken" in four languages). Number six connotes the identity of the campers: are they a family, a group, a couple, or a single? Finally, seven is the perceived time of day as that perception relates to access and availability of sites. For example, "early" means before most people try to get a site, and "late," after most have already tried. Of course, this judgment varies greatly from ground to ground. Late can be 7:00 AM at a popular location. For some isolated, no-fee areas, one can never be late.

There were five broad categories of markers: (1) written markers like paper platters, sack signs, or ticket displays; (2) equipment markers such as tents, trailers, or smaller items like camp stools, stoves, or ice boxes; (3) unit markers such as children's toys or insignia; (4) personal markers, for instance, clothes on line, food, toilet paper rolls nailed to a tree; and (5) blockages fashioned from rope, tires or garbage cans.

Table 12.1 Components of Meanings for Site Markers

1.0 Scarcity
    1.1 controlled access
    1.2 open access/little crowding
    1.3 open access/high crowding

2.0 Equipment Space
    2.1 recreational vehicle (RV)
    2.2 van (Campmobile)
    2.3 pick-up camper
    2.4 trailer
    2.5 tent
    2.6 van/tent
    2.7 trailer/tent
    2.8 RV/tent
    2.9 pick-up/tent

3.0 Site
    3.1 isolated/defined
    3.2 with view/defined
    3.3 woodsy/defined
    3.4 level/defined
    3.5 isolated/undefined
    3.6 view/undefined
    3.7 woodsy/undefined
    3.8 level/undefined

4.0 Commitment
    4.1 strong/impersonal
    4.2 weak/impersonal
    4.3 strong/personal
    4.4 weak/personal

5.0 Written Form
    5.1 yes
    5.2 no

6.0 Unit Identity
    6.1 single
    6.2 group
    6.3 couple
    6.4 family

7.0 Time of Day
    7.1 early
    7.2 late

RULES OF MARKER DISCOURSE,
OR HOW TO READ A SPARE TIRE

A marker is interpreted by people looking at a site in relationship to what they know about the various possible combinations of components. An object strategically displayed on a camp site becomes a message when it is read as such. The person who placed the marker and the person reading it establish an intersubjective sense regarding the intended message: "This site is taken"; "The site is taken, but we might be able to get it"; "This site is not taken"; "This site is definitely taken"; "Do not trespass!" Obviously, the test of effectiveness of the message lies in practical consequences—whether the message results in finding the site as it was left.

To see how markers function, we need to look at examples. A spare tire left in the middle of a parking space for a site is more than a blockage. The tire goes with a vehicle; it is out of place in the road. Since the item can be interpreted as an important part of the vehicle (no camper would travel far without a spare) and since special effort was required to remove the tire (over-sized spare tires in camper vehicles are often placed in hard-to-get-at places like inside a cabinet or under the chassis), such a marker is **strong**.

Interpretations of the meanings of markers vary according to three rules or conditions. The first is a scarcity condition: the more scarce the sites, the stronger the marker must be to function effectively. The second is the rule of equipment: equipment requires space for its use. The third is the rule of commitment, which is, the more risk a sender is willing to take in the display of a marker, the stronger the marker. Obviously, an item may be strong under one condition or rule and weak under another.

Early in the day, at a grounds that has open access and little crowding, for a site that is isolated and defined, virtually any item functions as a strong marker. For example, an empty six-pack on a table may be sufficient to mark a site. But late, in an area of controlled access, for a site with a view but undefined boundaries, a family may have to leave a tent and a blockage of bicycles and toys to protect a territory.

Scarcity: Condition I

When this condition is perceived as pertinent, the camper must carefully construct markers. Competition for sites is keen and one can count on another camper waiting to take your site at the first sign of vacancy. Hence, each marker must be selected so that it forms a configuration of the components appropriate to the condition. A child's toy, for example may function under this condition as either a strong or a weak marker. It would be a strong message sentence if it were used in a controlled access site (1.1) which was isolated and defined (3.1). It would show a weak but personal commitment to the site (4.4) communicated in an unwritten form

(5.2) connoting a family unit identity (6.4) early in the day (7.1). (See Table 12.1.)

Two components function to give this use of a toy strength as a message. First the message was left in a controlled access grounds in which sites have been assigned, and although there may be problems in knowing how long a person, group, or family intend to camp, at least if they are on the site, they are assumed to have priority. If it is early, the receiver reads a no urgency message. They have time to decide to stay another night. In this circumstance, all that is necessary is to mark with an item that displays occupancy: The family is in a van and they have driven off. The toy shows that they will be back. Hence the site is taken.

The same marker, still under condition I, becomes weak late in the day (7.2) or in the case of more free competition for sites (1.3).

Equipment: Condition II

Equipment defines it own environmental requirements. A large RV must have a level site and a trailer requires a long site. So when campers vacate a site, if the equipment left behind is large and complicated enough, it functions as a strong marker sentence regardless of other conditions. This is, of course, an advantage of a tent or trailer over a van or RV. An equipment marker sentence is like a zero-sum game. When present on the site, an RV is overbearing; when gone, no traces remain to serve as markers. RV owners, hence, develop markers to use under conditions I and III. A typical equipment marker sentence would be this: a tent left pitched on an open access site with little crowding (1.2) with isolated and defined boundaries (3.1). The tent (2.5) connotes a strong and impersonal commitment to the site (4.1) in unwritten form (5.2) for at least a group of people (6.2) late in the camping day (7.2).

A tent is expensive and difficult to "pitch and break down." Since it is assumed by campers that all other campers know this about tents, the tent can function as a strong marker. Smaller equipment or less expensive pieces must be used together with markers that operate under conditions I and III. A camp stool, for instance, could have been forgotten, does not require much effort to move, and, thus, carries a low potential as an equipment marker.

Commitment: Condition III

Under this condition a marker demonstrates that a person has a strong commitment to the site. The site might have sentimental importance to a family. It may afford a picturesque view, be the place where we always camp, or simply be "the place we want!" Commitment markers require that a sender display risk, that he or she purposefully become vulnerable to intrusion. This is accomplished by displaying of an expensive-looking yet light and uncomplicated movable item.

A fluorescent camp light placed on the cement table of a site would function as a strong marker even under background features which would render a less expensive piece of equipment a weak marker. Since this item is easily stolen, it conveys a strong commitment to the site. Lights, however, are not very personal. Bed rolls are, and so are pieces of clothing like underwear or bathing suits hanging on a rope tied from tree to tree. Although not expensive and not that vulnerable to theft, such items are regarded as highly personal and, therefore, function as strong, personal markers. Thus, we see that risk can be both personal and impersonal. To lose an icebox sets back the camper's budget, but to lose one's favorite sweatshirt is an affront. The strength of the marker is in proportion to the risk.

Conditions I, II and III work together, but any given marker gets its meaning from the dominance of one or the other of the conditions. Scarcity demands the use of equipment and personal markers of high commitment value, and equipment markers may be personal or impersonal. We say that a marker is successful whenever it conveys the intended meaning of the person who left it; in other words, whenever it is honored.

Campers establish the territories of temporary homes in a variety of ways. Identify the markers of home in this picture.

UNSUCCESSFUL MARKERS

There are three kinds of unsuccessful markers: (1) false markers; (2) weak markers; and (3) markers that result in misunderstanding and/or conflict.

False Markers

False markers are items left behind inadvertently, forgotten, or discarded that are wrongly perceived by site seekers as markers. A site that is cluttered with garbage can be mistaken as a marked site; or, pieces of forgotten equipment may preserve a site for days before someone decides the item is not a marker. Generally, false markers are found under conditions of low scarcity. When scarcity requires careful marking, an item not obviously displayed will rarely be recognized as a marker. For example, a camp stool by a tree near the back of the campsite will not be regarded as a marker under conditions of high scarcity. In one case at a little-frequented area however, a child's forgotten toy kept four site-searching families off a site for a full day. At the other extreme, in a very popular campground, campers ignored the presence of a small tent and set up camp around that piece of equipment.

The Problem of the Weak Marker

Often a camper will intentionally leave behind a **weak marker**. Since campers are itinerant, the certainty of the next night's site is always in doubt. Thus, they may hedge on the competition by leaving a weak marker at last night's site, while looking for a better site farther down the road. An expendable item may be worth the risk of loss. If, after arriving at a new site, campers find too much competition for sites, they can return to the marked site in hopes that the weak marker reserved their place. Using a weak marker allows the camper to think of this practice as "fair". After all, if sites become scarce everybody knows a weak marker will be insufficient to hold a site. On the other hand, if it works, there were plenty of places to go around anyhow. Because this kind of understanding prevails about the meanings of a weak marker, open conflict over a site rarely surfaces when a marker has been violated. The sender assumes the attitude "Well, it was worth the try."

In leaving items as contingency markers, the sender has to come to grips with burning questions like "How many miles is a skillet worth?" It depends on the skillet, of course. Grandma's old skillet, the one she used for those Sunday morning breakfasts on the farm, might be worth hundreds of miles of "backtracking." The $2.00 skillet from the Coast-to-Coast store in Kearney, Nebraska does not warrant a ten-mile setback in the day's travel. Since idiosyncratic values cannot be easily conveyed (one old skillet looks like any other) cheap items are used as weak markers.

One might fight over Grandma's skillet, but the loss of the $2.00 item simply does not matter that much.

Conflict and Misunderstanding

Flagrant intrusions upon marked sites are rare among campers. They do, however, occur. Sometimes novice campers or picnickers will disregard markers. This can be a matter of ignorance or defiance. For instance, a family in an RV goes into town to wash clothes and buy groceries. They mark their site with a tent. Upon returning, they find an elderly couple eating at the table on the site, their car backed into the parking space with the trunk lid up. The couple looks puzzled at the family peering out windows of their RV. The father, at the wheel, leans out the window and shouts "There must be some mistake here—this is our place!" The couple, without a word, pack their food, put it into the trunk, close the lid, and drive off, with a slight nod from the old man. The RV pulls into the site and recaptures "home."

Or, a family drives into town for the afternoon in their Volkswagon camper-bus. They are in a controlled access area and have paid for two nights and they have one to go. They mark the site with a small cheap backpacker's tent and cooking equipment on the table, including a stove. Upon returning they find an RV in their parking space. No one is around—the tent and other items are still in place. The eight-year-old son cries, "Someone took our place."

The mother of the family is cooler and more composed than the father, who keeps muttering something about "knocking blocks off," and proposes a discussion with the people who must be in the RV. The irate father insists upon avoiding a confrontation and wants to begin looking for another site. "It's not worth a fight—even if we do have the best view of the mountains." Finally, the mother wins. She approaches the RV with caution, gently knocking on the door. Another mother appears:

MOTHER 1: You have our site.

MOTHER 2: But the attendant gave us this number.

MOTHER 1: Wait, here's the ticket, we paid for this for tonight—didn't you see our things?

MOTHER 2: We're tired—my husband's asleep.

MOTHER 1: Well, what'll we do?

MOTHER 2: Go talk to the attendant.

MOTHER 1: OK, we'll be back—get ready to move.

The family, leaving markers in place, returns to the attendant's booth several miles down the road. There they produce the receipt and explain the situation.

ATTENDANT: Well, we had a new girl here helping out yesterday. Looks like she forgot to write you down for a second night. It's OK. We have a vacancy, site 13.

FATHER: The sign says full.

ATTENDANT: Well, we keep a few sites available to handle situations like this. You decide with the other family who gets 13.

Back at the site, the mothers resolve the problem—first come, first pick. After all, the site was marked. So, the markers function again, as the second family moves to site 13.

This conflict demonstrated three facts: (1) scarcity at this ground had resulted in formalized site distribution; (2) markers are still necessary to ward off picnickers and others who might "run the gate" to find an overlooked or extra site; and (3) conflicts and misunderstandings are anticipated by officials who, in turn, rely upon the informal marking system to aid in the mediation of conflict. Campers may be turned away as being "too late" even though, in fact, sites remain vacant. The safety valve function of the extra site is apparently worth the disgruntlement of would-be campers, and its successful application involves use of the marking system itself.

In the above case the markers were many and strong, but scarcity of sites overrode their communicative power. However, when the extreme condition of scarcity was lifted, the markers functioned normally. The markers were communicating even during the intrusion, and they warranted caution by the second family. They made no effort to move the things, for instance. Finally, the markers helped settle the question of who would take the less desirable site.

Studies of such mundane practices as the marking of campsites reveal how people establish territory in public places. They show how humans use available items in association with general and widely distributed knowledge to claim space temporarily. In the case of campsite markers, the general knowledge systems have to do with home and family. Privacy and sanctity are rights of the home. Within the home territory family-like activities may take place. To violate a marker and trespass into a camper's site is like entering a house without an invitation; the absence of walls does not mean the abandonment of home.

INTERACTIONAL TERRITORIES IN PUBLIC

Although the use of public space is generally fixed, there is still a considerable amount of freedom within boundaries for interactional territories and for individual variations in the meanings of usage. Goffman, Scott, Lyman, and others who led the way in the analysis of relations in public show that a dynamic exists between the official use of space and actual use of it. The accomplishment of territory varies not only with the

All the comforts of home.   The extent to which people will go in building territories they regard as appropriate to certain activities is sometimes remarkable.   The contrast between the difficulty of occupying temporary territory and the ease of occupying the permanent home is part of the appeal of camping.

physical aspects of urban settings but also with intentions and the competency of people who occupy the space.

Two studies graphically illustrate how the quality of interactional territory varies even in highly urbanized and presumably fixed public territory.   First, Melbin (1978) ingeniously demonstrates the extent to which a frontier spirit characterizes public life in the city at night, and second Nash (1981) shows how people's interpretation of weather translates into novel and fresh methods of interacting in an urban environment.

Night as Frontier

In a fascinating article, Melbin documents how human beings, through technological advantages in lighting, have become active creatures of the night.   He suggests that especially in America the nighttime is becoming a frontier in which human activity is expanding.   He defines a frontier as "a pattern of sparse settlement in space or time, located between a more densely settled and practically empty region" (Melbin 1978, 6).   He sees the nighttime as such a frontier, and he reasons that there should be similarities between frontiers of space and time.

Citing data which show that the nighttime populations of American cities are more sparse and more homogeneous than those of the daytime, Melbin builds his case.   In the night, he reasons, there are fewer social constraints and less persecution; these and other conditions, convince him that night is a frontier.

In a frontier, new styles of behavior emerge. While it is true there is more lawlessness and violence, helpfulness and friendliness can also be found in abundance. Each of these characteristics depicts both land frontiers as described by historians and time frontiers according to the data Melbin gathered.

Melbin set about cleverly to test whether or not night is a new frontier. The first test involved asking for directions from people on the street. In the second, he requested that a stranger consent to a brief interview. The third test involved color coding keys so that they could be traced to locations and placing the keys in conspicuous spots about Boston; each key had a tag on it listing a name and address of someone in a city several miles away and the request "Please return." In this test a measure of who returned the keys from where and at what time of the day could be constructed. The final test involved being sociable in the supermarket, where researchers frequented twenty-four-hour supermarkets in Boston at different times of the day and in different areas of the city.

Melbin analyzed the results of these tests and discovered that friendliness in giving directions, willingness to be interviewed and sociability in supermarkets were all significantly higher at night than at any other time. The key test, however, revealed that people were much less likely to return the lost keys that were found at night. Although it may appear that the results of the key test are not consistent with the hypothesis that nighttime behavior is more frontierlike, Melbin explains this finding in the following way:

> If someone finds a key and does not know the owner, he would guess that everyone who passed that way is equally likely to have lost it. Nighttimers, knowing they are few, assume on the weight of numbers that the person who lost the key is a daytimer...I suggest that the feelings of nighttimers toward daytimers resembles the attitudes of westerners toward easterners a century ago. They perceive they are different and resent the neglect shown by the day people toward them...Whereas frontier people readily help others whom they meet on the frontier, their sense of difference from unknown daytimers leaves them less concerned about the others' plights and they do not return many lost keys (Melbin 1978, 20).

Melbin conducted his research in public places. He discovered that the character of a place can change with those who inhabit it at different times. The lesson is clear: the quality of interaction varies with the interpretations people make of their involvements with others. Nighttime is a frontier, a time zone yet to be routinized and rationalized. In it people feel adventuresome, banding together to help each other and coping with the consequences of "relaxed" or absent rules of behavior. In the nighttime, certain kinds of people are encouraged to occupy city spaces, and they form associations that are not unlike "interest groups."

Melbin concludes his study by pointing out the role that expansion has played in the social changes in American society. He refers to the western frontier and its impact on American society and to the questions of policy that might emerge from increased understanding the nature of time as a resource. Since a frontier may be exploited, if it is governed and regulated more closely, will it lose its distinctive character? By conceiving of time as a social frontier we can see how interactional territories emerge from the sense people make of the situations in which they find themselves. Working nights, finding a location in the city one can claim, and seeking retreat from the routines of daytime city life are all attractions of the new frontier.

Relations in Frozen Places

Not only do people create new territories out of old ones in the opportunities that time affords, but they may also discover that other variations brought on by such natural occurrences as changes in the weather provide the raw materials of the social order. One of the reasons social psychologists have focused on public territories is because of the fragile and temporary character of these places. Since public places are essentially open to all, what happens there graphically demonstrates conflicts among various senses of "space" which people bring with them to their encounters with others. Tensions and changes in the public order reveal the underlying assumptions which support a general sense of social order, and they gauge the amount and nature of work that is going on. Frontiers are spaces in which an array of human activities takes place. The concept of frontier applies to space and time, but it may also apply to any change which affords people opportunities to work with and within a social order to achieve their own ends.

By studying public order, we find out that even the most routine aspects of everyday life, like walking past a stranger on the street or waiting for a bus, are tightly organized into social connections which together comprise the public order. Most researchers who look carefully at this order are interested in how it affects those whom it influences. For example, Goffman formulates a hypothesis that the more fixed the features of public order, the greater will be people's sense of alarm. Others have been interested in the affects of crowding and of the intermingling of strangers on **helping behavior**. They, therefore, may even stage a scene in which a person seems to be in distress to see if passersby will stop to give aid. This research generally shows that people tend to depend on the routines that they follow to get through the public domain, and are reluctant to modify those routines to help others. Helping others they fear may inconvenience them (by disturbing their established sense of order and the sense of protection that gives them) or be seen as an intrusion and violation of someone else's territory.

When the news stories appeared a few years ago about the brutal murders and assaults which took place within hearing and sight of passersby and of residents and who did not even call the police, people began to question the costs of the public sense of order. The impact of awareness of these problems has provided a more formal response mechanism for emergencies in large cities. Not only does the emergency 911 number allow fast response for city services, it also allows people to report incidences in convenient and anonymous ways. The public order is being rearranged to allow intrusion and helping behaviors consistent with the general character of public life, in other words, public ways to help.

But the question remains as to the degrees of opportunity that public life affords individuals for their "definitions of situations." Melbin's research shifts our perspective from looking at the impact of public life on people to people's impact on public life. We want to show that changes in the order brought on even by seasonal changes in the weather provide opportunities for the emergence of new versions of public order.

A study was conducted to document the effects of weather on public order (Nash 1981) focusing on the sense that people make of being out-of-doors in extreme winter weather. In order to gather materials, teams of researchers were organized and invested some 350 hours in observing those aspects of public life most obviously exposed to winter conditions. The study was conducted in the Twin Cities of Minneapolis and Saint Paul which are justifiably known as **winter cities**. Teams of observers concentrated on four settings: parks, streets, ski resorts (within the city proper), and recreational centers (principally skating rinks).

From the myriad observations gathered, several themes emerged. These themes can be thought of as organizing patterns of meaning that address the question, "What are we doing here?" The first deals with the communication of intention; Goffman calls nonverbal techniques which people employ to signal their intentions and motives for being in a public place **officious displays**. The second theme relates to the reduced numbers of people in public during winter. The third emerges from attitudes of festivity and celebration. The fourth theme deals with the adaptability of those who frequently use public territories. Finally, an important general theme emerged concerning the suspension of the norms that govern social order during the winter.

Officious Displays Goffman (1971, 130–32) writes of the "orientation gloss" which consists of gestures designed to communicate "official" purposes of behavior. The winter city study found that in winter such gestures became exaggerated. Waiting for the bus, people stand on benches, crane to look for the bus every few minutes, pace up and down and across the territory of the bus stop. They jump up and down and blow on their mittens or gloves as if to warm their hands.

Phone booths located near a stop may be used as stages for a ritual dance of warmth. By standing in the booth and jumping up and down, one can communicate waiting behavior and engage in "strange" movements within the semi-privacy of the booth. Such devices relate official messages about what the person is doing outdoors in such conditions, and most importantly, they show disdain for a public predicament.

A central theme of public behavior is active disregard for winter by "going about business as usual." Some people communicate this theme by underdressing. A businessman will walk from building to building in a "deliberate normal posture", upright slow gate with arms relaxed at his sides, but without a hat or coat. A school boy will wait for a bus, down vest unsnapped, in zero-degree weather. One observer, waiting for a downtown bus when the temperature hovered near zero, reported being "flashed" by an undaunted deviant.

Where Have All the People Gone? Observers recorded definite fluctuations in numbers of people outside according to weather conditions. "Weather conditions" refers not simply to temperature but to the sensation outdoors. In order to assess the relationship between weather and the numbers of people in public territories, the observers used an indicator frankly based on subjective judgment. A sunny zero-degree day with a low wind-chill factor could be judged as "nice" if it came after a week of cloudy, snowy, ten-degree days. Although "nice" days did bring out more people, it is important to note (1) that people were out even in the bitterest weather, and (2) that the peak days yielded numbers of people far below the summer averages.

The Festive Attitude Either during or after heavy snow, people in public often display a **festive attitude**. It is as if the weather itself is cause for celebration. One observer reported at a sledding hill after a heavy snow, "The routine glosses for parents are to stand around at the top of the hill, intervening on behalf of the smaller children, or to sit in an idling car with the heater on. Today it was different. Old ladies were laughing like crazy. Distinguished-looking, middle-aged men were guffawing in the snow. The sight of a grandma careening down the hill on a blue, plastic, space-age rocket sled was indeed extraordinary."

Another park observer noted the same phenomenon. After several weeks of bitter cold, the sun came out and the temperature rose into the teens. Gradually, the park filled with people. They were sledding, cross-country skiing, and even picnicking in the snow. Families and groups of young people spread blankets, buried six packs in the snow, and got out the food. It was like the Fourth of July.

The Big Country Complex The question arose: Do those who routinely use public space adapt well under winter conditions? Many, it seems, do. Runners reported their preference for wintertime training because of the openness of the roads. The outdoor skating rink is deserted on the bitter cold days; you can practice slap shots without fear of injury or reprimand.

One observer wrote, "I was standing on a hilltop watching a lonely cross-country skier, silhouetted against the city skyline, cut across the frozen golf course. I could sense a mastery over the environment. For the moment, the numbness of my fingers was a reminder that I had taken this expanse for my own. If I were tough, brave, reckless enough, this city turf was mine."

This intuititive relationship with the cityscape was reported by several other observers. The streets became personalized; walking down the middle of a traffic lane normally crowded bumper to bumper with automobiles, produced, for a fleeting moment, a sense of reclaiming that space. Using the ski areas, when others dared not, enhanced the experience of doing something special. (Skiers who refused to use headware—one observer called them "hatless wonders"—somehow demonstrated their mastery of the elements in admirable style).

The Democratization of Winter Space Public territories with fixed equipment and uses in the warm months often yield to a variety of uses in winter. It is as if democracy prevails out of season in questions of how to put the space to use. Bus stops offer more ready access to conversation. Benches may be stomped on. Phone booths may be occupied with no intent of making a call. A private country club opens its grounds to sledders and cross-country skiers—and hence goes public in the winter.

The meanings of public territories are not always fixed and unchangeable. In the winter city, people experience increased opportunities to redefine the appropriate use of public space, even if only temporarily. Here we see the frozen transformation of a city street.

People are allowed many norm violations. Some readily observable ones include the following:

1. Allowing bus waiters to stand inside buildings (often blocking doorways).
2. Relaxation of enforcement of "no alcoholic beverages" law in parks.
3. Late night practices of driving cars in such open spaces as parks, golf courses, and school yards.
4. A tolerance of the flagrant use of culs-de-sac and parking lots by couples seeking "in city" places to park.
5. Uncharacteristic leniency of the police in their use of crowd control techniques. (Noted an officer on duty at the massively attended funeral of a prominent politician, "If they choose to be out in this cold, they deserve to get a close look").

Our evidence points not just to single events or isolated occurrences of increased freedom, but to a general pattern. The wintertime order appears to operate on assumptions of temporariness, so that when winter conditions do prevail over long periods, a kind of anomie occurs while police and the private citizens alike wait for the "thaw."

In the data of this study, there are three implications. First, human attempts, however unsuccessful, to deny nature are distinguished by both the symbolic and literal withdrawal of the majority, and the exploitation of this withdrawal by an active minority. Second, the data suggest that space usages and policy directed at wintertime utilization should allow for increased individual freedom in definitions of territoriality. In short, planners should take advantage of the "cooled" sense of alarm that persons feel when using urban space during the winter. Finally, the winter city no doubt exhibits different organizational structures from other cities. Similarly, the consequent problems of transferring street layouts, architectural designs, and other features of city planning from warm to cold weather cities need to be more fully understood.

ALIENATION AND OPPORTUNITY

The examination of night and cold public places reveals a remarkable variety of unofficial usages. People construct social environments as overlays for physical ones. Their sense of appropriate usage depends on how they define their place in the environment. Of course, making sense out of public life involves conditioning by the larger cultural meanings in society. We have identified a consequence of mixing social forms as alienation. In chapter five, we learned how people cope in different ways with their feelings of estrangement. In fact, the entire question of fit between formal and informal group structure can be seen as the power of interpretations offered by people to each other.

When we study public life, we are dealing with a place of pre-eminent estrangement, where the very essense of social life involves using places and things which carry an official, ready-made definition of appropriate use. The contrast between different types of territories is one of finding "who can define meanings." In interactional, home and body spaces, people think they define the meanings themselves. The public meanings, on the other hand, are perceived as prefabricated structures, put in place by others. In public, then, people generally feel "out of place." Hence they hurry, avoid eye contact, and protect their bodies as vehicles which they can maneuver through "unfriendly" territory. Although there are many meanings of alienation in social science literature, this one is clearly a part of what is intended by those who use the concept.

However, what we see when we look closely at actual interaction in public space only partially supports its depiction as an alienated place. While it is true that strangers do not readily help each other, that night is a dangerous time in big cities, and that northern city streets are cold and barren in the middle of January, there is also evidence that public life in these alienated places are also places of opportunity for innovation. Nighttimers invent their own sense of belonging and wintertimers take advantage of suspended norms of public life to enjoy freedom in the streets.

The tension that we depict between alienation and opportunity has been documented in an exotic way by Douglas, Rasmussen, and Flanagan in their study of nude beaches (1977). While they discovered that the extremely private act of nudity in public did represent a novel use of the beaches, there were many aspects of the nude beach scene which resemble and illustrate the tension between alienation and opportunity.

For example, Douglas found that many people were motivated to visit and become a member of the "bareass" beach because they found the act of public nudity to be a "turn-on." He studied the use of the territories of the beach, how people exhibited themselves before one another, how sex acts were accomplished on the beach and the patterns of interaction that were located along the beach. Generally, he discovered that people attempt to cover-up interactionally in ways that enhance the tension between public and private. They do this by categorizing other members of the beach scene, by developing routine practices and, particularly in the case of females, by protecting themselves in small groups. In fact, he even suggests that the tension, which in this case derives from a novel use of public territory, was a basic attraction for the "bareass" beach phenomenon. He writes that most people who frequented the beach did so to escape the routine and boredom of everyday life. They were in search of excitement and adventure. What they often found was exciting but in a slightly different way than they had expected. Not only did beach goers have to learn to deal with a variety of people who had quite different ideas about the purposes of nude beaches, they also encountered the values of the larger society. They had to learn to cope with police and property owners. In his section on politics and the future of the nude beach, Douglas concludes that the nude scene depends on contact with and influence on the public world. Even in this extreme effort to creatively redefine the appropriate use of beaches, we see the tension between the need for order among strangers, and the opportunities for excitement and adventure that being in the presence of strangers provides.

SUMMARY

This chapter explores the social meanings people attribute to life in public places. We develop a conception of territoriality which appreciates the constructed, changeable, and situational character of human senses of place. There are home, interactional, public, and body territories. Each functions to establish a sense of location around the person's sense of him or herself.

All of these territories are mobile. We describe how the home territory is marked, and expand this notion to understanding the marking of temporary homes in the form of campsites. We discover that markers, both as physical things and as symbolic messages, communicate the intentions and motives of those who wish to establish a territorial claim.

We see how the idea of space and time come together in the frontier phenomenon. When we understand how certain features of space yield identifiable meanings, we can look for these meanings in places we might otherwise overlook. The night, according to Melbin, is a time frontier. Although overlooked as a territory because of our narrow definition of territory as space, time territories are concrete in the consequences they have for those who inhabit them. Nighttimers are friendly, willing to engage in conversation, and protective of their identities against the outsiders of the daylight.

Finally, the winter city has a distinctive public life, one characterized by bold officious display, decreases in the number of participants, festive attitudes, and increased freedom in usages for those who persist in the frozen order.

The tension between individual or informal senses of territories and collective or official senses results in oppressive environments which alienate people, but which do not always function as they are officially supposed to. The alienation which these tensions produce may provide the grounds for protection of informal senses of territory or the incentive for novel adaptations.

EXERCISES IN OBSERVING PUBLIC LIFE

1. Next time you are in a public place, start making a list of all the ways you see people marking territory. Keep this up for about a week. You should have a fairly long list. Now sort the list into categories according to how you think the markers are similar or dissimilar. If you have done a sufficient job at observing this aspect of public life, you should have described several distinctive marking behaviors. Make up names for the ways of marking.

2. Select one of Melbin's four tests for the hypothesis that night is a frontier. Repeat it at different times duing the day in your city. You might want to work in groups on this project. Of course, your city or town will have its own form of nightlife. We recommend that you stay as close as possible to Melbin's tests. It would be easy, for example, to repeat his key test on a small scale, or to visit "all-night" supermarkets and ask people for directions, or to consent to an interview. Be sure and record the time periods for your observations. The idea of this exercise is to see if your observations confirm Melbin's strong assertion that night is a frontier. You may wish to consult Melbin's article for details of the various tests.

3. Life in public places is rarely examined according to variations in weather. We have seen, however, that the sense people make out of weather is an important background feature for the way they act toward and judge the intention of others. Although you may not experience the winter extremes of Minnesota, most parts of the country have some distinctive weather phenomena—high winds, heat, thunderstorms, etc. Recall your own experiences with such extreme weather and see if you can describe some unusual things you might have done during this weather. For example, you may recall playing in the warm summer rain, or you may remember the special sense of community engendered by "special" weather. Do not use disasters for this exercise. Limit your examples to more or less ordinary weather, but weather that distinguishes your part of the country. Is there some association between territorial usages and weather variation?

KEY CONCEPTS

Public behavior
Norms
Territoriality
Public territory
Home territory
Interactional territory
Body territory
Marker
Strong marker
False markers
Weak marker
Helping behavior
Winter cities
Officious displays
Festive attitude

SUGGESTED READINGS

The subject of public life has been researched from many different perspectives. Anthropologists focus on the cultural aspects of marking territory; geographers have developed some fascinating concepts of public spaces, and architects pay close attention to relationships between environment and space. This chapter has followed the social psychological view that territories emerge out of the interaction taking place in public places. We recommend several readings which explore a wide range of topics within the perspective of this text.

First, we cite a collection of readings gathered by Helmer and Eddington. This reader contains excellent examples of the study of public life. Second, we direct the student to William H. Whyte's book in which he reports on the results of observational research he and his colleagues conducted in New York City. Finally, Aschcraft and Scheflen published a fine little book that summarizes the current state of knowledge about the making and breaking of human boundaries.

Ashcraft, Norman, and Albert E. Scheflen. *People Space: The Making and Breaking of Human Boundaries.* New York: Anchor Books, 1976.

Helmer, John, and Neil A. Eddington, eds. *Urbanman: The Psychology of Urban Survival.* New York: Free Press, 1973.

Whyte, William H. *The Social Life of Small Urban Spaces.* Washington, D.C.: Conservation Press, 1980.

Chapter Thirteen

Worlds of Emotion

Worlds of Emotion

It is the overwhelming sense of wanting to destroy something; it is a conviction that what is happening is beyond one's control. But there is warmth of belonging, and a satisfaction and near smugness that comes from having experienced the strongest feelings possible. As he watched his friend walk away, he felt the passion of his disappointment—a consequence, he knew, of expecting too much. He felt tenderness and anger at the same time. The passions were so intense and the contradictions so powerful, he could bearly contain himself. He could not be sure of even the relief he knew would come. Would it be in the form of cries and depression, or in the high tension of anger? The words of a country tune repeated themselves in his memory:

Sometimes some things are hard to face—
with me its reality . . .
It hurts so much to face reality.

From "It Hurts so Much to Face Reality" Tender Mercies, 1983.

I N our society, we believe feelings are biological in a way that thinking is not, and we regard thinking as somehow less permanent than feelings. When we want to discover a person's true self, we inquire of them how they feel rather than what they think; we assume a person can easily change his mind, but emotions are less easily feigned, and hence, genuine.

Such cultural beliefs influence scientific research. For example, many early researchers thought that nonverbal behaviors like gestures, eye glances, sweaty palms, and pupil contractions were much more accurate indicators of emotional stages than verbal reports (Modigliani 1971). They believed, in other words, that while talk and subsequent interaction deriving from talk could conceal many different motivations, designs, and schemes of action, nonverbal behaviors more directly reflected what was really going on inside the person. People may learn to lie straightfaced, but may not so readily control the perspiration of their skin. In a recent article, Kemper (1978) even suggests that the actual production of hormones in the nervous system is specifically associated with types of social relationships, these being primarily either power or status relations.

In our approach to social psychology, how people understand things is derived from their experiences. For us the important question is "how do people experience their relationships with each other?" That question we can answer with some confidence by simply asking people, observing them in social relationships, and exploring the meanings of our own experiences. We discover people believe that feelings reflect some genuine or authentic aspect of the self. They believe that feelings are not amenable to control. These beliefs are consistent both in the attitude of everyday life and in scientific or expert knowledge. In order to uncover some of the social meanings of emotions, our analysis begins with the vernacular expression: "Trust your feelings!"

Which feeling should we trust? We have already analyzed the role of many common emotions in social relations. We learned to appreciate love as a way of seeing relationships (Katz 1971). Anger, we found out, is associated with aggression, but we saw how people learn to control and even stage anger (Lyman 1981); and, from Homan's theory of group processes, we know that sentiments are linked systematically to the emergence of norms. Finally, the treatment of collective behavior emphasized the role emotions play in the emergence and maintenance of collective social forms (Lofland, 1981).

Emotions, when placed in social context, can be analyzed as a part of the meanings of interaction. For example, just as we understood the cognitive basis of interaction in terms of reciprocity of perspectives so we can understand emotional aspects of interaction as grounded in states of reciprocity. Just as we guess about what another person is thinking, so we guess about what he or she is feeling. In this chapter, the nature of social relationships is explored and viewed as worlds of feelings. We will follow Gordon's lead and focus on sentiment which he defines as "a socially constructed pattern linking sensations and expressive gestures with cultural meanings, organized around a relationship to another person" (1981, 592).

SENTIMENTS IN SOCIAL CONTEXT

When we say **sentiments** are constructed, we are calling on conceptual understandings we already have mastered. Regardless of the emotional state of the organism, we are focusing on the communication of feelings, what Gordon calls "expressive gestures." The meanings of feelings and the practical consequences of the communication of feelings make up the primary data of the social psychology of emotions, and the results of all these emotive interactions are many, layered worlds of feelings.

Every society is organized so that its members learn about the "proper" communication of feelings. Anthropologists have demonstrated how varied the expression of feelings can be from culture to culture. For example, Americans are typically puzzled by the outpouring of emotion, the explicit expressions of sorrow, they see occasionally on television coverage of a tragedy in the Middle East. Indeed, emotional conduct at burial ceremonies is a good indicator of the range of management and expression of emotions fostered by various societies. A funeral in some societies is almost a festive event, in others the expression of grief and sorrow is highly ritualized. Even the preparation of the body and a time and place for crying and loud wails of remorse are specifically defined and widely understood. In middle-class American society, the expression of emotion at funerals is controlled with almost stoic resolve. Members of the immediate family are often seated in a special section of the chapel so that they can not be directly observed by others at the service. Anyone who cries must do so discretely so as not to "interrupt" the service. Even the viewing of a body is seen as a time for the control and suppression of emotion.

Since worlds of feelings are a part of social realities, they can be analyzed in terms of the rules governing expression, and with regard to the consequences of staged emotions for subsequent interaction. In short, we are addressing the question of how people learn to recognize situations which have emotional import and how they move into and out of these situations.

ROUTINE FEELINGS

More than any other sociologist, Max Weber succeeded in characterizing the essential mood of modern society. Many recent scholars like Weigert (1981) have taken up his charge and offered detailed sketches of the way modern society controls and channels the expressions of emotions. All of these scholars, past and present, see modern society as a place where people are confronted with overwhelming complexity and diversity, yet the ways this complicated place confronts individuals can be described as having an ironic effect: life in modern society can be routinely boring.

Boredom, researchers contend, is a necessary result of modern life. Their argument goes like this: the simple pressures of numbers and diversity of people require that those things we all must do be quite simple. For instance, the rules governing traffic and safe driving call for minimal skills. Indeed, most traffic accidents do not happen because the driver does not know what to do, but because he or she seeks some break from the boredom of driving. Hence, speeding, wreckless driving, and inattention are all derived from the same condition, namely the boring state of ordinary driving. We can formulate a principle: *The greater the number of*

Boredom is partially a consequence of the organization of work in modern society.   What type of work do you suppose this woman is doing?

people doing some specific act, and the more diverse their background, the more likely that act will be organized in obvious and simple ways.

Crowd control techniques illustrate this principle, and the continual struggle between the necessity to "keep it simple" and the technical requirements of legal language for forms such as tax returns also embody this problem.

The process underlying this principle is **simplification**.   A correlative of simplification is rationalization.   We have discussed this feature of modern life before; it is cited now as a cause of boredom.   Weber used the phrase "disenhanced world" to refer to the consequences of rational social organization in everyday life.   Officially, the modern society is a world without magic.   Explanations are scientific and rational for virtually all human states of affairs.   This is not to say that people are literally trapped in boring life styles, just that their understanding of the world around them (physical and social) is generally rational.   Of course, people, can be excited by legal, scientific, or practical explanations, but that excitation is itself rationally understood (a scientist can be obsessed with finding a cure for cancer, for instance.) The problem of sustaining the rational view of the world is essentially one of coping with boredom. As the world becomes more understandable, it becomes more predictable and, hence, less surprising and enchanting.

Task differentiation and specialization also contribute to the problem of boredom. As work and play in modern society become more complicated, people receive more directed and specific instruction about how to conduct their affairs. Most people do tedious and repetitious work, and even their leisure time activities can become stale and staid.

In a study of the "meaning and demeaning of routine work," Garson (1975) interviewed workers in a variety of different jobs. The people she talked to were factory workers, assembly line operators, clerical and keypunch personnel, and others whose jobs were routine. A woman who worked in a tuna factory reported how she passed the hours by **fantasizing** about sex. She discovered the particulars of her task became less arduous and even sensual when she thought about more pleasant and exciting matters:

GARSON: What do you do all day?

WOMAN: I daydream.

GARSON: What do you daydream about?

WOMAN: About sex.

BOYFRIEND: I guess that's my fault.

WOMAN: No, it's not you. It's the tuna fish.

GARSON: What do you mean?

WOMAN: Well first it's the smell. You got that certain smell in your nose all day. It's not like the smell out there. Your fish next to you is sweet. And then there's the men touching you when they punch the tags on your back and maybe the other women on the line. But it's mostly handling the loins. Not the touch itself because we wear gloves. But the soft colors. The reds and the whites and the purples. The most exciting thing is the dark meat. It comes in streaks. It's red-brown. And you have to pull it out with your knife. You pile it next to your loin and it's crumbly and dark red and moist like earth (Garson 1975, 24).

As work becomes standardized and as place and time become more situationally defined, boredom is an inevitable consequence. The extremes to which workers go to escape this boredom and its consequences are remarkable.

Ironically, the very point at which society becomes complicated, people's understandings of it simplify. As we know more about the particulars of our small worlds, we know less about the particulars of others' small worlds. Modern citizens, therefore, are sophisticated about specific subjects, but often naive about general patterns and relationships among social worlds. The "hip" person (cf. Zurcher 1972) is tolerant about people "doing their own things," even if he or she has no idea what their thing entails. He or she may believe that great diversity exists when, in fact, it does not; or, conversely, that great similarity obtains among people, when from the various standpoints of the people, it does not. All of this leads to an inescapable conclusion: modern life both encourages boredom and is threatened by it.

WAYS TO BEAT BOREDOM

Our descriptive task is straightforward. What are the emotional mechanisms people have to cope with boredom? Put differently, how do people manage the sentiments that arise from interactions with large numbers of strangers? How do they deal with each other according to a formula of functional rationality, and how do they interpret life in the context of disenhanced and task-specific work and play?

Being Cool

According to the Beach Boys, "good vibrations" bring about "excitations." Long before rock 'n roll became an idiom for social criticism, Simmel noted that urban, modern life bombards the human senses. Noises and complicated everyday problems contrast with the press toward routine. In fact, when people follow routines, they are coping with the possibility of sensory overload. When we board a bus, instead of confronting the driver and passengers as unique people, we either follow a routine, if we know it, or try to find out what it is if we do not. The routine of putting coins in the meter, selecting a seat, and staring out the window insulates us from the impossible task of dealing with every detail in our interactional territory. As long as we remain safe inside our routine of doing-what-everybody-knows, we can retreat from an overwhelming state of excitation into boredom.

Boredom contrasts with excitation. We know that the siren from the passing ambulance means excitation. Disrupted routines can mean high levels of excitation, and in city life, excitation is always close by. We refer here to **excitation** as a condition of emotional exaggeration, where sentiments are heightened. These can be positive, like the heightened sense of emotions felt while watching a marching band parade by, or perhaps, more frequently, negative, as in the fear of being attacked or the fright from witnessing a crime or a serious accident:

I was driving my car to pick up my four-year-old son from his day school. I was traveling the same route I use every day. There's part of the three-mile drive where the road I use goes under the freeway. On this day, it was a little cold and there was moisture on the road, nothing really bad, just some puddles on the road under the underpass. I was driving along listening to the radio. I looked in my rearview mirror and saw a car approaching from behind at a high rate of speed. I just continued in my lane. The car cut between me and another car in the outside lane. It passed under the underpass, fishtailing and looking like the driver was really having a "good old time" with some fancy driving. All of a sudden, the car hit the water, went out of control, careened across the median into the path of a compact car. I saw the impact and the look on face of the driver of the compact car. It was sudden impact, and I felt the crash, and knew there was trouble. I stopped, got out of the car, stood motionless a few seconds in the middle of this busy city street. I didn't want to see what happened. Another driver had stopped, he approached me. We walked together to the wrecked cars. By this time, the driver of the bigger car was out of his car. He was young and, then, his passengers got out, all but one, whose legs were pinned under the dash. He was conscious and everybody else seemed OK. Then, we walked to the other smaller car. Inside, slumped over on her side was a young woman, no more than twenty-five years of age. She looked peaceful, no visible cuts. But she was dead, the impact had severed her aortic artery. Within minutes the paramedics were on the scene. They checked her and worked over her a few minutes. They could do nothing. I got back in my car as the police worked quickly to get traffic moving again. I drove on to the day school to get my son. I can't really describe how I felt inside, it was like everything inside me was reved up (Eye Witness Account from an Accident Report).

This description of an accident illustrates how suddenly excitement can overtake us in the complex modern society. While we may seek excitement in a scene of our choice, other kinds of excitement are less welcome. Lyman and Scott (1970) offer a way to understand the relationship between boredom and excitation. They stress how people manage the threat of danger and risk while maintaining a sense of being in control. They write of "Coolness in Everyday Life." We can think of the cool stance or "being cool" as a transformed state of boredom, a version of emotional readiness and an attitude toward one's surroundings in which the routines one has learned are doggedly performed. Lyman and Scott define **coolness** as "the capacity to execute physical acts, including conversation, in a concerted, smooth and self-controlled fashion in risky situations, or to maintain affective detachment during the course of encounters involving considerable emotion" (1970, 145).

They write of different kinds of risk—physical, financial, and social. **Risk** is any threat to the way persons want to present themselves to others. Hence, when people lose their cool, they show their emotional aspects as when a political candidate cries in public, a mother curses at her child while standing in line at the grocery store, or a student displays a "case of the nerves" during his research report to his senior seminar class.

According to Scott and Lyman, the essence of coolness is giving off the impression that one is "in control." A hallmark of coolness is the smooth performance. In our example of the person whose routine was interrupted by witnessing an accident, he maintained his cool by acting according to what he thought was an appropriate response: he simply looked at what happened and obeyed the authorities who requested that he "go about his business." Although he reports how he was emotionally anything but

Descending escapes. Escape attempts are efforts to redefine the meanings of everyday life in modern society. Such attempts are often organized to allow the participant to achieve the attitude of coolness.

cool, outwardly he gave off the appearance of being under control. The metaphor of "stage fright" has been used to depict the feelings associated with uncertainty about impressions given off, that is about how those around us will interpret who we are (Scott and Lyman 1970).

Coolness is an interpretation of emotions. It is the result of judgments made about a person's identity and status. When coolness is lost, performances are marred as when a "prop" fails. We have all "felt" for a speaker when he or she must deal with feedback noise in a public address system, or when a heckler intrudes on a performance. Embarrassment is a chief nemesis of coolness. When one is embarrassed, some interpretation of identity not desired or inconsistent with the performance at hand is made by one's audience. Hence, a speaker is embarrassed by a mispronounced word, as, for instance, a professor who wishes to give off the impression of being highly intellectual and urbane inadvertently reveals his lower class background by pronouncing *tire* and *tower* the same way.

One way to understand coolness as the management of emotion is to examine its loss. As Scott and Lyman write:

a failure to maintain expressive cool, a giving way to emotionality, flooding out, paleness, sweatiness, weeping or violent expressions of anger or fear are definite signs of loss of cool. On the other hand, displays of savoir faire, aplomb, sangfroid and especially displays of stylized affective neutrality in hazardous situations are likely to gain one the plaudits associated with coolness (1970, 149).

One can not really test for coolness in the routine situations of everyday life. It is under stress, in new and confusing circumstances that a person must work to maintain coolness. In short, it is precisely when a person is most likely to become emotional that he or she is supposed to remain in control. As we shall learn, one way to develop and display coolness is to seek out and even create situations of interaction which entail risk to body, pocketbook, or identity.

People do lose their cool; however, this does not mean emotions are beyond control. In fact, we discover that many popular, if not dramatically successful approaches to group therapy, rest on the assumption of the manageability of emotions. A common example used in such approaches goes like this: remember when you were at the fevered pitch of an argument with a "significant other," and the phone rang. What happened? In most cases, people report that they simply answered the phone in much like a normal tone of voice. The phone call is a summons from a stranger. It requires a response and the response must fit a formula, what some sociologists (Mehan and Wood 1974) refer to as the **answerer's greeting slot.** Filling this slot requires a simple "hello." Such a greeting triggers a sequence of conversational responses thoroughly a part of what everybody knows about appropriate ways to speak on the phone. One does not start a phone conversation with a high level of expressivity, for example.

The fact that most people can suspend or bracket their feelings when the occasion requires it, illustrates the essentially constructed character of emotions. Surely, the rituals of society help us to control emotions, but the manipulation of feelings sometimes is coded to enhance the accomplishment of an emotional display. For example, Barley (1983) describes in detail how funeral directors prepare bodies to achieve a posed and restful expression as a part of their occupation of dealing with emotional situations. The management and manipulation of emotions shows, at the very least, how the practical consequences of the expression of emotions creates fabricated worlds.

As therapists rightly contend, the ways in which we express emotions sometimes become so habitual we come to think of them as inevitable, simply the way things are. However, the most powerful feature of any approach to the management of emotions involves first changing situations to expose the constructed and artificial nature of the expression of emotion. In this fashion, one can learn to maintain cool.

We have discovered that emotions are inseparable from the context in which they are expressed. The relationship between being excited and being cool has been further explored by Buckholdt and Gubrium (1979) in their fascinating study of emotionally disturbed children. They entitle their study *The Caretakers* and stress how the behavior of the children labeled emotionally disturbed must be understood in social context.

In the home for children with behavior problems which they researched, an index of the child's emotional instability was their display of inappropriate behavior. Objectively, this behavior consisted of yelling, thrashing about, punching, and kicking. However, when careful observations were made of the kinds of incidents which got children into trouble, Buckholdt and Gubrium discovered that children and staff alike were using a gloss to cover a wide variety of emotional states which, taken together, evidenced the state known as being "emotionally disturbed." The gloss was **blowing up**. Whenever a child "blew up," he or she showed the reasons they were in the home. Invariably, blowing up got the children in trouble with staff, and conversely, a child's ability not to "blow up" was a positive sign which the staff interpreted as meaning progress was being made with the child's problem.

The book covers in detail the methods staff and children used to make complicated decisions about the progress or lack of it in the care of emotionally disturbed children. What is of primary importance to us is how this research documents the consequences of losing coolness. Of course, losing coolness can have negative consequences for adults as well as children. However, adults are assumed to have more control over their emotions, and even in anger, seem to have a measure of mastery over their feelings. Children, on the other hand, are allotted a degree of latitude because of their alleged "inability" to be cool. Also, they can be seen as victims of environments largely outside their power to manage. Sociologically, the problem faced by a child who blows up is that he or she has no reputation of coolness to fall back on. Adults in the everyday world who give off impressions of being normal are generally judged by those with whom they interact as being in control. Children, then, are at the mercy of those who decide the meanings of their behavior. A "blow up" is equated with the lack of control by parents and even by professional psychologists:

Consider an afternoon in cottage four as the boys are watching TV shortly after returning from class. James Brown and Lester Moceri furtively exchange derogatory names across the room when the cottage worker is not looking. Lester apparently intensified the exchange when he called James' mother a "whore." James crosses the room, stands briefly in front of Lester who is cowering, and warns him "not to say that again." As James returns to his seat, Lester whispers, "Black whore." James quickly turns around and runs toward Lester who buries himself beneath some pillows. James delivers several swift kicks to Lester's exposed legs. Lester begins screeching loudly, even before he is kicked, and calls for Jim Boyko, the cottage chief. Boyko emerges from the office

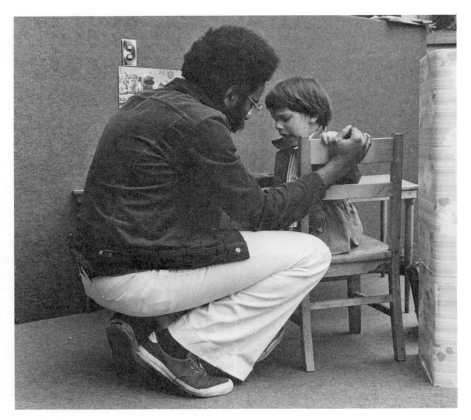

Learning the appropriate expression of emotions is a difficult interactional task. The right person can be a powerful influence on the acquisition of emotion-management skills.

where he was talking on the phone and asks Lester what is happening. Lester points to James who is still hovering over him and tells Boyko that James was kicking him and that it really hurts. As he walks back toward the office, Boyko commands James to return to his seat "right now." Lester again whispers, "black whore" and James leaps on top of him, kicking and hitting any accessible part of Lester's body. Boyko races across the room, grabs James, and restrains him. James struggles to get free from Boyko and return to Lester, who is peering from beneath his pillows, mouthing the same words that have so angered James. Boyko now calls for Amy Langley, the day worker in the cottage. When she arrives, Bokyo asks her to sit on James so that he can remove James' shoes and belt. A Cedarview rule requires that these two items be removed before a child is placed in the control room. James kicks and screams as his shoes and belt come off. He cries, "Get your fuckin' hands off of me! Nobody touches me!" Boyko then carries the still kicking James to the control room and locks him inside. When he returns, Amy asks him, "What happened?" Boyko replies, "He really blew. This is about the worst I've seen. He's so damn strong he could really hurt someone when he gets like this. Wild man, wild!" (Buckholdt and Gubrium 1979, 95–96).

Buckholdt and Gubrium report how children learn to both recognize and exert a measure of control over the "blow up." For example, children know that the staff regard the "blow up" as an indicator of emotional instability and they experience directly the consequences of "blowing up," even if at first they are not sure what constitutes "blowing up." They may protest the staff's judgment about what they did. They say that their behavior was not "blowing up", and in the act of so saying, provide the evidence that they did. Or, they may generalize "blowing up" to include a wide range of behaviors which cover routinely normal expression of emotions.

Even though the children's versions of inappropriate expressivity may differ from the adult staff's, this does not mean the children are totally out of control. Some children, it turns out learn to "stage" emotional displays. This is not particularly surprising given the ability of children to get what they want through the display of emotion. However, in this home, children had learned to get even with each other through the management of blowing up. They would, then, in order to get even with another child, mess up his bed, knowing that when he saw his bed in disarray he would yell and protest. They further knew that this behavior would result in the staff "isolating" the child for a "cooling down" period (this was seen as punishment by the children). In this fashion, children were managing not only their own emotions, but to a degree, those of their peers. They were manipulating the emotional displays of each other in efforts to establish their variety of social order under a constrained and close social control.

On the basis of the descriptive work we have reviewed and considering how closely tied emotional displays are to the quality of social relationships from which they derive, we conclude that expressivity, or the communication of emotions, is merely another part of whole social situations making up everyday life. Emotions are best understood as aspects of the meanings of everyday life. Some authors suggest that there are occasions in which these aspects can override all other meanings of a social encounter.

Being Erotic

In *Smut: Erotic Reality, Obscene Ideology* (1983), Murray S. Davis extends the idea of the layered meanings of social life to an assertion that there is a socially constructed reality of an erotic nature. What he means is that participants in any social interaction have, among the options open to them, the possibility of transforming their relationship into a sexual experience. Of course, this experience can be highly emotional.

Davis shows how the transformation to **erotic reality** is accomplished. The transformation depends on interactional work in which partners to the experience "lasciviously" shift from ordinary meanings or even from special ones like medical or artistic, to erotic. Through the sex act, they generate a reality with separate experiences of time, space, and most importantly of self. The **lascivious shift** functions to ready partners for the "sensual slide into erotic reality." Potential partners have ways to communicate to each other their social arousal, or readiness to begin a sexual experience. In some humorous passages, Davis depicts how this social arousal often generates problems in leaving ordinary meanings and entering the separate reality of the erotic.

Just as a couple slides into erotic reality, they may be "blown out" of this precarious state by such "factors" as "low status" behaviors from everyday life (farting) or idiosyncratic behaviors (chewing gum during intercourse), or "prop failures" (the bed falls down), or the intrusion of others (the phone rings, a family member walks into the bed room), or the intrusion of the environment (earthquakes, warning sirens), or a sudden transformation of one of the copulators themselves (one has a heart attack, stroke, or worse). Davis's analysis clearly shows that the most emotional state of all (making love) is dependent on individual competencies at moving from one reality to another, and on the support, or lack of it, from society. People learn to enter erotic reality. They think of this transformation in ways that make sense to them in terms of what they know about themselves and others. Hence, they use metaphors of everyday life to understand erotic reality.

Some people humorously refer to various sexual perversions in terms of upper-class Madison Avenue corporate abbreviations ("S and M," and "B and D," "AC–DC," "69") or lower-class service industry shop talk ("blow jobs," and "hand jobs"). Ghetto blacks even refer to normal sex as "taking care of business." Business metaphors for sex provoke laughter because they describe the human activities of erotic reality, which is supposed to be a refuge from the workaday world, in the most instrumental terms of everyday reality. Although such instrumentality has no place in erotic reality, it is required by the often difficult task of transporting both parties there from everyday reality. Thus humor can be used to relieve the tension created by the discrepancy between the unearthly ends of seduction and its mundane means. Both the incongruity and instrumentality of sex were nicely captured in the 1957 movie *The Fuzzy Pink Nightgown* when Jane Russell attempted to ward off a would-be seducer by exclaiming, "None of that 'funny business'!" (Davis, 1983:227–228).

This is not to suggest that the management of emotions during the shift and slide into erotic reality is easy, or even that everybody successfully negotiates the transformation. Davis simply amplifies the theme of multiple realities in social life and shows the stark contrasts between two of these, the everyday and the erotic. In many ways the starkness of the contrast depends on the control and expression of emotions during intimate forms of interactive encounters.

ESCAPE ATTEMPTS AS MODERN EXPERIENCE

Everyday life seems to be so potentially exciting that we cope by organizing our experiences in routine habits which produce the emotional effect of boredom. When we are excited, we try to appear bored or cool. And, as

Davis says "One of the melancholy aspects of human existence is that there are not enough lovables to go around" (Davis 1983, 28). We deal continuously with a dynamic dilemma between what we want and what we have, who we are, and who we wish to be, what we do, and what we imagine we could do. Little wonder that the worlds of feelings include fantasy.

Fantasy can function as a survival mechanism, as a safety valve for managing the tensions which are a part of daily life. When we use our fantastic imaginations to attempt escapes from everyday life, these escape attempts (cf. Cohen and Taylor 1978) become an integral part of the organization of what we have come to understand as modern society, and particularly modern experience.

In order to understand the nature of imaginative and emotional escapes from everyday life, we must analyze modern everyday life and what gives it distinctiveness. One way of doing this is by examining a recent and widespread phenomenon, the video experience.

Throughout this book, we have sketched a characterization of modern society. We saw how the dynamic between self and others changes as a society becomes complex and diversified. In sense, every chapter contains a part of the total picture of modern life. Before we can see the video experience as embodying some of essential features of modern life and hence as a reflection of the meanings of societal expressivity, we must have a clean definition of the global concept of modernity.

Global concepts are often provocative and controversial. **Modernity** is such a concept; it is defined in many ways in the literature of sociological social psychology, and more often than not these definitions embody ideologies. When writers use the concept, they may be discussing a new social order which they hope will "correct" the injustices of an older one, or they may be referring to an amorphous dark cloud of social change threatening the cherished values of the past. Because the video game symbolizes the modern society so thoroughly it provokes a similarly wide range of reactions and interpretations.

We draw on three characterizations for a working definition of modernity: (1) modernity can be seen as a distinctive style and organization of consciousness (cf. Schutz 1971; Berger, Berger, and Kellner 1973; Weigert 1981); (2) it can be depicted as the management of appearances (Goffman 1974, 1981; Cuddihy 1974); and, (3) it implies a certain range and type of social control (MacCannell 1976; Farberman 1980).

Berger and his colleagues highlight the impact of modern society on the thinking and feelings of individuals. By tracing the effects of industrial capitalism and the bureaucratic state on consciousness both in terms of content (packages) and processes (carriers), they sketch the "world view" that modern society fosters. Their sketch follows, though not directly, the demands of technology and bureaucracy. They list rationality, componentiality, multi-relationality, makeability, plurality, and progressivity as features of modern consciousness. They identify forms of thinking where

The loneliness of groups. It is an ironic fact of modern life that sometimes we feel most alone in the presence of many people.

society itself becomes "reality"; formal organizational principles, public, and private spheres are allocated, and human rights relate to bureaucratically identifiable rights. This characterization forces the consideration of the "discontents" of modernity:

> These discontents can be subsumed under the heading of "homelessness." The pluralized structures of modern society have made the lives of more and more individuals migratory, ever-changing, mobile . . . the individual migrates through a succession of widely divergent social worlds. Not only are an increasing number of individuals . . . uprooted from their original social milieu, but . . . no succeeding milieu succeeds in becoming truly home . . . A world in which everything is constant motion is a world in which certainties are hard to come by (Berger, Berger, and Kellner 1973, 184).

In the second characterization, our focus shifts to interactive phenomena and how these are said to be differentiated (Parson 1971; Cuddihy 1974, 10). Progressive differentiation has the effect of hollowing out the substance of interaction and reducing it to matters of appearance.

Goffman made clear, in increasingly eloquent statements, the precise ways in which appearances are formulated and presented. He theorized that one's place in society imparts meaning to interaction. This meaning presents the details of how people present themselves to each other in differentiated situations. Finally, in a thoroughly differentiated society, appearance is reduced to "forms of talk." A speaker has freedom to work, sometimes ingeniously, within the confines of ritual, participation frameworks, and the embedded identities of the audience, but the essence of talk is its ability to absorb these social matters into an organization for the exchange. Williams writes of Goffman's conception of talk:

It is the accommodative feature of conversational interaction that is one of its distinguishing features, this feature being brought about through the concatenation of ritual and communicative elements (1980, 230).

The final portion of the sketch portrays the ways in which modern society exerts control over its members. From Weber's metaphor of the iron cage to recent analyses of the role of fantasy, analysts stress that individuated and pluralized life worlds do not necessarily mean individual autonomy. In fact, the weakening of traditional social controls may bring out new and more tyrannical means of social control. These new modes may be more subtle, but they are as effective as the older symbols of order.

Farberman (1980) observes that everyday life is typically thought of as a "drag." The prospect of real action resides "elsewhere." He and others, notably Gouldner (1975), use the concept of everyday life in connection with consequences of modernity. Hence, a result of having adopted the modern world view is a dualism between ordinary and extraordinary, the authentic and the inauthentic. Individuals in such a state of mind can be easily moved into social arrangements that promise to provide the bright side of the dialectic; but these arrangements more often than not carry a price tag. They are, in the final analysis, modalities of rational exchange which embody the symbols of effective social control for society in general, that is, the very state from which escape was sought:

So, the circle closes, people escape the drag of everyday life by retreating epi-sodically into moral regions where they live out their dreams and fantasies which, like bait on a hook, land them in someone else's net. The dreams and fantasies that they use to transcend the world view now reinforce it (Faberman 1980, 20).

Modernity, then, means styles of thinking, ways of interacting, and modes of social control that typify societies highly differentiated according to rational criteria, and that have technologically sophisticated modes of production, and value individuated experiences. It is out of such societies that the experience we now examine emerges. The video experience— enjoyed and fussed over by millions of Americans—stands for modern meanings of interaction.

A STUDY OF A VIDEO PHENOMENON

In order to explicate the meanings of modern feelings, Nash and several student colleagues studied the act of visiting video arcades and playing the games. The video arcade experience and the video games themselves, we believed, provided us with a specimen in which all the properties of modernity can be found in an analyzable form.

We conducted a participation observation study. This method was appropriate because we needed data directly concerning the nature of the experience of video games and the emotions and meanings of players and their relationships. We began as naive observers having never played video games and being generally negative in our evaluation of them.

At first, when we frequented the arcades, we simply sat at tables in snack bar sections and watched others play, or we stood among the mostly

Electronic cool. Danger and the opportunities it affords for an attitude of coolness can be staged. The video game is particularly interesting because it can create interactional circumstances which provide a sense of overcoming danger exclusively through the manipulation of appearances.

male youngsters as they watched each other play the games. We appeared so out of place that it was common for managers to give us coins to encourage us to play. They did this partly because they had just opened under considerable criticism from residents in the neighborhood, and they were trying to establish the image of "family recreation" centers. We must have looked like the kind of people whose approval and patronage they wanted to cultivate. Typically, we gave the coins to players whom we knew.

After several months of gathering information in this fashion, it occurred to us that although we were learning about the occasions of visiting the arcade (cf. Sanders 1973), we were missing a lot of what was happening by not playing. Something was attracting and holding the players other than merely interacting with each other; and that something, we surmised, must have to do with the games themselves.

We began to play. Our initial reactions were frustration, confusion, and embarrassment at not being able to stand in front of the screen for more than a few seconds. The character of our notes and observations began to change, we picked up on the sounds of arcade environs. Before we tried to play, the place seemed merely loud, the noise serving as a background to cover conversations and to provide the appropriate ambiance for teenage interaction. Now we began to notice subdued rock music and we became more sensitive to the emotions of the scene. We were ready for our first **video experience**. It came while one of us was playing Zaxxon and it marked the beginning of our discoveries of the symbolic meanings of the games.

Unlike many games, Zaxxon cannot be played with any degree of expertise until the player learns to perceive depth through the graphics of the game. Of course, lucky reactions to obstacles might carry the player up to the first guarded opening, which is a niche in a brick wall blocked on the top by a force field. At this juncture, the player must see the hole and maneuver his shuttle craft through the opening. Quite suddenly after playing the game several times, one of us reported seeing the opening. Although our player did not successfully fly through it, at least he knew it was there.

We were excited and now knew the basic task of the video experience, namely to ascertain order from apparent chaos. The problem is one of figuring out which frame serves as the base portion of the organization of video experiences. This problem is distinctively modern in that it requires a mentality of cool detachment and the ability to function coherently against a strangely superfluous background. One way to apprehend this task is to think of it as learning the perceptual skills necessary to transform noise into music, or for some older members of society to appreciate hard rock music (cf. Curtis 1978). The experience is modern in a profound way because it is comprised totally of appearance. The game is essentially a manipulation of appearance. Experience itself is the commodity.

As MacCannell (1976, 21) puts it, a pure experience is the ultimate commodity, it leaves no traces. A short leap of imagination moves us to understanding that in the purchase of the experience the individual enters a modality of social control. But how does this transformation take place, and how is it cultivated; and in what ways are the content and form of this transformation essentially modern emotionally?

Learning and Cultivating the Experience

Learning and **cultivating** are two interdependent processes, but we must discuss them separately to achieve a detailed description. Learning to experience "video" depends on a player's mastery of five tasks: seeing the game, learning to play, controlling emotions, beating the game, and renewing the challenge.

We have already discussed the initial seeing of a game. To be sure, there are many variations of this tale. Some players, especially youngsters, seem to see the game almost immediately. However, playing is learned. We documented the progress of several players as they learned to play a "respectable" game. Their progress reveals the elements of seeing a game. In each case, in the beginning, the players were unable to sustain play for more than a few seconds. They observed other players, became engrossed in the images on the screens while others played, and, from indirect experience, they formulated vague ideas about how to play which provided for them a sufficient motive to play again. Specifically, their attitude allowed the learning of a few moves. Before discussing what it means to know how to "make a few moves," we must add that all this orientation and watching occurs with regard to a particular game, a focused encounter. The appeal of the game is, therefore, at least initially dependent upon the game's ability to present an image.

There are fantasy games with images of antiquity (Joust, Wizard of Wor, Tutankhamen); there are space games (Asteriods, Star Wars, Phoenix, Invaders); there are games dealing with everyday life (Pac Man, Dig Dug, Frogger); and finally, there are realistic games of war (Tanks, Frontline and NATO Command).

A player is attracted to a game that fits with his or her interests. This attraction process is basically a matter of the player selecting a game that is consistent with his or her likes and the perceptions of the likes of his or her peers. The selection of games according to the interests of the peer culture helps to account for the rise and fall in popularity of games as they move in and out of favor with age-specific groups of players.

After having selected a game, the next step is to learn to play. This is a matter of hands-on experience as well as watching others play. Hands-on experience consist of standing in front of the game long enough to get the feel of it. Players have difficulty articulating exactly how they learn to play. They say that it is a matter of getting inside of the game:

I like the graphics on Joust, the sounds are great too. After I started playing, got the feel of the joystick and the flap button. It's a question of anticipating the opponents and timing the collision just right. You can't wait to react like on some games, and I like that. You have to see the patterns, choose a place on the field and hang there ready to joust. Finally, I guess, I really got hooked when I was able to make plays off the screen (Fieldnotes 1982).

"Making plays off the screen" refers to this player's method of watching a figure exit the screen on one side and return at the exact position through the opposite side of the screen. The area of play in some games is not a traditional closed space like a football field, but is an interconnected universe. Players learn to set up moves by using the properties of the universe to catch opponents or to escape trouble.

There are many ways to learn to play the games. We have documented a few to show that idiosyncratic methods still have in common an element of symbolic interaction. They depend upon the ability to take on the attitude of both the game and its program and the other players whose skills are continuously made public through their play. In a strict sense, the player is interacting with the programmers of the particular game. He is attempting to figure out strategic moves and ways to anticipate the behavior of the characters in the game. Learning how to play, then, is a matter of learning how to interact, not so much with the machine, although that is a part of the process, but with the human elements of the games.

Our description of how players relate to the games parallels Goffman's (1974) notion of **keying**. Keying involves interacting at levels of "as if" experience—treating a serious remark as if it were a joke, or an error of speech as if it were intended. In order to play well, one must be able to treat the images on the screen as if they were alive, and so the player keys the game.

Since the programs for the games have become sophisticated, learning to play can be a frustrating affair. The games create the illusion of fresh movements essentially through a multiplication of possible reactions to player moves. For example, in Joust, if a players sits and waits for his opponents to appear at one end of the screen, the program for the game is written in such a way that they will appear at the other end. Thus, the games are programmed so that the moves of their characters appear intelligent and creative. As long as this image of freshness is vital to the player, the game maintains its appeal. However, the freshness of the game's behavior comes at the expense of the expressivity of the player.

Freshness of moves is achieved in part through a bombardment of the senses. Simmel (1971) noted that the modern city amounted to an environment in which the typical inhabitant experiences an assault on the senses. Video games overload the senses. In an episode of the popular television show "Taxi", Iggy, a burned-out refugee of the hippie movement, gets hooked on Pac Man. He is engrossed in the noises, the chase, and the obstacles of the chase. Bells, flashing lights, and unanticipated impediments capture his attention and he proclaims his first Pac Man game "the greatest experience of my life." Iggy's unflappability typifies coolness, but it also makes him vulnerable to a form of exploitation. He is "hooked" by the video experience and cultivates his habit through repeated play. Next payday his boss—who is also the proprietor of the video game machine—pays him with bags of quarters.

As we proceeded with this study we observed how important coolness is to the experience. Certainly, there are players who lose their cool, but we noticed patterns in the control and expression of emotions that can be understood only in terms of the symbolic context of the arcade. These reactions range from facial expressions to the use of expletives, to physical retaliation against the machine. The first reactions are clearly the most cool. A grimace, a facial contortion, a barely audible groan, allows one to communicate to his audience that he is aware of having been momentarily taken by the machine, but maintains his detached involvement with it. If he continues to play and ultimately amasses an impressive score, he will have achieved the highest state possible of the video experience. This state is the interactive outcome of learning to play and controlling emotions within the social context of the arcade.

The use of expletives is widespread among young arcade players and these words, of course, index emotionality. Although such outcries are not particularly cool, they are more often than not subdued and audible only to those close by. Of course, the background noise of the machines and the music of the arcade help to mute the cries of the players, and thereby enhance the accomplishment of coolness.

Finally, one can lose coolness altogether and strike the machine. Even here the notion of coolness helps us to understand these outbursts. "Totally uncool" is "blowing up" which is acting out of control and doing physical damage to the machines. Hence, a kid once broke the joystick of Dig Dug and another bent the steering wheel on Turbo. Although such feats are among the folklore of players, they are negative incidents; they get you kicked out of the arcade, or worse you may get the reputation of a hotheaded player. Everybody sympathizes with "blowing up," and might well "blow up" on a particularly frustrating occasion at the machine. But most players, when really frustrated by the game, strike the machine a glancing blow, usually with an open hand, on the controls (joystick or button) and under an attitude of control. There are cool ways to lose your cool. Mastering the range of ways to be cool, from supercool stances to the controlled blowup, comprise a major learning task in the experience of playing video games.

Next in the learning and cultivating of the video experience is beating the game which is both a triumph and a defeat. In fact, the modern condition of ambivalence is clearly exemplified in the phenomenon. At the very moment when the game is figured out, or when a quirk in the program allows the player to amass points in an easy way, the image of freshness disappears and the mechanical nature of the game becomes apparent. Players refer to this experience as "playing a pattern."

The first time we saw a "pattern" was on Pac Man. We watched a young player amass about 45,000 points. Some older players were standing around and noticed the boy's efforts. They remarked that the kid was the best "runner" they had seen (by this they meant he was playing by simply reacting to the characters, without a plan). They asked him if he would like to learn a pattern to which he enthusiastically replied, "Yes!" One of the men then instructed him to clear three boards which he did. Then the man traced on the face of the screen with his finger a route through the maze which the young player following with the Pac Man character. After a few trial runs, the boy memorized the pattern and improved his game by about 60,000 points.

Not all games lend themselves to this type of treatment, but most do. In Joust, for instance, on a particular wave of attacking knights, one can sit on the middle ledge while a bounder knight is captured by the lava troll and wait for the pterodactyl who will suicidally fly into your knight's lance. In this fashion, a player can get a thousand points per flying reptile.

These two cases show that players do figure out the games, and that they often display publicly the knowledge necessary to beat the games. The routine of following a pattern also aids in coping with the overload playing puts on the senses. Pattern players are necessarily cool players. Although the player enjoys amassing points and can be confident about his coolness, the freshness of the game is destroyed by this tactic, and the excitement of the game changes to a boring sameness.

At this point, coping with boredom, the final phase of cultivating the experience, operates. A player must learn to renew the challenge of the game. This is accomplished essentially by trying games that provide a new twist on the experience or playing old games in a new way.

Certain aspects of playing are transferable from game to game. For example, all video games require a high level of hand-eye coordination. More to the point, one's attitude about emotional conditions necessary for play is transferable. Having learned not to "blow up," the player is able to coolly approach a new game. He is confident that although he may not do well first time out, he will not commit a faux pas. His emotional display and his attitude toward it, is best described as "controlled panic." When the game overwhelms him as he knows it will, he is comfortable in the knowledge that he can rely upon the cool display to accomplish the image of being a player and to serve him as a take-off point for learning a new game. A negative instance illustrates this attitude. A young player was observed watching another player of Tempest. The player had assumed a posture in which she tilted her body to one side and repeatedly pressed the "fire" button while holding the movement of the character still. This tactic results in the successful accumulation of points. When the young player got his turn, he immediately assumed the posture but in an exaggerated style only to be rapidly "killed off". Those who saw this happen simply came apart with laughter. The young player had copied without fully understanding the basis of the tactic. He had inadvertently displayed the problem of **engrossability**, which is the problem of becoming too fully absorbed in the task. Just as one can be embarrassed by missing out on the flow of interaction because he is engrossed in a book, so a player can miss the purpose of a posture or a move by becoming engrossed in an isolated act of playing.

The player who has mastered a blasé attitude toward the game and who knows how to search for patterns can renew the challenge of the video experience by moving to new games or by altering play between patterned and spontaneous strategies. In patterned play, one tries to ignore impending danger and trusts the pattern. Hence, in Pac Man, although Winkie may be about to kill you, you know that at a certain spot on the board, he will change his direction and you can continue to follow your route. In Joust, it may appear that sitting without movement on a ledge means certain death to your knight, but you trust the pattern to avert death. Learning a new pattern can be very exciting. Learning a new game likewise reconstitutes the challenge of the game.

Environments of Feelings: Observations at the Arcade

A major contention of the sociology of emotion is that feelings derive from a social context. This study of playing video games illustrates how this experience evokes feelings distinctively modern. To fully appreciate the accomplishment of these feelings, we recorded observations over a six-month period at seven different arcades. I summarize these observations here to describe the background knowledge which shores up the meanings of video experiences. An arcade is first of all a location, a business. It has the features of a "hangout," and it provides youngsters and all players with access to the games, but, in a phenomenological sense, it is the place where video experiences occur. The place constitutes the social context for the characterization of games as symbols of modernity.

At arcades, players talk to the machines and to each other in front of the machines. Critics of video games have remarked that the machines have the effect of social isolation. To an extent this is true as we pointed out in the discussion of engrossability. However, it is blatantly false if isolation is taken to mean the absence of social interaction. Players accuse the machines of unfair moves, of playing cheap, and of taking advantage of unusual playing circumstances. On the offensive side of conversation, players may warn the machine of its impending defeat, talk to the joystick, and otherwise attribute human qualities to the parts of the machine. This practice of talking to the machine is recognized by game manufacturers, and they have put games on the market that not only make sounds, but that talk back as well. An advertisement for a home video game extols the fun of communicating with the game through the voice synthesizer: "Hear cheers, strategy, and taunting." A few games capitalize on the taunting and actually call the player names, deriding his skills whenever he fails. Of course, all of this is designed to enhance the accomplishment of controlled panic.

Players make gestures at the machine. Most of these are in response to unexpected termination of play. They communicate to others in the arcade and to the player him or herself in defiance and frustration. The symbolic value of the gestures is to inform others who are participating in the video occasion about the emotive states of the player.

A surprising amount of interaction takes place among the player and those spectators attracted to his or her performance. The principal forms of sociation taking place in front of the games are observing play, admiring and congratulating, and remedial remarks like "nice game," "nothing you can do about that," and "not bad." While it is true that much of this interaction is nonverbal, or consists of short verbal utterances, the communication system is nevertheless effective. Young players are encouraged or derided depending upon their performances. If a young player displays unusual skill at a game, older more accomplished players will recognize the player's potential. This is done either through direct remarks, or by comparisons. For instance, the older players may remark, "Wow, this kid's goin' beat my score," or, "Man, I never thought a little kid could play like that."

Much of this interaction functions to enhance the effects of play (excitation) and to establish status among the players. The effects of play are further amplified by spectators who could readily embarrass the player with deriding remarks. The status system at the arcade is primarily informal, but there is a formal dimension to it as well. Most machines allow high scoring players to record their initials on the machine display. These initials appear regularly on the screen of the game between play. Arcade goers know the initials of top notch players and struggle to beat, or at least get close to these scores. Through word of mouth, direct observation, and informal networks of peers, one's reputation as a player is established. All video players can quote their high score on their favorite games, and there seems to be a surprising amount of veracity in these self-reports. Even youngsters seven and eight years of age remember five- and six-digit scores.

Much of the interaction in and about the arcade is focused on financing play and transportation to and from the arcade. Among others, there is the practice of marking one's turn at the game with a quarter or token. It is a universally accepted practice to mark one's turn by placing a quarter up. This means simply putting a quarter on the face of the game. When arcades are busy and at popular games, there may be as many as ten quarters lined up. Players not only honor this system, but they remember whose quarter is up next. A player who wishes to play more than one game will put several quarters up. When he has played these, he usually has the option of "one last game." We have seen players skip over a quarter because they knew that the owner of that quarter was playing at a different game, then honoring that player's place when he returned. We have also seen players call for a queued player from across the room.

There are many ways to get money to play. Basically, adolescents in modern society are limited to lunch money, allowances, their own earned or procured money, or outright gifts from adults. For the purposes of this analysis it is not necessary to offer a detailed description of how funds are acquired; that the quarter is a basic symbol of the video experience seems self-evident, and its procurement is a necessary condition of the experience. Regular players carry many quarters with them so that they do not have to frequent the change machines. In this way, they may also avoid asking for change from an attendant. Someone without proper change has to approach an attendant who may be wearing a t-shirt that says "ask me for change." This practice is not particularly "cool", and will indicate a neophyte status. Hence, having quarters readily at hand is a hallmark of the regular player.

Transportation to and from the arcade is a part of the video occasion. In good weather, players will band together for the trip either on their bicycles or by foot. The trip itself is an occasion for sociability. The composition of the groups making the pilgrimage reflects the state of integration and organization of peer structure. Over the summer, for instance, who gets asked by whom to go to the arcade is a good indicator of the friendship structure of the group.

During inclement weather, rides are valued. They can be gotten from parents or from older adolescents. Generally, sixteen-year-olds with access to a car do not give rides to younger arcade-goers. The only exception to this rule is giving younger brothers or sisters rides. The major opportunities for rides comes from parents. Since parents often are not available to drive, kids can be observed traveling in bands towards the arcades even on the most inclement of days. The restrictions of travel that weather, bicycle, and foot impose on the players is a major factor in the next set of observations.

Each arcade takes on distinctive features depending on its social environs. Kene (1982) documented how laundromats have ethnic, racial, and class identities. The same may be said for arcades. In our study, there were three arcades owned and operated by the same franchise. In interviews with attendants, each was depicted according to its clientele. Number one was located in an upper-middle-class neighborhood and was regarded by the attendant as a "kid's place." In fact, he noted that the arcade has become a hangout. On Friday and Saturday nights, the arcade is a place to meet friends and members of the opposite sex. No serious video playing is done on these nights at this arcade by regulars. The arcade is crowded on "social" nights and most people simply stand in the middle of the floor between rows of games and engage in conversation. It is interesting to note mechanical games like table hockey have been introduced to the arcade. They are placed in the middle of the room and are the kinds of games which allow more talk and socializing to take place.

On "social nights," the atmosphere is party-like, the location becomes secondary to the flow of sociability. Attempts for high scores are made mostly by those not fully integrated into the peer culture or by those insiders who want to display their skills.

Another arcade was located in a neighborhood of mixed classes, light industry, and businesses. This location was characterized as appealing to more mature players who were often serious about their scores; indeed, a quick check of the displays on the games showed that the scores were significantly higher here than at the number one location. It was also not uncommon to find families with very small children in the arcade. The children would watch or totter around as their fathers played the games.

The third arcade was located in an area with a disproportionately black and transitory population. Here seven- to nine-year-old unsupervised kids could be seen just hanging out. It is also interesting to note that this arcade was the first in this franchise to change to token-operated games, in which every player must deal with the change machine which gives tokens or with the attendants. In this fashion, management thinks that it can control the arcade more effectively. Apparently, the need for this kind of close supervision is not perceived as existing at the other arcades.

Hence, an arcade may be interpreted as a space in which interactions of various content can take place. Although the rules of interaction are similar in all locations, there is still a distinctive character to each arcade depending on the way in which it attracts and functions for the local residents. Arcades as forms both absorb and reflect the background of socially significant variables that make up their social environments.

Conclusions of the Study

Video games can be interpreted as symbols of modern society. They embody meanings which parallel features of modernity especially with regard to the display of emotions in public places. The styles of thinking necessary to play well, the modes of interactions observed at arcades, the technology itself, and most importantly the nature of the experience manifest both the content and form of modernity.

The games require interactions of a complex nature with strangers. Sets of rules have been developed by players in order to maintain and enhance excitement and coolness, and these rules, though rational, promote a sense of membership and feelings of belonging. Arcades are essentially "hangouts" which absorb locally constructed social identities. The accomplishment of play is ephemeral and understandable only in terms of the situated context of video occasions. Finally, the order that emerges from the experience represents at least a nascent mode of control.

It is because the video phenomenon is essentially modern that it elicits a wide range of responses. These responses are hyperboles about modernity itself. The Surgeon General, C. Everett Knoop, declared the games an "aberration of childhood behavior" and links symptoms like tension, sleeplessness, destructiveness, and nightmares to playing, while Alex Comfort (1982) extolls the educational functions of the games. He remarks that children may be learning the principles of quantum physics through playing the games.

Although few would want to lay odds on such a claim as the latter, we can be assured of the quality of video game playing. The experience, we discover amounts to a framing practice in Goffman's sense of the concept (Goffman 1974). The player keys appearances and learns to master acting "as if." In this process, the technology of the computer is demystified, the routine and boring aspects of everyday life are temporarily escaped, and avenues for constructing social relationships are cultivated and practiced. What makes video games both attractive and repulsive to large numbers of people is the degree to which those games symbolize modern ways of experiencing life, a chief component of which is the framing of emotions.

SUMMARY

This chapter began by building a rationale for looking at emotions, a subject not usually considered a part of sociology. Emotions can be understood within the same general analytic framework which appreciates the constructed nature of social meanings. In order to apply this framework, it was first demonstrated that emotions are a part of the interactive problems making up everyday life.

At the heart of this demonstration is the thesis that feelings are at least partially bound in social context. Coolness, as an emotive state, for instance, is best understood as a synthesis, or neutralization of two polar states, excitation and boredom. Since both boredom and excitation are intrinsic consequences of modern social organization, coolness represents an emotional adaptation.

Even erotic experiences, typically understood from either a medical or moral stance, can be analyzed as the result of interactive work to establish a "reality" separate and distinctive from everyday life.

The chapter ended with a participant observation study of the recent phenomenon of video games and arcades. Through the observations reported it was seen that the games are best regarded as symbols of modern social order. They foster forms of interaction which are essentially cool, emotively.

Emotions, in this sense, must be woven into the social fabric not so much as a natural fiber, but as a synthetic.

EXERCISES IN OBSERVING FEELINGS

1. Watch a "day-time drama" (soap opera) on television. Video tape it with your school's equipment. Watch it several times and list the range of emotions displayed by the actors, and the situations in which they displayed these emotions. Describe the facial and verbal expressions which carry the display for each scene. Do they use props or other aids such as background music or scenery to enhance the effect? After you have a rather full descriptive account of several emotions, try to make generalizations about the relationship between emotions and the social contexts in which they are displayed for this form of drama.

2. Visit an arcade. Take notes on what you see (you might want to do this mentally to avoid attracting attention to yourself. You can always write down ideas and observations after you leave the arcade). Compare your data with that discovered by Nash and his students. Did you see "cool displayed"? Did you see the turn taking rules operate? How about the relationships between players and machines? If you find you have quite different observations, why do you think this happened? Think about changing social contexts and the essentially modern character of the video experiences.

3. Write down all the things that bore you, what you do to avoid being bored and how you escape boredom when you find yourself "trapped" in a boring routine. Organize into groups of three and compile a list from all the responses. Working as class in groups of three, you should be able to generate a list of "boring practices" and a variety of different escape attempts. Have the list for the entire class typed up and duplicated so that it can be distributed to each group. Then in group sessions, see if you can figure out what attributes "boring things" have in common, and what ways escape attempts are similar and different.

KEY CONCEPTS

Sentiments
Boredom
Simplification
Fantasizing
Excitation
Coolness
Risk
Greeting slot
Blowing up
Erotic reality
Lascivious shift
Modernity
Video experience
Learning
Cultivating
Keying
Engrossability

SUGGESTED READINGS

Scott and Lyman's article on "Coolness in Everyday Life" has become a classic. In it they develop in detail the hypothesis about the relationships among potential danger, its management and the control of it which we apply in the chapter. We recommend reading the original to reinforce one's understanding of this important insight into modern life.

In a richly descriptive book, Schwartz and Merten offer an account of the tender emotions of love and commitment as experienced by their informant, Cheryl. As she tells her story of love and commitment, we learn a great deal about the meanings of love and sex in American society. Noreen Sugrue, in a tightly reasoned paper, instructs her reader on a conception of emotion as property which can become an important "commodity" for negotiation. She relates a fascinating instance of a patient named Kathy who struggles with doctors over proper treatment and her emotional states.

Marvin Scott and Sanford Lyman, "Coolness in Everyday Life" in Lyman and Scott, *A Sociology of the Absurd* New York: Appleton Century Croft, 1970.

Gary Schwartz and Don Merten, *Love and Commitment* Beverly Hills, CA Sage Publication, 1980.

Noreen Sugrue, "Emotions as Property and Context for Negotiation" *Urban Life* Vol. 11 (Oct):280–292, 1982.

Chapter Fourteen

Conclusions and Directions

OUTLINE

Conclusions and Directions

The materials and perspectives presented and developed in the previous chapters come from a variety of different views of social psychology, all of which share common themes. In Chapter two, we acquired an appreciation of the origins and scope of social psychological thinking which places the analyst, in one sense or the other, in the place of the people who are experiencing social life. Throughout the various chapters and the topics examined, we repeatedly demonstrated the essentially "subjective" nature of the subject matter of social psychology.

Since the growth of the social sciences in general, there have been several groups of thinkers attempting to analyze the relationship between the individual and society. This last chapter will sort out the ways these analyses have developed, showing how each attends to different aspects of the task of understanding self-and-other relationships. And in the process of putting the theoretical house in order, we will acknowledge the various ways of social psychology.

THE WAYS OF SOCIAL PSYCHOLOGY

A social psychology which sets out to describe the nature and variety of social experience cannot, in this day and age, be composed of a single theoretical group. Instead, it moves on four distinctive fronts: phenomenological sociology; symbolic interaction; ethnomethodology; and dramaturgical sociology. Even these groupings, however, are not clearly separated from each other. A single author, for example, may identify his or her work by several of the labels at different times, for different analytic purposes. Several excellent books provide the interested reader with a full introduction to the range of social psychological theories. Morris (1974) refers to the social psychology of these thinkers as *Creative Sociology*. Meltzer, Petras, and Reynolds (1975) use *Symbolic Interaction* as a covering term for all four varieties of analysis, whereas some proponents of ethnomethodology and phenomenology often prefer to establish their domains of inquiry outside the boundaries of "conventional" sociology (cf. Handel 1981, and Psathas 1973).

With the awareness of the importance and diversity of social psychological thinking, however, has come an attitude of reconciliation among those who practice the analysis as well as increased efforts to articulate the pivotal concerns of social psychology. Douglas, et al. (1979) have made attempts in these directions, as has Weigert (1981). Both of these volumes emphasize the importance of the concept of everyday life, and similarities of analytic and methodological procedures among the ways of doing social psychology. This chapter will now introduce the four branches of "subjective" social psychology and focus on points of convergence.

Phenomenological Sociology

There are three interrelated goals for phenomenologically based inquiry: 1) the description of social realities, 2) the discovery of social essences within these realities, and 3) the investigation of the meaningful interrelationships among essences.

Phenomenological thinking depends on a particular way of philosophizing (Dickens 1979). Phenomenological inquiry focuses on human consciousness and offers a very broad conceptualization of existence. Our world, the phenomenologist contends, consists of many different phenomena understood according to the nature of consciousness. In the modern world, scientific consciousness tends to dominate all other forms, its principal rival being the attitude of everyday life or common sense.

In attending to the phenomenological variation of the social world, one must first describe what phenomena really are—what makes them different from one another. For example, what are the *essences* of scientific thinking, of commonsense knowledge, of religious belief, loving, aggression, or gender. Phenomenological sociology is the result of the application of a philosophy to primarily social psychological topics. Although phenomenological sociology can deal with societal experiences (most of Peter Berger's work exemplifies this), it is always connected with the task of appreciating the nature of human consciousness.

Such studies begin with consciousness as it is discovered by the analyst, in other words, as it is *given*. In order to conduct inquiry, we must suspend as best we can our own knowledge of the social world. Although we can never fully accomplish this, we use our imagination to doubt our knowledge about a given thing. This radical shift frees us from our accustomed ways of thinking; it allows us to look freshly at even the mundane world around us. Such methodological procedures are referred to as **bracketing**.

The phenomenologist wants to know what forms of consciousness or knowledge are taken for granted in the context of social life. He or she is interested in how knowledge is used in an unreflective fashion to serve as a basis for a sense of existence. Schutz illustrates this task by analyzing the classic story of Don Quixote.

Quixote lived in the fantasy world of knights, a world of history book chivalry which he resurrected several hundred years later. Quixote had a sidekick named Sancho Panza, his loyal manservant. Sancho was never fully converted to Quixote's way of seeing the world, but he dutifully followed, served and conversed with his master.

The story of one of Quixote's adventures shows clashes among three separate universes or phenomenological ways of experiencing existence: chivalry, common sense, and science. Quixote and Sancho are riding along a river and find a boat. To Quixote, the boat is special, capable of rapid travel to transport the knight to some noble person in distress. To Sancho the boat is ordinary. They tie up the donkey they have been riding and get into the boat. Shortly, Sancho hears the donkey braying and concludes that they have traveled but a short distance down the river. Quixote thinks they have traveled at least two thousand miles. They debate the question of distance traveled. To resolve the dispute, Quixote refers to the scientific knowledge of his time. Without proper measuring instruments, he does the next best thing; he evokes an empirical law. According to Spaniards and others who traveled over the sea to India, when crossing the equatorial line, lice die on everybody aboard ship. Quixote reckons they have traveled past the equator. To test this, he wants Sancho to pass "his hand over his head and see if he catches anything." Sancho objects. He can see and hear the donkey, and therefore, believes such a "test" to be unnecessary.

To this Quixote replies that as an unlearned man Sancho could not possibly have the knowledge of a scientist. He goes on to remark that if Sancho were to possess this knowledge, he would know they had traveled a great distance. Quixote says "once more I ask you, feel and fish!" To this Sancho obeys, he raises his head, looks at his master and says, "Either the test is false or we haven't got where your Worship says" (Schutz 1964, 151–52).

This example shows how three separate realities can operate within the same "objective" set of circumstances. Quixote thinks he is a knight and the boat is his enchanted transportation. Sancho is a common man. He knows only what he senses, and must rely on what his previous experiences tell him. Quixote shifts realities, becoming a scientist and reasoning "scientifically." Sancho understands neither the world of knights, or scientists, but knows he has caught lice.

A phenomenological study usually deals with thinking, its nature, and its social consequences. According to Schutz, the paramount reality of everyday life overrides, in the final analysis, all other realities. However, to fully understand the meanings of social life, one must still describe in detail and with fidelity, the coherence and sense (essences) of the varieties of experiences people have.

Phenomenologically informed inquiry focuses on the deep structures of social life. These structures are lived in and known about by virtually everybody, but understood by only those who can stand outside of experience and observe it. There is a philosophical flavor to this type of inquiry. Its goal is neither the codification of knowledge nor the production of research techniques. It pares forms of understanding to elemental and irreducible components. It offers profound, often extraordinary, and nonobvious understandings of obvious and ordinary occurrences.

Symbolic Interaction

The term **symbolic interaction** was coined by Hebert Blumer. He thought it was necessary because George H. Mead's terms of social psychology and social behaviorism were too easily misunderstood. Blumer did not intend to change Mead's conception of social psychology. He was just concerned that its distinctiveness was not properly reflected in its name.

Of the four branches of sociological social psychology, this one is probably the most difficult to depict. Authors and researchers who identify themselves as symbolic interactionists range from those who rely on phenomenological reasoning to those who seek empirically grounded generalizations about the organization and causality of self-concepts. However, there are two considerations that consistently set off the work of symbolic interactionists from that of phenomenologists. First, symbolic interactionist studies are invariably connected in an explicit way to the works of Mead, Cooley, Thomas, or others who stress the symbolic or communicative quality of interaction; and second, in this group, members place a strong emphasis on research or data-based theorizing. A symbolic interactionist will write of "data" and of "generalizations" about them while a phenomenologist will write of "bracketing procedures to arrive at essences."

Beyond these idiomatic differences, the symbolic interactionist is as clearly indebted to Mead as the phenomenologist is to Schutz. This means that a symbolic interactionist's work concerns the self as a focal concept. It also means that language and communication are understood in general and less technical ways among the symbolic interactionists. Their studies are often based on questions raised by Mead himself, and their task is to develop a version of social life which both appreciates Mead's self-theory and expands it in ways that are acceptable to, or at least conversant with, the concerns of sociology proper.

For some, the primary difference between their work and that of psychological social psychologists is in the kind of data they examine. Symbolic interactionists insist that data convey a "direct sense of what people are about" (Lofland 1971, 1). Others have expressed this idea through the proclamation that theory must be **grounded** (Glaser and Strauss 1968).

Theory is grounded through the researcher's total immersion in the experiences of others. This is accomplished through various techniques. Life histories and other autobiographical materials provide data with a valid perspective, as do interviews which require repeated exchanges between the researcher and the "subject"; and, of course, there is participant observation.

Each approach has its own advantages and disadvantages. In the first the observer can be certain of the "stance" of the data, but, there are always doubts about the veracity of self-reports, and even the completeness of the life accounts. In her recent work, McCall (forthcoming) has developed techniques which provoke people to write "life histories". These techniques allow the researcher a measure of control over the subject matter of life histories, something often lacking in historical and other incidental life accounts.

Interviewing can be effective and efficient, but there is always the danger of imposing the researcher's interests on those being queried. Again, Lofland and others have worked diligently to develop skills of interviewing and offer guidelines designed to avoid these problems. Lofland (1971) suggests what he calls **intensive interviewing** which amounts to a cross between interviewing in a formal sense and simply conversing with and observing someone.

Participating in what one researches assures the natural character of observations, but field observations are quite time-consuming, perhaps inefficient, and, on occasion, involve serious problems of ethics. For example, how much, if anything, should a researcher tell his subjects about what he or she is interested in, and to what degree should he or she become involved in the ongoing activities of the people studied, especially if these activities are illicit (see Georges and Jones 1980). How to use life histories, conduct an interview, or do participant observation are the important subjects of the methodology of social psychology, however.

I do not want to leave the impression that grounded symbolic interactionists contribute little to the theoretical and substantive growth of social psychology; I am merely trying to convey a sense of the kind of work that gets done under each branch of sociological social psychology. The phenomenologists devote effort to analysis with a decidedly philosophical tone, whereas the symbolic interactionists more likely begin, and perhaps end, with a "research project". These differences are not merely matters of taste, but derive from differences in what each regards as the pressing intellectual task of understanding.

Ethnomethodology

This style of social psychology dates from the publication of *Studies in Ethnomethodology* in 1967 by Harold Garfinkel. This method is a mix of several influences. It is phenomenological in origin, but shares with symbolic interactionism a concern for research. Born out of 1960s and 1970s professional sociology, **ethnomethodology** has a distinctively critical and confrontational bent. Although mellowed somewhat (see Handel 1982), the original intent of ethnomethodology must be considered. Many were attracted to it because they saw it as an alternative to traditional, survey, and experimental social psychology. In idiom and purpose, its audience is the graduate student and practicing sociologist; hence, much of this material is difficult for the beginning student to read. In fact, the members of the group have been called cultists (see Mehan 1976 for a reply to this charge).

Two themes run through most ethnomethodological studies; 1) a multi-realities conception stated in its extreme form which typically leads to the study of esoteric or unconventional topics; and 2) criticism of "normal" empirical social science.

Ethnomethodologists extend the idea of systems of knowledge into a position stating that all social reality is constructed, fragile, dependent upon constant work for its maintenance, and highly open to influence. More than the other schools, ethnomethodology draws out the implications of the notion of reflexivity.

Mehan and Wood (1974) contend all social realities are essentially "faithful" — they require that people believe in them. They refer to the articles of faith as **incorrigible propositions**, or beliefs which are necessary to a particular social reality. It is not that the knowledge derived from an incorrigible proposition is testable in a scientific sense, nor even that social reality is essentially opinions, but rather every system has a way of accounting for its version of reality. Systems may be far from "function-al," complete, or even practical, but they operate to explain away anoma-lies in the struggle with alternative ways of thinking and being.

In the struggle to uphold and live by perspectives, each system provides its own account of its existence and its own means of evaluating how it is doing. A socially constructed reality is, therefore, **reflexive**. The word reflexive is defined as "denoting an action that is reflected back upon an agent or subject", such as do reflexive pronouns—himself, herself, them-selves. Proponents of this view maintain that all social life, and ultimately all human life, has a reflexive quality; this point in a weaker form is Thomas's self-fulfilling prophesy. Ethnomethodologists, however, take this point to far-reaching conclusions. They suggest that talk itself is reflexive, by which they mean every utterance we make and every word or sentence we speak is heard not only by the person to whom we speak but by ourselves as well. In acts of self-monitoring, and through our imagina-tions of how "others" understand, we develop an understanding of how the social world is organized. Although other methodologists share this idea, only the ethnomethodologists turn their conceptual framework on themselves in a rigorous way. They insist that they must be subjects in the same sense as those whom they study.

In a recent book, therefore, David Sudnow (1980) examines the mean-ing, subtleness, and organization of the act of moving one's hand. He writes of the *Ways of the Hand* as he offers a technical but readable account of largely his own mastery of hand movements. His data consist, for the most part, of his own musing over the appearances of his hands at the tasks of typing and playing the piano.

Any social occurrence has a double quality to it: what it intends and the intender's judgment of the intention. All action is said to "fold back upon itself." Thus, ethnomethodologists can attend to the ways in which hands appear, or how a conversation unfolds. Invariably, they discover that social acts have several layers of meanings and these layers take on different practical consequences depending on the contexts of interaction. Mehan and Wood illustrate how reflexivity operates in a simple greeting:

> To say 'hello' both creates and sustains a world in which persons acknowledge that (1) they sometimes can see one another; (2) a world in which it is possible for persons to signal to each other, and (3) expect to be signaled back by (4) some other but not all of them. . . . When we say 'hello' and the other replies with the expected counter greeting, the reflexive work of our initial utterance is masked. If the other scowls and walks on, then we are reminded that we were attempting to create a scene of greeting and that we failed. Rather than treat this as evidence that greetings are not 'real,' however, the rejected greeter ordinarily turns it into an occasion for affirming the reality of greeting . . . [for example] . . . "he didn't hear me," (Mehan and Wood 1975, 13–14).

Such a theory highlights the importance of the researcher in the act of research and makes possible the use of "personal experience" (the other's or the researcher's) as primary data.

Ethnomethodological criticism of "conventional" research methods has opened up new vistas for inquiry through new ways of doing research. Although ethnomethodological literature is strong on critique, it is generally weak on clarity about how research is conducted. But, this is partially the result of the nature of the inquiry. Actually, much attention has been directed to the question of how sociologists do research. The question is framed by a broader consideration, namely, "How is social reality accomplished?" It follows that ethnomethodology is itself a social reality, and hence, can be described in terms of how *it* is established.

Look for mistakes, misfires, breaks in social order, or idiomatically, "breaches" in routine! This proclamation is the methodological maxim of ethnomethodology. It is essentially a methodology of confrontation. It is easy to be "blind to the obvious"; the trick is to learn to look at the obvious with a fresh perspective, one of readiness for surprise or discovery. The techniques that those who follow Garfinkel have used are ingenious. Some have resorted to mechanical devices such as prisms worn as glasses to "invert" the world; others have developed breaching devices like acting in an inappropriate fashion. Some of Garfinkel's students talked to an award-winning scientist at a university dining hall as if he were the maitre d'. Others acted as if they were strangers in their own homes. Purposive violations such as these of established, routine social realities provoke reactions in others. In turn, the meanings of these reactions reveal the essential features of the original reality. Generally, studies of this type use equipment breaches and contrived breaches, or they focus on settings of everyday life where there is some built-in ambiguity (these situations are sometimes referred to as **strategic interactive settings**). Examples of these are bus riding (Nash 1975), transsexuals (Garfinkel 1967), and door ceremonies (Walum 1974). Since these kinds of studies pioneer new ways of gathering and conceiving of data, they are often controversial and not well codified. They may, however, prove to be quite useful in a variety of research endeavors.

Mehan and Wood (1975) give a brief account of several innovative ways to "understand" everyday life. They cite the methods of **zatocoding** and **enjambing**. In zatocoding, one records observations of the scene of interest on cards or slips of paper, one observation per card. These cards are simply stored without any particular schedule or prearranged organization for a long period (the length varies with the nature and intensity of the social interaction being studied). After collecting many hundreds of seemingly disjointed pieces of information, one then tries to organize them according to how one believes a person in the scene would do so. Of course, the effect is to test whether or not the researcher has become competent as a member of the social reality being studied.

Likewise, with enjambing, transcriptions of interviews or conversations are prepared without punctuation or other customary ways of designating who is talking to whom in what fashion. The researcher must sort out this enjambed language, and punctuate it socially. Again, failure to do so indicates that the researcher has not yet "become the phenomenon." An underlying maxim for all these techniques is that social realities must be confronted by the researcher before they will reveal their true nature.

Ethnomethodology is critical, highly observational, and phenomenologically moored. Phenomenological inquiry supplements the scientific character of ethnomethodological work with connections between empirical investigations and investigations of wider philosophical meaning.

Dramaturgical Sociology

This approach is mentioned not so much because of its distinctiveness from the others, but because it illustrates another important aspect of social psychological inquiry into the meaning of experience. Here, understanding can be accomplished through the use of the metaphor. Metaphorical reasoning involves the use of "a word or phrase literally denoting one kind of object or idea in place of another by way of suggesting a likeness or analogy between them" (*Random House Dictionary* 1983). The social psychologist can look at a description of some social setting, then think about it as if it were something else. In this way, he or she can ascertain patterns and regularities that may lead to new insight about the social setting itself.

The name of Erving Goffman is usually associated with the analysis of social phenomena by metaphorical reasoning. In his early work, he suggested that the world is essentially stage-like. Persons play roles and enact scripts given to them by social organizations. However, there can be different purposes and intentions in role playing. Each person has a social mask, a **persona**, which he or she presents to others. Those others evaluate this mask and make judgments about its appropriateness for "playing out" or the "staging of" the social encounter. For example, in the book *Stigma: Notes on the Management of Spoiled Identities,* Goffman sets up a scheme for treating the way persons deal with discredited social identities. When a person's appearance communicates some negative meaning, that appearance becomes evidence that the person's persona is not acceptable. As is often the case with handicapped people, the discredited person must cope with a damaged persona.

Goffman relates example after example of the various ways in which this coping may develop: persons acquire stigmatized social identities and think of themselves as outcasts. They may even develop a biography or history as a type of person, a role to play that derives from "standard or starring performances." Goffman calls these patterns "moral careers" (1963, 32–40). He shows how information about the discredited and the discrediting person, and the processes of being discreditable and having a hidden identity that might be discreditable amounts to a high drama of everyday life, a dramatic enactment of protagonists and antagonists. Normality is the consequence of the management of impressions, according to Goffman. In society, we discover the script for acting out what it means to be "stigmatized."

Goffman offered a systematic version of his metaphorical social psychology in his classic *The Presentation of Self in Everyday Life.* In this book, he introduced the idea of actors varying in skills and script, in directorship and in supporting cast in the performances they give. This book has relied heavily on his work, and we have learned that in his recent works he drew on the findings of animal studies and on the abstraction of the form itself for yet other metaphors for social understanding.

Just as animals have territories which they defend and claim as their own, humans possess contrived and culturally relative, but nevertheless real, senses of "territories of the self" (cf. Lyman and Scott 1970). In a public place, for instance, a person may claim a "stall" which is the "well-bounded space to which individuals can lay temporary claim, possession being on an all or none basis" (Goffman 1971, 32–34). A telephone booth, a table with a view, or a place on the beach can be marked with a designation item—a purse or a phone off the hook for a brief time. Intrusions on claimed stalls often precipitate conflict and renegotiation of the space boundaries and time claimed.

Just as wolves mark their territorial boundaries, humans claim areas of public domains for themselves as to use, intentions, and relationship with other areas.

Goffman continuously up-dated the metaphors he used for social understanding. As we saw in the chapter on language, his latest work dealt with the ways in which formal analysis of language can and can not enlighten us as to the social foundations of human communication. It is important for us to recognize that Goffman does not use analogical reasoning uncritically. He uses it as a device, in much the same way the ethnomethodologists use devices, to further his analytic aims. Hence, on occasion, he finds it necessary to specify where analogical understanding distorts or falls short of complete descriptive validity. Hence, in *Frame Analysis,* he devotes a chapter to showing the ways in which theater and everyday life are not alike, and in *Forms of Talk* he makes it clear that formal linguistic analysis alone will not exhaust the meanings of human communicative exchange.

Goffman's contributions to understanding social life are immense. However, the reader should be cautioned about a danger of metaphorical understanding. The analyst, even if he or she is very careful, may become more interested in the model than in the phenomena themselves. Thus, Cicourel, commenting on Goffman's work, writes:

descriptive statements are prematurely coded, that is, interpreted by the observer, infused with substance that must be taken for granted, and subsumed under abstract categories without telling the reader how all of this was recognized and accomplished (Cicourel 1970, 20).

The metaphorical model can provide entrance into the world of first-hand experiences. It can be a handy device for organizing information, and a helpful tool for weaving one's way through the maze of detail that constitutes everyday life. If we are interested in achieving a sense of other people in their social environments, we must avoid mistaking the metaphor for the phenomenon. Goffman's work moves us toward understanding by heightening our analytic powers and, perhaps, most importantly, by teaching us the truth of the saying, "everything in the social world is significant." Goffman was the master of using *fait divers*. His books are full of the details that others overlook or discard as unimportant. Although he never developed what could be called a program for research, Goffman's contribution to social psychology is virtually immeasurable.

POINTS OF CONVERGENCE

The branches of social psychology we have briefly reviewed do differ from one another in some significant ways, and the reader is encouraged to pursue the theoretical issues raised by these differences in the many fine volumes devoted to this enterprise. However, it is the convergence among them that allows for a vital sociological social psychology. Although no true unified social psychology exists today, this book examines the common threads of theory woven into the fabric of inquiry, and closes by reiterating and recasting these threads.

The Significance of Subjective Meanings

Thomas wrote, "if situations are defined as real, they are real in their consequences." Although he did not show how these consequences and their objective antecedents are similar, he paved the way for the recognition of "social meaning" as the proper subject matter of social psychology. Psathas (1973, 14) puts it this way:

The world is not filled with objects that have appearance independent of humans who experience them, nor does subjective experience exist independently of the objects, events, and activities experienced. Subjective awareness of consciousness is consciousness of something. Whether that thing is real or imagined matters little in its impact on human experience. Subjective meanings are not found in psychological mechanisms of perception. They are experienced as being 'in the world'. Perception, therefore, can not be limited to what is received through the senses, but must include the meaning structures experienced by a knowing subject of that which is being perceived.

In all of the systems of thought we have reviewed, to say that something is subjective, known intuitively, or is part of cultural knowledge, in no way detracts from its significance. In fact, all agree that these aspects comprise the most important features of social life. This is not to say that objective considerations such as the number of people living in certain geographical areas (rural versus urban population destiny, for example) do not enter into the total understanding of individuals in society. However, like Psathas, they point out that all objects have meaning, at least a portion of which is attributable to human mental acts.

Everyday Life as Topic of Study

The social meanings we pursue can not be discovered in the theories of sociology, psychology, or another social science. Of course, each profession possesses a social meaning structure of its own. But sociological social psychology professes to study people and societies to the extent that understanding and experiencing become a part of the same meaning structure. Thus, what other sciences take for granted—the world of routine and day-to-day living—becomes a central subject matter. Phenomenologists say we start with the world as we find it "given in consciousness." Symbolic interactionists say we must anchor our concepts in the symbolic reality of real people in their real-life activities. Ethnomethodologists speak of "sense making" in everyday life. All point to the importance of focusing on the organization and content of everyday life.

In modern society, shifts take place continuously in everyday life, and we can not assume that patterns which depict one historical period will depict another. To understand how an individual connects with others, however, and how this connectedness makes up society, we must begin with descriptions of everyday life. If we are to understand, we must start with society as we find it; we must not study merely those things that interest us. The full range of the meanings encompassing everyday life must become the object of our inquiry.

Strategies for Observation

Although each branch of inquiry proposes different modes of research, a common ground for the characterization of these approaches to research can be sketched.

Suspicious Observations As much as possible, social psychologists should rid themselves of preconceptions about the form and content of the experiences being studied. This includes discarding hypotheses that derive from theories invented by sociologists about the nature of the subject. We pointed out earlier that without the bracketing of beliefs, without the stance of doubtfulness and suspicion, we have already decided what is important about what we study. If a social psychologist is overly confident about the nature of events, he or she may take for granted how the people being studied experience life, or some small portion of it. Such a stance toward research restricts the analyst to the discovery of the answers to a limited range of questions. Specifically, they can simply find out only if they are right or wrong.

We are after an answer to a broader question, "What really is happening, how is it happening, and what is its nature?" All of the branches of inquiry assume the critical importance of a descriptive attitude.

Naturalistic Attitude Serious interests in the description of phenomena lead to the naturalistic attitude. This refers to the mental stance of the researcher through which he or she purposefully seeks to discover the meaning of things in their natural surroundings. Just as biologists observe how animals behave in their natural habitats, social psychologists observe people at football games, in offices, running on tracks, eating in restaurants, or drinking at bars.

Most conventional, positivistic forms of social psychology require that people accommodate the researcher in some fashion. The survey researcher requests that people respond to his or her questions, taking time out from their routines to address sets of queries designed by the social scientist. This is also true, but in lesser degrees, of interview methods. And, of course, the experimenter brings people into the laboratory, in some cases, actually paying them to serve as subjects.

The varieties of social psychology presented here, in all four branches, turn this conventional research arrangement around. The researcher goes to the people and accommodates himself or herself to them. Matthew Speier writes:

Generations of students have been trained to talk about the social world without ever taking the trouble to actually look at it. It has become commonplace for students to develop very elaborate and highly abstract ways to talk and write about society . . . without making concrete observations (1973, 3).

Watching and wondering about people engaged in their ordinary affairs, going to them and attempting to understand them in their own terms, these are methodological maxims of sociological social psychology. Jane Goodall discovered that chimpanzees can be very brutal animals after she spent months in careful observation of chimpanzees in their natural habitat. It is now widely known that animals behave quite differently in captivity than they do in nature.

People, on occasion, capture each other and even live in a kind of captivity of their own design. And, there is a sense in which we can say laboratory studies, survey questions, and the like are a part of the humanly constructed social world. But Speier refers to the correspondence between what the researcher concludes and the nature of the settings in which he or she gathers information. Studying human social life simply requires being there.

Observational Tactics Because all of the branches of social psychology regard ordinary experiences as the base portion of analysis, the student of social life faces a unique problem. Linguists describing an exotic, unwritten language do not know that language before they begin study; likewise, biologists do not assume they know how chimps act. Social psychologists, however, are already a part of the phenomena being studied. They have friends, live with fellow human beings, and have several membership stances from which to draw. Hence, the methodological task of understanding is difficult. Without the special devices each branch offers (the zatocoding of ethnomethodology, the participant observation, interviewing, and life history techniques of symbolic interactionists, the radical description of phenomenologists, and the metaphor of drama), the analyst can become "blind to the obvious." No guarantees of insight come with any of the devices. Together, however, they provide us with an impressive set of tools, some of which we should be able to put to our own descriptive ends.

All aspects of the study of social meaning deal with another problem. After the analysis is finished, the researcher may be confronted with the feeling expressed in a popular song by the stylist, Peggy Lee, "Is that all there is?". Indeed, it is very difficult to do a good job belaboring something we presume we already know. We can see that people in other cultures know a great deal, tacitly, about how to think, feel and act within their own complicated contexts. We are fascinated by descriptions of "exotic" practices partly because they contrast so sharply with our own tacitly known worlds. Throughout, this book has employed the tactic of comparison. In the study of everyday life in modern society, this often amounts to focusing on "deviant" or "extraordinary" occasions and happenings. Of course, these social experiences can be designated "normal" or "unusual" only in terms of contrasts among several perspectives. This means that as soon as we succeed in depicting a typical understanding, we discover we have described a setting in which it would be accurate to say that "everybody knew that all along." Icheiser (1970) suggests that there is a paradox here because the more we penetrate into the hidden and obvious features of our existence uncovering commonsense knowledge, the more we create the impression of saying something which everybody knew all along:

The point to remember, however, is that the illusory impression arises only *after* the analysis has been completed and is simply the consequences of taking implicit awareness (immediate experience) to be explicit knowledge (Icheiser 1970, 11).

DIRECTIONS OF INQUIRY

Why is understanding so important? Isn't it enough to simply leave well enough alone? Why take tacitly understood experiences and go through the often arduous work of rendering them explicit and communicable? Why run the risk of becoming a disenchanted, cynical analyst? We answer these questions by following the same methodological maxims we outlined above.

Several scholars have attempted to describe the nature of scientific inquiry according to assumptions and tacitly understood knowledge structures that support it. Gouldner referred to the socially constructed, support experiences of science as **domain assumptions** (Gouldner 1970). Others, like Trent Schroyer (1970) have classified types of inquiry according to the purposes and aims of the inquirer. Each attempt makes clear in its own way that science, including social psychology, is a human activity and as such can be analyzed and understood in the same way other more mundane human endeavors are understood. This means that one way of making sense out of the efforts of inquiry is to see them as social experiences. The problems in analyzing and depicting social psychology as human experience, then, are no different than those entailed in, for instance, Lofland's analysis of being a member of the Divine Precepts cult.

Schroyer (1970), drawing on the work of some contemporary German sociologists, suggests that inquiry can be classified according to ends to which its proponents believe it should be put. First, there is the experience of inquiry as **strict science**. Those who live by this version of the reasons for inquiry state they are after the explanation of phenomena, by which they mean the ability to predict and control.

Why study human experience? Their answer is quick and to the point: to predict and control it. There are sophisticated arguments as to why prediction and control are the criteria for adequate explanation. These have to do with incorrigible propositions grounding this inquiry to the effect that there are canons of logic which in form alone are valid. Of course, we allude to symbolic logic and specifically deductive logic. If one starts with accurate descriptions, and these materials are arranged according to the formal properties of logic, then the conclusions reached will allow the "errorless" anticipation of similar occurrences; by implication, if one is in the position to prearrange the conditions engendering the phenomenon, that phenomenon can be controlled. We are describing a version of science known generally as **positivism**. Positivists experience inquiry as reducing to prediction and control of experience.

Secondly, inquiry can be experienced as leading to understanding. This entire text has been devoted to showing what understanding means. Like Jerzy Kosinski's character, Chance the Gardener, we rely on the powers of others to understand what we mean when we say "we understand." In his startling novel, *Being There,* Kosinski shows how people read into the experiences of others, the meanings they wish to see there. This process, of course, is the essence of social life itself. Inquiry can have as its purpose the understanding of understanding. Although profound and even entertaining, this is rarely all social analysts are interested in.

The third purpose, reflexivity, completes the program of inquiry. Gouldner used the term **reflexive sociology** to refer to inquiry which studied itself to uncover self-interests and to unravel the interconnectedness of interests in order to see who is and who is not benefiting from the inquiry. If we go back into the origins of social psychology, we will see that this aspect of inquiry has always been a crucial component in programs of understanding.

Many of the members of the Chicago school were concerned with the question of how to establish order from the disarray they saw in their own city from the turn of century through the Great Depression. Mead showed how in an expanded "generalized other" there is the possibility of tolerance and good will as a basis for a new and broader community. Gouldner admonished his fellow sociologists to express clearly the values they wished to maintain and promote.

But, of course, we always face the question, "Whose values?" A contemporary sociologist, Howard S. Becker, addressed this question in his article "Whose Side are We On?" We discussed this problem in the chapter on "deviancy." There we learned how the defense of values is bound up in the question of perspective. Understanding as the result of methodological and theoretic devices may be "context free," but the action we take on the basis of the understanding clearly is not.

Our inquiry can evoke in us a sense of what it is like to be the other person, but our understanding makes sense only in terms of the practical results which ensue from it. We can use our own understanding to write a book or an article, thereby serving our own interests as well as those of our readers. Or, understanding can become the basis for immediate experience, like political or social action. Our very program of inquiry teaches the impossibility of simply "understanding." We understand something or someone and do something on the basis of that understanding. This dimension to inquiry is most widely referred to as **critical**. Hansen expressed it well:

The invitation to critical sociology is an invitation to become an involved, critical explorer of human and societal possibilities ... In Mead, we find an invitation to self-and-other awareness. That awareness is seen as the groundwork of our personal freedom and creativity and of our personal responsibility, for neither our freedom nor our responsibility to ourselves can be untangled from the freedom of others and our responsibility to them (Hansen 1976, 12–13).

A direction of social psychology is to become critical. Although this volume can not deal with all the ethical aspects of critical social psychology, two values can be explicated here which seem to be widely distributed among social psychologists: tolerance and autonomy. These two values taken together, allow for a version of reciprocity sufficient to warrant the conclusion, "I understand what social psychology is really about."

Perhaps, better than any other twentieth century thinker, Mead expressed the problem of tolerance. Through increased awareness of self-and-other relationships, we see how in our differences we share a common humanity. However, Mead takes us much farther than this. He shows how tolerance is an outcome of understanding the dual nature of self and others. It is only in coming together with others that we recognize our unique qualities; yet as we express our unique qualities, we separate ourselves from the group. "Individuality requires order and destroys it" (Hansen 1976, 35).

Social psychology serves in the interest of tolerance—tolerance of differences of opinion, differences of bonds holding groups together, and finally differences of global social structures. But, this tolerance must be two-sided, coming from both the self and the other. Mead's legacy to the purpose of social psychology is a challenge to expand self-and-other awareness, and, at the same time, find grounds for an overarching bond, a system of solidarity which holds people of dissimilar backgrounds and interests together in an atmosphere of mutual respect. Using Mead's own terms, the ideal society is one in which the individual's I can grow and express itself without fracturing the me. In this sense, social psychology as developed in this book is an effort to grapple with the fundamental issues of what it means to be human. This book has presented some of the many-sided features of social psychology's responses to that challenge.

David Reisman (1950) raised the question of autonomy within the context of social pressures toward conformity. The way he thinks about the problem serves to illustrate another of the values of social psychology. Much of the content of social psychology is devoted to a demonstration of the forces that impinge on the individual. In understanding self-and-other relationships, we come to appreciate the necessity of control and the complicated mechanisms of socialization and external forces that result in uniformity of action among members of society. Still, the very act of trying to understand these forces implies the possibility of avoiding, adjusting to, coping with, or manipulating these forces. It is only from the vantage point of understanding them that the possibilities are known. Reisman talks about the forces of modern society in terms of their effects on individuals. He writes that the forces of modernity could result in people who are fine-tuned to the signals of approval or disapproval of others, people without inner guidelines for morality and self-worth. These kinds of people make up their minds, act, and feel only with reference to what they think others will think of them. Of course, this is the famous **"other-directed" personality**.

Although individualism is deeply ingrained in the American character (Derber 1979), and surely manifested itself in the narcissistic social order of the 1970's (Lasch 1978), Reisman's analysis still rings true. He focused on the value of inquiry by discussing the ways in which people use their understandings of the social forces which influence them. He suggested the concept of the **autonomous person** (1950, 239–60), one who is aware of both the possibilities of freedom and the requirements of group membership. In the duality of these stresses is a balanced position; it is not adjusting but is closer to what we have called adaptation, or a creative coping with the external and internal requirements of social life which allows persons to use competencies acquired in social interaction to further mutually perceived interests. Of course, a social psychological understanding is a necessary condition of autonomy.

Reisman writes:

Autonomy, I think, must always to some degree be relative to the prevailing modes of conformity in a given society; it is never an all-or-nothing affair, but the result of a sometimes dramatic, sometimes imperceptible struggle with those modes. Modern industrial society has driven great numbers of people into anomie, and produced a wan of conformity in others, but the very developments which have done this have also opened up hitherto undreamed-of possibilities for autonomy. As we come to understand our society better, and the alternatives it holds available to us, I think we shall be able to find a great many more alternatives, and hence still more room for autonomy (Reisman 1950, 257).

Social psychology as conceived of and presented here is a descriptive science with the goal of understanding. It is incomplete, however, without a critical dimension. Each person who travels the path of social inquiry must creatively and intellectually make a critical commitment to become involved in, and to explore the possibilities of human social interaction. These interests must be recognized. However, how a person becomes critically involved will vary according to the styles, values, and interests of that person's engagement with the people he or she studies. Having appreciated the layered, multiple, and diverse qualities of social interaction, and having recognized the act of inquiry as a form of social life, it should not be surprising that social psychology does not promise a single theory of human behavior, nor does it aim to establish a body of knowledge of invariant and stable validity. Its purposes are to be found in the meanings it discovers and the consequences of its discoveries.

EXERCISES IN VARIETIES OF SOCIAL PSYCHOLOGY

1. Next time you visit home, over a school vacation or on a holiday, try a zatocoding exercise. Buy a pack of 3 by 5 cards (any size will do) and write down one word or one phrase on each card for the impressions you have as you travel home, enter your home, greet your parents after a long absence, and so on. Continue this recording of words or phrases until you have compiled at least one hundred cards. Wait a few days, maybe until you return to school, and sit down with the cards and try to sort them into categories that make sense to you. Sort and resort until you have a system that makes some sense to you. Write a short paper in which you explain your reasoning for the sorting. This exercise will uncover many implicit things that you know about your home environment and will generate data for the description of the reality of your home.

2. Select a typical day in your life. Write a script instructing another person whom you do not know how to play the part of you in this routine day. Include at least some lines as well as instructions about props, setting, and the like necessary to produce a play about you.

3. Divide up into groups of three. Designate one person as an interpreter in the group. Follow the rule that two people will talk to each other through the interpreter, and that the interpreter can not simply repeat what has been said, but instead must rephrase and restate what is said. The principal conversationalists can not talk directly to each other. Try this for a few minutes, and then suspend the rules and discuss what you really meant to say and whether or not the interpreter actually represented what you intended. You should discover that the interpreter is in a strategic position to understand how the attempted communication is organized as social interaction. This may be a frustrating situation, but it should also generate some interesting data.

KEY CONCEPTS

Bracketing
Symbolic interaction
Grounded theory
Intensive interviewing
Ethnomethodology
Incorrigible proposition
Reflex
Strategic interactive settings
Zatocoding
Enjambing
Persona
Domain assumptions
Strict science
Positivism
Reflexive sociology
Critical inquiry
"Other-directed" personality
Autonomous person

SUGGESTED READINGS

To suggest readings for this chapter is to suggest readings that go beyond the scope of this book. As you know, there is an extensive literature in each of the branches of social psychology we have reviewed. I refer you to a range of sources. A recent book by Handel introduces ethnomethodology in a quite effective and readable fashion. Phenomenological sociology awaits a Handel to articulate its precepts to the uninitiated, but Berger and Luckmann did the job under the cover of "sociology of knowledge" in their book *The Social Construction of Reality.* Goffman should be read in the original, and his classic *Stigma: Notes on the Management of Spoiled Identity* is recommended.

Berger, Peter, and Thomas Luckmann. *The Social Construction of Reality.* Garden City, N.J.: Doubleday, 1966.

Goffman, Erving. *Stigma: Notes on the Management of Spoiled Identity.* Englewood Cliffs, N.J.: Prentice-Hall, 1963.

Handel, Warren. *Ethnomethodology: How People Make Sense.* Englewood Cliffs, N.J.: Prentice-Hall, 1982.

Appendix A

How to Organize Observations: The Methodology of Social Psychology

How to Organize Observations:
The Methodology of Social Psychology

I N social psychology, we try to discover, through observations, how people reason about their experiences. As observers, we must rely on more than just having the same experiences as those whose social lives draw our attention; otherwise, we would simply be satisfied with being able to interact like those whom we study. Of course, we may well require that our descriptions of meanings of social life be true to experiences of others, but all interaction is, after all, based on guesses about what others are thinking. The task of the social psychologist is a peculiar one. Not only must he or she preserve in description the reasonableness of the thinking, feeling, and doing of those studied, but he or she must communicate this understanding to an audience. Social psychologists are always a kind of "professional stranger" (cf. Agar 1980). They are a part of the worlds they study and yet they must maintain a detached attitude about their own experiences relating new insights to existing bodies of knowledge. Accomplishing valid understandings and effectively communicating them are the primary purposes of methodology.

Methodology is the rationale for the organization of observations and the means for developing understanding. In everyday life, all people concern themselves with methodology. Each of us has to figure out what is happening in the social world so that we can act in it. In the attitude of everyday life (the natural attitude), however, we are rarely called upon to make explicit the basis of our interactional work. In this closing note, I will present a sketch about how peculiar social psychology is—it requires exactly the opposite of the natural attitude. Whereas in everyday life, tacit assumptions often work best when they remain hidden, outside the critical eye of our fellows, in social psychology the precise means used to organize observations and the rules evoked to draw conclusions and assertions from these observations must be explicit. Although the way a social psychologist attempts to understand self and society may be painstaking and extraordinary, it is necessary for any claim for the validity of the undertaking itself.

Chapter one identified two ways to find out about the experiences of others: by asking or talking to them and by observing them. Both are indirect, both have advantages and disadvantages, and both, in their various forms, comprise the methodologies of social psychology.

HOW TO ASK PEOPLE ABOUT THEIR EXPERIENCES

In the natural attitude, we simply ask. But when we look critically at the act of asking, we see that asking is actually a method of finding out about the experiences of others. We must know the other person's language; we must ask their motivations; we must make judgments about their backgrounds and the skills they possess in interaction. Although we do not think about these things, they are the tacit basis of the work we are doing. Of course, in everyday life we get by without having to test each and every tacit aspect of social life. In the scientific attitude, we must explicate all pertinent aspects. Social psychologists have developed conventions for communicating their research with each other regarding the ways they went about their research (asking). Sometimes, they even insist on a rigid way of talking or writing while asking. We call this most heavily organized form of asking the **survey**.

In the survey, the precise wording of questions is carefully prepared before the researcher asks another person to tell of his or her experience. The social psychologist can only do this when he is very confident about the way people think and the subjects which people think about. Hence a survey question may ask people to respond to a sentence. Most often the way they can respond is restricted to versions of *yes* and *no*. Typical survey questions, for example, look like this:

Do you watch television?
_____ yes _____ no

How many hours a day do you watch? Check one
_____ 1 to 2 _____ 3 to 5 _____ 6 or more

or

The United States should be involved in the affairs
of Latin American nations.
Agree :____:____:____:____: Disagree

In most cases, the responses which people make to questions like these are coded and treated as comparable to other experiences they may have had, like having a certain kind of job or belonging to an ethnic group. The science of survey questioning has become very precise in recent years. It is possible, for example, to predict purchasing behavior, to anticipate the outcome of elections, and even to explain shifts in attitudes towards policy and political candidates from the use of survey questions.

However as has been stressed throughout this book, in order to survey, one must assume that people's responses mean the same (a "yes" is a "yes" for all those who so respond), that the background differences among respondents are irrelevant, and that experiences are similar enough to allow comparisons without adjustments for qualitative variations among them. Indeed, there are many subjects for which the survey question has provided valuable information for analysis. We learned a great deal about the experience of social class by surveying how people reacted to categories of other people, and, for example, that certain conditions of social life like health and even the quality of life are somewhat associated with the unitary meanings of gender.

Most social psychologists require more detail before they make assertions about the character and organization of experience. Hence, they rely on more intensive forms of questioning. As in the survey question, if they already know a great deal about the subject matter from previous studies or from their own experiences, they may be able to ask questions from a **prepared schedule**. Also, if the researcher is interested in questioning large numbers of people, he or she may give up some detail and flexibility in favor of the sheer bulk of information he or she can get from asking the same question of many different people. The difference between the survey question and the schedule is one of degrees of freedom in response. In the survey question, the respondent is limited to categories of responses defined by the researcher. In the interview schedule, a respondent may indicate what categories he is responding to in his response. The researcher may ask the same question of each of those studied, but does not prejudge the response categories. In fact, the categories are generated from the observed range of responses to the questions. For example, if we suspect that bigots are both intolerant and impervious to criticism, we may ask people suspected of bigotry to answer a question which we think will elicit responses manifesting both these characteristics. Such a scheduled question, if used with a white male, might be formulated as the following: How would you like it if your company assigned you to work under a black boss?

The respondent would be free to shape his response as he wishes. The researcher would have varying degrees of freedom to hear answers in the responses. Therefore, he or she may code what the respondent says as being "tolerant" or "open to criticism," or simply record responses under decoding procedures that are a part of what everybody-knows-who-knows-the-language, or in other words, the answers are ordinary instances of talking about the hypothetical situations.

Interviewing is a special case of simply asking people. It can vary from a way of asking that is organized according to the researcher's interests, to a version of asking that is virtually the same as conversational exchange. The open-ended interview is very often much like ordinary talking, but usually takes place at a single time in a situation which is officious and contrived. The problem with such conventional ways of interviewing is that they do not allow time for the questioner and the respondent to get to know each other, and, in many cases, the rapport established between the parties to the talk is important to the validity of the information gathered. Lofland (1971) proposes a technique he calls the **intensive interview**. In this form of talking with the other person, the researcher repeatedly visits the people being studied. He or she uses the responses from previous interviews to start subsequent sessions. In this way, Lofland claims that a greater amount of information that is also more accurate can be obtained.

Ethnographers also use a similar approach to talking with people. They insist upon repeated sessions in which the person being talked to (they call them "informants") teaches the questioner. Informants play an active role in shaping the information they give to the social scientist. Likewise, ethnographers have developed ingenious ways to elicit responses from informants and, after they have the responses, to categorize them for analysis. For example, Spradley (1979) advises that the first interview session should start with a "grand tour" question, one which requests that the informant orient the researcher, show him or her around in the domain of knowledge. A study may start with curiosity about some social phenomenon, a puzzle. A student notices men walking around her small suburban community dressed in buckskins. She inquires about the men and discovers they call themselves "muzzle loaders," after their primary interest in building and firing muzzle loading, flint and lock guns. She finds an informant and asks a "grand tour" question: "Tell me about muzzle loading."

This begins a long and often tedious process of depicting the cultural knowledge of this activity. The goal of the ethnographer is to describe in detail the organization of this knowledge and activity. The ethnographer, however, like the survey questioner, makes assumptions about the nature of this organization. The ethnographer believes the knowledge can be described in categories and these categories can be contrasted with each other in terms of features or components. The enterprise results in taxonomies and flow charts which allow the ethnographer to communicate what he or she has learned from the informants in a powerful, precise, and concise manner.

In social psychology, an amazing variety of ways to ask people about their experiences have been developed. In summary, we can list these in terms of fixed or flexible language in the questions and the degree of freedom the respondent has to formulate their answers. (See Table A/1)

Of course, we have simply outlined the forms of talking to people. When we discuss the process, the enacting of the talk, we move into

Table A/1   Flexibility in Questions and Answers for Ways to Talk to People

	Degree to Which Questions are Fixed	Degree to Which Answers are Fixed
Surveys	High	High
Interview Schedules	High	Moderate
Open Ended Interviews	Moderate	Low
Ethnographic Interviews	Moderate	Moderate
Intensive Interviews	Low	Low

another aspect of the methodology of social psychology. There are many excellent sources which give advice and counsel about how to gain entree to some setting, how to get official and unofficial approval for research, how to develop relationships with those being studied, and finally, even the "nuts and bolts" of taking notes and recording field observations (Emerson 1982).

Field research techniques are becoming increasingly sophisticated. Video and recording equipment can be used and the micro-computer is being used as an information storage and retrieval devise. Perhaps most importantly, with increased experience, researchers are sharing their knowledge about the problems of qualitative research. There are many complicated issues entailed in doing any kind of social science inquiry. For example, Douglas (1976) calls for an investigative attitude while talking to others in the act of research. He discovered that while people are often willing to discuss even intimate details of their lives, they have a variety of reasons for doing so. These reasons may shape and distort the information they give.

In his study of the nude beach, for instance, he happened to run across a person whom he had been interviewing for another project on sexual practices. This provided him with an opportunity to talk to others about this person. As it turned out, the middle-aged man in question had been serving as an informant for several months and had related detailed and seemingly creditable stories about his and others sexual experiences. Beach members gave different accounts about this man. He had said his daughter approved of his adventures and that she was even present at "swinging parties." Beach members said the man's daughter was repulsed by her father's practices. There were many other discrepancies between the man's stories and the accounts of those who know him. Douglas's point is well taken: The form and the content of talking are not also the same. Hence, he suggests that the role of researcher requires a healthy dose of skepticism and a critical eye able to see beyond the appearance of things; in short, an investigative attitude.

WAYS TO WATCH PEOPLE

The second major device for discovering the meanings of the experiences of others is to watch them act. This method provides either direct or indirect evidence of meanings, since we can watch people without necessarily talking to them, or we can join them in the activity while watching. In strict science, the model for watching is the experiment itself. Although we have learned that the literal application of the rational for experimental research does not aid in the explication of social meaning, we can still adapt this organization of observations to the purposes of social psychology.

In order to do this, however, we have to think about why one would want to experiment on others. Put simply, we want to see them do something that they either might not do in the routine of everyday life or might not allow us to see. An experiment is a kind of "set up." It is a way to "trick" people into doing things. Hence, Garfinkel's experiment in which he had students speak into a microphone under the false belief that a counselor would answer their questions (chapter one) is such a set up. The results of this set up revealed the ways in which students thought about the organization of their school-relevant experiences. We use such a device when we believe we can not otherwise see the meanings in routine life, or when we do not have the time to go into the field to see them.

The ethnomethodologist often writes of the breach, by which he or she means breaks in routines, occurrences which call into question the common sense basis of the immediate interaction. Students who act like strangers in their homes breach the ordinary meanings of family membership. Breaches can be natural or they can be contrived. A natural breach is something so out of the ordinary that it suspends the taken-for-granted knowledge used to make sense out of the occurrence. Disasters are natural breaches. But sometimes the social psychologist has the opportunity to introduce breaches.

In Sherif's (1961) study of conflict resolution, he organized Boy Scouts into distinct groups (eagles and snakes) so that they would develop strong senses of separate group identity. Then, he contrived situations like the breakdown of a jeep, forcing the groups to cooperate. He set up the students to see if a cooperative task would weaken their group identities which it did. This type of observation is sometimes referred to as a field experiment.

Of course, all devices of observations require that the researcher be there. Whether he has set up the situations of observations or has gone to the scene, he must, to a degree, be involved in the experiences of those studied. The classic example of this research is called **field research**. The most widely used type of field research is the participant observation study. Throughout, this book has relied on many such studies. However, simply being there does not imply participation. We can attempt to be a detached observer. Fishman's study of the conversation of the married couple illustrates this form of observation where the researcher is not actually present in person, but is present in the form of a tape recorder. The machine surely takes on meanings in the interactions of the couple ("Turn that thing off," or "Remember, we're being recorded"). Further, the use of concealed cameras or even concealed observers, as in the case of sitting in a warm building while watching people waiting for a bus, are forms of detached observation. In all of these cases, if the observer is detected, strategies for observation must change.

So we learn that observational devices vary from those requiring us to be a complete observer to those in which we are a complete participant. As a complete observer, we are detached from the experiences of others; as a participant we may literally become the phenomenon we study, and our own experiences can be taken as representative of those of other people.

Several years ago, Junker (1960) worked out a chart which illustrates the relationships of dimensions of participation and observation. (See Figure A/1)

From Junker's chart, we can see that observational devices involve both the "artificial" attitude of the researcher and the natural attitude of simply living in society. It is apparent, then, that the researcher has the advantage of his or her own experiences (cf. Rothman's 1982 book on natural childbirth) and, at the same time, must be able to separate the attitude of the researcher from that of the participant. The conventions of doing research help in the management of this continuing intrinsic problem. The trappings of the laboratory, the white coat of the researcher and the use of equipment—even if it is only a notepad and a tape recorder—enhance the attitude of detachment. Still, in the final analysis, the researcher is always to some degree participating in the experiences of those studied; and, a major part of the methodology of social psychology is given over to figuring out how this involvement is related to the understandings we have of social life. Techniques of research help us move from observation to participation and back, but they do not solve the problem of the intrinsic, inextricable connections among being there, knowing about it, and communicating it to others.

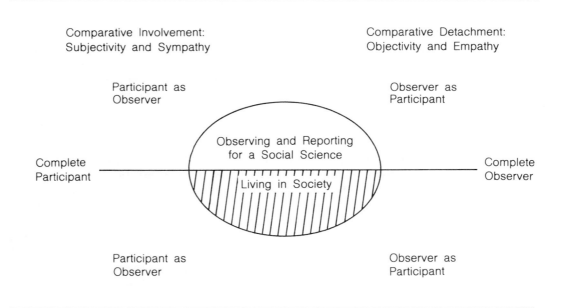

Figure A/1 The Relationships of Participation and Observation   (Adapted from Junker, Buford, *Field Work: an Introduction to the Social Sciences* Chicago: The University of Chicago Press 1960: 146)

UNDERSTANDING AT THE MOMENT AND OVER TIME

Conventionally, in the social sciences, a distinction is drawn between studies which focus on a phenomenon at a given time and those that follow the same phenomenon over several different "observational" periods. The first type of study is called **cross sectional** and the latter **longitudinal**. Although it is necessary to observe over time to assess causal links among phenomena, longitudinal studies are costly and very difficult to manage in societies where people are mobile, and generally protective of their private worlds. Hence, most social psychological studies are cross sectional. They define a set of phenomena to be observed and they are explicit about the time frame in which the observations take place.

Of course, cross sectional studies can be used to measure changes in phenomenon over time as long as the researcher can specify the sense in which the phenomena measured are comparable. For example, the Lynds first studied Muncie, Indiana, in the 1920s. They assessed the organization of the social lives of the residents on matters such as family life, leisure-time pursuits, and work. They returned in the 1930s to assess the impacts of the Great Depression on the social fabric of the community, and, most recently, a team of sociologists visited the town in the 1970s to see how family life compares today with what the Lynds observed (Lynds 1929, 1937 and Caplow, et al. 1982).

Obviously, most of the people who participated in the first or even the second study were not involved in the third. Although some of the high school students who answered the fixed language questions of the most recent researchers were related to the subjects of the original study, this study is not a longitudinal study in the strict sense. To be one, it would have to follow the same people through the decades, asking them questions and observing them at set intervals. Still, these Middletown studies, taken together, give us a view of the continuity of family and community life in America. We discover, for example, a surprising degree of stability over the decades in the meanings of work and leisure and most importantly, in the degree of importance attributed to family life. Much of the descriptive work of sociology can function as documents of the meanings of social life at particular conjunctions in history.

Since the goal of social psychology is understanding as a basis for action, we find that the ideas of strict science about causality can not be directly applied to social phenomena. As Fredrichs (1972) suggests, are we to say that Jonah's prophecy to the people of Nineveh was invalid because they heeded his advice and reformed to successfully avoid the prophesied fate of the destruction? To deal with the problem of change in meanings we can modify the ideas of cross sectional and longitudinal to fit the nature of social phenomenon.

The methodology used by linguists to assess language change, helps with the problems of understanding at the moment and over time. Linguists write of the way a language is structured and how it functions both at a given time and over time. They are able to show how the meanings of words change, and have quite different meanings at different times in the history of a language. We saw this in the chapter on gender when we discussed the sexist tendencies in the English language. But linguists take the analysis further; they illustrate how a single word or segment of language can be seen in terms of how it fits into the organization of contemporary usage and how it fits into the historical development of the language. The word *Mississippi*, for instance, is composed of a single unit of meaning (morpheme) when understood in terms of current usage (it means a specific river). When the word is examined in terms of origins (its roots in American Indian language), it has three distinct units of meanings (morphemes): Father of Waters.

Linguists call the study of language at a given time **synchronic analysis** and the study of the development of language **diachronic**. This distinction is particularly useful in the study of social phenomena. When we depict the experiences of others, we must be clear about our analytic point of view. We may be talking about the sense of experience at the particular moment, such as how a group of workers in a bank make sense of dress code (cf. Jackall 1977), or we may be attempting to put together a picture of major changes in how people understand their involvements with each other. The shifts we documented from "collective" senses of self to "individual" in the transitions from traditional to modern society represent this latter analytic stance. The version we give of understanding is inextricably tied up with how we conceive of time in relation to the problem at hand.

THE RESEARCH ACT

A research act is more than "doing a study." It entails that the researcher assume, master, and work within a form of consciousness in which he or she can employ devices for finding out about the experiences of other people. With these devices the researcher can imagine the practical consequences of various experiences in their social contexts, can "check out," according to some criteria, the extent to which the experiences have been described and preserved, and, finally, can communicate all this to an audience which, in turn, can be understood as a social phenomenon. The research act is, then, a commitment to information, perspective, and procedure (Denzin 1978). To commit such an act is to participate in social life as a kind of intellectual reporter, a person who tells stories about the way people think, feel, and act toward one another. The stories, however, are not "natural" because they are not told in "natural" language. They require the mastery of specialized idioms and attitudes. Schutz referred to the attitude of the researcher as that of the "expert."

As we have discovered in this book, it is often not so much what the social psychologist knows that allows the claim of being expert, but the way in which it is known.   The researcher's attitude is a heavy burden, requiring a suspension of commonsense perspectives for the purposes of understanding them.   Without the grounding that makes the processes of sense making uncritical in the "natural attitude," the researcher is set adrift in ways of thinking which blur distinctions between the obvious and the nonobvious, the commonplace and the extraordinary.   Although a project may delimit the focus of this consciousness (I am doing a study of children's play, for instance), the consciousness itself is critical, calling into question the very foundations of social life.

Certainly, the earlier thinkers like Mead and Thomas appreciated these points.   Just as the self and society are two sides of the same coin, so theory and research, observation and concept are binary pairs of the same reality.   The kind of thinking we depict as necessary to social psychology has been called **nonlinear** (Curtis 1978).   More conventional discussions of methodology leave the reader with a version of relationships stressing the things being related as separate and measurable, each with identifiable features.   This approach calls up images of causality and a straight-line progress of time (linearity).   The nonlinear approach, on the other hand, "resolves dichotomies ... into binary pairs, which interact and each term of which is equally necessary" (Curtis 1978, 22).

Since we are dealing with constructed, language-created phenomenon, the methodology we employ must be capable of appreciating the layered and interpenetrating character of social phenomena themselves.   Research acts are as much matters of consciousness as they are techniques for gathering information through observation.   What one sees in the social world is as much a result of how one thinks as it is a reflection of "what is out there."

In no way should this short treatise be constructed to mean that this approach to social psychology lacks rigor or standards in its methodology. Just the opposite.   Methodology means the pairing of theoretical consciousness with ways to get information, and it requires that the pairing make sense as a unit in and of itself.   It does mean, however, that no list of ways to ask questions and to observe can be presented for a given topic of study.   Methods and theory are binary.   The researcher may well discover that his or her odyssey from living in society to reporting about it necessitates the use of many different ways to gather information.   Further, as has always been the case with breakthroughs in science, new methods may have to be devised for developing pertinent data.   The creative search for new ways to get information about human experience has raised some provocative and serious questions of an ethical nature regarding methodologies of social research.

ETHICS AND UNDERSTANDING

Since so much of the subject matter of social psychology is simply "ordinary" life, and since ordinary life entails a full array of rules to follow and break, it should come as no surprise that questions about ethics of some of the methods of social psychology have been raised. If a researcher observes illicit and illegal acts, to what degree is he or she an accomplice? When an ethnographer uncovers how workers in a formal organization cope with rules they regard as "unfair," should that ethnographer tell management in order to increase the work output of employees? Or, the other side of that question, should the ethnographer teach others how to subvert and manipulate the official rules of an organization? (cf. Van Maanen 1979).

Often, these matters boil into bitter conflict. Members of a town which has been the subject of a research project may discover their secrets revealed to the literate world. Or, sociologists may fight among themselves over the proper ethical stance regarding a project. The most infamous case in recent years took place between a minister, turned sociologist, Laud Humphreys, who studied homosexuals by observing them in public restrooms (tearooms) and a prominent sociologist, Alvin Gouldner. Gouldner, it seems, was critical of the methodology employed by some sociologists in research on deviant behavior. He suggested that these researchers were more interested in their own professional advancement than in the plight of the deviants they studied. Professor Gouldner was accused of calling Humphreys a "peeping parson," while Gouldner was characterized by graduate students as a "bird that feeds on underdogs" (*The New York Times*, June 9, 1968). Although the problem was solved without seriously damaging the careers of either men, the incident shows the depth of emotions that research can evoke.

At issue, of course, is the degree of involvement which researchers should properly have in the lives of those they study. Gouldner argued that sociologists must deal with their own values in what he calls "reflexive sociology." Humphreys and others tend to be less judgmental in conducting research, taking a laissez faire attitude toward what is being observed. Both sides of this debate are concerned with the fate of those studied. Perhaps it is because their commitments were so strong that their disagreements over how to be involved became so bitter.

On another level, the federal government and institutions which support research on human subjects, often require that consent forms be filled out before a research project can be conducted. Of course, such precautions were designed to protect subjects in medical or psychological research. But clearly whenever we observe children at play, for example, the question arises whether they are our subjects, and should we receive consent from those responsible for them.

The matter of what has been called covert research has also received close attention in the literature. Some claim that studies in which the researcher's intentions and identity are concealed from those whom he or she studies should never be allowed (cf. Erickson 1967) while others argue that research of this kind holds more dangers for the researcher than for subjects (for a thorough discussion see Bulmer 1982).

These questions are indeed serious. They raise issues of invasion of privacy, the control of official information and more fundamentally of the interests and freedom of inquiry of both people being studied and those studying. We can summarize the positions as they have been articulated as two camps. Some argue that special caution and procedures are necessary to safeguard the rights of "subjects". They, therefore, generally oppose covert research and they support the use of consent forms and other legal guarantees of the rights of subjects. In the other camp, however, are those who maintain that the social psychologist who seeks understanding (as opposed to those who follow the model of strict science) is actually a part of the ongoing social interactions he or she studies. This means, consistent with our nonlinear methodology, that they are a binary pair and that each then affects and influences the other as people studying people.

Two conclusions can be drawn. First, the social psychologist enjoys no special privileges owing to his or her professional commitment. He or she is a citizen of the society as well as an expert on it. The laws of the land govern research in the same way they govern everyday life. This means liable and slander apply to the social psychological uses of knowledge. But, it also means that the obligations a researcher has to those studied are not completely a consequence of legal documents and contracts alone. They grow from the human contact inevitably experienced in acts of research.

Although professional bodies like the American Sociological Association should and do draft "code of ethics," the practice of these is a matter of interaction and must be understood as such. Lest we forget, our way of understanding as social psychologists contrasts with the natural attitude and hence we may, on occasion, fail to distinguish among our various stances of consciousness as clearly as we should like, and in the process, fail to see legal or organizational implications of our writing and talking about social life. When this happens, the professional may be judged. This occurred when a well-known sociologist received a suspended sentence for tape recording the deliberations of a jury. Or, a researcher may be vindicated as was Humphreys when he won his suit against his university which had fired him for his controversial research. The larger community and the people who belong to it will judge. They are the practical courts of ethical judgments, and the researcher must be aware of their potential action at each stage of research. The ethics of research, ultimately, are the ethics of everyday life.

References

Adams, Karen L., and Norma C. Ware. "Sexism and the English Language: The Linguistic Implications of Being a Woman." In *Women: A Feminist Perspective,* 2d ed., edited by Jo Freeman, 487–504. Palo Alto, Calif.: Mayfield, 1979.

Adorno T., et al. *The Authoritian Personality.* Harper and Row, 1950.

Agar, Michael. *The Professional Stranger: An Informal Introduction to Ethnography.* New York: Academic Press, 1980.

Allport, Gordon W. "The Historical Background of Modern Social Psychology." In *The Handbook of Social Psychology,* edited by Gardner Lindzey and Elliot Aronson, 1–80. Reading, Mass.: Addison-Wesley, 1968.

Altheide, David and John Johnson. *Bureaucratic Propaganda.* Boston: Allyn and Bacon, 1980.

Asch, Solomon E. *Social Psychology.* Englewood Cliffs, N.J.: Prentice-Hall, 1952.

Auletta, Ken. *The Underclass.* New York: Random House, 1982.

Ball, Donald. "Failure in Sport." *American Sociological Review* 41 (Aug. 1976): 726–39.

Baratz, Joan C. "Teaching Reading in an Urban Negro School System." In *Language and Poverty: Perspectives on a Theme,* edited by F. Williams, 11–24. Chicago: Markham, 1970.

Barley, Stephen R. "The Codes of the Dead: Semiotics of Funeral Work." *Urban Life: A Journal of Ethnographic Research* 12 (Aug. 1983): 3–31.

Bart, Pauline. "The Loneliness of the Long-Distance Mother." In *Women: A Feminist Perspective,* edited by Jo Freeman, 245–61. Palo Alto, Calif.: Mayfield, 1979.

Bateson, Gregory. *Steps to Ecology of Mind.* New York: Chandler Publishing Company, 1972.

Becker, Howard S. *Outsiders: Studies in the Sociology of Deviance.* New York: Free Press, 1963.

———. "Whose Side Are We On?" *Social Problems* 14 (1967): 239–47.

Berger, Peter L. *The Heretical Imperative.* Garden City, N.Y.: Anchor Press, 1979.

Berger, Peter L., and Briditte Berger. *Sociology: A Biographical Approach.* New York: Basic Books, 1974.

Berger, Peter L., Briditte Berger, and Hansfred Kellner. *The Homeless Mind: Modernization and Consciousness.* New York: Vintage Books, 1974.

Berger, Peter L., and Thomas Kellner. "Marriage and the Construction of Reality." *Diogenes* 46 (1964): 1–25.

Berger, Peter L., and Thomas Luckmann. *The Social Construction of Reality: A Treatise in the Sociology of Knowledge.* New York: Anchor Books, 1966.

Bernstein, Basil. "Elaborate and Restricted Codes: An Outline." *Sociological Inquiry* 36 (Spring): 126–33.

Blau, Peter. *Bureaucracy in Modern Society.* New York: Random House, 1961.

Blumer, Herbert. *Symbolic Interaction: Perspective and Method.* 1969. Reprint. Englewood Cliffs, N.J.: Prentice-Hall, 1975.

Brown, Roger. "Mass Phenomenon." In *Handbook of Social Psychology,* Vol. 2, edited by G. Lindzey. Cambridge: Addison-Wesley, 1954.

Buckholdt, David and Jaber F. Gubrium. *Caretakers: Treating Emotionally Disturbed Children.* Beverly Hills, Calif.: Sage, 1979.

Bulmer, Martin. "When is Disguise Justified? Alternatives to Covert Participant Observation." *Qualitative Sociology* 15 (Winter 1982): 251–64.

Caine, Lynn. *Widow.* New York: Bantam Books, 1974.

Callois, Roger. *Man, Play and Games.* New York: Free Press, 1961.

Cegala, Donald J. "An Examination of the Concept of Interaction Involvement Using Phenomenological and Empirical Methods." In *Interpersonal Communication: Essays in Phenomenology and Hermeneutic.* Washington, D.C.: University Press of America, 1982.

Centers, R. *The Psychology of Social Class.* Princeton, N.J.: Princeton University Press, 1949.

Cicourel, Aaron. "Basic and Normative Rules in the Negotiation of Status and Roles." *Recent Sociology,* No. 2, edited by Hans Peter Dreitzel, 4–45. New York: Macmillan, 1970.

———. *Cognitive Sociology: Language and Meaning in Social Interaction.* New York: Free Press, 1974.

Comstock, George S. "Types of Portrayal and Aggressive Behavior." *Journal of Communication* 26 (1977): 189–98.

Converse, P. E. "The Shifting Role of Class in Political Attitudes and Behavior." In *Readings in Social Psychology,* 3d ed., edited by Eleanor E. Malloby, T.M. Newcomb and E.L. Hartley. New York: Holt, 1958.

Cook-Gumperz, Jenny. "The Child as Practical Reasoner." In *Sociocultural Dimensions of Language Use,* edited by Mary Sanches and Ben G. Blount. New York: Academic Press, 1975.

Cooley, Charles Horton. *Human Nature and the Social Order.* 1902. Reprint. New York: Scribner's, 1922.

Cuddihy, John Murray. *The Ordeal of Civility.* New York: Dell Publishing, 1974.

Curtis, James M. *Culture as Polyphony: An Essay of the Nature of Paradigms.* Columbia: University of Missouri Press, 1978.

Dalton, Melville. *Men Who Manage.* New York: John Wiley and Sons, 1957.

Davis, Allison, Burleigh Gardner and Mary R. Gardner. *Deep South.* Chicago: University of Chicago Press, 1941.

Davis, Fred. "Focus of the Flower Children: Why All of Us May Be Hippies Someday." *Trans-Action* 5:10–18.

———. *Yearning for Yesterday: A Sociology of Nostalgia.* New York: Free Press, 1979.

Davis, Kingsley, and Wilbert E. Moore. "Some Principles of Stratification." *American Sociological Review* 10, No. 2 (1945): 242–49.

Davis, Murray S. *Smut: Erotic Reality/Obscene Ideology.* Chicago: University of Chicago Press, 1983.

Denzin, Norman K. *The Research Act: A Theoretical Introduction to Sociological Methods.* New York: McGraw Hill, 1978.

Derber, Charles. *The Pursuit of Attention: Power and Individualism in Everyday Life.* New York: Oxford University Press, 1979.

DeVilliers, Peter, and Jill G. DeVilliers. *Early Language.* Cambridge: Harvard University Press, 1979.

Dickens, Davis R. "Phenomenology." In *Theoretical Perspectives in Sociology.* New York: St. Martins, 1979.

Dillard, J. L. *Black English: Its History and Usage in the United States.* New York: Vintage Books, 1972.

Dollard, J. D., L. W. Miller and R. R. Sears. *Frustration and Aggression.* New Haven: Yale University Press, 1939.

Douglas, Jack. "A Sociological Theory of Official Deviance and Public Concerns with Official Deviance." In *Official Deviance,* edited by Douglas and Johnson, J. P. Lippincott, 1977.

Douglas, Jack, and John Johnson, eds. *Official Deviance: Readings in Malfeasance, Misfeasance and Other Forms of Corruption.* New York: J. B. Lippincott, 1977.

Douglas, Jack, et al. *Introduction to the Sociologies of Everyday Life.* Boston: Allyn and Bacon, 1980.

Dumont, Richard G., and William J. Wilson. "Aspects of Concept Formation, Explication and Theory Construction in Sociology." *American Sociological Review* 32 (Dec. 1967): 985–95.

Ellis, Donald, Leonard C. Hawes, and Robert K. Avery. "Some Pragmatics of Talking on Talk Radio." *Urban Life: A Journal of Ethnographic Research* 10 (July 1981): 155–77.

Erickson, Kai. *Everything in its Path: Destruction of Community in the Buffalo Creek Flood.* New York: Simon and Schuster, 1976.

Ervin-Tripp, Susan. "On Sociolinguistic Rules: Alternation and Co-occurrence." In *Directions in Sociolinguistics: The Ethnography of Communication,* edited by John J. Gumperz and Dell Hymes. New York: Holt, Rinehart and Winston, 1972.

Faberman, Harvey A. "Fantasy in Everyday Life: Some Aspects of the Intersection Between Social Psychology and Political Economy." *Symbolic Interaction* 3 (Spring 1980): 9–21.

Fabrega, Horacio, and Peter K. Manning. "The Experience of Self and Body: Health and Illness in Chiapas Highlands." In *Phenomenological Sociology: Issues and Applications,* edited by George Psathas, 251–304. New York: John Wiley and Sons, 1973.

Fishman, Pamela. "Interaction: The Work Women Do." *Social Problems* 25 (1978): 397–406.

Friedricks, Robert W. "Dialectical Sociology: Toward a Resolution of Current 'Crisis' in Western Sociology." *The British Journal of Sociology* 23 (Sept.1972): 262–74.

Furth, Hans G. *The World of Grownups: Children's Conception of Society.* New York: Elsevier, 1980.

Gardner, B. T., and R. A. Gardner. "Two-way Communication with an Infant Chimpanzee." In *Behavior of Nonhuman Primates,* edited by Shrier and Stollnitz. New York: Academic Press, 1971.

Garfinkel, Harold. "Common-Sense Knowledge of Social Structures: The Documentary Method of Interpretation." In *Theories of the Mind,* edited by Jordan M. Scher, 689–712. New York: Free Press, 1963.

———. "A Conception of, and Experiments with, 'Trust' as a Condition of Stable Concerted Actions." In *Motivation and Social Interaction,* edited by O.J. Harvey. New York: Ronald Press, 1963.

———. *Studies in Ethnomethodology.* Englewood Cliffs, N.J.: Prentice-Hall, 1967.

Garson, Barbara. *All the Livelong Day: The Meaning and Demeaning of Routine Work.* New York: Penguin Books, 1975.

Gecas, Viktor. "Contexts of Socialization." In *Social Psychology: Sociological Perspective,* edited by Morris Rosenberg and Ralph Turner. New York: Basic Books, 1981.

Gelles, Richard J. *The Violent Home.* Beverly Hills: Sage Publications, 1974.

Georges, Robert A. and Michael O. Jones. *People Studying People: The Human Element in Fieldwork.* Berkeley: University of California Press, 1980.

Glaser, Barney, and Anselm Strauss. *The Discovery of Grounded Theory, Strategies for Qualitative Research.* Chicago: Aldine, 1968.

Goffman, Erving. *The Presentation of Self in Everyday Life.* New York: Doubleday, 1959.

———. *Stigma: Notes of the Management of Spoiled Identity.* Englewood Cliffs, N.J.: Prentice-Hall, 1963.

———. *Strategic Interaction.* Philadelphia: University of Pennsylvania Press, 1969.

———. *Relations in Public: Microstudies of the Public Order.* New York: Basic Books, 1971.

———. *Frame Analysis: An Essay of the Organization of Experience.* Cambridge: Harvard University Press, 1974.

———. *Gender Advertisements.* Cambridge: Harvard University Press, 1979.

———. *Forms of Talk.* Philadelphia: University of Pennsylvania Press, 1981.

Gold, Ray. "Janitors Versus Tenants: A Status Income Dilemma." *American Journal of Sociology* 57 (1952): 486–93.

Goodman, F. "Disturbances in the Apostolic Church." In *Trance, Healing and Hallucination,* edited by F.D. Goodman, J. Henry, and E. Presel. New York: Wiley, 1974.

Gordon, David. "The Jesus People: An Identity Synthesis." *Urban Life and Culture* 3 (1974): 159–78.

Gordon, Steven L. "The Sociology of Sentiments and Emotions." In *Social Psychology: Sociological Perspectives,* edited by Morris Rosenberg and Ralph H. Turner. New York: Basic Books, 1981.

Gornick, Vivian. Preface for Erving Goffman, *Gender Advertisements.* Cambridge: Harvard University Press, 1979.

Gouldner, Alvin W. *Wildcat Strike: A Study in Worker-Management Relationships.* New York: Harper and Row, 1954.

Grimshaw, Allen. "Directions for Research in Sociolinguistics: Suggestions of a Nonlinguist Sociologist." *Sociological Inquiry* 36 (Spring 1966): 191–204.

Habermas, Jurgen. "On Distorted Communication." In *Recent Sociology,* No. 2, edited by Peter Dreitzel, 115–148. New York: Macmillan, 1970.

Hall, Edward. *The Hidden Dimension.* Garden City, N.J.: Doubleday, 1966.

Handel, Warren. *Ethnomethodology: How People Make Sense.* Englewood Cliffs, N.J.: Prentice-Hall, 1982.

Hansen, Donald. *An Invitation to Critical Sociology: Involvement, Criticism and Exploration.* New York: Free Press, 1976.

Heberle, Rudolf. *Social Movements: An Introduction to Political Sociology.* New York: Appelton-Century-Crofts, 1951.

Henslin, James M. *Introducing Sociology.* New York: Free Press, 1975.

———. "What Makes for Trust?" In *Down to Earth Sociology: Introductory Readings,* edited by James M. Henslin. New York: Free Press, 1972.

Hewitt, John P. and Randall Stokes. "Disclaimers." *American Sociological Review* 40 (Feb. 1975): 1–11.

Higgins, Paul C. *Outsiders in a Hearing World.* Beverly Hills: Sage, 1980.

Homans, George C. *The Human Group.* New York: Harcourt, Brace and World, 1950.

———. *Social Behavior: Its Elementary Forms.* New York: Harcourt, Brace and World, 1974.

Icheiser, Gustav. *Appearances and Realities.* San Francisco: Jossey-Bass, 1970.

Irwin, John. *Scenes.* Beverly Hills: Sage, 1977.

———. *Prisons in Turmoil*. Boston: Little Brown, 1980.

Jackall, Robert. "The Control of Public Faces in a Commercial Bureaucratic Work Situation." *Urban Life: A Journal of Ethnographic Research* 6 (Oct. 1977): 277–302.

Jacobs, Leo M. *A Deaf Adult Speaks Out*. Washington, D.C.: Gallaudet College Press, 1974.

Kaplan, Sidney, and Shirley Kaplan. "Video Games, Sex and Sex Differences." *Journal of Popular Culture* 17 (Fall 1983): 61–66.

Katcher, A. "The Discrimination of Sex Differences by Young Children." *Journal of Genetic Psychology* 87 (1955): 131–43.

Katz, Judith Milstein. "How Do You Love Me? Let Me Count the Ways (The Phenomenology of Being Loved)." *Sociological Inquiry* 46 (1976): 17–22.

Kemper, Theodore D. "A Sociology of Emotions: Some Problems and Some Solutions." *The American Sociologist* 13 (Feb. 1978): 30–41.

Kenen, Regina. "Soapsuds, Space and Sociability." *Urban Life: A Journal of Ethnographic Research* 11 (July 1982): 163–84.

Kerckhoff, A.C., and K.W. Back. *The June Bug: A Study of Hysterical Contagion*. New York: Appleton-Century-Crofts, 1968.

Killian, Lewis. "The Significance of Multiple-group Membership in Disaster." *American Journal of Sociology* 57 (1952): 309–14.

Klockars, Carl B. *The Professional Fence*. New York: Free Press, 1974.

Kockmann, Thomas, ed. *Rappin' and Stylin' Out: Communication in Urban Black America*. Urbana: University of Illinois Press, 1972.

Kohlberg, Larry. *Stages in the Development of Moral Thought and Action*. New York: Holt, Rinehart and Winston, 1969.

Kornhauser, William. *The Politics of Mass Society*. The Free Press of Glencoe, 1959.

Labov, William. "The Art of Sounding and Signifying." In *Language in Its Social Setting*, edited by William W. Gage, 84–116. Washington, D.C.: Anthropological Society of Washington, 1974.

———. "The Effects of Social Mobility on Linguistic Behavior." *Sociological Inquiry* 36 (Spring 1966): 58–75.

———. "The Logic of Nonstandard English." In *Language and Poverty: Perspective on a Theme*, edited by Fredrick Williams, 153–89. Chicago: Markham, 1970.

———. *Sociolinguistic Patterns*. Philadelphia: University of Pennsylvania Press, 1972.

Laing, R.D. *The Politics of the Family*. New York: Harper and Row, 1969.

Lefebrve, Henri. *Everyday Life in the Modern World*. New York: Harper, 1971.

LeMasters. E.E. *Blue-Collar Aristocrats: Life Styles at a Working Class Tavern*. Madison: University of Wisconsin Press, 1975.

Lemert, Edwin M. *Human Deviance, Social Problems and Social Control*. Englewood Cliffs, N.J.: Prentice-Hall, 1967.

Lever, Janet. "Sex Differences in the Games Children Play." *Social Problems* 23 (April 1976): 479–87.

Levi, Ken. "Becoming a Hit Man: Neutralization in a Very Deviant Career." *Urban Life: A Journal of Ethnographic Research* 10 (April 1981): 47–63.

Lindesmith, A.R., A.L. Strauss, and Norman Denzin. *Social Psychology*, 3d ed. New York: Holt, Rinehart and Winston, 1977.

Linton, Ralph. *The Study of Man*. New York: Appleton-Century, 1936.

Lofland, John. *Analyzing Social Settings: A Guide to Qualitative Observation and Analysis*. Belmont, Calif.: Wadsworth, 1971.

———. "Collective Behavior: The Elementary Forms." In *Social Psychology: A Sociological Perspective*, edited by Morris Rosenberg and Ralph Turner, 411–46. New York: Basic Books, 1981.

———. "Crowd Joy." *Urban Life: A Journal of Ethnographic Research* 10 (Jan. 1982): 355–82.

————. *Doomsday Cult: A Study of Conversion, Proselytization and Maintenance of Faith.* 1965. Reprint. Englewood Cliffs. N.J.: Prentice-Hall, 1980.

Lofland, John, and Rodney Stark. "Becoming a World Saver: A Theory of Conversion to a Deviant Perspective." *American Sociological Review* 30 (Dec. 1965): 862–74.

Lofland, Lynn. *World of Strangers.* New York: Basic Books, 1973.

Lorenz, Konrad. *On Aggression.* New York: Harcourt, Brace and World, 1963.

Luckmann, Bentia. "The Small Life-Worlds of Modern Man." In *Phenomenology and Sociology,* edited by Thomas Luckmann, 275–90. New York: Penguin Books, 1974.

Lyman, Stanford M. *The Seven Deadly Sins: Society and Evil.* New York: St. Martin's Press, 1978.

MacCannell, Dean. *The Tourist: A New Theory of the Leisure Class.* New York: Schocken Books, 1976.

Maccoby, E. E., and C. N. Jacklin. *The Psychology of Sex Differences.* Stanford, Calif.: Stanford University Press, 1975.

Mannhein, Karl. *Ideology and Utopia.* New York: Harcourt, Brace, 1938.

Marindale, Don. *The Nature and Types of Sociological Theory.* Boston: Houghton Mifflin, 1980.

Mayo, Elton. *Human Problems of Industrial Civilization.* New York: Macmillan, 1933.

McCall, Michal. "Life History and Social Change." *Studies in Symbolic Interactionism,* Vol. 6, Forthcoming.

McLuhan, Marshall. *Understanding Media: The Extensions of Man.* New York: McGraw Hill, 1964.

Mechanic, David. "Stress, Illness Behavior and the Sick Role." *American Sociological Review* 28 (1961): 51–58.

Mehan, Hugh, and Houston Wood. *The Reality of Ethnomethodology.* New York: Academic Press 1975.

————. "De-Secting Ethnomethodology." *The American Sociologist* 11 (Feb. 1976): 13–21.

Melbin, Murray. "Night as Frontier." *American Sociological Review* 43 (Feb. 1978): 3–22.

Meltzer, B.N., J.W. Petras, and L.T. Reynolds. *Symbolic Interactionism: Genesis Varieties and Criticism.* London: Routledge and Kegan Paul, 1975.

Merleau-Ponty, Maurice. "The Child's Relations with Others." In *The Primacy of Perception,* edited by James L. Edie. Evanston: Northwestern University Press, 1964.

Merton, Robert K. *Social Theory and Social Structure.* 1957 Reprint. Glencoe: The Free Press of Glencoe, 1963.

Mills. C. Wright. "Situated Actions and a Vocabulary of Motives." *American Sociological Review* 5 (1940): 904–13

Modigliani, Andre. "Embarrassment, Facework, and Eye Contact." *Journal of Personality and Social Psychology* 17 (1971): 15–25.

Morris, Monica B. *An Excursion Into Creative Sociology.* New York: Columbia University Press, 1977.

Myiamoto, Frank S., and Sanford M. Dornbusch. "A Test of Interactionist Hypotheses of Self-Conception." *American Journal of Sociology* 61 (March 1956): 399–403.

Nash, Jeffrey E. "Bus Riding: Community of Wheels." *Urban Life: A Journal of Ethnographic Research* 4 (April 1975): 99–124.

————. "The Short and the Long of It: Legitimizing Motives for Running." In *Sociology: A Descriptive Approach,* edited by Jeffrey E. Nash and James P. Spradley, 161–81. Chicago: Rand McNally, 1976.

————. "Decoding the Runner's Wardrobe." In *Conformity and Conflict,* 3rd ed., edited by James P. Spradley and David W. McCurdy, 172–85. Boston: Little Brown, 1977.

————. "Weekend Racing as an Eventful Experience: Understanding the Accomplishment of Well Being." *Urban Life: A Journal of Ethonographic Research* 8 (July 1979): 199–217.

———. "Lying about Running: The Function of Talk in a Scene." *Qualitative Sociology* 3 (Summer 1980): 83–91.

———. "Relations in Frozen Places: Observations on Winter Public Order." *Qualitative Sociology* 4 (Fall 1981): 229–43.

———. "The Family Camps Out: A Study of Nonverbal Communication." *Semiotica* 39 3/4 (1982): 331–41.

Nash, Jeffrey E., and Eric Lerner. "Learning from the Pros: Violence in Youth Hockey." *Youth and Society* 13 (Dec. 1981): 229–44.

Nelson, Margrette L., and Carol L. Jorgensen. "The Green Bag: The Uses of Ambiguity in Eliciting Covert Cultural Assumptions." *Human Organization* 34 (Spring 1975): 51–61.

Ogles, Richard H. "Concept Formation in Sociology: The Ordering of Observational Data by Observational Concepts." In *Theoretical Methods in Sociology: Seven Essays,* edited by Lee Freese, 143–74. Pittsburgh: University of Pittsburgh Press, 1980.

O'Neill, John. "Embodiment and Child Development: A Phenomenological Approach." In *Recent Sociology,* No. 5, *Childhood and Socialization,* edited by Hans Peter Dreitzel, 65–84. New York: Macmillan, 1973.

Ortega, Y. Gasset. *Man and People.* 1952. Reprint. New York: Norton, 1973.

Parson, Talcott. *The System of Modern Society.* Englewood Cliffs. N.J.: Prentice-Hall, 1971.

Phillips, Davis P. "The Impact of Mass Media Violence on U.S. Homicides." *American Sociological Review* 48 (Aug. 1983): 560–568.

Psathas, George. "Introduction." In *Phenomenological Sociology: Issues and Applications,* edited by George Psathas, 1–21. New York: Wiley, 1973.

Reisman, Davis. *The Lonely Crowd: A Study of Changing American Character.* New Haven: Yale University Press, 1950.

———. *Report of the National Advisory Commission on Civil Disorder.* New York: Bantam Books, 1968.

Riemer, Jeffrey W. "Work Setting and Behavior: An Empirical Examination of Building Construction Work." *Symbolic Interaction* 2 (Fall 1979): 131–51.

Rosenthal, R. *Experimenter Effects in Behavioral Research.* Appleton-Century-Crofts, 1966.

Rosenthal, R. and L. Jacobsen. *Pygmalion in the Classroom.* New York: Holt, Rinehart and Winston, 1968.

Rosow, Irving. "Forms and Functions of Adult Socialization." *Social Forces* (1966): 35–45.

Rothman, Barbara Katz. *Giving Birth: Alternatives in Childbirth.* New York: Penguin Books, 1982.

Sacks, Harvey. "Everybody Has to Lie." In *Socialcultural Dimension of Lanuage Use,* edited by Mary Sanches and Ben C. Blount, 57–80. New York: Academic Press, 1975.

———. "An Initial Investigation of the Usability of Conversational Data for Doing Sociology." In *Studies in Social Interaction,* edited by David Sudnow, 31–74. New York: Free Press, 1972.

———. "Notes of the Police Assessment of Moral Character." In *Studies in Social Interaction,* edited by David Sudnow, 280–93. New York: Free Press, 1972.

Schien, E.H., I. Schneier, and C.H. Barker. *Coercive Persuasion.* New York: W.W. Norton, 1961.

Schroyer, Trent. "Toward a Critical Theory of Advanced Industrial Society." In *Recent Sociology,* No. 2, edited by Hans Peter Dreitzel 210–34. New York: Macmillan, 1970.

Schulz, Muriel R. "The Semantic Derogation of Women." In *Language and Sex: Difference and Dominance,* edited by Barrie Thorne and Nancy Henley, 64–75. Rowley, Mass.: Newbury House Publishers, 1975.

Schur, Edwin. *The Awareness Trap: Self-Absorption Instead of Social Change.* New York: McGraw Hill, 1976.

Schutz, Alfred. *Collected Papers II: Studies in Social Theory.* 1964. Reprint. The Hague: Martinus Nijhoff, 1971.

Scott, Stanford, and Marvin B. Lyman. *A Sociology of the Absurd.* New York: Appleton-Century, 1970.

———. "Accounts." *American Sociological Review* 33 (Feb. 1968): 46–62.

Sherif, M. *The Psychology of Social Norms,* 1936. Reprint. New York: Harper and Row, 1948.

Sherif, M., et al. *Intergroup Conflict and Cooperation: The Robber's Cave Experiment.* Norman: Institute of Group Relations, University of Oklahoma, 1961.

Shotland, R. Lance, and Lynne Goodstein. "Just Because She Doesn't Want to Doesn't Mean It's Rape: An Experimentally Based Causal Model of the Perception of Rape in a Dating Situation." *Social Psychological Quarterly* 46 (Sept. 1983): 220–32.

Simmel, George. *George Simmel on Individuality and Social Forms.* Chicago: University of Chicago Press, 1971.

Smelser, Neil J. *Theory of Collective Behavior.* New York: Free Press, 1963.

Speier, Matthew. *How to Observe Face-to-Face Communication: A Sociological Introduction.* Palisades, Calif.: Goodyear, 1973.

Spilerman, S. "Structural Characteristics of Cities and the Severity of Racial Disorders." *American Sociological Review* 35 (1976): 627–49.

Spradley, James P. *You Owe Yourself a Drunk: An Ethnography of Urban Nomads.* Boston: Little Brown, 1970.

Spradley, James P., and David W. McCurdy. *Anthropology: The Cultural Perspective.* New York: John Wiley and Sons, 1975.

Stack, Carol B. *All Our Kin: Strategies for Survival in a Black Community.* New York: Harper and Row, 1974.

Stebbins, Robert D. "Studying the Definition of the Situation: Theory and Field Research Strategies." *Canadian Review of Sociology* 6 (1969): 193–211.

Stone, Gregory P. "Appearance and the Self." In *Human Behavior and Social Processes,* edited by Arnold M. Rose, 86–118. Boston: Houghton Mifflin, 1962.

Stouffer, Samuel A., et al. *The American Soldier: Adjustment During Army Life.* New York: John Wiley and Sons, 1949.

Strauss, Murray A. "A General Systems Theory Approach to the Development of a Theory of Violence Between Family Members." *Social Science Information* 12 (June 1973): 105–25.

Stryker, Syldon. "The Profession: Comments from an Interactionist's Perspective." *Sociological Focus* 12 (1979): 175–86.

Sudnow, David. *Ways of the Hand: The Organization of Improvised Conduct.* Cambridge: Harvard University Press, 1978.

Suttles, Gerald D. *The Social Order of the Slum.* Chicago: University of Chicago Press, 1968.

Sykes, G. and David Matza. "Techniques of Neutralization." *American Sociological Review* 22 (1959): 664–70.

Szasz, Thomas S. *The Myth of Mental Illness.* New York: Harper and Row, 1961.

Toennies, Ferdinand. *Fundamental Conceptions of Sociology.* New York: American Book Company, 1940.

Trudgill, Peter. *Sociolinguistics: An Introduction to Language and Society,* 1974. Reprint. New York: Penguin Books, 1983.

Tumin, Melvin M. "Some Principles of Stratification: A Critical Analysis." *American Sociological Review* 18 (Aug. 1953): 387–93.

Turner, Ralph. "Figure and Ground in the Analysis of Social Movements." *Symbolic Interaction* 6 (Fall 1983): 175–81.

Van Maanen, John, ed. *Qualitative Methodology.* Beverly Hills: Sage, 1979.

Vaz, Edmund W. *The Professionalization of Young Hockey Players.* Lincoln: University of Nebraska Press, 1982.

Wagner, Helmut R., ed. *Alfred Schutz: On Phenomenology and Social Relations.* Chicago: University of Chicago Press, 1970.

Walum, Laurel Richardson. "The Changing Door Ceremony: Notes in the Operation of Sex Roles." *Urban Life and Culture* 2 (1974): 506–15.

Warner, W. Lloyd. *Social Class in America: The Evaluation of Status.* New York: Harper and Row, 1960.

Weber, Max. *The Protestant Ethic and the Spirit of Capitalism.* New York: Scribner, 1958.

Weigert, Andrew J. "Alfred Schutz on a Theory of Motivation." *Pacific Sociological Review* 18 (Jan. 1975): 83–102.

———. *Sociology of Everyday Life.* New York: Longman, 1981.

———. "Identity: Its Emergence Within Sociological Psychology." *Symbolic Interaction* 16 (2 1983): 183–206.

Werthman, Carl. "Delinquency and Moral Character." In *Delinquency, Crime and Social Process,* edited by Donald Cressey and David Ward. New York: Harper and Row, 1969.

West, Candice and Don Zimmerman. "Women's Place in Everyday Talk: Reflections on Parent-Child Interaction." *Social Problems* 24 (1977): 144–72.

Whorf, Benjamin Lee. *Language, Thought and Reality.* Cambridge: The MIT Press, 1956.

Wieder, D. Lawrence. *Language and Social Reality: The Case of Telling the Convict Code.* The Hague: Mouton, 1975.

William, Frederick. *Language and Poverty: Perspectives on a Theme.* Chicago: Markham, 1970.

Williams, Robin. "Goffman's Sociology of Talk." In *The View from Goffman,* edited by Jason Ditton, 210–36. New York: St. Martins, 1980.

Wright, Sam. *Crowds and Riots: A Study of Social Organization.* Beverly Hills, Calif.: Sage, 1978.

Zeitlin, Irving M. *Ideology and the Development of Sociological Theory.* Englewood Cliffs, N.J.: Prentice-Hall, 1968.

Zimbardo, Philip C., C. Haney and W.C. Banks. "A Pirandellian Prison." *The New York Times Magazine.* April 8, 1973.

Zimmerman, Don. "Facts as a Practical Accomplishment." In *Ethnomethodology,* edited by Roy Turner, 128–43. London: Penguin, 1974.

Zurcker, Louis A. "The Poor and the Hip." *Social Science Quarterly* 53 (Sept. 1972): 357–76.

———. "The Staging of Emotion: A Dramaturgical Analysis." *Symbolic Interaction* 5 (Spring 1982): 1–22.

Glossary

Accentuation A practice in the thinking and behavior of children which exaggerates and overuses their simplified versions of the meanings of interactive situations.

Accommodation Interactive situations in which persons belonging to different domains distribute rewards according to their given social rankings, aiming to avoid both exploitation and competition.

Accounts Linguistic devices a person uses to either justify or excuse some untoward action attributed to him or her. Both excuses and justifications have many subtypes.

Acquaintance rape Sexual intercourse forced on a person by a partner whom the victim knows socially. Sometimes such rapes occur between persons who are "friendly" in nonintimate social circumstances.

Active deviancy A form of deviancy in which a person openly and actively enacts the identities associated with a deviant condition. In active deviancy, a person may try to change and even remove stigma.

Activity, Interaction, Sentiments and Norms Homans' four components making up the elementary organization of groups. These components are related so that an increase in the first increases the other three.

Alienation A feeling of being separated from oneself, one's environment, and one's social world. Often, alienation is a motivation for innovative responses in social life.

Anomie A condition of modern society in which no social norms exist to regulate the actions of individuals concerning matters of collective importance for society.

Anticipatory socialization Socialization that results from an individual anticipating membership in a group. The individual consciously shapes action, appearance and self-concept to fit what he or she imagines to be reflective of actual membership in the group.

Argots Sublanguages distinguished by specialized vocabulary, phrases, and other devices of language. Argots help define group membership and accomplish the goals of the group.

Ascribed and Achieved inequality Two methods of attributing rank that result in inequality. Ascribed inequalities are acquired from the taken-for-granted arrangements of domains of status. Achieved inequalities entail attributing motives and social qualities according to evaluations of the efforts of individuals or groups.

Assumption of typical experience A necessary condition for interaction in which it is assumed that experiences people have are similar for the practical purposes of everyday life.

Asymmetrical exchange An interactive encounter in which one partner speaks more, defines the form of the interaction, or otherwise contributes disproportionately to the meanings of the exchange.

Authoritarian personality hypothesis The idea that some people share a repressive socialization and are, therefore, susceptible to recruitment into totalitarian movements.

Autokinetic effect An effect of human perception. When a person stares at a pinpoint of light in a darkened room, the light will appear to move. The individual's judgments of the amount of movement can be influenced by group pressures.

Autonomous person concept Reisman's idea that through social scientific understanding of the social forces that impel people to behave in uniform ways, a person may gain a measure of control over those forces and, hence, a degree of autonomy as an individual.

Blowing up A category used in the judgment of emotional control. The person "blowing up" loses control of his or her emotions and erupts, letting out antisocial sentiments and disrupting existing social arrangements.

Boredom An emotional state of dullness. Boredom can be a result of modern life and the necessity for simple and obvious solutions to problems which implicate large numbers of people.

Bracketing A device of phenomenological analysis which requires highly developed critical powers. It helps an analyst discover the essence of a phenomenon. The analyst begins with a thorough description of the features of a given phenomenon and then mentally suspends each of these to discover whether that feature is essential to the quality of the phenomenon. The nonessential features are bracketed and the essence of the phenomenon remains.

Charisma The special qualities attributed to an individual or group. The social consequence of charisma is power for the person to whom the qualities are attributed.

Chameleon conformity The conscious and deliberate shaping of behavior which a person might do to achieve a reward or desired social position. In this case, the behavior which signifies conformity does not reflect the true self of the conformist.

Code telling Presenting information about a group in ways that both accomplish the goals and values of the group and separate members from nonmembers.

Code switching Verbally changing from one code of communication to another. Typically, code switching is associated with cross-modal communication and requires a speaker to have a repertoire of skills in various codes.

Collective behavior A behavior which involves relatively large numbers of people, has elements of spontaneity and significance, appears novel, and is innovative in ways not covered by the institutions of society.

Coolness An aloof attitude and demeanor in the face of risk. In modern society, coolness is a valued condition. Coolness must be achieved through means appropriate to a given social circle.

Competition An interaction in which the meanings of relationships are determined by the consequences of rule-governed conflict.

Conversion process Stages through which a person passes while experiencing conversion to a social movement, described by the interaction between social pressures and personality.

Counter-stigma A consequence of active deviancy in which a group aggressively counters the stigmatized meanings of their conditions of social life, often through advocating on behalf of the group.

Constructed social realities Stable and enduring features resulting from people organizing and interpreting their social experiences. Social realities are the beginning points of social interaction, and they ensue as a result of such interaction.

Cross-modal communication Communication between persons who routinely use different systems of talking. A person speaking cross-modally can either over- or undercorrect his or her speech in an attempt to be consistent with the listener's way of talking.

Crowds Minimally organized groupings of people in specific locations. Crowds have no definitive internal structure and may provide conditions necessary for collective behavior. Crowds can take on emotional qualities as in the case of angry or joyful crowds.

Deductive observations Observations organized according to concepts or clusters of concepts which serve to narrow and focus the meanings of the observed experiences.

Deference-confrontation Described by Goffman, a situation in which the ideology of a ritual is no longer taken for granted by its participants. With no consensus regarding the functional meanings of the ritual, participants either defer to or confront each other while enacting the ritual.

Definition of the situation The way an individual, group, or collectivity interprets and sets up the meanings for interaction in a given social circumstance.

Degradation ritual A standard practice followed within identifiable social boundaries for impugning the character of an individual or otherwise communicating a negative change in his or her status.

Democratization of space A generalization based on the observation that a tension exists between official and individual definitions of the use of public space. Whenever circumstances lessen the tension, such as in the winter city, people feel freer to use space as they see fit.

Descriptive attitude An approach to analysis which requires the analyst to suspend any values he or she may have about the subject matter and to describe from the point of view of those being studied.

Deviancy Actions labeled by groups of people as negative and unacceptable, and associated with moral, physical, and mental departures from the group's norms.

Disclaimer A statement made by a person trying to avoid anticipated negative consequences of what he or she is about to say. Disclaimers have many sub-types.

Distributive justice A sense of fairness that people have as a result of their interpretations of the ways in which rewards and desired social life-conditions are distributed among others. An important concept for describing the origins of relative deprivation.

Domain assumptions Basic assumptions social psychologists make about the nature of inquiry and explanation which guide, in subtle ways, the kinds of questions they ask and even their interpretations of "facts." Assumptions are specific to domains of inquiry although the same assumptions may ground many different domains.

Domains The groupings of thoughts, beliefs, and feelings that describe common sense perspectives of members of society. Domains are subject, topic, and relation specific.

Dramaturgical sociology A form of analysis which uses the metaphor of the stage and drama to understand social life.

Egoism A condition of modern society which promotes highly individualistic interpretations of the meanings of social life. Egoism suggests that individuals are at the center of all matters of responsibility and causation. Egoism inhibits an individual's recognition of social influences.

Ethnomethodology A type of inquiry which aims to understand social life by examining the complex methods for building and sustaining interaction employed by people in their daily existence. Its subject matter is often referred to as common sense knowledge. It emphasizes the thinking powers of humans and is an extremely relative form of scientific inquiry. Ethnomethodological studies often use innovative and unconventional techniques.

Erotic reality A version of the organization of human experience which is built on an erotic foundation. In an erotic reality, all aspects of human existence can take on sexual meanings.

Escape attempts All organized attempts to avoid or temporarily escape the demands of routine life (for example, through movies, fantasy games, tourism, sports, and entertainment).

Excitation A condition of emotional arousal. The experience is often contrived in modern society and is the opposite of boredom. The modern citizen according to the norms of many groups, should maintain an attitude of coolness during excited, emotional interaction.

Excuses A type of account which relieves the accused person of any responsibility for the act in question.

Exploitation An interaction in which one party controls the rules for access to rewards while the second party is kept naive or helpless with regard to access.

Fantasy An imaginative constructed version of experience which contrasts with everyday reality and which is normally either distinct from or complementary to everday life. Fantasizing is regarded as a consequence of routine and demeaning work.

Filling-in assumptions A state of mind necessary for social interaction in which vagueness in meaning, or the lack of detail about how others are thinking and what they are thinking about, is allowed to pass on the grounds that such detail can be "filled in" in future interaction.

Forms of conversation The organizational forms of talking between two or more people.

Forms of talking The social organizational principles which underlie ordinary talk.

Frame A type of analysis in which the organization of experience is thought of as a frame. Frames define the general meanings which specific actions can assume. They out-

line the possible meanings a person can attribute to everyday life. Frames are generally taken for granted.

Frustration-aggression hypothesis The idea that frustration arises from interference with the satisfaction of some need, either biological or social. Frustration results in anger and, in expressing anger, a person is rewarded, if only by reduced tensions. Reward, of course, reinforces aggression.

Functions of talk A concept which alerts us to the social consequences of communicative acts by focusing on how the presentation of information relates to the norms and values of group membership.

Gemeinschaft A nonmodern, folk, social organization. Gemeinschaft usually refers to small, rural, primary social units which collectively comprise a community.

Generational nostalgia The construction of a version of the past by persons who collectively experienced rapid social change at critical junctures in their life cycles.

Gender displays Behaviors rooted in emotional motivation and designed to communicate messages about the meanings of gender.

Gesellschaft A rational, modern form of social organization. Gesellschaft refers to impersonal, public and rational social exchanges which together comprise modern society.

Greeting slots Units into which a speaker may place a "piece of conversation," often used to describe openings in phone conversations.

Grounded theory The branch of symbolic interactionism which stresses that all theoretical concepts must be grounded in observation. Grounded theorists require inductive explanations. Hence, a researcher begins a project without theoretically preconceived notions and then grounds induced concepts in observations.

Gundecking A naval term for the practice of accomplishing an assignment or mission on paper only. A report, for example, may be "gundecked." The term generally refers to modifications of work and performance requirements within social organizations which are either too difficult for the group or are contrary to the informal qualities of that organization.

Hawthorne effect The commonly occurring effects of observation. People often act differently when they know they are being observed than when they do not realize they are part of a study. The effect was first reported in the Hawthorne studies in which workers modified their production output because they knew they were a part of a social scientific study.

Honored account An account accepted by others as either a reasonable or legitimate motive for the action in question.

Hypercorrection Efforts in cross-modal communicative situations in which a lower status person attempts to use the code of a higher status person (also known as overcorrection). "Mistakes" are usually made in the direction of using high status rules of grammar or pronunciation incorrectly.

"I" and "me" in social self Two components of the self. The "I" is the creative, highly individual character while the "me" represents the results of social influences on the formation of the self.

Iconographic speech A description of the way in which children formulate speech. Children use speech and its elements as literal representations of experiences when they speak "iconographically."

Ideal types A device used in social research to imagine the typical experiences of others. The device requires analysts to immerse themselves in the details of everyday life and then creatively construct ways of organizing the imagined experiences.

Incongruity procedure A rule police officers and others follow to make judgments about the moral character of others. It states that suspicion is warranted whenever conditions which ordinarily make up a social situation seem misaligned or organized in an incongruent fashion.

Incorrigible propositions Basic and elemental features of systems of believing and knowing which must be accepted before the reality these systems create can operate.

Inductive observations Observations which begin from experiences as given in the natural attitude. More general meanings are induced or inferred from the specific experiences.

Intensive interviewing A technique in which the interviewer repeatedly visits the person interviewed and devises questions for subsequent interviews based on the results of the previous. Intensive interviewing is designed to elicit detailed information from subjects.

Interruption patterns The distribution of interruptions by one partner in conversation with another. Interruption patterns in conversations are believed to be related to gender identities.

Intersubjective meanings A sense that the meanings a person attributes to his or her activities are the same as those attributed by others to the same experiences. The theory involves assumptions about shared meanings.

Invidious comparisons Comparisons among domains and systems of relevancy which cause animosity or resentment. The comparisons may be seen as offensive or unfair by one or both parties in a relationship.

Justification A type of account which allows the speaker to accept responsibility for an untoward action but modify the meaning of the act in terms of some positive or permissible values or norms. There are several types of justifications.

Keying Changing the tone, character, or subtle meaning of an interaction. According to Goffman, a "keyed" interaction is often not what it first appears to be. For example, a fight may be keyed play. The idea is similar to the musical concept of "key," as in playing a tune in another key.

Life plan The schemes, plans, and modes of interpretation which individuals use at a given time in their lives to impart the most general sense of direction to their social existence.

Life world The social circumstances which define all of a person's meanings for social existence at a given time in his or her life. Life world is a kind of parameter in everyday consciousness, a series of meanings a person has of a situation before he or she enters it.

Looking-glass self The image people have of themselves based on the way they imagine they appear to others.

Lascivious shift Devices used by persons to transform everyday reality into erotic reality. The lascivious shift functions to ready partners in interaction for a switch into the separate reality of the erotic.

Layered and laminated meanings Goffman's description of a given situation comprised of many social meanings, one on top of the other. Just as laminated wood is actually different kinds of woods in discrete layers, social situations may have distinctive meanings depending on which level the analyst looks at them.

Markers Any device (object, words, or gesture) which communicates territorial boundaries.

Mass collective behavior Collective behavior which takes place in mass society. Mass societies are characterized by distinctions between elites and nonelites and the availability and accessibility of information.

Membership stance An interpretation of the meaning of a social activity from the point of view of a person whose group membership is relevant to that activity.

Mixed group forms The organization of a group which exhibits both primary and secondary features. These features are often in conflict and such groups are dynamic.

Modernity A distinctive organization of social life which stresses the importance of the management of appearance, the necessity of rational and manipulative ways of thinking, and subtle modes of social control.

Moral career The regular and consistent ways in which a person or group acquires a commitment to and association with moral qualities. Careers exist through social time, although a person or group many shift from career to career.

Moral judge Persons or groups in a social order whose judgments determine the moral status of the actions of others, such as police officers, social workers, teachers, and others in positions of authority.

Neutralization A process of attributing social meanings to untoward actions in an effort to render the acts inconsequential.

Normal violence Aggressive and even injurious behaviors that are sanctioned in the organization of ordinary social life.

Normalization A process of attributing social meanings to actions in such a way that acts initially labeled deviant are cast as normal.

Nomic talk A specific, organized way of talking which functions within a given group to build the norms of that group.

Officious displays Exaggerated, nonverbal communication designed to tell people in public places one's official reasons for being there.

Passive deviancy A form of deviancy in which a person attributed with a deviant identity passively accepts the socially given meanings of that deviancy. Typically, in passive deviancy, the meanings of the actions in question are taken for granted.

Persona The character an individual communicates in association with others. An individual may attempt to employ many different personae in different situations.

Phenomenological sociology A version of sociology which stresses the nature of social phenomena and the discovery of essences and their relationships. It compliments symbolic interactionism, but is generally more philo-sophical and less researched oriented.

Primary group A group characterized by in-itimate, face-to-face communication, usually small and often having enduring and profound influences on its members.

Primary socialization The socialization pro-cess within a predominately primary context (family, friends, etc.).

Principle of least interest A generalization about romantically involved couples which suggests that the partner least interested in the relationship has more power.

Public behavior Behaviors in places where the use of space is defined by impersonal officials, where one's actions can be observed by strangers, and where interaction is typical-ly with strangers and for limited purposes. Public behavior contrasts with private life.

Rationalization A form of thinking in which the powers of the mind are given cen-tral significance over other human exper-iences. Rationalization is grounded in the belief that following explicit rules of thinking should be a primary mode of problem solving. In this sense, modern societies are rational.

Reciprocity thinking The kind of thinking in which a person assumes the point of view of another and thinks according to this as-sumptive stance. Important to this kind of thinking are the ability to assume the point of view of another and the assumption that one's thinking is a correct approximation of anoth-er's until some problem in interaction shows that it is not.

Reference group The real or imagined group an individual uses as a standard or point of reference for shaping his or her thinking, feel-ing, and acting.

Reflexive sociology A version of sociology in which sociologists turn their analytic and critical powers on themselves and on their science and question the idea of a pure or value-free inquiry.

Reflexivity A key concept in ethno-methodology referring to the feature of

human meaning systems in which elements are defined in terms of their own dimensions of meanings. It implies that all human sys-tems are self-sustaining and closed. Language is perhaps the clearest example of a highly reflexive system. Words get their meanings from their relationship with other words and are ultimately self-defining or circular.

Relative deprivation The feeling of being deprived of some desired reward or life-con-dition as the result of comparison with others who are thought of as similar and who are believed to possess the reward or condition of life. It is a sense of not having something relative to those who do.

Ritual identification A formal and highly stylized manner of identifying with persons, groups, or collectivities. Such identification often occurs in situations where a person, group, or collectivity strongly influences one's sense of belonging and self-expression.

Ritual of initiation Organized and regular practices within groups or other social entities which communicate the acceptance of new members.

Ritualization of belief A formal and highly stylized manner of expressing belief often oc-curring when people are subject to extreme stress or overt pressures to conform.

Ritualization of fighting An identifiable or-ganization to fighting (as in fighting at hockey games) which defines permissible aggressive behaviors in terms of social requirements and controls the destructive and disintegrative consequences of confrontation and combat.

Ritualization of the self The organization of ideals and qualities persons attribute to them-selves into rigid and formal patterns which mask what the individuals regard as true self states.

Ritualized lying A way of conversing among members of a group in which the truth of what is said is less important than the social consequences for the group of what is said.

Scenes Normatively governed activities, usually involving leisure time pursuits, which give members a strong sense of doing something distinctive. Scenes have a natural history, some going through all phases from articulation to the golden age, expansion, and stagnation. Some scenes effect core values of society as well as fads and fashions and are called grand scenes.

Secondary group A group in which interaction is impersonal and formal, and involves large numbers of people. It generally suggests a comparison with a primary group. Membership in secondary groups is instrumentally motivated. In the natural attitude, "secondary" connotes a degree of artificiality while "primary" connotes a degree of authenticity.

Secondary socialization The socialization process within impersonal, rational, and formal social settings.

Secondary violence Violence precipitated by lack of consensus about what constitutes "normal violence."

Self-fulfilling social expectations A common phenomenon in social life in which people act according to their expectations and in so doing create the circumstances which fulfill their expectations. The phenomeon is a variation of the Thomas Dictum, which states that situations defined as real are real in their consequences.

Sexual identity A sense people have of who they are based on widely distributed, common sense understandings of the meanings of gender.

Self-socialization Identities and acquired behaviors shaped by a person's own understandings of his or her social world. Although all socialization requires the individual to understand the social world, self-socialization is an extreme form of self-learning. Examples include children whose views of gender-appropriate behavior differ from "objective" descriptions of the gender arrangements in their own homes.

Signifying Ritual verbal insult, also known as "dozens," "sounding," and other terms which vary from community to community. Signifying is a kind of talking in which one

person comments on the moral, physical, and social character of another person or that person's relatives. The practice is governed by rules which are important to group membership.

Simplification When used to depict how a person perceives his or her social world, the term refers to the tendency to pare down themes of meanings to easily remembered formulas. Children often have simplified views of aspects of the adult world.

Situational propriety The idea that people learn to distinguish variations in circumstances which are associated with morally permissible departures from standard rules of action.

Situational violence The meanings of violence are associated with particular interactive settings and general definitions of violence are difficult to use in the description of what is experienced as violence. Thus, what is considered a violent act will, in some degree, vary from situation to situation.

Social constraint Pressure to follow the established modes of interpretation and action for a given social reality, form, or group.

Social integration The degree to which being a part of a social reality requires an individual to think of his or her identity in terms of belonging to the reality. People with high integration merge their collective and individual identities, while those with low integration can separate personal and social identities in their own minds.

Social movements Collective behaviors directed at changing or conserving core values of society, attracting people of disparate backgrounds.

Somantic categories Configurations of posture classified according to the social messages they convey.

Specimen case Deriving observationally grounded concepts by suggesting that the case under observation has characteristics which define the nature of the phenomenon. A specimen case allows for the characterization of social phenomena.

Stigma A direct or implied negative evaluation associated with some physical, moral, or social condition. A stigma is symbolized in some recognizable way: by dress, speech, appearance, or conduct.

Stratification system A general system of domains and relevancies which orders membership in society according to levels of status. Associated with each level, in common sense understanding, are distinctive attributes of everyday life.

Strict science The view of scientific inquiry which holds that prediction, explanation, and control are the final criteria for a true science.

Subjective meanings Interpreted experiences, or the sense people make out of their activities with others.

Symbolic interaction The view that one's social interaction consists of attributing meanings to persons and objects of one's environment, and then acting toward those persons and things according to the attributed meanings. The term is used in a general way to include all studies which emphasize the human ability to create and use symbols for social purposes.

Systems of relevancy People's thoughts, beliefs, and feelings organized into groupings of relationships or domains. These groupings are bounded; rules govern the items within groupings, and discrete items of thought, belief, and feeling are thought of as relevant according to how they fit into these systems of thinking.

Taking the attitude of the other The conscious act of imagining how others think and feel and then using this information as a part of an interactive exchange.

Temporality The sense of time in the experience of everyday life.

Territoriality A person's sense of place and the ways he or she uses place. There are many different sociological territories, including public, home, interactional, and body territories.

Truth telling The way ex-members of groups talk about the values and norms of their groups. The speakers use standard and widely accepted norms of conversation to reinterpret the specific codes of groups.

Typified knowledge The modal or typical way in which knowledge is organized.

Trivializing effects of words The idea that using words which connote negative or degrading meanings renders the referent of the words inconsequential. The idea is used most frequently in descriptions of devices used to denigrate women in society.

Underclass A category of people in society who are locked into low status and who may be second and even third generation representatives of the underprivileged life style. The term implies a permanency to the "down and out" status.

Undercorrection The practice of a higher status person communicating with a lower status person and attempting to talk like the lower status person. Usually the higher status speaker simplifies and incorrectly uses the lower status code. This is also called simplification.

Video experience The idea that in playing video games one learns how to organize experience in a special way so that the playing of the game becomes part of a larger mode of existence known as modern life.

Volcanic violence An aggressive and injurious interaction which seems to erupt almost spontaneously from seemingly routine social life.

Index

Photo Credits